Barbara Leigh Smith Bodichon
and the
Langham Place Group

WOMEN'S SOURCE LIBRARY

Series Editors:
Dale Spender and Candida Ann Lacey

This series brings together some of the most important, but still too little known, written sources which document the history of women's struggles for liberation. Taken from the principal women's archive in Britain, The Fawcett Library, and reprinted in full wherever possible, these pamphlets and papers illustrate major debates on a range of issues including suffrage, education, work, science and medicine as well as making the words of individual women widely available for the first time. Each volume contains a historical introduction to the material and biographical details of those campaigners who sought to improve the social, economic and legal status of women. The series was devised in collaboration with Catherine Ireland and David Doughan of The Fawcett Library, both of whom greatly assisted in the selection and compilation of material.

Other volumes in this series:

The Sexuality Debates edited by Sheila Jeffreys
The Education Papers: Women's Quest for Equality in Britain, 1850–1912 edited by Dale Spender

Forthcoming volumes include:

Women's Fabian Tracts edited by Sally Alexander
The Non-Violent Militant: Selected Writings of Teresa Billington-Greig edited by Carol McPhee and Ann Fitzgerald
Suffrage and the Pankhursts edited by Jane Marcus
The Lily edited by Cheris Kramarae and Ann Russo
The Revolution edited by Cheris Kramarae and Lana Rakow
Before the Vote was Won: Arguments For and Against Women's Suffrage, 1864–1896 edited by Jane Lewis

Barbara Leigh Smith Bodichon
and the
Langham Place Group

Edited by
Candida Ann Lacey

Routledge & Kegan Paul
New York and London

Published in the USA in 1987 by
Routledge & Kegan Paul Inc.
in association with Methuen Inc.
29 West 35th Street, New York, NY 10001

First published in Britain by
Routledge & Kegan Paul Ltd
11 New Fetter Lane, London EC4P 4EE

Set in Bembo 10 on 11pt
by Input Typesetting Ltd, London
and printed in Great Britain
by T. J. Press (Padstow) Ltd,
Padstow, Cornwall

Library of Congress Cataloging in Publication Data

Barbara Leigh Smith Bodichon and the Langham Place Group.

(Women's source library)
Includes index.
1. Feminism—Great Britain—History—19th century—
Sources. 2. Women—Great Britain—History—19th
century—Sources. 3. Women's rights—Great Britain—
History—19th century—Sources. I. Lacey, Candida.
II. Series.
HQ1596.B37 1986   305.4'06041   86–13121

British Library CIP Data also available
ISBN 0–7102–0947–9

Contents

Contents

Contents

Introduction

In 1849, when she was twenty-two, Barbara Leigh Smith complained that 'philosophers and reformers have generally been afraid to say anything about the unjust laws of society and country which crush women'. She added, optimistically, 'but now I hope that there are some who will brave ridicule for the sake of common justice to half the people in the world' (1849: pp. 1–2). It was this concern which made Barbara Bodichon, as she was to become, 'brave ridicule' herself and initiate the most important campaigns for women's rights to take place in Victorian England. Her pioneering schemes to improve the status of women would make the following twenty years some of the richest in debate and reform.

Never before had the 'woman question' been so widely discussed. Committees were formed and petitions demanding married women's property rights and, later, enfranchisement were presented to Parliament; from these committees, others developed and instigated further plans for practical and immediate changes – particularly in areas of education and employment for women – which were less dependent for their success on the attitude of the government or the state of Parliamentary business. *The English Woman's Journal*, which Barbara Bodichon had founded and financed, provided a public platform for the major feminist writings of the period whilst its offices, in Langham Place, formed the administrative centre of the Society for Promoting the Employment of Women. The task which faced the 'Langham Place Group', as Barbara Bodichon and her colleagues came to be known, was daunting. Before new ground could be gained, public opinion had to be changed. A wall of prejudice had to be dismantled brick by brick until the image of Victorian femininity crumbled, releasing women to claim their right to legal justice and a viable livelihood.

Most of the women at Langham Place accepted as axiomatic the need to convert their opponents by persuasion rather than by direct confrontation. How else would they win the parliamentary majority needed to support the controversial Married Women's Property Bill or to introduce the suffrage? Similarly, powerful sympathisers were needed if male-dominated professional and educational establishments were ever going to open their doors to women. It would be a slow process and, although significant gains were made, other changes would take much longer. The articles reprinted in this collection – articles published in *The English Woman's Journal*, papers read at the newly formed National Association for the Promotion of Social Science and pamphlets printed by Emily Faithful's task force of women compositors at the Victoria Press – are a testament to this struggle for slow and sometimes minimal rewards and an illustration of some of the difficulties involved in seeking to stretch the limits within which Victorian women were expected to live. Moreover, these articles reveal the complexity of that struggle: the diversity which quickly becomes apparent, not only in the range of projects which were undertaken but also in the attitude and political outlook of the women involved, denies us that temptation to reconstruct an idealised, unshakeable sisterhood. Particular circumstances and individual reasons brought each of these women into contact with the Langham Place Group; behind their common concern to improve women's rights, a welter of motives exists which would certainly reward further study and investigation. For it is in these different, and sometimes conflicting, voices that we can understand the strengths and the weaknesses of Victorian feminism. What emerges from the sample reprinted here is the comparative radicalism of Barbara Bodichon: both her clarity of purpose and her specific angle of vision, uncluttered by the social and political assumptions of some of her contemporaries, mark her as a forerunner of the modern women's movement.

Barbara Bodichon was an atypical Victorian woman; in many ways she was ahead of her time and enjoyed a liberty which was unknown to her peers. Her father had taken the unconventional step of providing each of his five children – daughters as well as sons – with a £300 annuity as soon as they came of age. Hence, Barbara's independence was assured and the image of this unorthodox freedom was reinforced two years after her twenty-first birthday when she and Bessie Rayner Parkes, her childhood friend who would become the editor of *The English Woman's Journal*, set off together for an unchaperoned tour of Europe. The advantage of an upbringing and an education (at the radical Westminster

School) usually reserved for male children could not erase the circumstances of her birth, however. Benjamin Leigh Smith, a Liberal MP, and Anne Longdon, a milliner's apprentice nearly thirty years his junior, were never married. Whether or not they would have married eventually is uncertain but when Barbara, their eldest child, was 7, her mother died. Social criticism and ostracism were inevitable: the Smith children were Florence Nightingale's illegitimate cousins and known as 'the tabooed family' (Haight, 1954–5, vol. II, p. 45). Mrs Gaskell once speculated as to the effect of Barbara's illegitimacy: 'she is – I think in consequence of her birth, a strong fighter against the established opinions of the world . . . I can't help admiring her noble bravery, and respecting – while I don't personally *like* her' (Chapple and Pollard, 1966, p. 607). Paradoxically, Barbara Bodichon would be relieved of the pressures which would hamper many of her colleagues: as an outsider, her radical ideals and endeavours were never curbed by the need for respectability and gentility. Other reformers, writing in *The English Woman's Journal* or working from the offices of 19 Langham Place, struggled to improve the status of women within the framework of traditional social values; Barbara Bodichon challenged those very values.

She initiated campaigns for both married women's property rights and the vote during the 1850s and 1860s; the first of her generation to become involved in these issues, she retained a keen sense of the long-term implication of such changes even when the goals appeared to be impossible. (In her lifetime, they were: she neither lived to see the final Married Woman's Property Act of 1893 nor to cast her vote in 1919.) Her concern for married women's property rights was directly linked to her unconventional views on marriage.[1] During her own honeymoon, she wrote:

> To believe in the transubstantiation or the divinity of the Virgin is not so perverting to the mind as to believe that women have no rights to full development of all their faculties and exercise of all their powers, to believe that men have rights over women, and as fathers to exercise those pretended rights over daughters, as husbands exercising those rights over wives. (1972, p. 63)

She was determined to retain her autonomy after marrying Eugene Bodichon and was adamant that this was recognised both materially and symbolically. Eight months after the wedding, she wrote: 'I do not think there is any law to oblige a woman to bear the name of her husband at all, and probably none to prevent her keeping the old name. To use it is very useful, for I have earned a right to Barbara Smith' (ibid., p. 134). It is interesting that her reflections on marriage predate John Stuart Mill's much publicised repudiation of the legal rights he would have obtained when he married Harriet Taylor in 1851 (see Elliot, 1910, vol. I, p. 58). Three years earlier, as a student at Bedford College, Barbara read Mill's 1848 work, *Principles of Political Economy*, and criticised the author for neglecting some important subjects: 'the Contract of Marriage is one; the Laws concerning Women is another, and there are many more' (1849, p. 1). She had been disappointed that 'one who carries so much weight' failed to mention 'the injustice of their [men's] laws to women and the absurdity of the present Laws of Marriage and Divorce', particularly as 'there never was a tyranny so deeply felt yet borne so silently' (ibid., pp. 1–2). Mill is customarily cited as the champion of women's rights; what is revealed in this unpublished notebook, however, is that it was more Barbara Bodichon's belief in the political purchase of Mill as a publicist than her faith in him as a philosopher which, seventeen years later, prompted her to capitalise on his position as an MP by asking him to present the petition for women's suffrage.

In 1854, Barbara Bodichon rectified Mill's omission by publishing her own critical consideration of the legal status of women: *A Brief Summary, in Plain Language, of the Most Important Laws of England concerning Women* was exactly that – a short, accessible and direct statement. At last, the stark facts were there for all to see. The position of married women, in particular, was a cause for grave concern: in accordance with English Common Law, the husband had absolute control over his wife's property and her earnings; she was unable to dispose of her possessions without his consent; if her property was stolen, *he* was the victim of the theft; the legal custody of her children, too, belonged to him. Many women had suffered and were suffering from this state of affairs. Mrs Gaskell, for example, received none of the income from her writing but had to depend on her husband giving her a small allowance. Furthermore, as had been demonstrated by Caroline Norton's plight, wives had no protection, nor legal redress, if their husbands failed to provide a sufficient allowance.[2] It was this vulnerability and the fallacy of the principle of protection ('women, more than any other members of the community, suffer from over-legislation') which Barbara Bodichon wanted to publicise (see p. 31). Her pamphlet was submitted to the Law Amendment Society and a report was drafted proposing the extension of women's property rights. The following year, Barbara Bodichon formed a committee of women to collect signatures in support of a Married Women's Property Bill. The petition was enthusiastically supported and the committee returned with 26,000 signatures, 3,000 of which came from London alone and included those of Elizabeth Barrett Browning, Harriet Martineau, Elizabeth Gaskell, Marion Evans, Anna Jameson, Mary Howitt and Geraldine Jewsbury.

Despite the failure of the Bill when it was introduced into Parliament by the Law Amendment Society in 1857, Barbara Bodichon had succeeded in drawing the attention of the public to this lack of 'common justice' for women. Although there were inevitable antagonists to the proposal (Margaret Oliphant declared that it was 'the merest nonsense which ever looked like reason' [1856, p. 387]), many women responded to the rallying call and continued to press for changes in legislation. Frances Power Cobbe, whose charitable work with prostitutes and paupers in Bristol's 'ragged schools' had given her a sharp insight into the poverty of the woman's lot, and brought her into contact with Barbara Bodichon's committee, recalled that she resolved 'to do everything in [her] power to protect the property, the persons, and the parental rights of women' (1894, vol. II, p. 526). In one of the articles Cobbe wrote for *Frazer's Magazine*, which is included here, she pointed out the blatant lie of the marriage ceremony: the groom promised to endow his bride with all his worldly wealth when, in reality, he was on the verge of appropriating hers. It was ironic, she argued, that women who fulfilled the role society required of them were subsequently treated in the same way as lunatics and criminals by the forfeiture of their legal rights and property (see pp. 378–401). Other women began to put their principles into practice. As a condition of her marriage to James Skelton Anderson in 1871, for example, Elizabeth Garrett insisted on taking legal control of her income as a medical practitioner.

The legal impact of redefining a married woman's relationship with her husband would be diluted by thirty-six intervening years and various reforms before the demands of the original 1857 Married Women's Property Bill were met in full. In the mean time, the valuable experience gained by those women agitating for property reform could be put to good use in the struggle for equitable suffrage. Although Harriet Taylor had called for the enfranchisement of women in 1851, the lack of a vote, at a time when only a small proportion of men were enfranchised, seemed less of a shortcoming than their financial hardships. However, the Reform Act of 1867 had doubled the electorate, by extending suffrage to many skilled working men, without making any concessions to women. The situation did not improve: seventeen years later, the third Reform Act introduced suffrage to *all* men over the age of 21 and served as a stark reminder of the *'deconsideration'* of women pointed out by Barbara Bodichon (see p. 107). Therefore, when the third edition of *A Brief Summary, in Plain Language, of the Most Important Laws of England concerning Women* appeared in 1869, fifteen years after the original, Barbara Bodichon had revised its contents and now stressed that exclusion from the franchise was the greatest disability suffered by women. The petition for Married Women's Property rights had won the support of many but the campaign for suffrage was a more divisive issue. Barbara Bodichon's cousin, Florence Nightingale, refused an invitation to join the suffrage committee, saying that,

> It makes me mad, the Women's Rights talk. . . . They don't know the names of the Cabinet Ministers. . . . They don't know who of the men of the day is dead and who is alive. . . . They cannot state a fact accurately to another, nor can the other attend to it accurately enough for it to become information. (quoted in Strachey, 1928, p. 25)

For Barbara Bodichon it was this very ignorance which demonstrated the necessity, rather than the denial, of the vote. As she explained in 1866, suffrage would emancipate women from their enforced insularity (see pp. 114–15); she denied the uniqueness of the qualities traditionally associated with women's 'indirect' influence on politics which was so often used as an argument against suffrage (see pp. 115–16). Her essentially progressive and bold vision of women's political potential set her apart from the other, more cautious, women at Langham Place. An article in *The English Woman's Journal*, probably written by Bessie Rayner Parkes, tentatively pressed for the vote in the following terms:

> Why may not a woman think about these great and practical subjects, and form opinions with regard to them intelligently and gracefully, in a manner suitable for a woman? And then why may she not give the world the benefit of these opinions by expressing them in a gentle, unobtrusive way? ('Women and Politics', 1863, p. 6)

Frances Power Cobbe was similarly constrained by notions of propriety and images of crinolined women. She was eager to circumscribe the kind of freedom Barbara had in mind, fearing that women might use this 'as a facility for licentiousness'. For Cobbe, political emancipation had less to do with the individual's right than 'a means – a very great means – of fulfilling our social Duty, of contributing to the virtue and happiness of mankind and advancing the Kingdom of God' (1881, p. 150).

Barbara Bodichon's call for women's suffrage came as a result of the paper she presented in 1865 at the Kensington Society, a woman's discussion group amongst whose members were Bessie Rayner Parkes, Elizabeth Garrett, Emily Davies, Frances Power Cobbe, Sophia Jex-Blake and Harriet Taylor. Emily Davies' comment on an early draft of the paper reveals the difference between the two women:

> In your paper there are two or three expressions I should like to have altered, e.g. I don't think it quite does to call the arguments on the other side 'foolish'. Of course they *are*, but it does not seem quite polite to say so. . . . I find nothing irritates men so much as to attribute tyranny to them. I believe many of them do really mean well, and at any rate as they say they do, it seems fair to admit it and to show them that their well-intended efforts are a *mistake*, not a crime . . . it is necessary to be careful. (quoted in Stephen, 1927, p. 108)

At the meeting, a resolution in favour of the paper was passed with a large majority and, although Emily Davies was apprehensive – 'My doubt is whether a safe Committee could be formed, and if wild people get upon it, who insist on jumping like kangaroos (the simile is not flattering), they would do harm' (quoted in Stephen, 1927, p. 109) – a suffrage committee was formed. A petition was presented to John Stuart Mill in June 1866 in the name of 'Barbara L. S. Bodichon and others' and, that October, her paper, *Reasons for the Enfranchisement of Women* was read at the Social Science Congress. However, after the rejection of Mill's proposed amendment to the Representation of the People Bill the following year, the committee split up. Emily Davies considered the dissolution and her own resignation as a narrow escape from the damage that such a contentious campaign could inflict on other ventures, namely, the promotion of women's education. Although both petitions initiated by Barbara Bodichon had failed and any gains from either the Married Women's Property Act or suffrage seemed remote, the women involved in these campaigns had been alerted to other injustices. They responded with the sense of urgency Adelaide Anne Procter described in her poem, 'Now', and it was from these efforts to secure further education, vocational training and a viable employment for women, that results were forthcoming.

Barbara Bodichon's concern and aims for education were undoubtably influenced by her own schooling. At Westminster School, which her father had helped to establish, she had been taught by a former teacher at Robert Owen's New Lanark school, James Buchanan. There she helped with the younger pupils and gained first-hand experience of Buchanan's teaching methods. As a result of the transference of the deeds of Westminster School, which she had inherited from her father when she was 21, she was able to re-open it in 1854. A year later there were 113 pupils. Perhaps the most unorthodox aspect of Portman Hall, as the new school was named, was its secularism and mixed classes: Jewish children mixed with Catholics and girls with boys. Difficulties arose not only because of the preconceptions of most teachers (a problem she discusses in 'Middle Class Schools for Girls' in this collection) but also as a result of traditional assumptions about the propriety of educating girls in the same manner, and in the same subjects, as boys. But Barbara Bodichon insisted that girls, too, should be trained for adequate and suitable employment. At the National Association for the Promotion of Social Science in 1860, she attacked the appalling standards of existing schools and argued that, in addition to fulfilling their practical needs, a sound general education for girls would eliminate the incalculation of 'vanity, false ideals of what is lady-like and every shallow, showy accomplishment' (see p. 77).

The problems of convention and propriety with which Barbara Bodichon had to contend in the running of Portman Hall in the 1850s was paralleled a decade later in the campaign for women's higher education. Emily Davies and her colleagues fought against a tide of inaccurate but dogmatic opinion. They had to convince their antagonists that education was intrinsically valuable rather than inherently harmful for women. Furthermore, they felt that the only way to succeed was to avoid arousing their opponents' hostility. In her struggle for a woman's college (which would come to fruition with the opening of Girton in 1873), Emily Davies' overriding concern was that the higher education committee should not be associated with the suffrage movement or any 'radicals'. Barbara Bodichon's name was thus omitted and, in the first public meetings called to discuss women's education, Emily Davies carefully placed only pretty and meek-looking women in the front rows (Stephen, 1927, p. 162; Caine, 1982, p. 547).[3]

The campaign for medical education could not be stage-managed so easily. The idea of women studying to become doctors was greeted with hostility and steadfast opposition. In 1863, Elizabeth Garrett was refused admission as a candidate in the matriculation examinations at London University for no other reason than because she was a woman. Femininity and learning were incompatible. Not only was education morally wrong (women should be concerned with their duties as potential wives and mothers) but it also went against the grain of conventional medical wisdom: mental exertion surely would result in physical breakdown, for women were biologically unsuited to academic work. In America, the situation was the same: Elizabeth Blackwell had been turned away by every medical school in Philadelphia and New York as well as by Harvard, Yale and Bowdoin. She had no choice but to study anatomy privately before, eventually, she was accepted by Geneva College. Travelling to London nine years after she qualified, in 1858, in order to help advance professional opportunities for medicine in Britain, she met Barbara Bodichon and Bessie Rayner Parkes. They helped her to organise lectures and published extracts from her writings in *The English Woman's Journal*. A year later, Elizabeth Blackwell became the first woman to have her name entered on the Medical Register of the United Kingdom. The effect of this breakthrough was not immediately apparent to aspiring medical students, however. Inspired by Blackwell's lectures, Elizabeth Garrett resolved to become a doctor only to find herself refused by all the medical schools in England and Scotland. She, too, studied privately. Six years later, in 1865, after a heated debate (to which Emily Davies refers in 'The Influence of University Degrees on the Education of Women'), she was finally allowed to sit the examinations of the Society of Apothecaries. Although she was now qualified to practise, it would take another four years and further struggles before she was able to sit for the full M.D. degree and have her name entered on the British Medical Register.

Opponents had to be persuaded continuously. Many of the apologists justified women's medical education in terms of their conventional nurturing role: in her article, 'What Shall We do with Our Old Maids?', Frances Power Cobbe defended the cause on the grounds that women needed this knowledge in order to care for their children and for other members of the household; Emily Davies used a similar argument in 'Female Physicians', saying that a medical education would help women to realise their true responsibilities whilst, for many patients, 'the sympathy and tenderness of a woman would be absolutely more curative than the possibly superior skill of a man' (see p. 408). Only Barbara Bodichon explicitly argued that the most important benefit of medical training would be experienced by women themselves: as she pointed out, in *Women and Work*, at last women would be able to consult doctors of their own sex. Unlike Davies and Cobbe, who believed that nursing was a vocation, Barbara Bodichon insisted that both medicine and nursing were simply two of a number of occupations which should be immediately opened to women.

The question of women's employment had become a subject of public debate from the early 1850s. Reports from the Sadler Committee, the Factory Commission and the Children's Employment Commission had exposed not only the grim conditions which working women and children had to bear but also the extent of their employment. At the same time, the circumstances of middle-class women were publicised, largely as a result of the 1851 census which had revealed that 'the number of females of marriageable age, in Great Britain, will always exceed the number of males of the same age to the extent of half a million'. It was a statistic which, as Bessie Rayner Parkes correctly surmised, effectively destroyed the 'doctrine that married life is a woman's profession' (see p. 177). And yet parents rarely provided for their daughters either by endowment or education (the latter being positively discouraged). The only occupations available to a single, middle-class woman were those deemed to be respectable. She was not spoilt for choice: she could become either a governess or a needlewoman. Both situations were overcrowded and the 'surplus' of women applying for too few jobs had the result of lowering already derisory wages. Without the benefit of an education, these women were unable to command a higher salary and, to make matters worse, they were demeaning themselves in the eyes of society by having to work at all. To become a governess was to 'retire from all the pleasures of life, of rational intercourse, equal society, peace and hope, to penance and mortification for ever' (Austen, 1816, p. 179). Jane Austen's comment was as true in mid-century as it had been when *Emma* was published. Although the Governesses' Benevolent Institution was founded in 1843 in an attempt to furnish these destitute women with loans, annuities and retirement homes, such methods of alleviation could not keep pace with the rapid growth of the problem. Barbara Bodichon continually bemoaned the conditions and restrictions of women's employment. The plight of 'distressed needlewomen . . . the decayed gentlewomen and broken-down governesses' had been exposed and her solution to the problem was unequivocal:

> Apprentice 10,000 to watchmakers; train 10,000 for teachers for the young; make 10,000 good accountants; put 10,000 more to be nurses under deaconnesses trained by Florence Nightingale; put some thousands in the electric telegraph offices all over the country; educate 1,000 lecturers for mechanics' institutions; 1,000 readers to read the best books for

working people; train up 10,000 to manage washing-machines, sewing-machines, etc. (p. 44)

In 1858, in the first issue of *The English Woman's Journal*, Bessie Rayner Parkes confirmed the need for better conditions and new opportunities for women: only an education, a training and a wider choice of employment could offer some degree of financial independence and set about 'getting rid of this particular form of destitution arising in great measure from the overcrowding of the Profession of the Teacher' (1858, p. 2). She and Barbara Bodichon had established the journal in an attempt to publicise 'the present industrial employments of women, both manual and intellectual, the best mode of judiciously extending the sphere of such employments, and the laws affecting the property and conditions of the sex' ('Domestic Life', 1858, p. 75). Another member and activist of the Married Women's Property Committee, Isa Craig, had recently taken up the position of Assistant Secretary to the National Association for the Promotion of Social Science. The appointment of a woman, together with the admission of women to the meetings, was a radical development which delighted the staff of *The English Woman's Journal*. The connection enabled them to secure both the attention of influential men and the publicity they needed so badly; it provided a platform for their papers on education, employment, working conditions and on a range of social problems, from hospital nursing to the causes of insanity, many of which they subsequently published.

One young woman, Jessie Boucherett, caught sight of a copy of *The English Woman's Journal* in a railway station bookstall; she was so enthusiastic about its contents that she travelled to London in order to meet its editors. A year later, in 1859, she and Adelaide Anne Procter who, as a close friend of Bessie Rayner Parkes, had been involved with the journal from its inception, established the Association (later Society) for Promoting the Employment of Women. This was intended 'for girls and young women, where they may be specially trained to work in shops by being thoroughly well instructed in accounts, book-keeping, etc.' ('Association for the Employment of Women', 1859, pp. 58–9). An employment register was set up and soon various enterprises were under way. Printers would not accept women apprentices so, in 1860, Emily Faithfull, the Society's Secretary, started the Victoria Press to employ women compositors; henceforth, *The English Woman's Journal* was printed there. The Victoria Press was immediately successful and, six months later, Emily Faithfull was appointed Printer and Publisher in Ordinary to Queen Victoria. In 1863 she founded the *Victoria Magazine*, a magazine of general and literary interest which consistently upheld women's rights, frequently publishing articles by Frances Power Cobbe and Emily Davies.

The Society for Promoting the Employment of Women struggled against apathy, prejudice and the enmity of men's trade unions. But, by 1861, Jessie Boucherett, who had started a remedial school in arithmetic and accounting, and her colleagues had found situations for women under photographers, lithographers and dial-painters and as shop assistants, hotel managers, watchmakers, clerks, telegraphists and nurses. Maria Rye opened a Law Engrossing Office at Lincoln's Inn and employed women to copy legal documents; she, too, was involved in founding the Victoria Press and, with Isa Craig, ran the Telegraph School, teaching women how to operate the new technology. So many women were applying for work through the Employment Society and the Telegraph School that Maria Rye sought new ways in which to deal with the problem of unemployed English women: in 1861 she founded the Female Middle Class Emigration Society, whose aims she outlined in the article included here. For the next eight years she helped to organise jobs for countless women in Australia, New Zealand and Canada – countries where cooks, governesses and needlewomen were urgently required and the wages were high. The Society for Promoting the Employment of Women could boast other successes including encouraging women to learn to swim (the Committee persuaded the manager of St Marylebone Baths to admit women on Wednesday afternoons) and establishing The Ladies' Sanitary Association in an effort to raise standards of hygiene and educate women about basic principles of health.

Because the urgency to improve the employment situation arose from the recent revelation about and implications for 'surplus women', women like Bessie Rayner Parkes, Jessie Boucherett and Frances Power Cobbe were eager to change public opinion by proving that other trades need not be demeaning. They argued that work did not necessitate a fall from grace and Victorian ideals but, on the contrary, that it encouraged positive virtues such as self-reliance and industry (Boucherett, 1863; Parkes, 1865; Cobbe, 1881). Emily Davies claimed that industry and domesticity *could* co-exist: 'it is certainly not easy to see why it should be unfeminine for a girl to sit in her father's office, under his immediate eye (and protection if needed) gradually acquiring some experience' (1910, p. 11).

Protagonists, as well as antagonists, were finding the need to progress from philanthropic to paid work difficult to accept. Philanthropy had been the traditional occupation of middle-class women; with only gratitude as its reward, this was considered to be a suitable and natural pastime. Charitable deeds were recommended by such popular and well-known reformers as Anna Jameson. For Bessie Rayner Parkes, too, the provision of work which did not resemble paid labour was an important consideration as can be seen in 'What Can Educated Women Do?' and 'The Condition of Working Women in England and France'. And, although Frances Power Cobbe admitted that charitable acts were no longer a sufficient means to an end, she wanted to stretch the possibilities for philanthropy so that a woman would be able to 'devote herself . . . to relieve the miseries of mankind' (1863, p. 106). Such notions of what women's work should entail were staunchly guarded. In 1859, a young student at Queen's College was offered a teaching position. When her father discovered that the job was waged, he wrote in dismay:

> I have only this moment heard you contemplate being *paid* for the tutorship. It would be quite beneath you, darling, and I *cannot consent* to it. Take the post as one of honour and usefulness, and I shall be glad. . . . But to be *paid* for the work would be to alter the thing *completely*, and would lower you sadly in the eyes of almost everybody.

Sophia Jex-Blake replied that she had 'fairly earned' the payment and asked 'why should I not take it? You, as a man, did your work and received your payment, and no-one thought it any degradation. . . . Why should the difference of my sex alter the laws of right and honour?' (quoted in Todd, 1918, pp. 67, 68–9). But the logic of her argument failed to convince him; the future physician and founder of the London Medical School for Women was permitted to accept her first job on condition that she refused the salary.

Only Barbara Bodichon insisted on a woman's right to *paid* work. She argued that women were degraded not by financial independence but, on the contrary, by their customary dependence on the benevolence of their nearest male relative (see p. 41). Her earlier concern to establish women's economic rights, in her battle to reform the legislation concerning married women's property, remained central to her argument for women's employment. Unlike other Victorian reformers who considered that 'it is endemic and the ambition of women to be considered in all relations, all the conditions of life, domestic and social, as the helpmate' (Jameson, 1859, p. 346), Barbara Bodichon not only pointed out that gratitude was poor remuneration for women who were in need of money but she also disagreed with the principle of philanthropy itself. On this subject, as in all her writings, she attacked the notion that women needed no other occupation than marriage and denied that they were necessarily content to be financial dependents. Because she carved away at the very foundations of women's subordination, her task was formidable and the results were slow to take shape. But it was her bold ambition which remained the driving force behind the Langham Place Group and made the achievements of others possible. Adopting a more radical stand than her colleagues, Barbara Bodichon remained adamant in her demands:

> To sum up. Women want work for the health of their minds and their bodies. They want it often because they must eat and because they have children and others dependent on them – *for all the reasons that men want work.* (p. 64)

Candida Ann Lacey
Brighton, December 1985

NOTES

1 In 1855, Barbara had considered entering into a permanent relationship with John Chapman, the editor of *The Westminster Review*, who was married with children. Although she decided against such a move and, two years later, married the French doctor whom she had met in Algiers, the marriage was hardly conventional, particularly as she spent six months of each year apart from her husband in order to continue working in London. Hester Burton's (1949) biography of Barbara Bodichon omits significant evidence of her non-conformity: her illegitimacy and her affair with Chapman, for example. Recently, Sheila Herstein (1986) has provided a more accurate picture.

2 Caroline Norton (1808–77), the granddaughter of Richard Brinsley Sheridan, left her violent husband in 1836 but, as the law stood, she was unable to obtain a divorce. George Norton refused to give his wife an allowance and, since all her property had passed into his legal possession, she was penniless. She turned to writing and won considerable acclaim; as soon as her literary efforts bore fruit, George Norton asserted his right to his wife's earnings. The final blow came after he had unsuccessfully sued Lord Melbourne, then Prime Minister, for damages on the grounds of adultery with his wife: as a married woman, and therefore a legal nonentity, Caroline Norton was unable to appear in her own defence at the trial; her helpless situation was compounded when George Norton abducted their three young sons and refused to let his wife see them. The first of Caroline Norton's pamphlets, which pointed out the gross injustice of her situation and appealed for legal reform, helped to win the passage of the 1839 Infants Custody Act

which gave mothers certain limited rights to their children. See Forster (1984), pp. 15–52.

3 Although Barbara Bodichon was not a member of the original Committee in 1867, she was actively involved in its progress and donated the largest single sum – £1,000 – to the College fund.

REFERENCES

'Association for the Employment of Women' (1859), *The English Woman's Journal*, IV (September), pp. 54–60.

Austen, Jane (1816), *Emma*, rpt. Penguin, Harmondsworth, Middlesex, 1969.

Bodichon, Barbara Leigh Smith (1849), 'Remarks on Mill's *Political Economy*', Unpublished notes, The Leigh Smith Papers, Girton College Library.

Bodichon, Barbara Leigh Smith (1972), *An American Diary, 1857–8*, ed Joseph W. Reed, Jr, Routledge & Kegan Paul, London.

Boucherett, Jessie (1863), *Hints on Self-Help: A Book for Young Women*, S. W. Partridge, London.

Burton, Hester (1949), *Barbara Bodichon, 1827–1891*, John Murray, London.

Caine, Barbara (1982), 'Feminism, Suffrage and the nineteenth-century English Women's Movement', *Women's Studies International Forum*, 5(6), pp. 537–50.

Chapple, J. A. V. and Pollard, A. (eds) (1966), *The Letters of Mrs Gaskell*, University of Manchester Press, Manchester.

Cobbe, Frances Power (1863), *Essays on the Pursuits of Women*, Emily Faithfull, London.

Cobbe, Frances Power (1881), *The Duties of Women: A Course of Lectures*, William and Norgate, London and Edinburgh.

Cobbe, Frances Power (1894), *The Life of Frances Power Cobbe*, 2 vols, Houghton, Mifflin and Co., Boston and New York.

Davies, Emily (1910), *Thoughts on Some Questions Relating to Women, 1860–1908*, Bowes and Bowes, Cambridge.

'Domestic Life' (1858), *The English Woman's Journal*, II (October), pp. 73–82.

Elliot, Hugh S. R. (ed.) (1910), *The Letters of John Stuart Mill*, 2 vols, Longmans, Green and Co., London.

Forster, Margaret (1984), *Significant Sisters: The Grassroots of Active Feminism, 1839–1939*, Secker and Warburg, London.

Haight, Gordon S. (ed.) (1954–5), *The Letters of George Eliot*, 7 vols, Oxford University Press, London.

Herstein, Sheila R. (1986), *A Mid-Victorian Feminist: Barbara Leigh Smith Bodichon*, Yale University, New Haven, Connecticut.

Jameson, Anna (1859), 'A Letter to Lord John Russell', *The English Woman's Journal*, III (July), pp. 343–52.

Oliphant, Margaret (1856), 'Laws Concerning Women', *Blackwood's Edinburgh Magazine*, LXXIX (April), pp. 379–87.

Parkes, Bessie Rayner (1858), 'The Profession of the Teacher', *The English Woman's Journal*, I (March), pp. 1–13.

Parkes, Bessie Rayner (1865), *Essays on Woman's Work*, n.p., London.

Stephen, Barbara (1927), *Emily Davies and Girton College*, Constable, London.

Strachey, Ray (1928), *The Cause: A Short History of the Women's Movement*, rpt. Virago, London, 1978.

Taylor, Harriet (1851), 'The Enfranchisement of Women', rpt. in Alice S. Rossi (ed.), *Essays on Sex Equality*, University of Chicago Press, Chicago and London, 1970, pp. 91–121.

Todd, Margaret (1918), *The Life of Sophia Jex-Blake*, Macmillan, London.

'Women and Politics' (1863), *The English Woman's Journal*, XII (September), pp. 1–6.

Adelaide Anne Procter
(1825–64)

The eldest child of Anne Skepper and Bryan Waller Procter, Adelaide Anne Procter was better known as a poet than as a feminist reformer in her own lifetime. She began a long connection with Charles Dickens's *Household Words* when she was twenty-eight (initially under the pseudonym of 'Mary Berwick') and five years later published her collected poems in two volumes entitled *Legends and Lyrics*. Reputedly Queen Victoria's favourite poet, she sold more volumes of her poetry than any other contemporary poet except Tennyson. It was her concern for women's rights, however, which won her a place on the National Association for the Promotion of Social Science's committee in 1859 to consider fresh ways of providing employment for women. At the same time, she helped to establish the Society for Promoting the Employment of Women with Bessie Rayner Parkes and Jessie Boucherett. Shortly afterwards she contracted tuberculosis and, after fifteen months as an invalid, died in February 1864. Jessie Boucherett selected this poem for her obituary in *The English Woman's Journal*.

Now

Rise! for the day is passing,
  And you lie dreaming on;
The others have buckled their armour,
  And forth to the fight have gone:
A place in the ranks awaits you,
  Each man has some part to play;
The Past and the Future are nothing
  In the face of the stern To-day.

Rise from your dreams of the Future –
  Of gaining some hard-fought field;
Of storming some airy fortress,
  Or bidding some giant yield:
Your future has deeds of glory,
  Of honour (God grant it may!)
But your arm will never be stronger,
  Or the need so great as To-day.

Rise! if the past detains you,
  Her sunshine and storms forget;
No chains so unworthy to hold you
  As those of vain regret:
Sad or bright, she is lifeless ever.
  Cast her phantom arms away;
Nor look back, save to learn the lesson
  Of a nobler strife To-day.

Rise! for the day is passing;
  The sound that you scarcely hear
Is the enemy marching to battle –
  Arise! for the foe is here!
Stay not to sharpen your weapons,
  Or the hour will strike at last,
When, from dreams of a coming battle,
  You may awake to find it past!

ADELAIDE ANNE PROCTER

Barbara Leigh Smith Bodichon

(1827–91)

The eldest of five children, Barbara Leigh Smith was the daughter of Anne Longden, a milliner, and Benjamin Leigh Smith, a Radical MP for Norwich whose house was frequently used as a meeting-place for abolitionists and political refugees from Europe. In 1849, she enrolled at the newly formed Ladies' College in Bedford Square where she studied law, political economy and art. Shortly after-wards she founded and taught in the innovative Portman Hall School where children from different classes and religious back-grounds were educated together. In 1854, she began her career as a writer and feminist reformer with the publication of the provoca-tive and highly successful *A Brief Summary, in Plain Language, of the Most Important Laws of England concerning Women*. It is not surprising, since with its particular reference to married women's property rights the pamphlet implicitly cast doubt on the merits of matrimony, that it was at this time that Barbara was considering a permanent extra-marital relationship with John Chapman. However, her father refused to countenance the proposed arrange-ments and the affair ended. Barbara left for Algiers where she met Eugene Bodichon, whom she married in 1857. Together they embarked on a tour of America where they met leading abolition-ists and prominent figures in the American Women's Rights Move-ment. Barbara Bodichon was overwhelmed by the implications of American liberty but she vigorously attacked the great paradox of slavery, publishing several articles in *The English Woman's Journal* on the subject. Her other interests included painting: she gave her profession as 'artist' on her marriage certificate. She was a prolific artist, competent enough to have studied in Corot's studio and frequently exhibiting her work. When she died she left £10,000 to Girton College, the proceeds from the sale of her paintings.

A Brief Summary, in Plain Language, of the Most Important Laws Concerning Women: Together with a Few Observations Thereon

(1854)

Legal Condition of Unmarried Women or Spinsters

A single woman has the same rights to property, to protection from the law, and has to pay the same taxes to the State, as a man.

Yet a woman of the age of twenty-one, having the requisite property qualifications, cannot vote in elections for members of Parliament.

A woman duly qualified can vote upon parish questions, and for parish officers, overseers, surveyors, vestry clerks, etc.

If her father or mother die *intestate* (i.e., without a will) she takes an equal share with her brothers and sisters of the personal property (i.e., goods, chattels, moveables), but her eldest brother, if she have one, and his children, even daughters, will take the *real* property (i.e., not personal property, but all other, as land, etc.), as the heir-at-law; males and their issue being preferred to females; if, however, she have sisters only, then all the sisters take the real property equally. If she be an only child, she is entitled to all the intestate real and personal property.

The church and nearly all offices under government are closed to women. The Post-office affords some little employment to them; but there is no important office which they can hold, with the single exception of that of Sovereign.

The professions of law and medicine,[1] whether or not closed by law, are closed in fact. They may engage in trade, and may occupy inferior situations, such as matron of a charity, sextoness

23

of a church, and a few parochial offices are open to them. Women are occasionally governors of prisons for women, overseers of the poor, and parish clerks. A woman may be ranger of a park; a woman can take part in the government of a great empire by buying East India Stock.

A servant and a master or mistress are bound by a verbal or written agreement. If no special agreement is made, a servant is held by the common custom of the realm to be hired from year to year, and the engagement cannot be put an end to without a month's notice on either side.

If a woman is seduced, she has no remedy against the seducer; nor has her father, excepting as he is considered in law as being her master and she his servant, and the seducer as having deprived him of her services. Very slight service is deemed sufficient in law, but evidence of some service is absolutely necessary, whether the daughter be of full age or under age.

These are the only special laws concerning single women: the law speaks of men only, but women are affected by all the laws and incur the same responsibilities in all their contracts and doings as men.

Laws Concerning Married Women

Matrimony is a civil and indissoluble contract between a consenting man and woman of competent capacity.

These marriages are prohibited – A widower with his deceased wife's sister; a widow with the brother of her deceased husband; a widower with his deceased wife's sister's daughter, for she is by affinity in the same degree as a niece to her uncle by consanguinity; a widower with a daughter of his deceased wife by a former husband; and a widower with his deceased wife's mother's sister. Consanguinity or affinity, where the children are illegitimate, is equally an impediment.

A lunatic or idiot cannot lawfully contract a marriage, but insanity after marriage does not make the marriage null and void.

A lunatic may contract a marriage during a lucid interval. Deaf and dumb people may marry by signs.

The consent of the father or guardians is necessary to the marriage of an *infant* (i.e., a person under twenty-one), unless the marriage takes place by banns. The consent of the mother is not necessary if there be a father or a guardian appointed by him.

A second marriage while a husband or wife is living is felony, and punishable by transportation.

An agreement to marry made by a man and woman who do not come under any of these disabilities is a contract of betrothment, and either party can bring an action upon a refusal to complete the contract in a superior court of Common Law.

Marriages may be celebrated as a religious ceremony after the requisite public proclamations or banns, or as a secular form.

The object of the Act for authorising civil marriages was to relieve Dissenters and those who could not conscientiously join in the formulary of the Church. Due provision is made for necessary publicity, and the marriage can be legally contracted in a Register Office. Marriages in the Church of England (without banns or licence), marriages of Quakers, Jews, Dissenters, and Roman Catholics, and marriages according to the civil or secular form, must be preceded by a given notice from one of the parties to the Superintendent-Registrar of the district.

The marriage law of Scotland is founded upon the *Canon* Law (i.e. rules drawn from Scriptures and the writings of the Church). In Scotland there are regular and irregular marriages. Irregular marriages are legal without any ceremony, and are of three sorts.

1. By a promise of marriage given in writing or proved by a reference to the oath of the party, followed by consummation.

2. By the solemn mutual declaration of a man and woman, either verbally or in writing, expressing that the parties consent to take each other for husband and wife.

3. By notorious cohabitation as man and wife.

Persons living in England and having illegitimate children, cannot by going to Scotland, there marrying, and then returning, legitimatise their children in England. A domicile (or abiding home) in Scotland, and a marriage of the father and mother, legitimatises the children in Scotland whenever born.

Lawful marriages in foreign countries are valid in England unless they are directly contrary to our laws.

Marriage with a deceased wife's sister is valid in England, if it has been celebrated in a country where such marriage is legal, provided the parties were at the time of the marriage domiciled in such country.

A man and wife are one person in law; the wife loses all her rights as a single woman, and her existence is entirely absorbed in that of her husband. He is civilly responsible for her acts; she lives under his protection or cover, and her condition is called coverture.

A woman's body belongs to her husband; she is in his custody, and he can enforce his right by a writ of *habeas corpus*.

What was her personal property before marriage, such as money in hand, money at the bank, jewels, household goods, clothes, etc. becomes absolutely her husband's, and he may assign or dispose of them at his pleasure whether he and his wife live together or not.

A wife's *chattels real* (i.e. estates held during a term of years, or the next presentation to a church living, etc.) become her husband's by his doing some act to appropriate them; but, if the wife survives, she resumes her property.

Equity is defined to be a correction or qualification of the law, generally made in the part wherein it faileth, or is too severe. In other words, the correction of that wherein the law, by reason of its universality, is deficient. While the Common Law gives the whole of a wife's personal property to her husband, the Courts of Equity, when he proceeds therein to recover property in right of his wife, oblige him to make a settlement of some portion of it upon her, if she be unprovided for and virtuous.

If her property be under £200, or £10 a year, a Court of Equity will not interpose.

Neither the Courts of Common Law nor Equity have any direct power to oblige a man to support his wife – the Ecclesiastical Courts (i.e. Courts held by the Queen's authority as governor of the Church, for matters which chiefly concern religion) and a Magistrate's court at the instance of her parish alone can do this.

A husband has a freehold estate in his wife's lands during the joint existence of himself and his wife, that is to say, he has absolute possession of them as long as they both live. If the wife dies without children, the property goes to her heir, but if she has borne a child, her husband holds possession until his death.

Money earned by a married woman belongs absolutely to her husband; that and all sources of income, excepting those mentioned above, are included in the term personal property.

By the particular permission of her husband she can make a will of her personal property, for by such a permission he gives up his right. But he may revoke his permission at any time before *probate* (i.e. the exhibiting and proving a will before the Ecclesiastical Judge having jurisdiction over the place where the party died).

The legal custody of children belongs to the father. During the lifetime of a sane father, the mother has no rights over her children, except a limited power over infants, and the father may take them from her and dispose of them as he thinks fit.

If there be a legal separation of the parents, and there be neither agreement nor order of Court, giving the custody of the children to either parent, then the *right to the custody of the children* (except for the nutriment of infants) belongs legally to the father.

A married woman cannot sue or be sued for contracts – nor can she enter into contracts except as the agent of her husband; that is to say, her word alone is not binding in law, and persons giving a wife credit have no remedy against her. There are some exceptions, as where she contracts debts upon estates settled to her separate use, or where a wife carries on trade separately, according to the custom of London, etc.

A husband is liable for his wife's debts contracted before marriage, and also for her breaches of trust committed before marriage.

Neither a husband nor a wife can be witnesses against one another in criminal cases, not even after the death or divorce of either.

A wife cannot bring actions unless the husband's name is joined.

As the wife acts under the command and control of her husband, she is excused from punishment for certain offences, such as theft, burglary, housebreaking, etc., if committed in his presence and under his influence. A wife cannot be found guilty of concealing her felon husband or of concealing a felon jointly with her husband. She cannot be found guilty of stealing from her husband or of setting his house on fire, as they are one person in law. A husband and wife cannot be found guilty of conspiracy, as that offence cannot be committed unless there are two persons.

Usual Precautions Against the Laws Concerning the Property of Married Women

When a woman has consented to a proposal of marriage, she cannot dispose or give away her property without the knowledge of her betrothed; if she make any such disposition without his knowledge, even if he be ignorant of the existence of her property, the disposition will not be legal.

It is usual, before marriage, in order to secure a wife and her children against the power of the husband, to make with his consent a settlement of some property on the wife, or to make an agreement before marriage that a settlement shall be made after marriage. It is in the power of the Court of Chancery to enforce the performance of such agreements.

Although the Common Law does not allow a married woman

to possess any property, yet in respect of property settled for her separate use, Equity endeavours to treat her as a single woman.

She can acquire such property by contract before marriage with her husband, or by gift from him or other persons.

There are great difficulties and complexities in making settlements, and they should always be made by a competent lawyer.

When a wife's property is stolen, the property (legally belonging to the husband) must be laid as his in the indictment.

Separation and Divorce

A husband and wife can separate upon a deed containing terms for their immediate separation, but they cannot legally agree to separate at a *future* time. The trustees of the wife must be parties to the deed, and agree with the husband as to what property the wife is to take, for a husband and wife cannot covenant together.

Divorce is of two kinds:

First, divorce à mensâ et thoro, being only a separation from bed and board.

Second, divorce à vinculo matrimonii, being an entire dissolution of the bonds of matrimony.

The grounds for the first kind of divorce are, first, Adultery, second, Intolerable Cruelty, and third, Unnatural Practices. The Ecclesiastical Courts can do no more than pronounce for this first kind of divorce, or rather separation, as the matrimonial tie is not severed, and there is always a possibility of reconciliation.

The law cannot dissolve a lawful marriage; it is only in the Legislature that this power is vested. It requires an act of Parliament to constitute a divorce à vinculo matrimonii, but the investigation rests by usage with the Lords alone, the House of Commons acting upon the faith that the House of Lords came to a just conclusion.

This divorce is pronounced on account of adultery in the wife, and in some cases of aggravated adultery on the part of the husband.

The expenses of only a common divorce bill are between six hundred and seven hundred pounds, which makes the possibility of release from the matrimonial bond a privilege of the rich.

A wife cannot be plaintiff, defendant, or witness in an important part of the proceeding for a divorce, which evidently must lead to much injustice.

Laws Concerning a Widow

A widow recovers her real property, but if there be a settlement she is restricted by its provisions. She recovers her chattels real if her husband has not disposed of them by will or otherwise.

A wife's paraphernalia (i.e., her clothes and ornaments) which her husband owns during his lifetime, and which his creditors can seize for his debts, becomes her property on his death.

A widow is liable for any debts which she contracted before marriage, and which have been left unpaid during her marriage.

A widow is not bound to bury her dead husband, it being the duty of his legal representative.

If a man die intestate, the widow, if there are children, is entitled to one-third of the personalty; if there are no children, to one-half; the other is distributed among the next of kin, among whom the widow is not counted. If there is no next of kin the moiety goes to the crown.

A husband can, of course, by will deprive a wife of all right in the personalty.

A right is granted in Magna Charta to a widow to remain forty days in her husband's house after his death, provided she do not marry during that time.

A widow has a right to a third of her husband's lands and tenements for her life. Right of dower is generally superseded by settlements giving the wife a jointure. If she accept a jointure she has no claim to dower.

Laws Concerning Women in Other Relationships

A woman can act as agent for another, and, as an attorney, legally execute her authority. A wife can so act if her husband do not dissent.

An unmarried woman can be vested with a trust, but if she marry, the complexities and difficulties are great, from her inability to enter alone into deeds and assurances.

A single woman can act as executrix under a will, but a wife cannot accept an executorship without her husband's consent.

A woman is capable of holding the office of administratrix to an intestate personalty, and administration will be granted to her if she be next of kin to the intestate. But a wife cannot act without the consent of her husband.

If a man place a woman in his house, and treat her as his wife, he is responsible for her debts.

Laws Concerning Illegitimate Children and Their Mothers

A single woman having a child may throw the maintenance upon the putative father, so called to distinguish him from a husband, until the age of thirteen.

The law only enforces the parents to maintain such child, and the sum the father is obliged to pay, after an order of affiliation is proved against him, never exceeds two shillings and sixpence a week.

The mother, as long as she is unmarried or a widow, is bound to maintain such child as a part of her family until such child attain the age of sixteen.

A man marrying a woman having a child or children at the time of such marriage is bound to support them, whether legitimate or not, until the age of sixteen.

The rights of an illegitimate child are only such as he can acquire; he can inherit nothing, being in law looked upon as nobody's son, but he may acquire property by devise or bequest. He may acquire a surname by reputation, but does not inherit one.

The only incapacity under which he labours is that he cannot be heir-at-law nor next of kin to any person, nor can he have collateral heirs, but only lineal descendants; if he acquire property and die without a will, such property will go to the crown unless he have lineal descendants.

Remarks

These are the principal laws concerning women.

It is not now as it once was, when all existing institutions were considered sacred and unalterable; and the spirit which made Blackstone an admirer of, rather than a critic on, every law because it was *law*, is exchanged for a bolder and more discriminating spirit, which seeks to judge calmly what is good and to amend what is bad.

Philosophical thinkers have generally come to the conclusion that the tendency of progress is gradually to dispense with law –

that is to say, as each individual man becomes unto himself a law, less external restraint is necessary. And certainly the most urgently needed reforms are simple erasures from the statute book. Women, more than any other members of the community, suffer from over-legislation.

A woman of twenty-one becomes an independent human creature,[2] capable of holding and administering property to any amount; or, if she can earn money, she may appropriate her earnings freely to any purpose she thinks good. Her father has no power over her or her property. But if she unites herself to a man, the law immediately steps in, and she finds herself legislated for, and her condition of life suddenly and entirely changed. Whatever age she may be of, she is again considered as an infant – she is again under '*reasonable restraint*' – she loses her separate existence, and is merged in that of her husband.

'In short,' says Judge Hurlbut, 'a woman is courted and wedded as an angel, and yet denied the dignity of a rational and moral being ever after.'

'The next thing that I will show you is this particularitie of law; in this consolidation which we call wedlock is a locking together; it is true that man and wife are one person, but understand in what manner. When a small brooke or little river incorporateth with Rhodanus, Humber, or the Thames, the poore rivulet loseth her name, it is carried and recarried with the new associate, it beareth no sway, it possesseth nothing during coverture. A woman as soone as she is married is called covert, in Latine nupta, that is vailed, as it were clouded and overshadowed she hath lost her streame. . . . I may more truly farre away say to a married woman, her new selfe is her superior, her companion, her master. The mastership shee is fallen into may be called in a terme which civilians borrow from Esop's Fables, Leonina societate.'[3]

Truly 'she hath lost her streame', she is absorbed, and can hold nothing of herself, she has no legal right to any property; not even her clothes, books, and household goods are her own, and any money which she earns can be robbed from her legally by her husband, nay, even after the commencement of a treaty of marriage she cannot dispose of her own property without the knowledge of her betrothed. If she should do so, it is deemed a fraud in law and can be set aside after marriage as an injury to her husband.

It is always said, even by those who support the existing law, that it is in fact never acted upon by men of good feeling. That is true; but the very admission condemns the law, and it is not right that the good feeling of men should be all that a woman can look to for simple justice.

There is now a large and increasing class of women who gain their own livelihood, and the abolition of the laws which give husbands this unjust power is most urgently needed.

Rich men and fathers might still make what settlements they pleased, and appoint trustees for the protection of minors and such women as needed protection; but we imagine it well proved that the principle of protection is wrong, and that the education of freedom and responsibility will enable women to take better care of themselves and others too than can be insured to them by any legal precautions.

Upon women of the labouring classes the difficulty of keeping and using their own earnings presses most hardly. In that rank of life where the support of the family depends often on the joint earnings of husband and wife, it is indeed cruel that the earnings of both should be in the hands of one, and not even in the hands of that one who has naturally the strongest desire to promote the welfare of the children.

All who are familiar with the working classes know how much suffering and privation is caused by the exercise of this *right* by drunken and bad men. It is true that men are legally bound to support their wives and children, but this does not compensate women for the loss of their moral right to their own property and earnings, nor for the loss of the mental development and independence of character gained by the possession and thoughtful appropriation of money; nor, it must be remembered, can the claim to support be enforced on the part of the wife unless she appeals to a court of law. Alas, how much will not a woman endure before she will publicly plead for a maintenance!

Why, we ask, should there be this difference between the married and unmarried condition of women? And why does marriage make so little legal difference to men, and such a mighty legal difference to women? In France it is somewhat more equal; married women have a right, if they marry without a marriage contract, to claim at the death of a husband half of whatever he possessed at the time of marriage, or may have gained afterwards. If a woman have property of her own, she may if she please marry under the 'régime de séparation de corps et de biens', in which case she has the entire control of her own fortune, and has no need of trustees. But usually marriages in France are of another description, or under the 'régime dotal', in which case a portion of the property of the wife is left at the disposal of the husband, and the rest placed in the hands of trustees, much as it is with us in England. The choice which the French law allows is however a great improvement on our law.

In Turkey, daughters succeed equally with sons in houses and landed property, and always take one-third of the personal property. A widow receives one-eighth of the personal property, and must be provided for during her life by the heirs. Women control their own inheritance when married; the husband has no power over the inherited portion of his wife or wives.

In Hungary, the common law, before 1849 (the German law is now introduced), made a broad distinction between *inherited* and *acquired* property, whether landed or personal. Whatever was inherited went to the heirs; it could not be subject to a will.

As to *acquired* property, the law only interfered to give half to the wife; it was her absolute property, of which she might dispose in any way during life or by will. Among the nobility this law did not obtain. In cases where inherited property had been so left by the will of the first *acquisitor* as to exclude the female sex, the brothers were obliged to give a handsome sum if they married to their sisters, and provide for them in a becoming way if they remained single.

The rights of a widow were great; she was guardian of children, administrator of property, and, as long as she bore the name of her husband, she could exercise all the political rights of a man; she could vote in elections of county officers, and in those of the Deputies to the Diet.

Single females, according to the Hungarian law, were considered as minors, who became of age upon marriage, and by marriage came into full control of all their estates. They were not liable for the debts of their husbands; they were not even bound to provide for the domestic expenses, the care of providing for the house and the education of the children being incumbent on the husband. Wives could make wills and sign deeds without the consent of the husbands. If a wife died intestate, her property went to her children or collaterals.

In fact a wife was not regarded in Hungary as a minor, her husband was not her guardian, nor were there trustees appointed for her property. 'None of my countrywomen would ever have submitted to such a marriage settlement as is usual in England,' said a Hungarian lady, well known for her genius and reputation. With the one exception of considering all unmarried women as minors, the Hungarian law is very much in advance of ours.

The laws in the United States are generally much the same as ours. As a general rule married women cannot make a devise of real estate. In some of the States there are more reasonable laws, and a married woman may make a will and devise lands in the same manner as men. These States are Ohio, Illinois, Connecticut,

Mississippi, and Louisiana. In Ohio the laws are remarkably liberal to women. The first section of the statute of wills in Ohio declares that any person of full age and sound mind and memory may make a will. By the statute of Ohio it is expressly provided that the will of an unmarried woman shall *not* be revoked by her subsequent marriage.

What changes we find in the American laws are improvements upon ours. Is there not evidence in our English laws of old opinions relating to women which are passing away with the old state of things which engendered them? In the early times, when women were obliged by the violent state of society to be always under the guardianship of father, brother, or husband, these laws might be necessary; but in our peaceful times, such guardianship is proved to be superfluous by the fact of the secure, honourable, and independent position of single women who are sufficiently protected by the sanctuary of civilization.

Since all the unmarried women in England are supported either by their own exertions or by the exertions or bequests of their fathers and relations, there is no reason why upon marriage they should be thrown upon the pecuniary resources of their husbands, except in so far as the claims of a third party – children – may lessen the wife's power of earning money, at the same time that it increases her expenses. Of course a woman may, and often does, by acting as housekeeper and manager of her husband's concerns, earn a maintenance and a right to share in his property, independent of any children which may come of the marriage. But it is evident that daughters ought to have some sure provision – either a means of gaining their own bread, or property – as it is most undesirable that they should look upon marriage as a means of livelihood.

Fathers seldom feel inclined to trust their daughters' fortunes in the power of a husband, and, in the appointment of trustees, partially elude the law by a legal device. Also, the much abused Court of Chancery tries to palliate the Common Law, and recognises a separate interest between husband and wife, and allows the wife alone to file a bill to recover and protect her property, and trustees are not necessary if there has been an agreement.

Why should not these legal devices be done away with, by the simple abolition of a law which we have outgrown?

We do not say that these laws of property are the only unjust laws concerning women to be found in the short summary which we have given, but they form a simple, tangible, and not offensive point of attack.

NOTES

1 Elizabeth Blackwell, M.D., received her diploma in America before she walked [into] St Bartholomew's Hospital in London.
2 With regard to the property of women, there is taxation without representation, for they pay taxes without having the liberty of voting for representatives, and indeed there seems at present no reason why single women should be denied this privilege. *Note to Christian's Blackstone.*
3 The Lawe's Resolutions of Women's Rights, A.D. 1682.

Women and Work

(1857)

For we are all the children of God by faith in Christ Jesus; for there is neither Jew nor Greek, there is neither bond nor free, there is neither male nor female, for ye are all one in Christ Jesus.

St Paul

> Be sure, no earnest work
> Of any honest creature, howbeit weak,
> Imperfect, ill adapted, fails so much
> It is not gathered as a grain of sand
> For carrying out God's end. No creature works
> So ill, observe, that there he's cashiered.
> The honest, earnest man must stand and work;
> The woman also; otherwise she drops
> At once below the dignity of man,
> Accepting serfdom.

Elizabeth Barrett Browning

PREFACE

This Tract is addressed especially to men and women who live by the work of their hands or heads; their ears are always the most open to reason; they are the main mass and the hope of our country; and it is they who are the most to blame in not training up their daughters to work.

I beg all of you who read, to think seriously over my words; if they have truth in them, it is a matter between God and your own souls that you act upon them.

Women Want Professions

Cries are heard on every hand that women are conspiring, that women are discontented, that women are idle, that women are overworked, and that women are out of their sphere. God only knows what is the sphere of any human being.

Again, we hear cries that the world is going wrong for want of women, that moral progress cannot be made without their help; that Science wants the light of their delicate perceptions; that Moral Philosophy wants the light of their peculiar point of view; Political Economy, their directness of judgment and sympathy with the commonalty; Government, the help of their power of organising; and Philanthropy, their delicate tact. Hospitals must have them, asserts one; Watches must be made by them, cries another; Workhouses, Prisons, Schools, Reformatories, Penitentiaries, Sanatoriums, are going to rack and ruin for want of them; Medicine needs them, the Church calls for them, the Arts and Manufactures invite them.

One great corresponding cry rises from a suffering multitude of women, saying, 'We want work.'

Women are God's children equally with men. In Britain this is admitted; because it is a Christian country: in Mahommedan countries this is denied. We admit it as a principle, but we do not admit all that can be deduced from it: in practice we deny what we affirm in theory. If we are God's children, we owe certain duties to Him. The life of most women is a practical denial of such duties.

God sent all human beings into the world for the purpose of forwarding, to the utmost of their power, the progress of the world. We must each leave the world a little better than we found it. Consider all the evils in the world; you will see they are such as God has given us power to cure. We could not prevent good if we set about it, but evil we can hinder; it has in it the seeds of death, while all good influences are protected by God. This is a striking example:

'In the present state of ethnological science these principles are established:

First, between two races which mix, the more beautiful repro-
duces its type, in preference to the more ugly.

Second, two ugly races who mix, produce, nevertheless, a cross
finer than their father and mother.

This generic law ought not to surprise us, for nature tends
without ceasing to perfectionate humanity.'[1]

One duty in this world is to try and make it what God intends
it shall become: we are His tools. By working for the salvation of
this world, we may chance to achieve our own in another, but
never by any other means. To set to work to save our own souls
is as foolish as for a man on horseback to try and pull up his fallen
horse, or endeavour to use a lever without a fulcrum. To do God's
work in the world is the duty of all, rich and poor, of all nations,
of both sexes.

No human being has a right to be idle, no human being must
use the earth as a stable, and 'eat off his own head'. Whatever
comes under our hands should be bettered by the touch of our
fingers. The land we own we should drain and make more fertile
for ever. The children who are in our power should be educated.
If a sickness falls upon our town, we must try to stop its progress,
and to alleviate the sufferings it occasions. If an old roof lets in the
rain, we must new-slate it. If an old pot comes to us to mend, we
must mend it as best we can. *And we must train ourselves to do our
work well.* It is a good thing to ask ourselves daily the question,
'Have I eaten my head off to-day?' Women must, as children of
God, be trained to do some work in the world. Women may not
take a man as a god: they must not hold their first duty to be
towards any human being.

Never, since the world began, have women stood face to face
with God. Individual women have done so, but not women in
general. They are beginning to do it now; the principle that Jesus
Christ laid down is beginning to be admitted. Young women
begin to ask at the age of sixteen or seventeen, 'What am I created
for? Of what use am I to be in the world?' According to the answer
is often the destiny of the creature.

Mothers! the responsibility lies with you: what do you say in
answer? I fear it is almost always something to this purport: 'You
must marry some day. Women were made for men. Your use is
to bear children; to keep your home comfortable for your husband.
In marriage is the only respectable life for woman.'

If a girl has a religious or an inquiring mind, she will be much
dissatisfied with this answer, and say, 'But if no one ask me to
marry whom I can love? or suppose I do not want to marry?

38

Suppose my husband dies? or what am I to do all the years I have to wait for a husband? Is there nothing I can do for anybody?'

The newness of the world and the vigour of young life will prevent some years from being absolutely miserable. Among the rich, music, languages, drawing – 'accomplishments', in fact, fill up much of life, and stop the questionings and discontent of heart. In so far as they do this they are pernicious. In so far as they are amusements only, they are killing to the soul. It is better far to hear the voice of the hungry soul loud and crying. It is better to have the bare fact of idleness, than to be busy always doing nothing. Accomplishments, which are amusements only, do more harm than good. Do not misunderstand: all 'accomplishments' may be works, serious studies; and may, by helping others to bear life better, and giving pleasure to those who have none, be made worthy work for women; but for this end they must be studied faithfully and with self-devotion.

Women in modern life, even in the humblest, are no longer spinsters. Their spinning is all done by the steam-engine; their sewing will be soon all done by that same mighty worker. The work of our ancestresses is taken away from us; we must find fresh work. Idleness, or worse than idleness, is the state of tens of thousands of young women in Britain: in consequence, disease is rife amongst them; that one terrible disease, hysteria, in its multi-form aspects, incapacitates thousands.

There is nothing in the world so sad, so pitiful to see, as a young woman, who has been handsome, full of youthful joy, animal spirits and good nature, fading at thirty or thirty-five. Becoming old too soon, getting meagre, dried up, sallow, pettish, peevish, the one possible chance of life getting very uncertain, and the mind so continually fixed on that one hope that it becomes gradually a monomania.

It is difficult for fathers and mothers when they look at their daughters young, charming, full of cheerfulness and life, to think that they can change; but alas! probably they will in ten years change sadly. No cheerfulness that does not spring from duty and work can be lasting.

I believe more than one-half the women who go into the Catholic Church join her because she gives work to her children. Happier far is a Sister of Charity or Mercy than a young lady at home without a work or a lover. We do not mean to say work will take the place of love in life, that is impossible; does it with men? But we ardently desire that women should not make *love their profession.*

Love is not the end of life. It is nothing to be sought for; it should come. If we work, love may meet us in life; if not, we have something still beyond all price.

If women were in active life mixing much with men, the common attraction of sex merely would not be so much felt, but rather the attractions of natures especially adapted to each other.

> Whoever says
> To a loyal woman, 'Love and work with me',
> Will get fair answer, if the work and Love,
> Being good themselves, are good for her, the best
> She was born for. Women of a softer mood,
> Surprised by men when scarce awake to life,
> Will sometimes only hear the first word, Love,
> And catch up with it any kind of work
> Indifferent, so that dear Love go with it.
> I do not blame such women, though for love
> They pick much oakum.

'Certainly it would make unmarried women happier to have professions. But is it not discouraging to give a girl a training for a trade when we know that if she marries she will most surely give it up? She must, you know, if she has children, and nine out of ten women do marry and have children.'

Taking your statement as true, which, by the bye it is not, (for, of women at the age of twenty and upwards, forty-three out of the hundred in England and Wales are unmarried) we can answer that it is worth while. Firstly, a girl will make a better wife for having had such serious training. Secondly, your daughter may not marry. It is your duty to provide for that possibility; and she will surely be ill, miserable, or go mad, if she has no occupation. Thirdly, it may be years before your daughter finds a husband. It is your duty to give her worthy work, or to allow her to choose it; and certainly she is more likely to be attractive and to get a good husband if she is cheerful and happy in some work, than if she, being miserable and longing for a change, clutches at the first offer made her. Fourthly, suppose the man she may love is poor, by her labour she can help to form their mutual home. Birds, both cock and hen, help one another to build their nest. Fifthly, your daughter may be left to act as both father and mother to children dependent on her for daily bread.

But is it certain that a girl will give up her occupation when married? Are there not quite enough women carrying on business, professions, different works after marriage, to prove that it is possible, and much for the benefit of husbands and children? It is absurd to look to remote consequences and possibilities; all we can do is to walk straight on the little bit of way we see clearly with our foggy vision? If it be right for girls to ask for work, give it to them. If your daughter says, 'Teach me a trade', you have no right to refuse her. She may have to earn her own living; and hard indeed will be the struggle, if with no training, no habits of work, she enters into competition with the skilled workers of the world, and those who have habits of hard application.

Every human being should work; no one should owe bread to any but his or her parents. A child is dependent on its parents for bread as a child: idiots and imbeciles must be fed all their lives; but rational beings ask nothing from their parents save the means of gaining their own livelihood. Fathers have no right to cast the burden of the support of their daughters on other men. It lowers the dignity of women; and tends to prostitution, whether legal or in the streets. As long as fathers regard the sex of a child as a reason why it should not be taught to gain its own bread, so long must women be degraded. Adult women must not be supported by men, if they are to stand as dignified, rational beings before God. Esteem and friendship would not give or accept such a position, and Love is destroyed by it. How fathers, knowing men, can give up their daughters to be placed in such a degrading position, is difficult to understand. Human nature is better than human institutions; and there is, in spite of all the difficulties and dangers, a good deal of happiness in married life in Britain. But how much misery that might be prevented! Women must have work if they are to form equal unions. Work will enable women to free themselves from petty characteristics, and therefore ennoble marriage. The happiest married life we can recall ever to have seen is the life of two workers, a man and a woman equal in intellectual gifts and loving hearts; the union between them being founded in their mutual work.

Women who act as housekeepers, nurses, and instructors of their children, often do as much for the support of the household as their husbands; and it is very unfair for men to speak of supporting a wife and children when such is the case. When a woman gives up a profitable employment to be governess to her own family, she earns her right to live. We war against idleness, whether of man or woman, and every one is idle who is not making the best use of the faculties nature has given them.

How often dreary years of waiting for marriage might be saved by the woman doing just so much work as would keep her soul alive and her heart from stagnation, not to say corruption! We know an instance, a type of thousands. B, a young man was

41

engaged to M; they were both without fortunes. B worked for years to gain enough money to marry upon. M lived as young ladies usually do – doing nothing but reading novels and 'practising'. She became nervous, hysterically ill, and at last died of consumption. B, overworked and struck with grief, became mad. I could add a score of such cases. Ask medical men the effects of idleness in women. Look into lunatic asylums, then you will be convinced something must be done for women.

Think of the noble capacities of a human being. Look at your daughters, your sisters, and ask if they are what they might be if their faculties had been drawn forth; if they had liberty to grow, to expand, to become what God means them to be. When you see girls and women dawdling in shops, choosing finery, and talking scandal, do you not think they might have been better with some serious training?

Do you think women are happy? Look at unmarried women of thirty-five – the prime of life. Do you know one who is healthy and happy? If you do, she is one who has found her work: 'Blessed is he who has found his work, let him ask no other blessedness.' 'My God! *if I had anything to do,* I could bear this grief,' said a girl whose lover was just dead. Another living only in her lover who was a sailor, saw a false statement in a newspaper, that he was drowned – she lost her reason instantly and never recovered it. We do not say that if she had been a medical student or a watchmaker that the grief might not have turned her brain; but most certainly she would have had a stronger and a stouter reason, and some cause to wish to live. It is a noble thing even to make good watches, and well worth living for.

For our part, when we think of the lives of most women, how they are centred and bound up in human affection, living no life but that of love, we cannot wonder at reason going when love is lost. 'Oh! that I had now what you men call the consolations of philosophy', said a woman whose heart was sorely tried. The consolations of philosophy which men have, are indeed great when philosophy means the knowledge of God's works, but not enough unless some branch of the philosophy involves work. The man who works to discover the habits of an insect, or the woman who watches the growth and means of nourishment of a polyp – whoever works, is consoled. I have a great respect for the young lady, who being desperately in love, and having to give up her lover, went through the first four books of Euclid that she might not think of him. But I think it must have been heavy work, and that if she had been studying to be an architect, her purpose would have been better answered. It is surprising to see girls study so much as they do, considering how constantly the idea is put before them that they must give it up some day.

We were talking with Dr Emily Blackwell a little while before she left England to join her sister, Dr Elizabeth, in New York, as to the possibility of married women continuing in the exercise of professions if they had many children. She said: 'Granting women want to be doctors, and that medical science has need of women, women must, and will, enter the profession. I think it most probable that women will modify the practice of medicine; they will, probably, practise in groups, taking different branches; but we can hardly tell what effect the introduction of women may have upon the medical profession. We shall see in time; depend upon it, it will be good.'

Our gracious Queen fulfils the very arduous duties of her calling, and manages also to be the active mother of many children. Each woman must so arrange her own life as best to fulfil all her duties. Women can be trusted to do the best for their young children: maternal love is too strong ever to be weakened by any love of a science, art, or profession. As the human being is larger and nobler, so will all the natural affections be larger and nobler too. Let women take their places as citizens in the Commonwealth, and we shall find they will fulfil all their home duties the better.

There are now many trades open to women with good training in bookkeeping and knowledge of some especial branch of business, not difficult to acquire, if fathers would help their daughters as they help their sons. Two or three young women together might enter upon most shopkeeping businesses. But very few young women know enough arithmetic to keep accounts correctly.

We remember seeing two young women who kept a shop in a country village, slaving to answer the perpetual tinkle tinkle of the shop-bell, dealing out halfpennyworths of goodies, bacon, or candles – who, when asked how much they were paid yearly for the hard work of attending the shop, hardly understood the question, and only knew that *generally* they did not have to pay more for their goods than they sold them for, and got their food into the bargain, week by week. 'But how do you make your other expenses out?' 'By letting lodgings', said they.

It is unjust to say sneeringly, 'If women want to work, why don't they?' It is not an easy thing for a boy brought up to manhood to expect a large fortune to gain his livelihood if he be suddenly deprived of every farthing he possesses; and much is the pity lavished upon him. Probably friends lend him some hundreds of pounds for him to live upon, while he prepares for some profession. The case of most women who are left destitute is much harder, and there are fewer paths open to them, and these are choke full. We are sick at heart at the cries that have been raised about distressed needlewomen, and decayed gentlewomen, and broken-down governesses. Much sympathy has been felt, but little solid thought given to the subject.

There is no way of aiding governesses or needlewomen but by opening more ways of gaining livelihoods for women. It is the most efficacious way of preventing prostitution. 'It is a terrible incident of our social existence,' says *The Times*, in a leader, Wednesday, February 11, 'that the resources for gaining a livelihood left open to women are so few. At present the language practically held by modern society to destitute women may be resolved into Marry – Stitch – Die – or do worse.'

Apprentice 10,000 to watchmakers; train 10,000 for teachers for the young; make 10,000 good accountants; put 10,000 more to be nurses under deaconnesses trained by Florence Nightingale; put some thousands in the electric telegraph offices over all the country; educate 1,000 lecturers for mechanics' institutions; 1,000 readers to read the best books to the working people; train up 10,000 to manage washing-machines, sewing-machines, etc. Then the distressed needlewomen would vanish; the decayed gentlewomen and broken-down governesses would no longer exist.[2]

It is only fathers and mothers who have the power to effect this change. Remember the next generation is ours to form and model as we will. If all fathers and mothers were faithfully to discharge their duties to their daughters, the next generation would see women healthier, happier, and more beautiful than women have ever yet been.

WORK – not drudgery, but WORK – is the great beautifier. Activity of brain, heart, and limb, gives health and beauty, and makes women fit to be the mothers of children. A listless, idle, empty-brained, empty-hearted, ugly woman has no right to bear children.

To think a woman is more feminine because she is frivolous, ignorant, weak, and sickly, is absurd; the larger-natured a woman is, the more decidedly feminine she will be; the stronger she is, the more strongly feminine. You do not call a lioness unfeminine, though she is different in size and strength from the domestic cat, or mouse.

If men think they shall lose anything charming by not having ignorant, dependent women about them, they are quite wrong. The vivacity of women will not be injured by their serious work. None play so heartily as those who work heartily. The playfulness of women which makes them so sympathetic to children, is deep in their nature; and greater development of their whole natures will only increase this and all their natural gifts.

It is often said, it is wrong of daughters to leave their parents to follow this or that pursuit. Mothers and fathers say nothing, if their daughters leave them to be married. It is much more important to the welfare of a girl's soul that she be trained to work than that she marry. It is very hard for children to battle against this feeling in mothers and fathers, even when they feel it most unreasonable. Generally, daughters have neither the courage to choose work, nor the resignation to submit with cheerfulness to be children all their days. Oh, girls, who are now suffering in this battle, remember your sufferings when you have children, and do unto them as you would you had been done unto!

Children who spend their lives in ministering to the little fancies and whims of a father or mother, who, from the old habit of childish obedience, cannot break through the slavery of home-life, should remember that by wasting their lives in such trivial duties they weaken their own intellects and hearts, and will as surely one day or other be dependent upon such attentions themselves. Far be it from us to say that children do not owe deeds of reverence and duty to their parents – they do, most certainly. All that ennobles women will make them discharge these more faithfully. But for two or three daughters to remain at home idle, with the pretence of attending on a father or mother who is not even always old, infirm, or ill, is absurd. The pretence breaks down as soon as a 'good match' offers. There are, moreover, many professions, such as medicine, many branches of decorative art, wood-cutting, engraving, watchmaking, etc., which, after some time of apprenticeship, can be carried on at home. The alteration of the laws concerning married women's property will make a great difference in the public feeling as regards women working after marriage. The 60,000 women who have signed petitions for the alteration of the law, and which alteration will give them a right to their own earnings after marriage, have quite settled the question as to whether women want to earn money or not. Women *do* want work, and girls must be trained for professions.

Professions Want Women

Ask the thousands of soldiers who passed under the consoling hands of Florence Nightingale and her noble band, what profession wants women! The profession of nursing wants women, and will have them. I think those same soldiers, if they could vote, would elect women to fill the whole commissariat department.

Ask the emigrants who went out to Australia year after year under the careful and wise system of Caroline Chisholm's colonisation, how women can organise and what professions they should fill. I think they would answer, 'As organisers of colonisation, emigration, secretaries to colonies', etc.

Ask those interested in the reform of juvenile criminals. They will say, 'Mary Carpenter is appointed by nature to be establisher and inspector of such schools. Women are wanted in the vast vocation of reformation.'

Miss Dix of New York is another appointment by Divine command. She established and improved lunatic asylums in all parts of the Union, prompted by her own mission to the work. At present she is aided, and power delegated to her, by the United States Government.[3]

But women of far more ordinary power than Miss Dix show their capacity for managing the insane. In the January number of the *Psychological Journal*, is an account of an Asylum for female lunatics at Ghent, which is managed by a 'Sœur Supérieure' and her assistant Sisters of Charity (the physicians are non-resident). 'The number of resident lunatics under treatment, on the day of my visit,' writes Dr Webster, 'amounted to 269 altogether, of whom 201 were considered incurables. No person was under restraint of any kind whatever, nor in seclusion. Indeed, it may be added, that physical coercion in any form is very seldom employed at this establishment; the great object constantly kept in view being to amuse and occupy the inmates, whereby tranquillity becomes promoted, at the same time that such means tend to improve their mental condition. In one apartment, upwards of a dozen young females – all idiots or imbeciles – were assembled at their singing lesson, under the tuition of a zealous "Sister". These poor girls sang delightfully, accompanied by their teacher on the piano, which made quite a musical treat; and as several juvenile performers were blind or dumb, while their execution hence seemed more surprising, this unexpected performance, by intellectually bedimmed and unfortunate fellow-creatures, caused us greater satisfaction.'

Madame Luce, the first establisher of schools for Moorish girls, is another instance of an appointment by nature.

'Madame Luce,' writes a lady who has recently visited her school in Algiers, 'came to Algiers shortly after the conquest, and has resided here ever since – viz., twenty-seven years. She was a teacher, probably in the family of some one of the resident functionaries, of whom the French mode of government entails so many upon all countries under her care. In 1845 she was a widow, Madame Allix, though, for the sake of avoiding confusion, we have always called her by the name she now bears. She was also poor, having only a small sum of money on which to commence an undertaking upon which her heart had been long set – a school in which girls of Mohammedan family should be taught the language, and somewhat of the civilisation, of the conquering race. The government had already established schools for instructing native boys in French, etc. But these institutions were not flourishing, the Mohammedans dreaded intrusting their children to Christians, more particularly if the Catholic priests had any share in the work; and one Muphti, a Mohammedan ecclesiastic, was actually deported to the Ile Ste Marguerite for contumacy upon this subject. As to the girls, nobody ever thought of them; and, indeed, any European who came to know the ways and customs of the Moresques, the religious and social tyranny under which they suffer, and their own utter debased ignorance, might well despair of effecting any sort of good among them. The lower ranks walk about the streets closely veiled, excepting a narrow slit for the eyes; but the upper class of Moorish women rarely stir out except to the bath or the cemetery. Three or four times a year to the mosque completes their part in the religious ceremonies enjoined by the Koran. They have very little to do with religion; active charity is impossible under the multitude of restrictions amidst which they exist; they can neither read nor write, and they are not taught any manual art by which women deprived of other means of subsistence might gain their daily bread. Neither can they be said to be housewives. The simple *manière d'être* of the Eastern nations, their fine climates, their scanty furniture, their idle slovenly existence, give no sort of scope to the virtues of a farmer's or of a mechanic's wife. To "suckle fools" is indeed the duty of mothers all the world over; but the corresponding occupation of "chronicling small beer" is no part of the vocation of a Moresque. To wash their linen and hang it out to dry either on the rails of their court or on the terrace-roof which is possessed by every house; to clamber over the said roof and its partition on to her neighbour's (the received way of paying calls in Algiers), there to drink coffee and to offer the same in requital; to dress up very fine upon occasion – gauze, silk, ribbons, and jewels – and very shabbily and dirtily on other occasions in the *débris* of former splendour; such seems to be the idea of life entertained by, or permitted to, these poor creatures. In sickness it is still worse; they refuse to take the commonest precautions, preferring the "will of

Allah" to any of the alleviations of science and skill. They object to being visited by French medical men, because the intruder is of the other sex; and, even if they did not object, it would probably bring them into great trouble with their husbands. Whole families die off for want of vaccination, or proper separation of sick and well in fever. They do not know their own ages, in which they are no worse than the men; for it is only of late years that the French have procured the regular registration of children, male and female; while, for the crowning affliction and degradation of their lives, they are liable to be sold in marriage at the age of eleven or twelve, while yet merely children: they assume the veil when eight years old. We read in Mr Morell's book upon Algiers that "Moorish women are valued by *weight!*" – a somewhat singular standard of feminine elegance; and that "marriages among the Moors, as with most other Mussulmans, are contracted through third parties and gossips – the young people never meeting till the wedding-day."

Such was the human material which Madame Luce dared to conceive of as capable of being raised to something approaching the condition of her European sister. This was the way in which she set to work, being profoundly persuaded that till something was done to alter the social spirit of Moorish interiors, no true amalgamation with the conquering race could ever take place.

While collecting her small funds, and laying her large plans, she perfected herself in the knowledge of the native language; and in 1845, fifteen years after the conquest, she commenced a campaign among the Moorish families of her personal acquaintance, endeavouring to persuade the fathers and mothers to intrust their little girls to her care for a few hours every day, that they might be taught to read and write French, and also to sew neatly – an accomplishment in which the Moresques are as deficient as they are in Latin and mathematics. By dint of coaxing, presents, entreaties, and the most solemn assurances that she would not interfere with the religion of the children – by using, in short, her personal influence with all the energy of a philanthropist and the tact of a Frenchwoman, she contrived to get together four little girls, whom she installed in a house she hired for the purpose, and she began to teach them without an hour's delay. In writing this account I follow a long memorial addressed by her to the Minister of War, corroborated by my own personal observation on the present state of the school. By degrees, as the rumour of her plan spread among the Mussulmans, one child after another dropped in upon her, till the numbers ran up to thirty and to forty. Finding it answer beyond her hopes, she then began to demand support from the local government – the same support which they gave to the education of boys – telling the officials that it was in vain to hope to rear a better, a more rational and civilised race of Mussulmans, so long as their wives and the mothers of the next generation were left in worse than the ignorance of the brutes, to whom God has given sufficient intelligence for the performance of the simple duties and the enjoyment of the simple pleasures of their state. But the Algerine officials saw no manner of good in educating Moorish women; they could not understand that "as the wife is, so the husband is", reversing Tennyson's well-known stanza in *Locksley Hall*; and though they complimented Madame Luce upon her energy, they declined allowing her pecuniary assistance. She, who had counted on demonstrating to them the value and the success of the experiment, was almost in despair. The expenses were heavy, and altogether defrayed by her; the children had to be bribed to come – to be helped, such as were of poor families, by food and clothing, lodging, school-books – all fell upon small means; and though the school answered in all its moral and intellectual ends, there seemed nothing for it but to close it, and lament over the failure of so noble an experiment and the waste of much time and money. The 30th of December, 1845, came, on which day the Council of Administration was to meet. She waited in breathless suspense, hoping something would be said about the school. Evening came: she learnt they had not even mentioned her; and on New Year's day 1846 the school was *closed!* Perhaps the reader will think she was at last daunted, being deserted by the local authorities, and being upwards of 900 miles from the central government, to reach which was a far longer, more difficult, and expensive journey than it is at present. Madame Luce had little or no money; and though some of the heads of affairs at Algiers had offered her a small sum as indemnification to herself, she had absolutely refused it, saying it was not personal help she wanted, but support to an undertaking of great national importance.

What, then did she do next? She pawned her plate, her jewels, even a gold thimble, the gift of a friend, and set off for Paris, which she reached early in February, and there she at once sent in to the Minister of War that memorial from which we have taken the preceding details. She also visited in person most of the influential deputies, and endeavoured to prepossess them in favour of her plans. In Paris she found the official mind more sympathising than in the military colony, and at last saw daylight begin to break. They gave her 3,000 francs for the cost of her journey, and she also came in for 1,100 from some property belonging to her dead husband, M. Allix (1,000 francs amount to £40). They also urged her to return to Algiers and recommence operations, and promised to give her further support. So she set out on her way home, and reached Algiers once more in June, when she reopened her school amidst great rejoicings from parents and children. But here again came in the spirit of official delay, and seven more months elapsed before her school was fairly adopted by government, with a proper salary to herself and defrayal of expense. During these seven months the school kept rising in numbers, and she was put to the greatest shifts to keep it together. M. the Abbé Pelletan, curé of Algiers, gave her a little money and a great deal of sympathy; and Count Guyot, a man high in office, helped her from his own private purse, having always felt a great personal interest in the undertaking. To him, when the necessities of the day pressed too heavily, she sent one of her negresses, for she was obliged to keep two to attend to the house and to fetch and reconduct the pupils. Count Guyot would then send a small sum for her assistance. He also one day gave a small bag of money left by the Duc de Nemours for the benefit of a journal which had at that time ceased to exist, telling her she might have whatever it contained. She opened the bag and found 200 francs inside; "And this money," said she, "appeared to me to come from Providence." So she got along, "from hand to mouth", as the saying is, with an increasing school; and she engaged an Arab mistress, formerly teacher in the family of Hussein Bey, and a remarkable instance of native cultivation, to assist her in the instruction of the pupils, also to superintend their religious exercises; "For," says Madame Luce, "it does not do to leave children without any religion"; so that being, by the very fact of the existence of her school at all, debarred from teaching them her own faith, she preferred their being properly instructed in that of their parents – a faith which contains some of the elements of Christian verity, inasmuch as it inculcates a profound belief in, and reverence for, one only God, and impresses a sense of moral responsibility in regard to right and wrong.

My readers will remember that Madame Luce had in this matter no power of free action, as she would not have got a single child but for her sacredly pledged vow that she would not endeavour to instil her own religion. At length, in January 1847, the storms were weathered; the school was formally adopted by Government, and received its first visit of official inspection, at which Count Guyot was present. The inspector declared himself more than satisfied with the condition of the children, not thinking it possible that so much progress could have been made in instructing Mores-

ques. On this occasion the gentlemen were received by thirty-two
pupils and the Arab sub-mistress *unveiled*, which Madame Luce
considered a great moral triumph. She always works against the
use of the veil, thinking, and truly thinking, as it seems to us, that
it is far from conducive to true modesty of bearing, which should
be simple and straightforward, of that purity which "thinketh no
evil".

Since 1847 Madame Luce has pursued her path of usefulness.
The school numbers at present 120, of all ages between four and
eighteen.

Madame Luce at one time established a workshop, where the
elder pupils executed work for the ladies of the place, and earned
in this way a considerable sum of money; learning at the same
time to appreciate the value of labour. They had always a week's
stock waiting for them in advance, when the Government put an
end to it – whether for the sake of economising the salary for the
sewing-mistress who superintended it, and which did not amount
to more than £35 a year, or whether for the sake of exclusively
favouring some similar institution set on foot by the nuns –
Madame Luce does not know; but she greatly regrets the stoppage,
as she considers it one of the most useful parts of her whole
scheme. She is obliged to pay great attention to the intellectual
training of her pupils, because the gentlemen-inspectors think far
more of a well-turned French phrase than of a neatly-sown frock;
but she individually feels more anxious about the industrial
education than anything else; thinking it of the utmost importance
that Moorish women should possess some means of gaining a
respectable livelihood, to say nothing of the eminent need in their
own homes of neatness and order, and the power of making and
mending their own and their husbands' clothes.

I must add that there is nothing very elaborate or first-rate in
the management of this school. It seems to be a system alternating
between kindness and a many-thonged leathern whip, of which
the wild young folk did not seem particularly to stand in awe.
Living, as they all do, at home, fetched backwards and forwards
every day by negresses specially attached to the school for this
task, and being, moreover, condemned to all the evil influences of
possible early marriages, more than a certain amount of good
cannot be done. They must still be rough and savage, and distress
the looker-on by the coarse expression of face which two generations of training cannot remove. But they are actually taught to
read and write in a foreign language, to do the first few rules of
arithmetic, to sew, and to be proud of Madame Luce. They learn
to conceive of their own sex as of rational and responsible beings,

to think that they can earn money and support themselves. The present Moorish teacher is a young woman, who in all ways looks like a French woman. She has passed a regular examination, and taken out her diploma; indeed, I was astonished to find that she was a Moresque and a Mussulman. Some of the older girls had been many years with Madame Luce, and are monitors.

Every Moresque thus educated carries into her home the seed of a better state of moral thought and feeling, germs of a kindlier sentiment towards the conquering race, and a prospect that her own little daughters will have to contend with fewer social prejudices in working out a good and useful career. There is another school of the same sort now in Algiers, and I believe more than one in the provinces of Algeria, established by government after the example of the original founder. But in looking at the advance of female education in Algeria, those who may chance to visit this beautiful land should never forget that the first seed was sown by a woman, poor, and without the aids and appliances which rank bestows; that, by her unaided energy, she not only set afloat the principle of education for native women, but with expenditure of time, trouble, and limited means, forced the government also to recognise its value; finally, that the boys' schools have themselves succeeded much better since the impetus given by her to the idea of intellectual advancement in the minds of Moors and Arabs. Let us, therefore, in Britain learn, and hold in respect, the name of MADAME LUCE.'

Madame Marie Carpentier Pape, who for twenty years has devoted herself to establishing and conducting infant schools in France (*Salle d'Asiles*), led to the work by the peculiar gifts of her nature, is another example. As a private individual she began, gradually extending her sphere of usefulness: her book *Conseils sur la Direction des Salles d'Asile*, was crowned by the French Academy, and authorised by the Conseil Royal de l'Université, and after years of difficulty and hard work she is now at the head of the Normal School in Paris.

As an illustration of the power evinced by women sometimes in still more unusual directions – we cannot refrain from the pleasure of quoting from the *Daily News*, March 18th, the following story:

One day last month the people in the streets of New York observed a litter, evidently containing a sick person, carried up from the shipping to the Battery Hotel. Beside the litter walked a young creature who, but for her careworn countenance and her being near her confinement, might have been taken for a little school-girl. Her story soon became known, and it had presently reached all hearts. She is now twenty. At seventeen she had married a sea-captain – a gallant young fellow of five-and-twenty, she being a softly-reared young lady of East Boston. Just after the marriage, Captain Patton was offered the command of a ship – the *Neptune's Car* – prepared for the circumnavigation of the globe, and ready to sail that day but for the illness of the commander. Captain Patton declined the offer, declaring it impossible to leave his bride so soon and suddenly for so long a time. He was told that he would be allowed to take her with him. She agreed; and they were on board within twelve hours from the first question asked. During that voyage she learned whatever her husband could teach her; and especially she became practised in taking observations, and in keeping the reckoning of the ship. She studied navigation, in short, to some purpose. The voyage lasted seventeen months. Last August the captain and his wife sailed in their old ship for San Francisco, being so proud of the vessel as to pique themselves on reaching California sooner than two others which took their departure at the same time. It was this rivalship which first disclosed to Captain Patton the evil quality of his first mate, who was not only lazy and negligent to a dangerous degree, but ill-disposed. He was evidently bent on carrying the ship into Valparaiso, for purposes of his own. Anxiety and toil told on the captain's health before Cape Horn was reached. He there deposed the first mate from office, and, in the effort to discharge the duty himself, sank down in fever which soon issued in congestion of the brain. Before he lost his reason he declared positively against going into Valparaiso, saying, that the men would desert, and the cargo be lost before the consignees could arrive; and his honour and conscience were concerned in going on to the right port. This was enough. His wife determined that it should be done. As soon as her husband became hopelessly delirious, the first mate attempted to assume authority, and wrote a letter to Mrs Patton, charging her with the responsibility of all their lives if she opposed him. She told him that her husband had not trusted him while he was well, and that she would not trust him now her husband was ill. She assembled the crew, told them the facts, and appealed to them to disregard the first mate, to accept her authority in her husband's place, and to obey the second mate in the working of the ship. Every man of them agreed; and they sustained her well, as far as their power of support went. They looked with pity and reverence upon her as they saw her through the cabin-windows at her desk, keeping the reckoning, and making entries in the log. Noon and midnight she was on deck taking observations. She marked the charts, made no mistakes, and carried the ship into port, in the best condition, on the 13th of November. She had studied the medical books on board, to learn how best to treat her husband's case; and she never left him, day or night, but to perform his duties.

Happily he was a Freemason: his brother masons at San Francisco were kind, and sent them back by the first practicable opportunity to New York. There they arrived wholly destitute – the husband blind, deaf, delirious, dying – the wife worn and grave, but active and composed. She was anxious to reach Boston before her confinement; but, by the last accounts, she was disappointed by her husband being too ill to be removed.

The New York underwriters sent her an immediate gift of a thousand dollars; and the owners of the vessel and others are taking measures to testify their sense of the conduct by which a vast amount of property has been saved, and their interests and those of their crew have been conscientiously considered under singular extremity. With our Lady Fanshawes, Lucy Hutchinsons, and Catherine Mompessons, may now rank the Mary Patton of a kindred nation. It needs no other Freemasonry than that of the universal human heart to secure her reverence and welcome in every port she may put into henceforth in the rough voyage of life.

We might multiply instances. The work which women do on the press is considerable. It is difficult to know how much, but two facts we can state which are significant: Two-thirds of the writers in *Chambers's Edinburgh Journal* are women; Mrs Johnson of Edinburgh was for years the real editor of the *Inverness Courier*, the principal paper in the north of Scotland.

Perhaps there is no profession which so calls for women as that of medicine. Much suffering would be saved to young women if they had doctors of their own sex, who with friendly counsel and open speaking would often prevent many forms of severe disease by attending to first symptoms. On this point we let Dr Elizabeth Blackwell speak for herself:

In *An Appeal in behalf of the Medical Education of Women*, after referring to the establishment and opening of medical schools for women in Philadelphia, Boston, and other towns of the

United States, in the nine years since 'the first woman was admitted as a regular student to a medical college, and graduated with the usual honours'; she says, 'In all these places public opinion has expressed itself heartily in favour of the action of the colleges. The majority of the female graduates have entered upon the practice of their profession, and many of them have already formed a large and highly respectable practice. The intense prejudice which at first met the idea of a female doctor, is rapidly melting away. If further evidence were needed of the vitality of the new idea and its adaptation to a real want in the community, it might be found in the character of the practice which has come to those physicians now most firmly established. Intelligent, thoughtful women, of calm good sense, who appreciate the wide bearing of this reform, and foresee its important practical influence, have been the first to employ the new class of physicians in their families, and encourage them with their cordial approbation. The young also form a large portion of present practice, and there is no woman physician who has not felt her heart swell with satisfaction in the perception of the truly womanly nature of her work, when ministering to the necessities of delicate young womanhood.

To meet the great want, which women now feel, in relation to the study and practice of medicine, a very different method of education *from anything yet attempted is necessary*. A few short courses of lectures are quite insufficient to fit any one for the responsibilities of a physician's life, and yet this is the chief part of the college system.

The great need of women now is a large woman's hospital, which shall form a centre for all women who wish to pursue a thorough medical education.

In 1854 a charter was obtained for the organisation of the New York Infirmary and Dispensary for Women and Children. Under this charter a Dispensary has been organised in one of the most destitute sections of the city. This has been opened for the visits of those needing medical advice and medicine. It has been gratuitously attended by Dr Elizabeth Blackwell, Drs Parker, Cammann, Kiszam and Taylor, acting as consulting Physicians. More than three hundred poor women have received assistance from this institution; and instruction as to healthy habits of life, and friendly counsel, has been often added to the medical advice and medicine.

The time has now arrived for the extension of this charity

so as to make it the foundation of the Institution so urgently needed; and it is proposed to do this, by the enlargement of the out-patient department, and the organisation of the Hospital department, as contemplated in the charter.

All classes of non-infectious disease will be admitted, and there will be very full provision made for midwifery and the diseases of women – branches in which, from their very nature, it is particularly difficult for women as students in general hospitals to obtain satisfactory instruction, although they form necessarily so large a part of their practice, and in which, among the poor, the aid of educated women-physicians would be so valuable.

Students attending the hospital will be divided into small classes for practical instruction, and will serve by turn in each department, among the out-patients, and in the maternity charity. These classes will be small, so as to keep them completely under the supervision of the professor, to enable him to acquire a full acquaintance with the ability and needs of each individual student, and to allow the latter to obtain that special aid of which the want is so much felt by those who have been members of a large hospital class. This will also enable the physicians to save the feelings and ensure the welfare of the patients, and avoid their being ever injured by the indiscriminate admission of crowds of students. As soon as possible a laboratory and good anatomical rooms will be added to the hospital, which shall afford thorough practical facilities to students. The Institution must be endowed. The length of time requisite for a complete course of study renders it more expensive than the means of most women allow. They have generally more time than money; yet it is extremely important that every inducement to study thoroughly should be held out to them. The fees for the course must therefore be very low, and as the highest talent must be engaged in the service of the Institution, and the fullest illustration in all departments must be provided, a large endowment is indispensable.

In this way, by organising a large and well-arranged outpatient department, and a hospital department, small at first, but to be increased as rapidly as the funds collected will justify, the great want now felt by women engaged in the study of medicine, and by those engaged in their instruction, will be met, and a system of medical education provided which will afford women proper opportunities for study, and ensure to the community the services of a class of capable women-physicians.

Another object which it is hoped will be accomplished by this Institution, is that of raising the standard of the education and training of nurses. The want so strongly felt by all those who have anything to do with medicine, a body of thoroughly-trained nurses, filled with a high sense of the moral responsibility of their profession, will never be fully met until woman's true position in medicine is recognised and granted.

It will not be forgotten that a hospital is not merely a scientific school, that, though the promotion of science and scientific education is a most legitimate object, it should never encroach on the physical and moral welfare of the patients. It will be remembered that the poor who resort to a hospital, ignorant, degraded, even vicious, as they too often may be, are, nevertheless, not beyond the possibility of moral as well as material aid – that to such a class of women, the practical advice and counsel of educated women might be invaluable in spreading some wiser views with reference to their own health and life, and the rearing of their children, that they should leave the Institution, if possible, better in every respect than they entered; and that, for this reason, the character of the nurses who are constantly with them is of the highest possible importance, and, while every influence that could even most remotely be held to be of a sectarian character, will be sedulously avoided, an effort will be made to secure the assistance, as nurses, of women not only of respectable character and intelligence, but also of a truly religious spirit, so that the Institution, while the usual rules adopted in general hospitals for securing absolute freedom from any sectarian influence whatever will be strictly observed, shall fulfil, as far as possible, the highest idea of a hospital, that of a Christian charity for the poor.

If the Institution can be made what is desired in this respect, it is believed that it may be so arranged as to receive young ladies also, who desire to obtain practical knowledge in relation to sickness and health.

It would be a blessing to the race if young persons could find an opportunity, through such a hospital, of acquiring presence of mind, skill in tending the sick, acquaintance with the proper management of infancy, a knowledge of the difference between real and fancied ailments, and learn to guard their own health, and the health of those dependent on them.

This could only be *effectually accomplished* in a hospital, but a hospital may be rendered attractive instead of repulsive; and the relations which might spring up between the rich and the poor, when brought together in a truly Christian union, would be of lasting service to both.

A department of this Institution will be arranged for the reception of patients, whose means are too limited to obtain proper medical and other care, at their own homes. By the payment of a small weekly sum, their sense of independence will be preserved, while they are, at the same time, surrounded with every care which their condition requires.

It is a Women's Hospital, founded on these principles, and striving to accomplish these ends, that is now needed. In such a hospital, women students would feel at home; it would be their medical centre, and give them support throughout their professional career.

In order to accomplish its purpose, it must enlist the sympathies of the whole community, and be truly the Union Hospital for women. It is simply on account of its central position, and great facilities for medical study, that New York is chosen as the seat of this Institution. The city, as the great immigrating port of the United States, contains a larger number of sick poor than any other city in the Union. The statistics of immigration for the last five years stand as follows:

1851	262,590
1852	255,895
1853	284,947
1854	319,223
1855	136,233

making a total of 1,258,888 immigrants landing in New York during the last five years.

Large as the number of public charities in New York is, it by no means meets the wants of the needy population; and an unrivalled opportunity is presented for establishing a hospital, affording that wide range of observation necessary to the medical student.

It would be an excellent way of assisting this movement, and aiding our poor fellow countrywomen cast sick upon the shores of a new country, to establish an English ward for English immigrants. Can the funds be raised? Let us remember that this hospital will be accessible to Englishwomen, and may be a means of enabling them to get that medical education which they may have to wait for here in England for another quarter of a century.[4] America and England every year draw closer and closer together. New York will soon be but a few days from London. All that makes English and Americans co-operate, helps forward the world.

It is delightful to see two Englishwomen beginning in America this good work. Let us help them with all our power.

Many of the evils of our workhouses and prisons might be avoided by the introduction of well-paid women.

Mrs Jameson, in her admirable Lecture on the 'Communion of Labour', says, 'I come now to an institution peculiar to ourselves; and truly can I affirm, that if ever the combination of female with masculine supervision were imperatively needed, it is in an English parish workhouse.

'I have seen many workhouses, and of all grades. The regulation of details varies in different parishes. Some are admirably clean, and, as far as mere machinery can go, admirably managed; some are dirty and ill ventilated; and one or two, as we learn from recent disclosures, quite in a disgraceful state; but whatever the arrangement and condition, in one thing I found all alike: the want of a *proper moral supervision*. I do not say this in the grossest sense; though even in *that* sense, I have known of things I could hardly speak of. But surely I may say there is want of proper *moral* supervision where the most vulgar of human beings are set to rule over the most vulgar; where the pauper is set to manage the pauper; where the ignorant govern the ignorant; where the aged and infirm minister to the aged and infirm; where every softening and elevating influence is absent, or of rare occurrence, and every hardening and depraving influence continuous and ever at hand.'

In support of such views stands the valuable testimony of the Rev. S. Brewer; we extract it from an excellent article on the 'Employment of Women'[5]: – 'I have often thought how much more the gentle influence and silent teaching of an earnest and meek lady would be effectual, especially with her own sex, beyond all that I could say or do. I have often thought that the very contrast would teach more than the most impressive argument, that the insensible conviction thus conveyed to the minds of those who had never seen the best of their sex – certainly had never seen them engaged in a mission of mercy to themselves – would be effectual above all other methods.'

Women can be designers, and with proper training show themselves remarkably apt at ornamentation. To compete with Swiss watches, women are wanted in the watchmaking trade.

Mr John Bennett of Cheapside, who, with as much benevolence as intelligence, has so perseveringly endeavoured to open a new means of employment for women in watchmaking, reiterates: 'My complaint as an Englishman, is this – viz., not that the Swiss make too many watches, for their consummate ingenuity deserves its full reward; but that we produce comparatively so few. The Paris Exhibition must have opened the eyes of all but the wilfully blind to the startling fact that, quality, strength, and elegance considered, the Swiss are nearly 40 per cent under our prices. So striking was their superiority, except in our first-class watch, that I took my own eyes for a month through their principal manufacturing districts. There I found causes in active operation that explain the whole matter. From three leading manufacturers I learnt that 1,500,000 watches were made last year (1855) in the Neufchâtel district, and this over and above the produce of the Geneva district. They declare, too, that their powers of production have doubled in the last seven years. The marvellous ingenuity of their tools, and their skilful economy of labour, fully confirm this statement. Thousands of women are at this moment finding profitable employment at the most delicate portion of watchwork throughout the district round Neufchâtel. The subdivision of labour is there wisely made so minute as to adjust itself precisely to the special capabilities of every woman's individual dexterity. The watch is composed of many distinct parts, some require force and decision in the hand of the workman, while many are so exquisitely delicate that for them the fine touch of the female finger is found to be far superior to the more clumsy handling of the man. Now, within the London district, including every dealer who professes and calls himself a watchmaker, we had, in 1851, but 4,800 in the trade; while I learn from the Goldsmiths' Hall that only 186,000 were stamped last year of British manufacture. This number is so contemptible as to be far below our home consumption, if we would but make them at a very moderate price. In 1854, duty was paid on 79,209 watches; in 1855, on 90,670. Now why should not our English women be employed upon a labour for which their sisters in Switzerland prove themselves so eminently adapted, and thus provide to a large extent a remedy for the distresses of our labouring female population, and open out a new channel whereby they may elevate their condition and benefit mankind? In London 50,000 females are working under sixpence per day, and above 100,000 under one shilling per day. So long as nearly every remunerative employment is engrossed by men only, so long must the wretchedness and slavery of women remain what it is. For any man to declare, whatever his motive, that the women of London are sure to do badly what the Swiss women are now doing so well, is an insult and a fallacy in which I refuse to join.

No factory system is necessary for the successful manufacture of this very beautiful little machine. The father has but to teach his own daughters, wife, and female relatives at his own home, and then, just as their leisure suits, they can perform each her part without necessarily interfering with the most indispensable of her domestic duties.

Thus the whole family is well provided for, and by the reduction of the cost of the watch, the sale would be increased indefinitely, and this increase would give additional employment to men and women in about equal proportion.

Working watchmakers have no need to fear the introduction of female labour, the large demand that necessarily would ensue, when watches were materially cheapened in price, would, doubtless, more than compensate any loss they might temporarily sustain; the change it would effect would be found not only a moral good and an immense social blessing, but would satisfy the indispensable requirements of a strong commercial necessity.'

Women should teach languages and oratory. Aspasia taught rhetoric to Socrates. The voice of women is more penetrating, distinct, delicate, and correct in delivering sounds than that of man, fitting her to teach both oratory and languages better.

All the work of philanthropy is imperfect unless women co-operate with men.

When we are down in the strong black tide of ignorance and misery in Westminster or St Giles, we exclaim –

> Oh, that we now had here
> But one ten thousand of those *wo*men in England
> Who do no work to-day!

And so in all places might we say, if women were but fitted to the work.

Great is the work to be done in the world, but few are the skilled labourers.

Two Fallacies

It seems hardly worth while to say that there is a prejudice against women accepting money for their work. But there is one, therefore it is as well to say a few words upon it.

Money is only a convenient representative of desirable things;

'and what every woman, no less than every man, should have to depend upon, is an ability after some fashion or other, to turn labour into money. She may or may not be compelled to exercise it; but every one *ought* to possess it. If she belong to the richer classes, she *may* have to exercise it; if to the poorer, she assuredly *will*.'6 It would be well if all should part with what they make, or what they do well, for money; they will then know that some really want what they produce. What they produce will go to the right people, and they, the producers, will gain a power; for money is a power. Money may be a power to do good. If for your needlework you get money, you know that your work goes to someone who wants it. You are not always sure of that if you give it away; and you gain a power of sending a child to school, of buying a good book to lend to the ignorant, of sending a sick person to a good climate, etc. We may give this power up to another whom we consider can use it better than we, but money is a power which we have not the right lightly to reject. It is a responsibility which we must accept.

Of course, we may give our labour, our work, our money, where we think right; but it is as well to exchange them sometimes for money, to be sure we are as valuable as we think. Some work is beyond all price, and many prices are far beyond the value of the works.

Most of the work of the world must be done for money. It is of the utmost importance to make that work 'stuff o' conscience'. To make all work done for money honourable, is what we should strive for. To insist on work for love of Christ only, to cry up gratuitous work, is a profound and mischievous mistake. It tends to lessen the dignity of necessary labour; as if work for daily bread could not be for love of Christ too! Mrs Jameson, in her beautiful and wise Essay on the 'Communion of Labour', has, we think, made a great mistake in this respect, of work for love and work for money. Well-done work is what we want. All work, whether for love or money, should be well done; this is what we should insist upon. 'Ill-done work seems to me the plague of human society. People are grasping after some grandiose task, something "worthy" of their powers, when the only proof of capacity they give is to do small things badly. Conscience goes to the hammering in of nails properly, and how many evils from trying one's temper to tearing one's garment, have come of imperfect hammering.'

Another common fallacy: It is often said that ladies should not take the bread out of the mouths of the poor working-man or woman by selling in their market.

The riches and material well-being of the country consist in the quantity of stuff in the country to eat and to wear, houses to live in, books to read, rational objects of recreation and elevation, as music and pictures, etc. Anyone who puts more of any of these things into the country, adds to its riches and happiness. The more of these things, the easier is it for all to get. Do not think of money until you see this fact. This is why we bless steam-engines; this is why we would bless women. Steam-engines did at first take the bread out of a few mouths, but how many thousands have they fed for one they have starved!

Concluding Remarks

One of the practical impediments in the way of women working is the inconvenient modern dress, which is only suited to carpeted rooms, where it appears graceful and proper; in the streets, it is disreputable, dirty, and inconvenient. As long as women will not get out of their 'long clothes', they deserve to be treated as babies. There are signs that the

> just medium will be found
> A little lower than the knee, a little higher than the ground.

The ladies of the aristocracy, when they lead an active life in the country, do not go about with draggle-tail petticoats, like the working-women in our towns, but in short petticoats, thick-ribbed, brown, blue, or barred stockings, and solid Balmoral boots.

How many girls are prevented from continuing their attendance at school, college, workshop, atelier, musical academy, or Marlborough House, by colds caught from going without proper waterproof clothing!

No woman ought to be without a waterproof cloak with a hood. The best can be procured for £2, common ones for £1. Winter boots should always be made with a layer of cork between the two soles; this keeps the feet perfectly dry, and, by adding thickness to the soles, lifts the boot from the mud without adding to the weight.

To sum up. Women want work both for the health of their minds and bodies. They want it often because they must eat and because they have children and others dependent on them – *for all the reasons that men want work*. They are placed at a great disadvantage in the market of work because they are not skilled labourers, and are therefore badly paid. They rarely have any training. It is the duty of fathers and mothers to give their daughters this training.

All experience proves that the effect of the independence of women upon married life is good.

The time has arrived when women are wanted in the Commonwealth. John Milton said the Commonwealth 'ought to be but one huge Christian personage, one mighty growth and stature of an honest man, as big and compact in virtue as in body'. Our idea differs from this grand but incomplete conception. We rather think the Commonwealth should be

> Inclusive of all gifts and faculties
> On either sex bestowed, knit up in strengths
> Of man and woman both; hers even as his,
> And tempered with the finest tenderness
> Of love betwixt these two.

Many have sneered and sneer at women entering professions, and talk of the absurdity of their being in the army, mixing in political life, going to sea, or being barristers. It is not very likely many women will enter these professions; women will rather prefer those nobler works which have in them something congenial to their moral natures. Perhaps we may say that women will only enter those professions which are destined to be perpetual, being consistent with the highest moral development of humanity, which war is not. The arts, the sciences, commerce, and the education of the young in all its branches – these will most strongly attract them.

NOTES

1 'Etude sur l'Algérie et l'Afrique,' par Bodichon, Docteur Médecin à Alger.

2

WHITE SLAVERY
To the Editor of The Times

Sir, Will you permit me through the medium of your valuable paper to make known one of the many cases of cruelty and insult to which governesses are exposed? I was one of about fifty ladies (most of whom were accomplished gentlewomen) who applied last week in reply to an advertisement in *The Times*, for a situation as governess in a family in the neighbourhood of Kingsland.

The applicants went from all parts of London and its environs, many were in consequence quite overcome with fatigue, having walked long distances to save expense.

After having been kept standing in a cold, draughty hall more than an hour, I at last obtained an interview with the lady, and learnt that the duties of the governess would consist in educating and taking the entire charge of the children, seven in number, two being quite babies, to perform for them all the menial offices of a nurse, make and mend their clothes; to teach at least three accomplishments, and 'fill up the leisure hours of an evening by playing to company'.

For these combined duties the munificent sum of £10 per annum was offered! I ascertained for a fact, that the two domestic servants in the same family were paid respectively £12 and £10. Surely in a country like ours some employment besides that of teaching could be found for educated women, or at least better treatment might be expected for those to whom is entrusted the responsible duty of forming the minds and manners of the rising generation. As the best means of correcting this evil, may I beg you, Sir, to wield your powerful pen in behalf of this much-abused class of individuals?

A POOR GOVERNESS

3 Miss Dix was left dependent on her own resources at twelve years of age, and until she became possessed of a moderate competency upon which now she lives, she supported herself by teaching, contributing besides to the maintenance and education of two relatives.

As soon as her means permitted her to give up her profession, she devoted herself to philanthropic objects, and for a short period (about two years, we believe) she spent her time chiefly in visiting prisons. It was there that her attention was drawn to the miserable condition of lunatics, for whose proper care scarcely any provision had then been made throughout the United States. The plan of farming them out individually to those who would admit them into their homes had been tried, but abandoned in consequence of the horrible suffering to which the poor creatures were subjected, often from the impossibility of restraining them, by any but painful means, from injuring themselves and others. In the almost total absence of asylums, the workhouse was the only refuge for the harmless insane, while the violent were sent to prison. Shocked by this confounding of misfortune with crime, and by the hopelessness of cure which such treatment involved, Miss Dix thenceforth gave herself up entirely to the cause, wherein her labours entitle her to be regarded as the apostle of the insane. Nineteen asylums have been established in her native country, at her instance; they are supported partly by funds granted by Government, and partly by donations obtained by her from private individuals, one of which amounted to 40,000 dollars. She has been the means of passing thirty-two Acts of Legislature for the better care of the insane, appearing publicly in none, but taking all details upon herself, and not trusting a word of her clauses to clerks or official men. Her efforts, however, have not been limited to establishing asylums only, but she has, by constant inspection throughout the United States, satisfied herself that no abuses exist in their management, or, if found to exist, that they are speedily remedied.

Having long laboured in America, she crossed the Atlantic a few years ago, and since then has visited, we believe, every country in Europe, except Spain and Portugal; investigating, so far as it was possible, the condition of the insane in each, and making herself acquainted with the state of the prisons and charitable institutions.

She met, as might be expected, with great variety in the treatment of lunatics, and sometimes found them subjected to cruelty and neglect; but in numerous instances she saw them admirably cared for in the governmental asylums, and that occasionally in countries, as for example Russia, which we are accustomed to consider as backward in social improvement.

As regards *private* asylums in all countries, Miss Dix expresses a most unfavourable opinion. Even in England, she has found them to be the scene of fearful abuses; and though she knows that many are well managed, and under the superintendence of most humane and enlightened men, we have heard her say, that she would herself on no account place any patient elsewhere than in a public institution. It is most consolatory to find that her extensive experience of insanity has led her to the conviction that, with judicious treatment, and by attacking the malady in time, ninety-five cases per cent are curable, without danger of relapse.

Miss Dix returned to America in September last to resume her philanthropic labours in her own country. They necessitate constant travelling from place to place; and the fact that for twelve years past she has had no settled home will help us to estimate their extent.

It is peculiarly appropriate to the object these pages have in view to state that Miss Dix believes no duty is more urgent, or more completely within the power of educated women to fulfil, than that of investigating and watching over the treatment of the insane. Few probably could so wholly devote themselves to it as she has done; but by many labouring in the same path great benefit might be conferred on this most unhappy class of our fellow-creatures.

The results she has achieved may appear apocryphal to strangers, but are readily understood by those acquainted with her untiring zeal, persuasive eloquence, and indomitable resolution. These qualities, beside enabling her to operate on the minds and hearts of the sane, give her also great influence over the lunatic; and instances have frequently occurred, in which raving madmen, whom no-one else dared to approach, have been rendered calm by her.

4   *The Observatory, Glasgow,*
March 3d, 1857

Dear Barbara,

Your letter requesting an account of the attempt made by M — and myself to obtain a thorough medical education in England reaches me on my lecturing tour; I cannot, therefore, send you all the letters and documents, but I think the enclosed will answer your purpose.

My desire to study medicine originated in the constant care required of me by my little brother, who, owing to some deficiency in the system, has broken his legs sixteen times, and by Ricciotti, Garibaldi's boy, both lame. On one occasion, when the former broke his leg early one Sunday morning, his own doctor being out of town, the child objected to a stranger being called in, and I had to set the broken bone myself. On Monday evening, the surgeon sent by Dr Little commended the operation, and laughingly offered me a certificate for the Crimea. I asked him, instead, to assist me in obtaining an entrance to one of the hospitals – for study – but this he declined, and I continued the process of splint-making and bandaging for both boys as usual.

When, however, I consulted Dr Little, he entered warmly into my project, gave me several introductions, and exerted his influence with his own medical friends. By his advice I made a formal application for admission to all the London Hospitals – fourteen in number.

The following are fair specimens of the questions sent to, and the answers received from, each. (See Appendix, No. I.)

The request for private anatomical instruction was made at the suggestion of Dr Bence Jones, who foresaw that in this department practical difficulties might arise. I owe him cordial thanks for the energy and generosity with which he advocated my cause throughout the discussions. On the day following the receipt of my letter, I received a long visit from Dr ——, the head doctor of St George's. From his conversation I augured favourably of the result, and was disappointed to receive the following. (See No. II.) Of course, the Weekly Board of Governors acted according to the advice of the Committee. Meanwhile, I called upon several influential doctors and surgeons connected with the different hospitals. Some received me kindly, and a few promised their vote. One individual informed me that even if the Committee should consent to admit me to the hospital, the door of his ward should be for ever closed to me. Another reproached me with the indecency of my demand: in no single case did I receive either a sensible or logical reply to my question, 'Why may not a woman study medicine?'

You will see by Mr Balfour's letter, that even had I succeeded in entering the hospitals and in obtaining certificates, the Diploma necessary for commencing practice would have been denied. (See No. III.)

One more letter from St Bartholomew's, and I think you will be convinced, that a little alteration in Dr Johnson's lines gives the only reason why I was denied admission:

> We shan't admit you, Mistress Fell –
> The reason why we cannot tell;
> But this we all know very well,
> We shan't admit you, Mistress Fell! (IV)

Throughout May, June, and July, when I was receiving refusals from all the hospitals, one hope cheered me, namely, that the University of London, quite the most liberal community of modern times, would admit me as a candidate to the Matriculation Examination. Until such an examination has been passed, of course no degree can be taken. Moreover, I hoped that a promise of examination from the Senate would influence the decision of some of the Hospital Committees, or at least, should I present myself again, after having passed such an examination, they might choose to reconsider such a decision.

To my formal application I received the following letter (V), and a few days after, Dr Carpenter's (VI), to which I replied (VII). A long silence followed. I knew that I had one very influential friend in the Senate, and that several others were disposed to accede to my request. I received, too, private information, that the pervading feeling was that a woman *would* be admitted as a candidate for examination if she presented herself prepared to pass, but that the authorities did not choose to commit themselves to a promise. Now, though quite disposed to matriculate on the chance of being *then* admitted to study in the hospitals, I could not afford to pass at least a year in the society of Xenophon and Livy, etc. on the chance of being allowed to matriculate. I still pressed for an official answer, and received the following. (See No. VIII.)

The receipt of this letter then dashed all my hopes of obtaining a thorough medical education in England. As I wished you know for a profession, as a means to an end, rather than as an end in itself, as I am preparing myself for future work in Italy, conceiving that the way to make other women work is for us each to achieve some practical work ourselves. I shall not therefore go to America for that education which England denies me. But for many reasons I am glad to have made the experiment. Several medical men have assured me that if a band of women were now to apply for admission at one or more of the hospitals, such has been the feeling excited among some of the most liberal-minded in the profession by the discussions following on my request, that it is improbable they would be refused.

Others have since told me, that on receiving the above letter I should have applied to the Court of Queen's Bench for a writ of Mandamus compelling the University of London to admit me to examination. The expense involved precluded the possibility of this in my own case. But why, if other women feel inclined to make the experiment, should we not raise a fund to meet the law expenses, since the question involved is of importance to us all? Read the charter of the University carefully – take the clause in which 'Victoria, by the grace of God, of the United Kingdom of Great Britain and Ireland, Queen, Defender of the Faith', revokes the Letters Patent of William the Fourth, 'deeming it to be the duty of our royal office, for the advancement of religion and morality, and the promotion of useful knowledge, *to hold forth to all classes and denominations of our faithful subjects without any distinction whatsoever* an encouragement for pursuing a regular and liberal course of education' – read this and the succeeding paragraphs, showing our Queen's motives for constituting the University of London, and I believe you will agree with me, in thinking that it will be difficult to exclude women legally from sharing in the benefits of said University. Considering, as we do, that the first step towards the amelioration of society is to find work for women, and women for work, we ought, I think, to make efforts in this direction.

If, after further trials, it be found that prejudice is too strong to admit of women studying in the hospitals now existing, I believe that some of the best teachers and lecturers would agree to hold classes for women apart, and as there are some hospitals not frequented by students – the practical knowledge necessary might be so obtained. In this, as in other things, if we cannot have all we want at once, we must take as much as we can at a time.

I believe the study and practice of medicine to be particularly calculated to call forth the highest and truest womanly faculties; on the other hand, it is a sphere of labour evidently requiring women workers. Consequently, I feel it to be our duty to clear the distance as much as possible between the supply and demand.

In other branches we may obey the somewhat sarcastic bidding of our noble sister poet, and '*do* our work', claiming the right in the deed; but as in England no one can lawfully 'cure the plague' until he or she be a legal 'leech', we must preach and agitate until we may be thus legalised. So, let any woman or women come forward, desirous of fitting herself for a doctor, and if she be unable to meet the enormous expense it will involve, let us each do our part to help her, and to advance our common cause through her.

I, for one, will willingly do my share,

Ever, affectionately yours,

Jessie Meriton White

To Miss Leigh Smith
5 *North British Review*, January, 1857.
6 *North British Review*, January, 1857.

APPENDIX

No. I

To the Secretary of St George's Hospital

Sir,

I wish, with another lady, to attend a three-years' course of lectures, and surgical and medical practice, commencing the October Term, in St George's Hospital.

I presume my being a woman will prove no obstacle, as I can furnish you with certificates as to character and capacity from known London physicians.

Will you inform me whether I can have private anatomical instruction, and on what terms? An answer will oblige

Yours, respectfully,

JESSIE MERITON WHITE

7 Upper Gloucester Place, Dorset Square,
May 9th, 1856

No. II

13 Manchester Square,
Saturday, May 17th, 1856

Dear Madam,

Your letter of the 9th instant, containing an application for permission 'to attend with another lady a three-years' course of lectures, and surgical and medical practice, commencing the October Term, in St George's Hospital', has been submitted to the Medical School Committee; and I am requested to inform you that the Committee, not having the po͟ tꞋ grant that permission, have referred your letter to the Weekly Board of Governors. At the same time, the Committee wish me to add that, having carefully and maturely considered the subject of your application in all its relations, they are of opinion that so many practical inconveniences would result from the admission of women as pupils of the Hospital and School, that they do not intend to advise the Weekly Board of Governors to accede to your application.

I have the honour to be, Dear Madam,

Your obedient Servant,

HENRY WILLIAM FULLER, M.D., *Hon. Sec.*

Miss Jessie Meriton White

No. III

Royal College of Surgeons,
May 17th, 1856

Madam,

In reply to your letter of the 10th inst. inquiring, 'Can a woman on producing certificates of having attended during three years the lectures and the medical and surgical practice in one of the London Hospitals, be admitted to examination for a diploma in surgery and midwifery?' I am desired by the Court of Examiners to acquaint you, that there is no instance of this College ever having admitted a female to examination for either of the said diplomas, and that the Court considers it would not be justified in adopting such a course.

I am, Madam,
Your very obedient Servant,
EDM. BALFOUR, *Sec.*

Miss White

No. IV

St Bartholomew's Hospital,
May 30th, 1856

Madam,

I have the honour to inform you that, this afternoon, at a meeting of the Medical Officers and Lecturers of this Hospital, your letter of the 19th inst. was read and considered; and, in reply to it, I am requested to state, that, in the opinion of the meeting, it is not expedient to admit ladies as students of the hospital.

I remain, Madam,
Your faithful Servant,
JAMES PAGET

Miss Jessie Meriton White

No. V

University of London,
Burlington House, May 12th, 1856

Madam,

I have the honour to acknowledge the receipt of your letter of the 10th inst. The inquiry contained in it, however, being a novel one, I should wish to consult the Senate on the subject of it, which I will endeavour to do at their next meeting, and will communicate the result to you without delay.

I am, Madam,
Your most obedient Servant,
H. MOORE

Miss Jessie M. White

No. VI

University of London,
Burlington House, May 22nd, 1856

Madam,

I am directed by the Senate to forward you a copy of the minutes of its proceedings on the 14th inst., by which you will perceive that your letter has been brought under its consideration with a view to a decision upon the question proposed in it, at an early meeting.

In the meantime, I beg to direct your attention to the regulations to which candidates for degrees in medicine are required to conform; and especially to those relating to the Matriculation Examination. These you will find in the Calendar herewith sent, pp. 35–41 and 58–60.

Should increased knowledge of the requirements of the University make any alteration in your views, I shall be obliged by an intimation to that effect.

I am, Madam,
Your obedient Servant,
WILLIAM B. CARPENTER, *Registrar*

Miss J. M. White

No. VII

7 *Upper Gloucester Place,*
Dorset Square, May 23rd, 1856

Sir,

I thank you for your letter just received, and for the Calendar.

Before addressing you, on the 10th inst., I was aware of the regulations to which candidates for degrees in Medicine are required to conform, and shall be prepared to comply with all the requirements of the University should the Senate decide to admit me for examination.

I am, Sir,
Respectfully yours,
JESSIE MERITON WHITE

Dr William B. Carpenter

No. VIII

University of London,
Burlington House, July 10th, 1856

Madam,

I am directed by the Senate to inform you, that, acting upon the opinion of its legal advisers, it does not consider itself as empowered, under the Charter of the University, to admit females as candidates for degrees.

I have the honour to be, Madam,
Your obedient Servant,
WILLIAM B. CARPENTER, *Registrar*

Miss Jessie M. White

Middle-Class Schools for Girls

(a paper read at the National Association for the Promotion of Social Science, October 1860 and reprinted in *The English Woman's Journal*, November 1860)

It is very easy to find fault with our National and British Schools, and with our whole system of Government aid to education; and also with the vast body of masters and mistresses sent out all over the country from the great training schools and colleges supported by public funds; and it is not difficult to say, with much apparent truth, that these crammed and certificated ladies and gentlemen are not giving a very good practical education to the working people of England. Perhaps the very first observation you make is that they do not keep in view the very end of education, the very point to be aimed at – to teach the children to help themselves – to help themselves to think rightly, and to carry their right thoughts into right action; to make rational beings with good habits. You will perhaps say that for the most part these masters and mistresses only strive to pour out the learning so lately poured into themselves. You have, no doubt, visited National Schools, and have laughed at the answers given by the children to your questions, showing the utter want of any instruction in the art of thinking; of which want the reply lately made by a pupil may be taken as a specimen. I stopped a child in the midst of a chapter in the Bible as she gabbled 'and His coming was foretold by the prophets'. 'Who were the prophets?' I asked. The girl stared me in the face and said, 'What father makes in his shop.' And another girl, after naming glibly all the countries in Europe, confessed that she did not believe in their existence! Indeed, a very little examination will prove that children do not *believe* in half they are taught. But although it is easy to find fault with the education England is giving her people, fault-finding and criticism are useless without the exercise of comparison. We must not take the ideal instead of the possible and the practicable as our test – and when we find fault with National and British Schools, do we compare them with others? Not often, I believe. How many of those who visit and criticise these establishments have ever thought of examining *what the education is which the mass of the people provide for themselves?* I speak of those who can provide for themselves; the class who can afford to pay more than 2*d.* a week.

I believe it to be inferior in every respect to the education given in the National and British Schools. I do not think any advocate of the voluntary system can deny the fact.

The little cheap, private day-schools, academies, institutes, and 'collegiate establishments for young ladies and gentlemen', have proverbially a low character, unknown as such regions are to the higher classes, and would, we believe, have a still lower character if they were known. They are often conducted by incompetent, brokendown tradespeople, who, failing in gaining a livelihood in a good trade, take in despair to what is justly considered (in consequence of the competition of the schools assisted by Government) as a very bad business.

I speak generally of the schools charging from 6*d.* a week to 15*s.* a quarter, opened for the children of small shopkeepers and mechanics who are too rich or too 'genteel' to go to the National Schools. Such academies abound in the cheap quarters of all towns, and are usually held in small private houses, only manifesting their scholastic character by a brass plate or a large board, and only maintaining it by pretentious ignorance. I have good reason to believe that the education given in these places for 6*d.* and 1*s.* a week is inferior to the twopenny education given in the popular schools. It is very difficult to investigate this matter, but I wish to draw special attention to the subject, so that it may be inquired into by all who have the opportunity. The number of these schools is enormous, and their influence on the future welfare of England very considerable; so that it is well worth while to know something about what passes within them. Does the Government aid to the National Schools injuriously affect these schools? What is the education and training of the mistresses? What education is usually given? What books and apparatus are used? etc. These and other questions should be inquired into, but it is exceedingly difficult to visit such establishments: they are *private,* and I have found the mistresses exceedingly jealous of inspection, most unwilling to show a stranger (and quite naturally) anything of the school books, or to answer any questions. The first school of this class which I visited was in a large country village, to which the small farmers and shopkeepers sent their daughters. It was considered a most respectable and superior establishment; the lady principal boasted of having an accomplished Indian lady to teach languages and music; I went with a farmer's daughter, who was an old pupil, and whose extraordinary deficiency in reading and writing at the age of thirteen quite excited my curiosity. The lady principal was a poor sickly creature utterly unfit for anything, but who had been obliged to do something for a livelihood. She had a certain kind of flabby ladylike manner which quite awed my blunt honest farmer friends. The school was conducted on the most old fashioned system; the books were out of date, and the children were taught after this fashion, that there were four elements, earth, air, fire, and water! The Indian lady, the boast of the establishment, was a negress, a dashing, ignorant American, who thought the most important part of her duty was to teach deportment and the small manners and vanities supposed to transmute the little female clodhoppers into *elegant* young ladies.

Other schools which I visited proved as bad; and of the many of which I have received reports from trustworthy persons, few have been much better. The teachers have little knowledge, and no idea that there is a difficult art called teaching which must be *learnt*.

Mistresses of such schools have often told me they *were not used to work – were ladies, and quite unfit for this sort of thing!*

We have heard of harshness and the indulgence of tyranny unchecked by any supervision or any public inspection; cases of extreme atrocity are fresh in the minds of all. In one day I heard of two cases of blows being given for mistakes in reading; and I am convinced that these ignorant, disappointed, and soured teachers oftener act harshly and misuse their despotic power than is at all supposed. Despotic power over children, without a parent's natural and restraining affection, is a dangerous thing.

Parents sometimes send their children to National and British Schools, often having tried private schools and found them fail; we have often questioned children from these schools, and generally found them terribly ignorant.

One of the greatest evils is the insufficient room and ventilation; to make these cheap schools pay it is necessary to cram the children as close as possible, and the rooms of a common, small dwelling-house are not fit or healthy for a school. This is a very serious consideration; for children cannot learn in an impure atmosphere, the vitiated air makes them feverish or drowsy, cross or stupid. A chemist in a small street in London being asked where he sent his children, said, 'Oh! to the pious old girl next door.' On examining the school in question, it was found that the mistress had been the teacher of a National School, but gave it up because the work was too hard (she said), and started a school charging three times as much – 6*d*. a week, and extra for grammar and other things. It was curious to see the inefficient or incapable teacher raising her price because of her inefficiency or incapacity! She professed to teach anything the pupils wanted to learn, her house was crammed with disorderly children, and the emanations from so many bodies was anything but pleasant.

In country towns we have known families of sisters left destitute, and starting private schools without any training at all, and charging 6*d*., 9*d*., and 1*s*. a week, honestly confessing that their instruction was not so good as that of the monitors in a common National School.[1]

This class just above the labouring one which touches it, influences the latter more than the higher branches can do, and it is a very sure and sound way of helping the lower classes, to educate those who are richer than themselves, but in immediate contact with them. To give good sense and refinement to this class would indeed be a great boon. If we could make these women high-minded, intelligent, and simple in their tastes, instead of leaving them to be brought up to vanity, false ideas of what is lady-like, and every shallow showy accomplishment, it would indeed be a blessing! At present, their contact with those above them is just of that external character which causes them to imitate their dress, and the vanities and follies of those they call real ladies. Although they touch the lowest, they aim at pushing their way into the upper classes, and, judging by the past history of English society, they will inevitably accomplish their aim. It is, therefore, of vital importance to educate them rightly and highly.

I will now take for granted (though everyone who is interested in this subject ought to prove it for himself by inspection), that the existing schools for the middle class are bad, and worse than those assisted by Government. The difficult question then arises, how to provide better.

Several of those mentioned by the Rev. J. S. Howson in his paper read before this Association last year have been, he says, successful. The Birkbeck Schools established by Mr William Ellis admirably supply the want as far as they go. But they are not specially for girls. Others have been founded by committees and by private efforts with more or less success. But there is no organised effort, no society devoted to this purpose, and not the particular attention turned to the subject which it deserves.

These schools do not so much want money given towards their foundation, as the thought and experience of competent people.

The next question is, ought these schools to be self-supporting?

The self-supporting principle is very admirable, and it is desirable to make as many of these schools self-supporting as possible. A very admirable principle, but why should it be especially applied to girls?

Magnificent colleges and schools, beautiful architectural buildings, costing thousands and thousands of pounds, rich endowments, all over England, have been bestowed by past generations as gifts to the boys of the higher and middle class, and they are not the less independent, and not a whit pauperised.

Neither Christ Church, Eton, nor Oxford are supposed to degrade those who are educated by them, yet they are in a great measure charities! Too much will not be given to girls, and we are not afraid to urge that some foundation schools, some noble halls and beautiful gardens, be bestowed on them also. Giving education, the very means of self-help, is the safest way of being charitable. Charity is a gracious thing, but we must give with judgment. The more freely knowledge is diffused the better, and no narrow view should prevent us from giving good gifts to all with whom we come in contact.

I believe that educated ladies who have the will, the intellect, and the money wherewith to help their fellow-creatures, cannot begin a better work than by interesting themselves in the education of the girls of the middle class; girls who certainly ought to be sensibly and practically brought up, as they are destined to as hard trials as either their richer or poorer sisters; if these girls could see that ladies above them had solid knowledge, as well as superficial accomplishments, it would do them an immense good – example is always better than precept.

The rich do much harm in giving advice; they understand little of the true wants and sympathies of the recipients. When the givers are vastly higher in station, it is much easier to make the poor into servile beggars and canting hypocrites than to do any solid good. The same danger does not apply to assistance rendered to the middle class. They are very independent, and though they will willingly accept help, they cannot endure patronage.

Now a great power is wasted in the quantity of time and knowledge which rich young English women have on their hands. I cannot help thinking that it might be organised, and usefully employed. A vast number draw well from nature, a greater number still are good musicians and good French scholars – why should not this teaching power be used for the benefit of the public? If some of the ladies who are wearied with study – seeing no point for their efforts – would club together their talents, and make a sort of joint stock company, some subscribing money, some lessons in various branches, they could themselves establish these better sort of schools. In fact, we want an application of the volunteer movement; but a trained mistress, always in the school, would be absolutely necessary.

Good schools for 6*d*. a week will not pay, but 1*s*. a week from 150 children can be made to pay expenses without profit. Probably schools charging £1 a quarter could be made to pay a profit.

It is very desirable that a society should be formed for the establishment of such schools in connection with such an institution as the Queen's College, and that paid or volunteer teachers should procure certificates, and the schools established might avow themselves in connection with some well-known and authorised academy. Some Journal should also be open to the monthly reports of such schools (*The English Woman's Journal* for instance) and opportunities be given for the interchange of questions and comparisons by meetings of teachers at stated times. Publicity of every sort should be afforded for the exertions and various experiments of these societies of ladies, not only for their own improvement, but also to give parents a fair opportunity of understanding the comparative advantages of different schools. These should also be open to inspection, at least on certain fixed days. The attention of the wealthy and charitable should likewise be drawn to the importance of endowing a certain number of day-schools for girls, to correspond to the grammar schools so richly endowed for boys.

Again, every effort should be made by the friends of education to raise the standard of the mistresses, and to give them opportunities of steady improvement, and some public recognition of their efficiency. It is desirable to extend simultaneously all the agencies at work for the better education both of teachers and pupils, and nothing would more promote it than the opening to them of 'the University Examinations of Students who are not Members of the University'. At Cambridge there is an examination every year for students who are not more than sixteen years of age, and another for students who are not more than eighteen years of age. The subjects of examination are English Language, including reading aloud, spelling, dictation, etc., history, geography, the Latin, French, and German languages, arithmetic, mathematics, natural philosophy, etc. The students who pass the examinations will receive certificates.

'After each examination the names of the students who pass with credit will be placed alphabetically in three honour classes, and the names of those who pass to the satisfaction of the examiners, yet not so as to deserve honours, will be placed alphabetically in a separate class. Marks of distinction will be attached to the name of any candidate who may specially distinguish himself in any particular parts of the examination. After the name of every student will be added his place of residence, the school (if any) from which he comes to attend the examination, and the name of his schoolmaster.'

Such is the system pursued at Cambridge, the extension of which to female teachers would prove a great guarantee to the parents of pupils. I have looked over the Examination Papers for 1859–60, and do not think that they need in any way be changed if women were included among the students. There need be no terrible publicity to shock and frighten the female candidate, for we read that 'an examination will be held in any place where it can be ascertained that there will be thirty candidates for examination'.

I will now proceed to make a few remarks on the sort of education which would be really valuable to the middle class, and at the same time attractive to them. In the first place, it is very desirable to adopt the method of teaching in classes by means of object-lessons, which is habitually pursued in National Schools. The apparatus and the museum are essential to good teaching. To acquire a string of names by heart, with no ideas or with wrong ideas attached to those names, does not increase a child's real knowledge. To do this you must place the actual object before the child's eyes whenever possible. In girls' schools this is rarely thought of; I remember a London girl in a 'boarding-school for young ladies' who had repeated the word *hay* for twelve or thirteen years, in prose, poetry, and conversation, and who had a vague idea that hay was composed of leaves of trees mixed with bits of stick; yet this was a very accomplished girl who could play well on the piano. It is worth while to follow in our minds the consequences of a false idea of hay, that we may feel the utility of *real knowledge*. How very much she lost by her ignorance, misunderstanding the beauty and meaning of every passage in the Bible about grass; knowing nothing of mowing, and ignorant of the meaning of the word scythe! Vague incorrectness of thought about natural objects is very common in the minds of girls, who have, generally, fewer opportunities than boys possess of absolute contact with the earth and the water. Real knowledge develops not only the observation, but the imagination and the poetical faculties; while, on the other hand, nothing so much takes away from the solidity and intensity of a character as the habit of using *words* without knowing the *things* they signify. It breeds intellectual and moral unfaithfulness. Schoolmistresses so little understand this very evident law in education, that they expect their girls to feel an interest in poetry full of similes about things they have never seen, and to learn hard tasks in natural science without witnessing experiments or handling specimens. How many lessons are given on the chief products of the countries of Europe, and how few products are ever shown in young ladies' schools. Professor Brodie would not teach chemistry to young men unless he could show them substances and solutions, yet children are expected to learn, and punished for not learning, on a system too stupid, too obsolete to be applied to young men.

All who have heard Mr Shieles' admirable object-lessons at the Peckham Birkbeck Schools will readily understand what a difference this method of teaching makes to the pupils in exciting their interest, and bringing out the powers they delight to exercise. In addition to the usual branches of education, and to these object-lessons, drawing should also be taught with great care to all the children, and taught from nature as well as from copies. It is easier to teach drawing than writing, if the lesson be made interesting and really beautiful; and delicate drawings can be executed by mere children, of leaves, of bits of architecture, of vases, etc., and copies be made from engravings of more complicated things. Pupils of twelve or thirteen should be able, after two years' instruction, to draw the branch of a tree with its leaves, so as to give pleasure to the beholder.

The drawing lesson can be elevated into a lesson on art, and the beauties of form in antique vases and statues can be pointed out, and plants, flowers, and fruits be brought in illustration, aided by fine etchings.

Singing from notes and in parts must enter into the course of instruction; children always delight in joining together to sing, and very soon enjoy the best music. French lessons will distinguish the scholars in these schools from those who pay only twopence a week in National Schools, and must be taught not only because it is useful to know the language of our neighbours, but also because it is extremely desirable that children should know that there are other names for things besides those they use themselves, and because English grammar is best acquired in connection with that of another language. Moreover, not only is a great saving of time thus effected, but a strong desire to learn French exists in the middle class, which must be taken into account.

In addition to arithmetic, girls should be taught to make out bills, to keep accounts, and to understand book-keeping. From the very first they should be taught how to apply their arithmetical knowledge, and it is of the greatest importance to teach girls to know when and how to set about calculation. Most girls (and all we say is true of boys, *ceteris paribus*) are pushed forward into rules which they have not the remotest idea how to apply to real life, and which they probably do not believe to be of any practical use. For instance, not long ago I dictated this question to a class of girls in a highly esteemed school: 'If you earn a penny a day, how much will you earn in a year?' 'Oh! that is too easy!' cried the children; yet not half gave the right answer, and one of them wrote ·9 (*decimal point nine!*). Yet most of these children were very far advanced in the arithmetic book. A clever teacher, with a quick original mind, will turn all lessons to practical account, and finding out what will be the probable future of her pupils, prepare them for it and keep it before their minds.

While the essential duties of these future women as mothers, housekeepers, and governors of families must always be kept in view before and beyond every other object, the fact that most of the girls will probably have to work during some years for their own livelihood must not be lost sight of. The advantages and disadvantages of the different employments for women ought to be laid before the elder pupils, and the principles of social and political economy taught to them. They should above all be taught the vast resources of our colonies, and fitted to be emigrants by giving them independent habits, quickness to help themselves in emergencies, and an intimate acquaintance with the countries they may visit. The history of our colonies, their geography, and prod-ucts, should be familiar to them; then there would be no danger of girls refusing, as I have known many do, to leave England, fearing everything of which they know nothing. I have known numerous instances of brothers and husbands departing alone for Australia, the Cape, and America, because their sisters and wives drew back with horror from daring the utterly unknown. The daughter of a nursery gardener, about thirty years of age, told me tremblingly that she had consented to go with her family to Australia, 'but how she was to get through the earth to the other side, where she understood Australia to be, she did not in the least know'. This is only to be equalled by a schoolmistress who wrote to me that she actually did pass through three regions to arrive at the Cape of Good Hope – the region of ice, the region of fire, and the region of wind!

In these middle-class schools for girls, no public exhibitions, or prizes, or displays, should be encouraged. If any public examin-ations are thought necessary, they should be very cautiously conducted, as such examinations are generally productive of more moral mischief than intellectual good. No schools should be entirely closed to the public. It is a good plan to examine the children by dictated written questions as well as by vocal questions; and these written questions and answers should be kept and compared at stated intervals; in this manner progress in writing, spelling, and general neatness can be tested, as well as the proficiency of the children in special branches of knowledge. A clever teacher will make of these dictations a very useful lesson, and also a thorough test of the general intelligence of the pupils. These questions should cover a wide field of thought and observation, and care should be taken to make the children sometimes answer by means of drawing plans and forms from memory.

I will conclude by reiterating the main points of this paper.

Firstly, that it is desirable to investigate the education which the girls of the middle class are receiving.

Secondly, that the establishment of schools at 6*d*. or 1*s*. a week is much needed, which schools must be assisted by charitable efforts.

Thirdly, that schools at a higher rate, say 15*s*. or £1 a quarter, might be made to pay a profit.

Fourthly, that the Queen's College, and similar London Societies, should encourage and continue to correspond with such schools.

Fifthly, that they should be open to inspection.

Sixthly, that reports of the various exertions and experiments should be published in some periodical.

NOTE

1 If any lady will take the trouble to learn something of her tradespeoples' daughters, she will probably find that they are not receiving so good an education as the workmen she employs. The gardener's daughter will probably write, read, and sum better than the grocer's or butcher's children, and is probably receiving a more practical and solid education than the class a grade above for less than half the price.

Of Those who are the Property of Others, and of the Great Power that holds Others as Property

(reprinted from *The English Woman's Journal*, February 1863)

There is no doubt that in the gigantic war going on in the West, the sympathies of England *en masse* are for the South as against the North. For this there are more reasons than one, but the principal reason is that we imagine they have been oppressed by the North. Strangely enough, the people of England have, in their intense sympathy for the oppressed South, forgotten almost that the South are systematically the greatest oppressors on the face of the whole world.

We will give a sketch of what slavery is in America, and then of what have been the actions of the slave-owners as a Power, that this may be clearly demonstrated.

Slavery existed in all ancient nations, and one of the great differences between the ancient and modern world is this institution of slavery. 'And when Abraham heard that his brother was taken captive, he armed his trained *servants*, born in his own house, three hundred and eighteen, and pursued them unto Dan.' These servants were slaves, most likely in a state of perpetual and unconditional slavery. The slaves of the Hebrews were prisoners taken in war, or kidnapped from neighbouring nations. The story of Joseph, who was sold by his brothers to Arabian merchants, and then sold by them into Egypt, is an example.

The laws of Moses were not rigorous, for slave laws – and there were many ways allowed for a bondsman to redeem his liberty (see Leviticus xxv). Compared to the laws of the Southern States of America, they were kind and considerate indeed.

The Romans and the Greeks held slaves, called *servi*. In the heroic times of Greece the slaves were absolute slaves, in the American sense of the word, but the bondsmen of the Doric States, who were principally employed in cultivating the soil, were not slaves but serfs; they could not be separated from their families, and were allowed to acquire property. The commercial States of Greece appear to have had an immense slave population, far outnumbering the freemen. The Roman system of slaves was much lighter than that of the commercial States of Greece, until the later times of the Republic, when it became much more cruel and hard. The Emperors made many efforts for the slaves, and the Christian Emperors especially. Christianity did not, for centuries, touch the question of slavery, but its influence bettered the condition of slaves.

The Northern tribes which invaded the Western Empire had slaves. During the Saxon period in England, slaves were sold out of England; even as late as 1102, the English were sold as slaves to strangers, principally to the Irish. About this time slavery may be said to have died in Europe, but the Venetians continued to sell Slavonians to the Mussulmans until much later.

In Mohammedan countries slavery continued to our own time; we have all heard of Christians being sold as slaves in Algiers, and even after the conquest of Algeria, negro slaves were permitted to be held by the natives, until the much abused Government of 1848 abolished slavery in all the French Colonies. The interference of the nations professing Christianity has abolished slavery in Barbary, Egypt, and the Ottoman Empire. Where then must we look if we wish to study this ancient institution? We must turn, not to the 'barbarous Turk', or the cruel Moors of Africa, if we wish to examine how men and women live together where some are the property of others, who can buy and sell them like cattle, but we must turn Westward to a Christian nation. Never in a Mohammedan country has bondage been such pure and unmitigated slavery as it is now in the Western World.

When America was discovered, the Spanish and Portuguese, finding the Indians weak and indolent, imported African slaves; and it is Charles V, the Catholic and Christian Emperor, who has the honour of being the first to authorise a large importation of blacks into the West Indies. This was the commencement of the infamous slave trade, all the horrors of which used to be so familiar to us in England, but which we seem lately to have forgotten. It is this horrible system of kidnapping and traffic which the Southern States wish now to re-establish.

The terrible sufferings of the slaves during their journey to the coast, the manner in which they were packed on board the vessels, their sale on arrival, and their condition, exposed to the power of men who were absolutely their owners and masters – these topics were discussed and written about over and over again, during the last century and the beginning of this. The horrors of the slave *trade* principally occupied Thomas Clarkson and other philanthropists of that time, because the constant supply of slaves increased tenfold the cruelties of slavery. It was then the interest of the master to get as much work out of his slaves as possible, and as soon as he had worked them to death, to buy newly imported ones. It is evident that to keep up the stock in the natural way, enforces a certain amount of humanity, which is not necessary when men, women, and children, can be bought 'ready reared', imported fresh from Africa.

The slave trade was abolished in 1807, but it was not until 1834 that slavery was abolished in our colonies. The English reformed Parliament may well be proud of that vote of twenty millions as compensation to the slave-owners. This act will be prominent for ever in the history of our country. France did not emancipate her slaves until the Provisional Government of the Republic in 1848.

Of the state of those who are the property of others in America, we can judge by considering the laws. In old countries the laws do not give us the habits of the people in the same manner as in the American Republic, where the laws are all modern and made by the people themselves, we may say as the result of their yesterday's experience and practice. In all the Slave States, slaves are absolutely the property of their masters, and everything they have belongs to their masters. In no State can a slave make a marriage which is legally indissoluble. The children always belong to the master of the female slave. A slave can be leased or mortgaged at the will of his owner. He can be seized by creditors or legatees. His master may determine absolutely the quantity of labour he shall be subjected to, and what food he may have, and may inflict any punishment he thinks proper. There is no way in which a slave may redeem himself, or institute any action against his master, no matter how atrocious his master's conduct may have been. These laws are in many respects much harder than any slave laws which the world has ever seen. In Mohammedan countries the children of slave women do not follow the condition of the mother, and thus some of the worst and most cruel consequences of slavery are avoided. Considering the slave as a member of civil society (the expression seems like a joke), we find he cannot bear witness against a white person, or be a party in a suit; all means of education are withheld from him; submission is enforced from the slave, not only to his master, but to all white people. The penal laws are harder on him than on the whites, and in most of the States even the trial of slaves on criminal accusations is different from the trial of whites. Emancipation is not encouraged as in the ancient world, but is hedged round by all sorts of difficulties, and those who have emancipated themselves are not often allowed to remain in the Slave States.

Thus you have, in a few words, the spirit of the laws of the States concerning slaves. A very little reflection will convince any one that with such laws the condition of the slave and his happiness must depend on his master's disposition, and it is evident the position of the master, with such laws to back the devil in him, must increase any natural inclination towards cruelty and oppression. The most atrocious cruelty is possible, and it is enough to say that nothing in 'Uncle Tom' is overdrawn, though the cases as bad as Legree are rare. The laws are as bad as Legree, and we will give a few instances to show what the laws can do. In these cases no violent passions need have been roused, and all was done in cold blood.

We have said that many difficulties are thrown in the way of any master who would free his slaves.

Not many years ago in North Carolina a free coloured man, who was very industrious, saved enough money to purchase his wife, who was a slave, and the children which had been born up to that time. They had several other children. Now by the law of the State the wife and all his children were his slaves. Unfortunately, he became involved in debt, his creditors obtained judgments against him, and his wife and children were sold into perpetual slavery![1]

A citizen of Mississippi, named Elisha Brazealle, held a coloured woman as a slave. She had a son called John Brazealle, of whom her master, Elisha Brazealle, was the acknowledged father. Elisha Brazealle went into Ohio and there emancipated this woman and her son, and then returned to his house, Jefferson County, Mississippi, where he lived until his death. By his will, executed after the deed of emancipation, he recited the fact that such a deed had been executed, and declared his intention to ratify it, and devised his property to the said John Brazealle, *acknowledging him to be his son*. The heirs at law of Elisha Brazealle filed a bill in Chancery claiming all the estate which had belonged to him in his lifetime, on the ground that the deed of emancipation was void as being contrary to the laws and policy of Mississippi, and that being so, the said John Munroe Brazealle was still a slave and incapable of taking by devise or holding property. The decision was for the heirs. Appeal was made to the highest court in the State, and the decision was the same: 'John Munroe and his mother are still slaves and a part of the estate of Elisha Brazealle.'

We might go on with page after page of such extracts from

cases of the working of the slave laws in the States, but we have not space, and could not detail some cases, which are too shocking even to be printed in our Journal.

What can be expected with such an institution as slavery in a society? The laws must be atrociously unjust, if there are laws at all regulating it. The slaves themselves are very much what any human being would be under such a system, only that in the African nature there is a fund of gentleness, and patience, and cheerfulness, exceeding that of all other races. Their indolence and their disposition to lie are to be accounted for by their position. They have no motive to work but fear, and fear makes a man conceal his powers, and fear also is the great master of lies. They are loving and agreeable as servants in a house, if well treated, and their affection to children is quite wonderful.

One of the most remarkable English women of this century resided in the Southern States for many months, and assured us that she found more pleasure in the society of negroes than any other society after that of the very best in England. After the experience of our residence in the South we almost agree with her. They have a certain genius of geniality which is peculiarly charming: no people so soon respond to kindness. This cheerfulness of the negroes misleads visitors to the Slave States, and they almost begin to think slavery may be the cause of it, as they are told incessantly that it is.

The negro race is very affectionate, and the ties between parents and children strong and deep. What, then, must be the suffering of mothers and children when they are exposed to separation at any moment, on the whim or necessity of the master! While in America, I asked many old female slaves where were their children, and I never recollect a single instance of an old woman having all her children with her or near her; generally she was alone, and her children dispersed, she knew not whither. In the slave depots at New Orleans, and in the auction rooms, I never saw families sold together; often a mother and one child put up together, when the child was young, but not often a mother and a child above six or seven. Scenes I saw in negro sale rooms cannot be related, they were so atrocious, so shocking to all feelings of decency as well as justice. Such is this peculiar institution. 'But I never saw such things,' said a lady of New Orleans to me. 'You should not have gone to such places,' said another. Yes, it is easy to live in New Orleans and see nothing; but for all that these things exist. And for all the smooth appearances in the Southern States, there is a fearful amount of misery and heartbreak caused by the necessary action of the slave laws. Of the amount of domestic tyranny and cruelty it is more difficult to judge, but I am convinced it is very great. In my small circle at New Orleans I knew of two cases, and the number I heard of was very great.

The system of slavery might be, perhaps, upheld logically if the negro race could be proved to be not men, but a kind of monkey race made to wait on men. But facts are too strong, and the Southern upholders of slavery have never attempted to prove that; what they do say is that the negroes are inferior and cannot govern themselves; that slavery is a 'divine institution' for civilising and Christianising these savage African races. As regards the alleged inferiority, I am convinced the negro is superior in some qualities, and how far inferior in others cannot be asserted until he and the white man are placed in exactly the same position. Where they have been, the negro has not acquitted himself discreditably. We will now go on to say something of the actions of those who hold others as property.

At the time when the Federal Union was established there was a strong feeling against slavery and a strong party for emancipation. And if Washington, Jefferson, and the North had been firmly determined to have no union with Slave States, it is probable slavery never would have been increased to its present dimensions. But fear of England made the leaders consent to union, which was almost necessary to their existence as a nation.

The Northern States had cast off slavery, and it is probable the leaders thought slavery in the South would be more easily got rid of at a future time than at that moment; but, in my very humble opinion, Washington committed here a great fault. The introduction of the culture of sugar and cotton suddenly increased the extension of slavery. The Slave States demanded more power and territory, and almost the whole of the politics of America became slavery politics. Political parties became parties for or against slavery or the extension of slavery, and almost the whole mental activity of the people has been turned to the question of the negro.

The great quarrels have been about the territory or new lands, which, of course, the South has always desired to form into Slave States and too often successfully, as in the case of Missouri and Texas. The nature of slavery makes the Slave States by necessity aggressive. Slave labour exhausts the soil and makes fresh land a necessity to slave communities; the position, too, of slave-owners makes their passion for power naturally dominant. And the increase of Slave States naturally is sought for to give power in the central government.

When Missouri was received into the States as a Slave State, a compromise was made for the Free States, that slavery should not be carried north of the parallel of 36° 30′ of north latitude. This was a triumph to the South, and so the Southern States went on triumphing over the North, until the election of Lincoln in 1860.

In spite of the Missouri compromise, they tried hard to seize Kansas, which was north of the boundary then agreed on, and in every way showed their ill faith and their one determined aim to go on increasing the Slave States. After disgraceful scenes of war, Kansas decided herself, in spite of Southern ruffians, on being a Free State.

After the affair of Kansas, the North began to wake up to the designs of the South, and anti-slavery principles became much more generally accepted. The atrocities of the South had absolutely frightened the North. It was then that the Republican party was formed; their policy was to prevent the extension of slaves into any new territory. In 1856 this party, though defeated, and Buchanan the Southern President elected, still showed by its power that the slave dominion was no longer submitted to in the North without a protest. The leaders of the South felt that this was a sign of a coming struggle, and they girded themselves for the fight. The real cause of their defeat in Kansas was the want of power of colonisation.

A slave population cannot compete with a free people in colonisation. The South had taken the ground with her hordes of hired ruffians of 'white trash', but could not hold it against the free settlers of the North, who poured in with their families.

The South then felt the necessity of a disposable population, and turned its face towards the African slave trade, closed since 1808, and it became strongly their interest to re-open it. The South now declared it was unconstitutional to close it; in 1857 the governor of South Carolina said so. In 1858 the newspapers of the South advocated the opening of this market, and there were cargoes of negroes from Africa landed at the mouth of the Mississippi when we were at New Orleans in the spring of 1858.

At that time the governors of the Southern States spoke openly of their hostilities to the North, and I remember in the address of the governor of Alabama to the State Assembly at Montgomery, he urged the increase of the State army, to resist the North if it encroached on their rights. In 1859, associations were formed to re-open the slave trade, and every effort made to disseminate this new doctrine in the States. A Mississippi paper, the *True Southern*, offered a prize for the best sermon in favour of free trade in human flesh!

More and more slaves, *in spite of the law*, were landed in the

South in 1859 and 1860, and in fact now, practically, the slave trade is established.

We must just touch here on the decision in the momentous case of Dred Scott, in which Chief Justice Janey of Missouri pronounced Dred Scott a slave, although he had been freed by a residence in a Free State. The Chief Justice went the whole length of the encroachment of the new party in the South, and pronounced that there was no difference between a slave and any other property; and secondly, that all American citizens might settle with their property in any part of the Union in which they pleased. By this decision the Union might be peopled with slave-owners, and New York and Massachusetts (*all their laws being set aside*) become really Slave States!

The Southern aggressors became more insolent, and even the democratic party refused to go the whole lengths of the 'thorough' party formed in the South, much as they desired to preserve the Union; they therefore separated, and this split in the Southern camp was the real cause of the victory of the Republicans in the election of Lincoln. As soon as the Slave States saw they stood alone, with no party to abet them in the North, they decided on secession.

The democratic party was for free trade State rights; that is, it was for not meddling with slavery in the State, and it inclined always for the rights of slave-owners: yet the South was not satisfied with this policy, and wanted something more than free trade as we understand it, and as the Democrats understood it; and we must not suppose, as many do in England, that the desire for free trade was the cause of the war, or why did the South break with the free trade Democrats? Free trade in human beings, the Democrats would not have supported, but that is one of the points the South is determined to gain.

Slavery alone is the question at issue between the North and the South. Slavery has been the cause of all their differences, and it is slavery that will be the cause of an everlasting feud as long as it remains on the same continent with the Free States.

In the admirable book of Mr Cairnes, he professes his belief that secession will be favourable to the growth of slavery, and says the leaders of the South would not fight for it if they were not convinced of this, and that they may be admitted to know their own advantage. On the other side, it is certain that the abolitionists have thought conscientiously that union with slave-owners was iniquitous, and believed the constitution to be a compact with slavery, which being against Christianity, ought not to be upheld; and in 1844, Mr Lloyd Janison, as President of the American Anti-

Slavery Society, wrote an address, which, in the strongest possible language, insists on this point. In large letters, as our eye runs down this address, which is signed by the President, and by Wendell Philips and Maria Weston Chapman, we see, 'NO UNION WITH SLAVEHOLDERS, etc. MERCILESS TYRANTS, BLOODTHIRSTY ASSASSINS. Circulate a declaration of DISUNION FROM SLAVEHOLDERS throughout the country. Hold mass meetings, assemble in conventions, nail your banners to the mast, etc.'

In the works of W. E. Channing, we find that he believes 'no blessings of the Union can be a compensation for taking part in the enslaving of our fellow-creatures, nor ought the bond to be perpetuated if experience shall demonstrate that it can only continue through our participation in wrong-doing'. To this conviction the Free States are tending.

Theodore Parker thought the Union iniquitous, and believed it necessary for the safety of the South. 'The Union protects that property. (The property in men.) There are 300,000 slaveholders, owning thirteen hundred millions of dollars invested in men. Their wealth depends on the Union.' We might multiply passages from the writings of the anti-slavery party to show that they believed the Union ought to be broken; and from slave-owners, asserting that *the dissolution of the Union was the dissolution of slavery*, that *they looked to the North to protect them* from the *stupid depraved savages, a dangerous class of beings.* Such were the opinions of the anti-slavery party, and such were the opinions of the slave-owners until quite lately, almost until the war broke out. I believe the anti-slavery party did not change until after the war began. Secession it was thought would be the death of slavery; both North and South agreed in this. It is not then astonishing that we in England should have been puzzled for some time to know where to look for emancipation. But we ought never to have hesitated about the character of the South.

John Stuart Mill, Professor Cairnes, and other authorities, think the North was obliged to accept the challenge to battle with the South. Some of the Northerners felt it their duty to fight for the Union, some that those who might wish to join the North, should have fair play, and be able to express themselves, free from the terrorism of the South. In this the North has been successful, and there is little doubt that Maryland, Virginia, Missouri, Kentucky, by the war will be able to join the North. The facts are clear, though *The Times* has done all it can to misrepresent them. The North, in spite of all mismanagement, has gained much. The South, in spite of its frightful sufferings and good management, has not been able to prevent its States from being invaded, and

New Orleans taken. Supposing the South could drive out the Northern army from all its States (which seems to us perfectly impossible), what would be its career as an unrestrained State, Republic, or rather Slave-Aristocracy?

Mr Cairnes proves in his book that the very nature of slave culture exhausts the lands and demands new territory. We have shown how the South has gone on acquiring by foul means new states. Missouri was gained by a compact they did not mean to keep. Texas was positively stolen. It was not for want of blood-thirsty ruffians that Kansas was not gained, but simply after many struggles the free settlers so largely outnumbered the slave popu-lation, that they could not be refused admittance as a Free-State.

Then the South asserted the right of making slaves like any other property, with which they might settle anywhere. Then the slave trade was approved of and absolutely practised. This has been the career of the South to 1860, when by a split in their own camp, caused by the 'Thorough' party, going too fast, even for the Democrats, the republican candidate was elected; this election, in which the South of course voted, they would not submit to, and declared for secession.

What may we expect by this past for the future? Slavery, they have asserted, is to be the cornerstone of the new Union, unfettered by any restrictions.

Where there is slavery, industry is despised, and the new Union will have five millions of whites who, called 'mean whites', have no calling, but live an uncertain and almost savage life, always ready for any piratical expedition. They will have an economic necessity for extension of territory and a determination to settle newly acquired territory with African stock. But let us quote from Prof. Cairnes' book, the opinion of the Vice-president of the Southern Confederation. 'We can divide Texas into five Slave States, and get Chihuahua and Sonora, if we have the slave popu-lation, but unless the number of the African stock be increased we have not the population, and might as well abandon the race with our brethren of the North in the colonisation of the Territories. Slave States cannot be made without Africans.' 'Take off,' says Mr Gaulden of Georgia, 'the worthless restrictions which cut off the supply of slaves from foreign lands . . . take off the restrictions against the African slave trade, and we should then want no protec-tion.' With the slave trade as well as slavery, with the 5,000,000 of mean whites, what could be expected from the new Union, cut off from the restraining North, all Christendom against her; with the lust of power as her predominant character almost by necessity? What could be expected from her career if she triumphs over the

North? A Union of tyrants, whose hand will ever be against the weak, whose aim abroad would be power and dominion, and whose pet institution, once called 'peculiar', now become 'Divine', would be *slavery*.

With such a prospect, ought we not to look anxiously for the success of the North? and, knowing what the South has done and will do, so well as the Northern people do, it is not astonishing that they should think us cool and indifferent to the most vital question of the world.

They have decided it to be right to fight the South. They have decided that now they will not let the slave power domineer longer if they can help it. They have decided now to do what we have abused them for fifty years for not doing. They have decided to alter the constitution even, that sacred legacy of Washington and their great patriots. Yet England has not shown any sympathy for the North and her frightful inherited difficulties.

The war so far has done so much for the cause of freedom in the North, that even secession could be allowed now, in 1863, with much greater loss to the Slave States and gain to the North than in 1860.

That the North regard the war as a war against slavery, there cannot now be the slightest doubt. The North see more clearly now than ever what slavery really is. When she was a partner with slavery she was almost bound to defend it; now – now for the first time, the Slave and Free States are separated, the North is free to think without prejudice, and does think, and does make rapid progress towards a determination to do all it can to rid itself of that horrible stain and scandal.

I have a letter before me from one of the most distinguished members of the Abolitionist party, and as it shows in what light the war is regarded in North America, I will insert some passages. 'This terrific war' – 'I believe it will humble the haughty spirit of America, check her vain boasting, and enlighten her to see that all her glory as a nation has been darkened by the plague spot of slavery, that her vaunt of being a united people was but a fable to deceive European nations. Union was impossible between slavery and freedom: from the first Congress to the last, slavery has been the cause of ceaseless strife; our political history is but a tissue of encroachments on one part, and of mean subserviency on the other. Happily, as John Brown said, while awaiting his execution – "There is no night so dark as to prevent the dawn of day, no storm so furious as to prevent the return of warm sunshine and cloudless sky." We shall probably have to wait long for the sun, but when he rises it will be on a nation cleansed of slavery with its concomitant vices, and crimes, and miseries, and my settled conviction has long been, that a ten-years' war will inflict less suffering and less moral degradation upon us than the continuation of slavery. Hence I rejoice in the war, seeing in this fearful calamity our only chance of regeneration and salvation. "With what measure ye meted it shall be measured to you again." If, as a nation, ye have torn asunder the tenderest ties of humanity – parents and children, husbands and wives, brothers and sisters have been parted, to endure a fate infinitely worse than death – now behold the recompense of your works. War is desolating your homes and wringing your hearts, your beloved are taken from your midst, and the perils of war encompass them, your hearts may never again throb against each other. But mark, yours are lighter sufferings: those who leave you breathe air of freedom; the slave is consigned to mental as well as physical torture, he writhes in his chains. Go now to your battlefields and your hospitals – behold the ghastly wounds, the lacerated bodies, the maimed and bleeding forms of those who went voluntarily to fight and to perish for the phantom of a Union laid in iniquity and cemented by cruelty and oppression. Turn then to the prison-house of the South. Behold her scorpion lash, her thumbscrews, her various instruments of cruelty, designed to crush out of human beings their noblest aspirations, to turn God's crowning work of creation into a soulless automaton, and tell me if the sufferings of your sick and wounded soldiers do not faintly shadow forth the sufferings of your slaves, and cry to you in a voice of warning and of woe, if not of repentance, "The measure ye meted to others is being measured to you again." See ye not in this desolating conflict the just retribution of your hypocrisy and your barbarity? . . . Slavery will be abolished, the South will let the oppressed go free, but the vile prejudice against the negro, so rampant at the North, will not be abolished. It is no less a crime than slavery, and must meet its recompense in humiliation and suffering. It almost makes me despair of my country when I see her thrusting back the confiding slave into bondage, using him as a tool and denying to him the right of every man to confront his enemy and to battle for freedom, his own freedom, for the privilege of asserting his manhood and saving himself from contempt and degradation. Oh, my dear friends, I can offer no other prayer but this, "Let not thine eye pity, nor thy hand spare, until judgment has brought the victory of Righteousness." Let not the wound of this people be healed slightly – Oh, my country, my country! mayest thou know in this the day of thine adversity the things which belong unto thy peace, ere they be hid from thine eyes.'

It is a moment of deep solemnity in the history of the free white people, our brethren in America. It is a moment full of the most important consequences to the whole African race, and we ought not lightly to judge in this tremendous struggle. We should not be led away by a show of 'pluck' and daring, to sympathise with the South, or be turned in disgust from the cause of the North because of the barbarities of any one leader, or the rapacity of any number of Government officials.

There is a *cause* in this struggle, and we are responsible to give the whole weight of our opinion, to help either the right or the wrong. I grant there has been much to confuse us, and much we can with difficulty understand, amid all the conflicting accounts, and the sudden changes of opinion in America; but of this we may be sure, the South is in the wrong; the South is dangerous. The cause of the war is slavery.

There is one consideration which regards England particularly – it is that of opening afresh the slave trade. There is a future cause of war for us with the South, which hates England with a bitter and intense hatred as the land which has set the example of a great sacrifice made for the freedom of the slave.

NOTE

1 These cases we have abridged from *A Sketch of the Laws relating to Slavery in the several States in the United States of America*, 2nd edition, by George M. Stroud, Philadelphia, 1856.

Accomplices

(reprinted from *The English Woman's Journal*, February 1864)

That terrible history of the young girl 'worked to death' has made fine ladies, and ladies not fine at all, pause and think, 'Am I to blame? Am I in any way an accomplice in causing this wretched girl's misery?' A young lady with tears in her eyes told me she had often had her bonnets from Madame E., and, that in consequence, she felt she was implicated in this horrid system; I could not deny she had some cause for the feeling, though not much for remorse.

Physicians and others who have witnessed the deadly effects of the manufacture of common lucifer matches,[1] and of artificial flowers in which emerald green is used, have written very detailed reports, and all those who have taken the trouble to read the evidence, must be convinced that these employments are always unhealthy and sometimes fatal. Now when fully convinced that the production of certain articles causes terrible disease and suffering, are we justified in using or wearing such articles, and causing, through our demand for them, this misery?

Probably no man or woman will answer, 'Yes'; therefore, we will take for granted that we have no right, when we *know* we are causing misery – to cause it. We all admit in this matter that knowledge gives some responsibility; that knowledge makes this difference – that if we *know* these girls and women are dying with terrible ulcers and inflammations, and if we continue to aid in their dying, we are sinful; but if we do *not* know, we are not sinful, though we cause as much misery. '*But if we do not know, we are not sinful*', let us consider if our ignorance is sinful or not.

You will admit that the acquisition of some kinds of knowledge is a duty; but what kinds? Religious knowledge, a knowledge of our duties to God – moral knowledge, the knowledge of our duties to men, would rank first; then the knowledge of how to preserve health, and how to acquire wealth; and following at some distance, in importance, the knowledge of the characteristics of other countries, of the animal world; and still farther off, knowledge of the past history of the earth. Most rational beings consider it a duty to acquire some, if not all these, and a great many other kinds of knowledge, and perhaps sinful *not* to have acquired them if we have had the opportunity.

The most important of all our duties except one, the knowledge of our duties towards men, includes many things; whenever we have power, we have duties and responsibilities; whenever we can influence the fate of our fellow men, we have moral duties which it is incumbent upon us to study. We ought to have a knowledge of the effects of our actions, and do nothing which affects our fellow-creatures, without considering if it be for good or for evil.

Now because the facts do not pass before their very eyes, few people remember they are employing the flesh and blood of human beings when they spend money, and that they influence the destinies of all those people they employ; really the exercise of this influence for good is one of our first duties, and the ignorance of this duty certainly culpable.

No lady would set the task to her own maid to powder artificial grapes with a poisonous substance, and yet few ladies think it their duty to know anything about the people whom they thus employ, when they go to shops and buy their artificial flowers. In a very simple state of society, where most things used in a household are made at home, it is easy to see with your own eyes, whether you are causing human beings to do anything prejudicial to them; if every bit of influence or power exercised by the master and mistress is good and not harmful. An old lady in New England once described to me how, about fifty years ago, everything which the family ate or wore, was made on the farm, the only things bought were tools, nails, hatchets, etc. They grew their own flax and hemp, and spun and wove it; they tanned their own leather, and made their own shoes; they dyed their linen, and in fact had a very profound knowledge of the manufacture of almost everything with which they came in contact: they were not surrounded by unknown conditions. A state of things with immense disadvantages and drawbacks, but with this advantage, the master would not have let his servants make poisonous ornaments, and his family could not be accessory to that kind of suffering and wrong, and so on.

With us, in our crowded and complicated life, arise new duties and new sins. Not the less are we responsible for all the labour we

employ than the man on the New England farm. It is one of the
kinds of knowledge which it is a sin not to acquire. We ought to
know the history of what we buy for use, for clothing, or food;
its manufacture, and whether the people we employ when we buy
their work are healthy and happy. Surely this knowledge is more
important to us and our country than a knowledge of Roman
History, or most other learning. I remember standing years ago
in the Water-Colour Exhibition, long before Ruskin wrote his
ideas of Political Economy, with a Member of Parliament, who
was buying drawings, and was known for his great benevolence
and equal sagacity, and ranked with the political economists and
reformers of his country. 'I like to spend my money in this way,'
said he, 'better than in fine furniture, and the usual luxuries of life,
because I think that water-colour painting is a noble and healthy
pursuit, and I have as much satisfaction in helping the lives of
these artists as enjoyment in what they produce.' Here is the whole
pith of the question: it is a question which should be taught in
schools, and how interesting the study of the effects of their actions
might be made to the young. For instance, if a boy wanted to buy
cardboard to make models, the occasion might be taken by the
real educator to show him the manufactory, and point out to him
how the cardboard was made, and the people who made it; and
he would indicate the unhealthiness of the occupation of making
certain kinds of cardboard, and leave it to the boy to choose to
use that which did not cause disease in its manufacture. A hundred
useful and interesting moral lessons of this kind could be given.

It is quite clear our ideas of morality have not become complex,
acute, and subtle enough in proportion to the advance of civilisation. Education it is true has been pushing on, but not always to
the point, and has been striving after *elegant learning*, or *profitable
knowledge*, rather than after that other kind of knowledge much
more important; how to do good and avoid doing harm to our
fellow-creatures in this complex civilised life.

I think our church should have taught us how to cultivate our
moral responsibilities, to meet and be equal to the complexities of
modern life; but as far as I know, the church has been utterly
dumb on this point.

Now how far is this responsibility of searching into the effects
of our actions to carry us? – Is it to make us prefer going without
seemingly necessary things, to employing, and so producing
suffering anywhere, even far away? Yes, I think so, we ought to
make *any* sacrifice if we are sure of our principle.

There are certain things which we all know are not only produced by suffering, but which are absolutely produced by stolen

labour, by being forced by fear to work under the most frightful system that the world has ever seen. Are we not morally committing a great sin to encourage such a system?

When Mrs Stowe came to England, after the great success of *Uncle Tom*, she proposed that we should abandon the use of slave-grown cotton, sugar, etc., as a means of getting rid of the horrible evil – slavery.

This proposition was not listened to for a moment seriously, and why not? Would it have answered the purpose if all England had refused to wear slave-grown cotton? Certainly it would have discouraged slavery to the same extent that our demand has encouraged it. Slavery is only profitable in the production of a few commodities, and cannot, like free labour, be rapidly applied to different kinds of production, and in as far as these goods were not saleable, slavery would have diminished. I do not see any reason why we should complain at being obliged to use flaxen, hempen, and woollen goods produced by free labour to serve so good a cause as the abolition of slavery.

Why was Mrs Stowe's proposal met with a smile, as if it were an amiable, womanly, impracticable plan? Simply because it was out of the pathway of usual thought; we had never been taught to think of applying our consciences to this sort of everyday work of buying and selling. We had always been taught that our only duty when we went to market was to get our goods as cheap as possible: that may be a duty, but as we have seen, it is certainly not our only duty; and reasoning by analogy, we are really as much accomplices in perpetuating slavery as long as we buy slave-grown goods, as we are accomplices in creating disease when we buy emerald-green ornaments.

When all the individuals of a country act in habitual forgetfulness of their duties of moral responsibility, suffering must ensue. The country goes into partnership with something which has evil and death in it. It becomes dependent on something wicked. Wicked institutions do not go on in peace, but are subject to violent revolutions, disturbances, and miseries, in which the partners are involved; – so Manchester is punished with New Orleans. We ought not to have allied ourselves with slavery, on the high moral ground that it is a great injustice to our fellow-men, but it is also plain, such is the *solidarité* of human kind, that we cannot encourage it without in the end suffering the punishment which surely overtakes evil, even in this world.

This war is not the only evil that was imminent in such a state of society as that of the Slave States. A slave insurrection is always possible. When, four years ago, I stood in the auction room, at

New Orleans, and after hearing the bids for a steam-boat, I saw men and women sold, sometimes with their little children, and as often, separately – women examined like horses, their mouths opened by the would-be buyers to look at their teeth, their flesh felt to see if it were firm and healthy – the whole sense of what slavery was came over my heart and head, and the horror of it almost made me faint on the spot. No descriptions that I have read of a slave sale equals the revolting, brutal reality. Just at this present time, we in England are apt to forget what slavery is, therefore I say this for my testimony as an eye-witness, having lived nine weeks in New Orleans, and many months in the Slave States, that the institution is degrading alike to masters and slaves, and that progress and Christian virtues are incompatible with its existence.

Now have we in England done all that we can do to exterminate this terrible outrage on human beings? Are we not accomplices in many ways?

'Why are you such a decided partisan of the South?' I asked a pleasant, well-bred English lady, whom I met travelling abroad a few months ago.

Miss D. 'Oh, because I know so many pleasant people who are Southerners; didn't you know Mrs Y. at Rome?'

'Yes, and she was a merry elegant little creature; but why do you think slavery right?'

Miss D. 'Oh, you see I have never met any Northerners I liked at all, and I do so like the real Southerners of family, they are charming!'

'And so because you liked pretty Mrs Y. and five or six other people from the South, you uphold that slavery is right?'

Miss D. 'Why yes! you see it can't be so bad; and I have not thought much about it, and I know I hate the abolitionists, and I do admire Stonewall Jackson!'

Amusing and melancholy to hear an intelligent being, thirty-five years of age, born with every advantage of influence, money, and position, upholding that four millions of people, because they have darker skins and tenderer natures than some of us, should be property like sheep and cattle! You will say, perhaps, that her opinions do not matter, and I am sure she did not think they did in the least; but I say her opinions, and your opinions, and all our opinions *do* signify. For whatever we do, and do not do, depends on what opinions we hold, and there is nothing more humiliating than the stupid indifference of women, and the small value they set on their own influence. The importance of the formation of right opinion is not felt as it ought to be; it is forgotten, how close upon the heels of opinion, action treads. Miss D. did not believe her opinions wrong, and yet what actions they lead to!

The women of Spain laughed to see heretics burn, and the state of mind which could so stifle all womanly pity was produced by false opinion. It seems not even vice can so degrade a character or produce greater misery!

In some ways, too, from their usual position of living a little apart, and withdrawn from the active business of the world, women should find it easier to form wise judgments. Of a man intensely occupied in active life, one may predict his opinions almost certainly by knowing what are his interests and surroundings.

It is to be ardently desired that women should make use of the opportunities they have – to be ardently desired also, that they had wider opportunities, but we would gladly see in the heads of households some dim discerning of what a grand place a woman holds even *now*, if she would but seize it!

To return to Miss D. and those like her, whose opinions are only formed by the influence of some few agreeable people, and are like caterpillars who take their colour from the food on which they feed. What a good thing it would be, if such lightly taken opinions were but lightly held; but alas! the greater part of mankind and womankind do not hold them indifferently, but often quite strenuously and positively, and are ready to ally themselves for better and worse to men and parties fighting for those opinions. Why cannot people when they have not the time or the head to investigate a subject, say, 'on that I have no decided opinion?' words very rarely, alas! used. There is very little relation between the grounds of any opinions, and the rigour with which it is upheld. For example, Miss D. had made up her mind slavery was right (on what grounds you have seen), and would, all things permitting, have had no objection to marry a Southerner, and invest her fortune in human chattels; and once her interest on that side, what a partisan she would have become!

Now to return to the question of cotton. Can we expect the slave-owner to give up his slaves, when we rush with our money to buy the produce of this stolen labour? Slavery is surely a greater crime than the modern robbery of pockets; it includes the greatest of all robberies, the robbery of man, of his labour, his wife, his children. If you bought knowingly stolen pocket handkerchiefs, you would be branded as an accomplice of the thief! Does no one think of blaming every one in England for buying the produce of stolen labour?

NOTE

1 'Shortly after the introduction of phosphorus in the manufacture of matches it began to be observed, especially on the Continent, that a peculiar affection of the jaw was apt to come on, in those who were engaged in the match-factories, especially in those most exposed to the fumes arising from the composition employed; and it was soon established that the proclivity to this disease, though varying in intensity in different manufactories, was a special evil common to all. The disease, it was noticed, began usually with aching in one of the teeth, causing marked, and when fully established, great and almost intolerable pain, rendering sleep almost impossible. The gums and face swell, the teeth ultimately perish, or fall out. As the disease progresses, the swelling of the face grows larger, and extends to the neighbouring glands: the gums spongy and red, give forth at frequent openings a most offensively smelling matter; abscesses form over the jaw and break, whence issues the same sort of corrupt discharge, sinuses are established, and the livid gums shrink and retire from the bone, which thus becomes exposed, and is found on probing, to be rough and diseased; portions of bone scale off, and then, either the disease becomes checked, and the mutilated patient recovers, or more frequently, the whole jaw becomes involved, the patient's strength gives way, he pines, becomes subject to diarrhoea, and to low fever, and after lingering for a longer time than would be thought possible under such an affliction, is at length worn out and dies. . . . Were "amorphous phosphorus" substituted for the usual kind, there would be no danger at all, but manufacturers find no sale for matches so made, as they are a trifle dearer. The matches of Messrs Bryant and May deserve their name of 'safety matches' for they will not ignite except upon the box, and the phosphorus disease is not amongst the possible incidents of their manufacture.' – *Report of the Medical Officer of the Privy Council, with Appendix.* – 1862. *'Meliora', for October,* 1863.

Reasons for the Enfranchisement of Women

(a paper read at the National Association for the Promotion of Social Science, October 1866)

That a respectable, orderly, independent body in the state should have no voice, and no influence recognised by the law, in the election of the representatives of the people, while they are otherwise acknowledged as responsible citizens, are eligible for many public offices, and required to pay all taxes, is an anomaly which seems to require some explanation, and the reasons alleged in its defence are curious and interesting to examine. It is not, however, my present purpose to controvert the various objections which have been brought forward against the extension of the suffrage to women. Passing over what may be called the negative side of the question, I propose to take it up at a more advanced stage, and assuming that the measure is unobjectionable, I shall endeavour to show that it is positively desirable.

Mr Anthony Trollope, speaking in reference to the restrictions on voting in some departments of the Civil Service, says: 'A clerk in the Customhouse, over whom no political ascendancy from his official superior could by any chance be used, is debarred from voting. I once urged upon a Cabinet minister that this was a stigma on the service – and though he was a Whig, he laughed at me. He could not conceive that men would care about voting. But men do care; and those who do not, ought to be made to care.' The case is very similar as regards women. Many people, besides Cabinet ministers, are unable to conceive that women can care about voting. That some women do care has been proved by the Petition presented to Parliament last session. I shall try to show why some care – and why those who do not ought to be made to care.

There are now a very considerable number of open-minded unprejudiced people, who see no particular reason why women should not have votes, if they want them, but, they ask, what would be the good of it? What is there that women want which male legislators are not willing to give? And here let me say at the outset, that the advocates of this measure are very far from accusing men of deliberate unfairness to women. It is not as a means of extorting justice from unwilling legislators that the franchise is claimed for women. In so far as the claim is made with any special reference to class interests at all, it is simply on the general ground that under a representative government, any class which is not represented is likely to be neglected. Proverbially, what is out of sight is out of mind, and the theory that women, as such, are bound to keep out of sight, finds its most emphatic expression in the denial of the right to vote. The direct results are probably less injurious than those which are indirect, but that a want of due consideration for the interests of women is apparent in our legislation, could very easily be shown. To give evidence in detail would be a long and an invidious task. I will mention one instance only, that of the educational endowments all over the country. Very few people would now maintain that the education of boys is more important to the State than that of girls. But as a matter of fact, girls have but a very small share in educational endowments. Many of the old foundations have been reformed by Parliament, but the desirableness of providing with equal care for girls and boys, has very seldom been recognised. In the administration of charities generally, the same tendency prevails to postpone the claims of women to those of men.

Among instances of hardship traceable directly to exclusion from the franchise and to no other cause, may be mentioned the unwillingness of landlords to accept women as tenants. Two large farmers in Suffolk inform me that this is not an uncommon case. They mention one estate on which seven widows have been ejected, who, if they had had votes, would have been continued as tenants. The following letter is from the unmarried sister of these gentlemen, herself a farmer in the same county:

> It is not perhaps sufficiently considered how large a proportion of women occupy and cultivate farms entirely on their own account, nor how sensibly a share in the suffrage would affect their interests. In strictly agricultural counties, like those of Norfolk and Suffolk, it is a thing of daily occurrence for leases to be granted or renewed to the widows, daughters, or sisters of farmers, and many tenant-farmers are unwilling to hire of landlords who, as the phrase is, 'turn out the women'. In these districts the agricultural class is richer than almost any other, and the female portion of it

receive as a rule, a much better education than the daughters of clergymen and the poorer professional men. In fact they receive the best within reach. I think you would find very few farmers who do not consider their wives or daughters quite as capable of voting as themselves, and would not show their faith in their business capacities by making them executrixes and administrators of their property. Land proprietors, as a rule, however, like, and with reason, to have their estates represented in Parliament – and here I come to the chief point I would urge upon your attention. Instances daily occur of the widow of a deserving tenant being ejected from her farm with a large young family unprovided for, simply because she cannot vote. Farming is a healthful, easy, and natural profession for women who have been brought up in agricultural counties, and have thus been learning it from childhood. Moreover, for holders of capital, it is a tolerably lucrative one. I know many and many a single woman living upon the narrow income derived from a fair property invested in the funds, who would gladly hire land instead, and thus obtain a higher interest for her money. It seems to me not a little hard that a woman possessing capital should be deprived of the privileges other capitalists enjoy, but it seems harder still that she should be robbed of her livelihood, simply because an anomalous custom has shut her out from such a privilege.

Take for instance the following cases which have come under my own notice, which show the working of the law both ways: The other day a widow was left with a large family, in a farm her husband had occupied for years. The landowner was one of those gentlemen who highly estimate parliamentary influence; his unfortunate tenant was only saved from want by a generous public subscription. People might say – if she had sufficient capital to carry on a farm, how was it that she was in need of assistance? But such a question shows an utter misconception of the subject. Anyone at all acquainted with farming will understand how ruinous is a sudden ejection, admitting as it does no oppor- tunity of preparing for high valuation; and any one acquainted with general business will understand what an advantage it is for capital to be used. A sum quite adequate for carrying on a moderate sized farm would bring in a miserable income, if 'safely' invested.

Take another case. My next door neighbour, a respectable widow lady, has gained a competent living for herself and daughter, on a farm she has occupied since the death of her husband, twenty years ago. Had she been ejected then, she must have eked out a miserable income by keeping a third-rate school, or thrown herself upon friends. As it is, she has maintained a respectable and independent position, and has of course, employed her capital to the utmost advantage. It seems a little hard that this lady, who in every way performs the duties of an employer, should have no vote, whilst the keeper of a low beerhouse close by, who demoralises labouring men, and is hardly able to write his name, exercises the right from which she is denied.

In conclusion, I beg to say that I have been a farmer for some years, that I know few parishes in which women are not owners or occupiers of land, and that every practical farmer with whom I have discussed the subject of the extension of the franchise to women, has recognised the justice of such a claim. They certainly see no reason why we should be entrusted with property, and not entrusted with the influence pertaining to it. The only wonder is that the attention of the public has not been drawn to this matter before.

M. B. Edwards

The case, as stated by Miss Edwards on behalf of farmers, is scarcely less strong as regards all women, who, as heads of a business or a household, fulfil the duties of a man in the same position. Their task is often a hard one, and everything which helps to sustain their self-respect, and to give them consideration and importance in the eyes of others, is likely to lessen their difficulties, and make them happier and stronger for the battle of life. The very fact that, though householders and taxpayers, they have not equal privileges with male householders and taxpayers, is in itself a *deconsideration*, which seems to me invidious and useless. It casts a kind of slur on the value of their opinions, and I may remark in passing, that what is treated as of no value is apt to grow valueless. Citizenship is an honour, and not to have the full rights of a citizen is a want of honour. Inconspicuously it may be, but by a subtle and sure process, those, who without their own consent and without sufficient reason, are debarred from full participation in the rights and duties of a citizen, lose more or less of social consideration and esteem.

These arguments, founded on considerations of justice and mercy to a large and important class, might, in a civilised country and in the absence of strong reasons to the contrary, be deemed amply sufficient to justify the measure proposed. There remain to be considered those aspects of the question which affect the general community. And, among all the reasons for giving women votes, the one which appears to me the strongest is that of the influence it might be expected to have in increasing public spirit. Patriotism, a healthy, lively, intelligent interest in everything which concerns the nation to which we belong, and an unselfish devotedness to the public service – these are the qualities which make a people great and happy; these are the virtues which ought to be most sedulously cultivated in all classes of the community. And I know no better means at this present time, of counteracting the tendency to prefer narrow private ends to the public good, than this of giving to all women, duly qualified, a direct and conscious participation in political affairs. Give some women votes, and it will tend to make all women think seriously of the concerns of the nation at large, and their interest having once been fairly roused, they will take pains, by reading and by consultation with persons better informed than themselves, to form sound opinions. As it is, women of the middle class occupy themselves but little with anything beyond their own family circle. They do not consider it any concern of theirs, if poor men and women are ill-nursed in workhouse infirmaries, and poor children ill-taught in workhouse schools. If the roads are bad, the drains neglected, the water poisoned, they think it is all very wrong, but it does not occur to them that it is their duty to get it put right. These farmer-women and business-women have honest, sensible minds and much practical experience, but they do not bring their good sense to bear upon public affairs, because they think it is men's business, not theirs, to look after such things. It is this belief – so narrowing and deadening in its influence – that the exercise of the franchise would tend to dissipate. The mere fact of being called upon to enforce an opinion by a vote would have an immediate effect in awakening a healthy sense of responsibility. There is no reason why these women should not take an active interest in all the social questions – education, public health, prison discipline, the poor laws, and the rest – which occupy Parliament, and they would be much more likely to do so if they felt that they had importance in the eyes of Members of Parliament, and could claim a hearing for their opinions.

Besides these women of business, there are ladies of property, whose more active participation in public affairs would be beneficial both to themselves and the community generally. The want of stimulus to energetic action is much felt by women of the higher classes. It is agreed that they ought not to be idle, but what they ought to do is not so clear. Reading, music and drawing, needlework, and charity, are their usual employments. Reading, without a purpose, does not come to much. Music and drawing, and needlework, are most commonly regarded chiefly as amusements intended to fill up time. We have left, as the serious duty of independent and unmarried women, the care of the poor in all its branches, including visiting the sick and the aged and ministering to their wants, looking after the schools, and in every possible way giving help wherever help is needed. Now education, the relief of the destitute, and the health of the people, are among the most important and difficult matters which occupy the minds of statesmen, and if it is admitted that women of leisure and culture are bound to contribute their part towards the solution of these great questions, it is evident that every means of making their co-operation enlightened and vigorous should be sought for. They have special opportunities of observing the operation of many of the laws. They know, for example, for they see before their eyes, the practical working of the law of settlement – of the laws relating to the dwellings of the poor – and many others, and the experience which peculiarly qualifies them to form a judgment on these matters, ought not to be thrown away. We all know that we have already a goodly body of rich, influential working-women, whose opinions on the social and political questions of the day are well worth listening to. In almost every parish, there are, happily for England, such women. Now everything should be done to give these valuable members of the community a solid social standing. If they are wanted, and there can be no doubt that they are, in all departments of social work, their position in the work should be as dignified and honourable as it is possible to make it. Rich unmarried women have many opportunities of benefiting the community, which are not within reach of a married woman, absorbed by the care of her husband and children. Everything, I say again, should be done to encourage this most important and increasing class, to take their place in the army of workers for the common good, and all the forces we can bring to bear for this end are of incalculable value. For by bringing women into hearty co-operation with men, we gain the benefit not only of their work, but of their intelligent sympathy. Public spirit is like fire: a feeble spark of it may be fanned into a flame, or it may very easily be put out. And the result of teaching women that they have nothing to do with politics, is that their influence goes towards extinguishing the unselfish interest – never too strong – which men are disposed to take in public affairs.

Let each member of the House of Commons consider, in a spirit of true scientific inquiry, all the properly qualified women of his acquaintance, and he will see no reason why the single ladies and the widows among his own family and friends should not form as sensible opinions on the merits of candidates as the voters who returned him to Parliament. When we find among the disfranchised such names as those of Mrs Somerville, Harriet Martineau, Miss Burdett Coutts, Florence Nightingale, Mary Carpenter, Louisa Twining, Miss Marsh, and many others scarcely inferior to these in intellectual and moral worth, we cannot but desire, for the elevation and dignity of the Parliamentary system, to add them to the number of electors.

It need scarcely be pointed out that the measure has nothing of a party character. We have precedents under two very different governments, those of Austria and Sweden, for something very similar to what is now proposed. With regard to voting in Austria, Major Noel, who has resided many years in Germany, writes as follows: 'In all the so-called "crown and hereditary lands" of the Austrian empire, the principle has been established by the Imperial Patent of 1864, of the representation of classes and interests in the respective Diets. One class represented is that of the large landed proprietors. In this class all females, whether of noble or citizen blood, if they possess the property qualification, have votes just the same as males. Women in their corporate character, as stifts-damen or nuns, have the franchise too, if their revenues are derived from land. As regards the representation of citizens proper (towns-people), I know that in some of the electoral districts, widows carrying on business, or spinsters possessing houses and paying the necessary taxes, vote likewise. But when I made more particular inquiries on this head last January, Count Thun wrote me that the law as regards the female franchise, with the exception of the class of large landed proprietors, was very vague and undecided. It was the intention of the Government, however, to introduce laws for the acceptance of the various Diets, whereby independent women should have votes like males in every one of the represented classes. Whether such laws have been introduced and carried, I know not. I must mention, however, that in the Hungarian Constitution of 1848, when so many democratic changes were introduced, there is an express clause *excluding* women of any class of society from the franchise.'

In Sweden the Reform bill passed in December, 1865 gave the election of members of the Upper Chamber to municipal and county bodies, called *Stads-full-mäktige*, and *Landstingsmän*. In the election of these bodies, women take part. In order to be an elector, a woman must be unmarried or a widow, and must have attained her majority (twenty-five years), and be possessed of more than 400 riksdalers riksmynt (about £22) per annum.[1]

In England, the extension proposed would interfere with no vested interests. It would involve no change in the principles on which our Government is based, but would rather make our Constitution more consistent with itself. Conservatives have a right to claim it as a Conservative measure. Liberals are bound to ask for it as a necessary part of radical reform. There is no reason for identifying it with any class or party in the State, and it is, in fact, impossible to predict what influence it might have on party politics. The question is simply of a special legal disability, which must, sooner or later, be removed.

It was said by Lord Derby, in his speech on entering upon the office of Prime Minister last Session, in reference to Reform – that 'there were theoretical anomalies in our present system which it was desirable, if possible, to correct; that there were classes of persons excluded from the franchise who had a fair claim and title, upon the ground of their fitness to exercise the privilege of electors; and that there was a very large class whom the particular qualifications of the Act of 1832 excluded.' I venture to submit, that the exclusion of female freeholders and householders from the franchise is an anomaly which it is very desirable, and not impossible, to correct; that there is no class of persons having a fairer claim and title upon the ground of their fitness to exercise the privileges of electors; and that whatever may be deemed expedient with regard to other classes, this class, at any rate, should not be excluded by the particular qualifications of the Reform Act of the future.

NOTE

1 Article 15 of the Italian Electoral law, provides, 'That the taxation paid by a widow, or by a wife separated from her husband, shall give a vote to whichever of her children or relations of the first or second degree of propinquity she may select. In the same way, a father, who pays direct imports in several electoral districts, shall be able to delegate his vote in the one which he does not inhabit himself, to either of his sons he may select. These delegations of power can be cancelled at will.'

Objections to the Enfranchisement of Women Considered

(1866)

The following Petition was presented to Parliament on June 7th, 1866:

> *The humble Petition of the undersigned, sheweth,*
> That it having been expressly laid down by high authorities that the possession of property in this country carries with it the right to vote in the election of representatives in Parliament, it is an evident anomaly that some holders of property are allowed to use this right, while others, forming no less a constituent part of the nation, and equally qualified by law to hold property, are not able to exercise this privilege.
>
> That the participation of women in the government is consistent with the principles of the British Constitution, inasmuch as women in these islands have always been held capable of sovereignty, and women are eligible for various public offices.
>
> Your petitioners therefore humbly pray your Honourable House to consider the expediency of providing for the representation of all householders, without distinction of sex, who possess such property or rental qualification as your Honourable House may determine.

This petition was signed by 1,499 women, including many whose names alone are sufficient to entitle them to a respectful hearing. It has given rise to discussion in many households, and articles have appeared in newspapers and magazines, some containing arguments for the prayer of the petition and some against it. As I think the onus of proof lies with those who say women ought not to vote, I will proceed to consider the arguments I have met with on that side of the question.

Among these, the first and commonest is – women do not want votes. Certainly that is a capital reason why women should not have votes thrust upon them, and no-one proposes compulsory registration. There are many men who do not care to use their votes, and there is no law compelling them either to register themselves or to vote. The statement, however, that women do not wish to vote, is a mere assertion, and may be met by a counter-assertion. Some women do want votes, which the petitions signed and now in course of signature, go very largely to prove. Some women manifestly do; others, let it be admitted, do not. It is impossible to say positively which side has the majority, unless we could poll all the women in question; or, in other words, without resorting to the very measure which is under discussion. Make registration possible, and we shall see how many care to avail themselves of the privilege.

But, it is said, women have other duties. The function of women is different to that of men, and their function is not politics. It is very true that women have other duties – many and various. But so have men. No citizen lives for his citizen duties only. He is a professional man, a tradesman, a family man, a club man, a thousand things as well as a voter. Of course these occupations sometimes interfere with a man's duties as a citizen, and when he cannot vote, he cannot. So with women; when they cannot vote, they cannot.

The proposition we are discussing, practically concerns only single women and widows who have 40s. freeholds, or other county qualifications, and for boroughs, all those who occupy, as owners or tenants, houses of the value of £10 a year. Among these there are surely a great number whose time is not fully occupied, not even so much as that of men. Their duties in sick rooms, and in caring for children, leave them a sufficient margin of leisure for reading newspapers, and studying the *pros* and *cons* of political and social questions. No-one can mean seriously to affirm that widows and unmarried women would find the mere act of voting once in several years arduous. One day, say once in three years, might surely be spared from domestic duties. If it is urged that it is not the time spent in voting that is in question, but the thought and the attention which are necessary for forming political opinions, I reply that women of the class we are speaking of, have as a rule, more time for thought than men, their duties being of a less engrossing character, and that they do, as a fact, bestow a considerable amount of thought and attention on the questions which occupy the Legislature. Social matters occupy every day a larger space in the deliberations of Parliament, and on many of these questions women are led to think and to judge in the fulfilment of those duties which, as a matter of course, devolve upon them in the ordinary business of English life. And however important the duties of home may be, we must bear in mind that a woman's duties do not end there. She is a daughter, a sister, the mistress of a household; she ought to be in the broadest sense of the word, a neighbour, both to her equals and to the poor. These are her obvious and undeniable duties, and within the limits of her admitted functions, I should think it desirable to add to them – duties to her parish and to the State. A woman who is valuable in all the relations of life, a woman of a large nature, will be more perfect in her domestic capacity, and not less.

If we contemplate women in the past, and in different countries, we find them acting in addition to their domestic part, all sorts of different *roles*. What was their *role* among the Jews and the Romans? What was it in the early Christian churches? What is it amongst the Quakers? What is it in the colliery districts – at the courts of Victoria, and the Tuileries? We can conjure up thousands of pictures of women, performing different functions under varying conditions. They have done, and do, all sorts of work in all sorts of ways. Is there anything in the past history of the world, which justifies the assertion that they must and will do certain things in the future, and will not and cannot do certain other things? I do not think there is.

But to return to my argument, and supposing that there were enough data in the past to enable us to predict that women will never take sufficient interest in politics to induce even widows and single women to wish to vote once in several years, should we be justified in realising our own prediction, and forbidding by law what we declare to be contrary to nature? If anyone believes, as the result of observation and experience, that it is not a womanly function to vote, I respect such belief, and answer – only the future can prove. But what I do not respect is the strange want of toleration which says 'you shall not do this or that'. We do not want to compel women to anything; we only wish to see them free to exercise or not, according as they themselves find suitable, political and other functions.

The argument that 'women are ignorant of politics', would have great force if it could be shown that the mass of the existing voters are thoroughly well informed on political subjects, or even much better informed than the persons to whom it is proposed to give votes. Granted that women are ignorant of politics, so are many male ten-pound householders. Their ideas are not always clear on political questions, and would probably be even more confused if they had not votes. No mass of human beings will or can undertake the task of forming opinions on matters over which they have no control, and on which they have no practical decision to make. It would by most persons be considered a waste of time. When women have votes, they will read with closer attention than heretofore the daily histories of our times, and will converse with each other and with their fathers and brothers about social and political questions. They will become interested in a wider circle of ideas, and where they now think and feel somewhat vaguely, they will form definite and decided opinions.

Among the women who are disqualified for voting by the legal disability of sex, there is a large number of the educated class. We shall know the exact number of women possessing the household and property qualifications, when the return ordered by Parliament has been made. In the meantime, the following calculation is suggestive. In the *London Court Guide*, which of course includes no houses below the value of £10 a year, the number of householders whose names begin with A is 1,149. Of these, 205, that is more than one-sixth, are women, all of whom are either unmarried or widows.

The fear entertained by some persons that family dissension would result from encouraging women to form political opinions, might be urged with equal force against their having any opinions on any subject at all. Differences on religious subjects are still more apt to rouse the passions and create disunion than political differences. As for opinions causing disunion, let it be remembered that what is a possible cause of disunion is also a possible cause of deeply founded union. The more rational women become, the more real union there will be in families, for nothing separates so much as unreasonableness and frivolity. It will be said, perhaps, that contrary opinions may be held by the different members of a family without bringing on quarrels, so long as they are kept to the region of theory, and no attempt is made to carry them out publicly in action. But religious differences must be shown publicly. A woman who takes upon her to change her religion – say to go over from Protestantism to Romanism – proclaims her difference from her family in a public and often a very distressing manner. But no-one has yet proposed to make it illegal for a woman to change her religion. After all – is it essential that brothers and sisters and cousins shall all vote on the same side? For let me mention once again, we are not discussing the expediency of giving votes to wives.

An assertion often made, that women would lose the good influence which they now exert indirectly on public affairs if they had votes, seems to require proof. First of all, it is necessary to prove that women have this indirect influence – then that it is good – then that the indirect good influence would be lost if they had direct influence – then that the indirect influence which they would lose is better than the direct influence they would gain. From my own observation I should say that the women who have gained by their wisdom and earnestness a good indirect influence, would not lose that influence if they had votes. And I see no necessary connection between goodness and indirectness. On the contrary, I believe that the great thing women want is to be more direct and straightforward, in thought, word and deed. I think the educational advantage of citizenship to women would be so great that I feel inclined to run the risk of sacrificing the subtle, indirect influence, to a wholesome feeling of responsibility, which would, I think, make women give their opinions less rashly and more conscientiously than at present on political subjects.

A gentleman who thinks much about details, affirms that 'polling-booths are not fit places for women'. If this is so, one can only say that the sooner they are made fit the better. That in a state which professes to be civilised, a solemn public duty can only be discharged in the midst of drunkenness and riot, is scandalous and not to be endured. It is no doubt true that in many places polling is now carried on in a turbulent and disorderly manner. Where that is unhappily the case, women clearly must stay away. Englishwomen can surely be trusted not to force their way to the polling-booth when it would be manifestly unfit. But it does not follow that because in some disreputable places, some women would be illegally, but with their own consent, prevented from recording their votes, therefore all women, in all places, should be without their own consent, by law disqualified. Those who, at the last election, visited the polling places in London and Westminster, and many other places, will bear me out in asserting that a lady would have had no more difficulty or annoyance to encounter in giving her vote, than she has in going to the Botanical Gardens or to Westminster Abbey.

There are certain other difficulties sometimes vaguely brought forward by the unreflecting, which I shall not attempt to discuss. Such, for example, is the argument that as voters ought to be independent, and as married women are liable to be influenced by their husbands, therefore unmarried women and widows ought not to vote. Or again, that many ladies canvass, and canvassing by ladies is a very objectionable practice, therefore canvassing ought to be the only direct method by which women can bring their influence to bear upon an election. Into such objections it is not necessary here to enter.

Nor is it needful to discuss the extreme logical consequences which may be obtained by pressing to an undue length the arguments used in favour of permitting women to exercise the suffrage. The question under consideration is not whether women ought logically to be Members of Parliament, but whether, under existing circumstances, it is for the good of the State that women, who perform most of the duties, and enjoy nearly all the rights of citizenship, should be by special enactment disabled from exercising the additional privilege of taking part in the election of the representatives of the people. It is a question of expediency, to be discussed calmly, without passion or prejudice. It has been my desire to meet, in a candid spirit, those, who without jealousy or distrust, are willing to extend to women any privilege which is likely to conduce to their advantage or the public good, but who reasonably shrink from precipitate action in a delicate and difficult matter. Such persons I would invite to a serious consideration of the question in all its bearings, confident that in proportion as the investigation is deliberate and searching, the conclusion will be in accordance with sound expediency.

Authorities and Precedents for giving the Suffrage to Qualified Women

(reprinted from *The Englishwoman's Review*, January 1867)

Twenty-five years ago a very clever and remarkable article appeared in the *Westminster Review*, advocating among other changes, the measure we propose. We will extract some sentences which will show the drift of the writer:

> On one material point, however, there is now a general agreement – that there is no good in female ignorance.

Again,

> We are indeed fully persuaded that the progress of civilisation will discover, nay, has discovered many faults and defects in the laws which concern women, and it would be hard indeed to adhere to the wisdom of our ancestors only with regard to them.
>
> Ever since the Reform Bill – that era of better hope – it has appeared to us a needless, if not prejudicial, inequality to exclude women altogether from representation. 'In the English Reform Act,' says Mr Baillie, who has devoted a chapter in his *Rationale of Representation*, to consider very seriously and philosophically the propriety of the limitation of the elective franchise by sex, and has given it strongly as his opinion, that there should be no such limitation. 'In the English Reform Act a very small concession, without disturbing the legal relations in which the sexes stand to each other, would have saved the appearance of injustice to females. No evil, in fact, could have arisen from placing men and women on such an equality in regard to the franchise, as the present system of law would admit. Wives, and sisters, and daughters, living under the same roof with husbands,

and fathers, and brothers, would have been excluded, not on the ground of sex, but on account of not being householders, sharing in this respect the condition of sons residing with their fathers, and of other mere lodgers. It would have been only widows or single women, keeping house or possessing the requisite amount of property, that could have been entitled to vote, and it is difficult to conceive the shadow of a reason why they should be debarred from the privilege, except the tumultuous proceedings which are the unruly progeny of unskilful arrangements.'

Compared with the general community, such persons (few in number to be sure) have yet a direct interest in the economy of public establishments, in the security of property, in the administration of justice, in a word, in all the objects of government. While they contribute to its support, and are not exempted by the weakness of their sex from paying taxes, it seems to us a plain case that they should have a voice in the management of the revenue, or at least be able, like other loyal subjects and citizens of the same grade in society, to 'lay this flattering unction' to their souls; and we agree with Mr Baillie that it might be made quite consistent with female delicacy to register and go to the poll, as consistent, at any rate, as to go to the cess office, or to receive the visits of the tax-gatherer or rate-collector.

Any objections that we have heard against the permitting females who possess the requisite qualifications to enjoy this first and lowest degree in political power, have appeared to us extremely slight, if not wholly groundless.

The possible sway of male relations has been made an objection. At most this could only neutralise the biassed votes of females, and, acting indifferently on all classes, could not be turned to the advantage of one party more than another.

This objection was urged by Fox, and used as an illustration of the disadvantages of universal suffrage on occasion of Mr Grey's motion for a reform in Parliament, May, 1826.

'In all the theories and projects of the most absurd speculation, it has never been suggested that it would be advisable to extend the elective suffrage to the female sex; and yet justly respecting, as we must do, the mental powers, the acquirements, the discrimination, and the talents of the women of England, in the present improved state of society – knowing the opportunities which they have for acquiring knowledge – that they have interests as dear and as important as our own – it must be the genuine feeling of every gentleman who hears me, that all the superior classes of the female sex of England must be more capable of exercising the elective franchise with deliberation and propriety, than the uninformed individuals of the lowest class of men to whom the advocates of universal suffrage would extend it. And yet why has it never been imagined that the right of election should be extended to women? Why! but because by the law of nations, and perhaps also by the law of nature, that sex is dependent on ours, and because, therefore, their voices would be governed by the relation in which they stand in society.'

This argument, good in the main, is not, however, strictly applicable to the class of women whose rights to representation we are disposed to advocate; for of such it cannot be said that they are directly influenced, any more than they are represented by men.

It must be observed that Fox did not admit the objection of incapacity, the only one we can think of besides a general alarm of danger to the state, and detriment to our hearths and altars, which we do not feel it necessary to combat.

We do not expect that the greatest legislators, or most profound politicians, will be found among female house-holders, after the elective franchise has been extended to them. The Reform Bill, however, does not proceed on the supposition that the knowledge or wisdom of a statesman is required in an elector, but on this, that within certain limits of intelligence, and opportunities of instruction, every one understands his own interests best, and has a right to let them be known by the fittest deputy he can find. Now wherever we see a woman able, by her own exertions, unassisted by the stronger arm, or head of man, to place herself in a situation which would entitle him to have a vote in the choice of a member of parliament, we think it clear that such a woman is not without the necessary qualifications. We have not this assurance so completely in a higher class of women employed in only the *dolce far niente*. Yet, granting between a lady and her coachman an original difference of capacity (in favour of the latter for the affairs of government), we think it is making too much account of it in its undeveloped state to give him the right, and withhold it from his mistress.

The argument of incapacity loses much of its force at present, when 'a woman sits at the helm of government in England'. This was well shown before the event had taken place, in a clever article in the *Monthly Repository*, p. 638.

'It is not strange that the egregious anomaly should have been felt of institutions which sometimes invest women, educated in very unfavourable circumstances, with the state and amplitude of supreme political authority, and which, nevertheless, uniformly deny to women, though trained in the most favourable circumstances, the exercise of the very lowest and simplest political function, that which is essential to political existence, the elective franchise. In the common opinion of common statesmen, the fitness of women to vote for an individual's elevation to the temporary dignity of a legislator in the House of Commons, is a mere joke; yet her naming scores of persons legislators for life, and all their heirs legislators too, through all generations, is an essential portion of that perfection of ancestral wisdom under which we live. She is vested with the entire power of the state, or not entrusted with its meanest fraction.'

The writer further very happily observes that – 'Sundry aggravations of the discrepancy are scattered about society, with that beautiful contempt of uniformity which the Reform Bill so happily copies from our older institutions, in order that the constitution may not go to total wreck and ruin. There are sundry little clubs and dignities about the country, in selecting for which a woman's judgment, if she possess property, may be legitimately exercised. She may have her portion of parochial representations in the vestry, she is perfectly competent to pronounce on the skill of a physician who may save or sacrifice life, on a large scale, in the county hospital. She helps to elect the sovereigns of India, who hold their sittings in Leadenhall street. All this is reasonable and constitutional, but vote for a member of Parliament – preposterous! What makes this matter still more odd is that a man does not vote because he is a man, still less because he is an honest man, or a wise man, but because he is a ten pounder or upwards. There, and there alone, is his qualification. But though the woman be a fifty pounder and upwards, and both honest and wise into the bargain, yet it availeth not. Truly it is very mysterious.'

We feel persuaded that if this use of their capacities were once permitted to women, it would do something to improve them, and would rather diminish than increase the number of those ignorant meddlers who now go by the name of female politicians. Although the injustice of not being allowed any voice in the legislature can only be substantially made out in the case of a few individuals of the sex, it is not, perhaps, too much to say that, in as far as their exclusion affects public opinion, the inequality is felt by all of them, implying and helping to produce an inferiority of rank in the social scale. And in this point of view the removal of the limitation by sex might prove a general benefit to society.

In July, 1851 another article appeared in the *Westminster*, from which we make the following extracts. This article was subsequently reprinted in Mr John Stuart Mill's *Dissertations & Discussions*, and though not written by him, yet has received his warmest commendation.

It was written on the occasion of a public meeting having been held at Massachusetts, US in order to obtain the right of suffrage for women, on the ground that every person 'whose property or labour is taxed for the support of the government is entitled to a direct share in such government'. The writer remarks upon this.

Not only to the democracy of America the claim of women to civil and political equality makes an irresistible appeal, but also to those radicals and chartists in the British islands, and democrats on the Continent, who claim what is called universal suffrage as an inherent right unjustly and oppress-ively withheld from them. For with what truth or rationality could the suffrage be termed universal, while half the human species remain excluded from it? To declare that a voice in the government is the right of all and demand it only for a part – that part, namely, to which the claimant himself belongs – is to renounce even the appearance of a principle.

The chartist who denies the suffrage to women, is a char-tist only because he is not a lord: he is one of those levellers who would level only down to themselves.

Even those who do not look upon a voice in the govern-ment as a matter of personal right, or profess principles which require that it should be extended to all, have usually traditional maxims of political justice, with which it is impossible to reconcile the exclusion of all women from the rights of citizenship. It is an axiom of English freedom that taxation and representation should be co-extensive.

Even under the laws that give the wife's property to the husband, there are many unmarried women who pay taxes. . . . Apart from maxims of detail which represent local and national rather than universal ideas, it is an acknowledged dictate of justice to make no degrading differences, without necessity. . . . A reason must be given why anything should be permitted to one person and interdicted to another.

Further on the writer remarks, with regard to the intellectual capacity of women for politics –

Women have shown fitness for the highest social functions, exactly in proportion as they have been admitted to them. By a curious anomaly, though ineligible to even the lowest offices of state, they are in some countries admitted to the highest of all, the regal; and if there is any one function for which they have shewn a decided vocation it is that of reigning. Not to go back to ancient history, we look in vain for abler or firmer rulers than Elizabeth, than Isabella of Castile, than Maria Theresa, than Catherine of Russia, than Blanche, mother of Louis IX of France, than Jeanne d'Albret, mother of Henri Quatre. There are few kings on record who contended with more difficult circumstances, or overcame them more triumphantly than these. . . . In the middle ages, when the difference between the upper and lower ranks was greater than even between women and men, and the women of the privileged class, however subject to tyranny from the men of the same class, were at a less distance below them than anyone else was, and often in their absence represented them in their functions and authority – numbers of heroic chatelaines, like Jeanne de Montfort, or the great Countess of Derby as late even as the time of Charles I, distinguished themselves not only in their political but their military capacity. In the centuries immediately before and after the reformation, ladies of royal houses, as diplomats, as governors of provinces, or as the confidential advisers of kings, equalled the first statesmen of their time; and the treaty of Cambray, which gave peace to Europe, was negotiated in conferences, where no other person was present, by the aunt of the emperor Charles V and the mother of Francis I.

Towards the end of the article some remarks are made which explain why, until lately, so few women have come forward to ask for the rights to citizenship.

We have left behind a host of vulgar objections, either as not worthy of an answer, or as answered by the general course of our remarks. A few words, however, must be said on one plea, which in England is made much use of for giving an unselfish air to the upholding of selfish privileges, and which, with unobserving, unreflecting people, passes for much more than it is worth. Women, it is said, do not desire – do not seek, what is called their emancipation. On the contrary, they generally disown such claims when made in their behalf, and fall with *acharnement* upon any one of themselves who identifies herself with their common cause.

Supposing the fact to be true in the fullest extent ever asserted, if it proves that European women ought to remain as they are, it proves exactly the same with respect to the Asiatic women; for they too, instead of murmuring at their seclusion, and at the restraint imposed upon them, pride themselves on it, and are astonished at the effrontery of women who receive visits from male acquaintances, and are seen in the streets unveiled. Habits of submission make men as well as women servile-minded. The vast population of Asia do not desire or value, probably would not accept, political liberty, nor the savages of the forest, civilisation; which does not prove that eithermof those things is undesirable for them, or that they will not, at some future time, enjoy it. Custom hardens human beings to any kind of degradation, by deadening the part of their nature which would resist it. And the case of women is, in this respect, even a peculiar one, for no other inferior caste that we have heard of have been taught to regard their degradation as their honour. The argument, however, implies a secret consciousness that the alleged preference of women for their dependent state is merely apparent, and arises from their being allowed no choice; for if the preference be natural, there can be no necessity for enforcing it by law. To make laws compelling people to follow their inclination, has not hitherto been thought necessary by any legislator.[1] The plea that women do not desire any change, is the same that has been urged, times out of mind, against the proposal of abolishing any social evil – 'there is no complaint'; which is generally not true, and when true, only so because there is not that hope of success, without which complaint seldom makes itself audible to unwilling ears.

The position of women is like that of the tenants or labourers who vote against their own political interests to please their landlords or employers; with the unique addition, that submission is inculcated on them from childhood, as the peculiar attraction and grace of their character. They are taught to think, that to repel actively even an admitted injustice done to themselves is somewhat unfeminine, and had better be left to some male friend or protector.

To be accused of rebelling against anything which admits

of being called an ordinance of society, they are taught to regard as an imputation of a serious offence, to say the least, against the proprieties of their sex. It requires unusual moral courage as well as disinterestedness in a woman, to express opinions favourable to women's enfranchisement, until at least, there is some prospect of obtaining it. . . . The professions of women in this matter remind us of the state offenders of old, who, on the point of execution, used to profess their love and devotion to the sovereign by whose unjust mandate they suffered.

Griselda herself might be matched from the speeches put by Shakespeare into the mouths of male victims of kingly caprice and tyranny; the Duke of Buckingham, for example, in Henry VIII, and even Wolsey.

From Mr Mill's work on *Representative Government*, the following extracts are of the highest interest, as bearing on this question:

We need not suppose that when power resides in an exclusive class, that class will knowingly and deliberately sacrifice the other classes to themselves: it suffices that, in the absence of its natural defenders, the interest of the excluded is always in danger of being overlooked; and, when looked at, is seen with very different eyes from those of the persons whom it directly concerns. *Page* 22.

Rulers and ruling classes are under a necessity of considering the interests and wishes of those who have the suffrage; but of those who are excluded, it is in their option whether they will do so or not, and however honestly disposed, they are in general too fully occupied with things which they *must* attend to, to have much room in their thoughts for anything which they can with impunity disregard. *Page* 67.

In the preceding argument for universal, but graduated, suffrage, I have taken no account of difference of sex. I consider it to be as entirely irrelevant to political rights, as difference in height, or in the colour of the hair. All human beings have the same interest in good government; the welfare of all is alike affected by it, and they have equal need of a voice in it to secure their share of its benefits. If there be any difference, women require it more than men, since, being physically weaker, they are more dependent on law and society for protection. . . . Women do not need political rights in order that they may govern, but in order that they may not be misgoverned. . . . Nobody pretends to think that women would make a bad use of the suffrage. The worst that is said is, that they would vote as mere dependents, at the bidding of their male relations. If it be so, so let it be. If they think for themselves, great good will be done, and if they do not, no harm. It is a benefit to human beings to take off their fetters, even if they do not desire to walk. It would already be a great improvement in the moral condition of women to be no longer declared by law incapable of an opinion, and not entitled to a preference, respecting the most important concerns of humanity.

There is something more than ordinarily irrational in the fact that when a woman can give all the guarantees required from a male elector, independent circumstances, the position of a householder and head of a family, payment of taxes, or whatever may be the conditions imposed, the very principle and system of a representation based on property is set aside, and an exceptionally personal disqualification is created for the mere purpose of excluding her. When it is added that in the country where this is done, a woman now reigns, and that the most glorious ruler whom that country ever had was a woman, the picture of unreason, and scarcely disguised injustice, is complete. Let us hope . . . that the opinion of Bentham, of Mr Samuel Bailey, of Mr Hare, and many others of the most profound political thinkers of this age and country (not to speak of others), will make its way to all minds not rendered obdurate by selfishness or inveterate prejudice; and that, before the lapse of another generation, the accident of sex, no more than the accident of skin, will be deemed a sufficient justification for depriving its possessor of the equal protection and just privileges of a citizen. *Page 74 to page 76.*

Some strong passages on this subject are to be found in *Social Statics*, by Mr Herbert Spenser.

Whoso urges the mental inferiority of women, in bar of their claim to equal rights with men, may be met in various ways. . . . But let it be granted that the intellect of woman is less profound than that of man – that she is more uniformly ruled by feeling, more impulsive and less reflective than man is – let all this be granted; and let us see what basis such an admission affords to the doctrine that the rights of women are not co-extensive with those of men.

1. If rights are to be meted out to the two sexes in the ratio of their respective amounts of intelligence, then must the same system be acted upon in the apportionment of rights between man and man. Whence must proceed all those multiplied perplexities already pointed out.

2. In like manner, it will follow, that as there are here and there women of unquestionably greater ability than the average of men, some women ought to have greater rights than some men.[2]

3. Wherefore, instead of a fixed allotment of rights to all males and to all females, the hypothesis itself involves an infinite gradation of rights, irrespective of sex entirely, and sends us in search of those unattainable desiderata – a standard by which to measure capacity, and another by which to measure rights.

In another place Mr Spencer observes:

The extension of the law of equal freedom to both sexes will, doubtless, be objected to, on the ground that the political privileges exercised by men must thereby be ceded to women also.

Of course they must, and why not?

Is it that women are ignorant of state affairs? Why, then, their opinions would be those of their husbands and brothers; and the practical effect would be merely that of giving each male elector two votes instead of one.

Is it that they might by-and-by become better informed, and might then begin to act independently? Why in such a case they would be pretty much as competent to use their power with intelligence as the members of our present constituencies.

We are told, however, that 'woman's mission' is a domestic one – that her character and position do not admit of her taking a part in the decision of public questions, that politics are beyond her sphere. But here raises the question, who shall say what her sphere is? Amongst the Pawnees and Sioux it is that of a beast of burden; she has to carry the baggage, to drag home fuel, and to do everything that is menial and laborious. In slave countries it is within woman's sphere to work side by side with men, under the lash of the taskmaster.

Clerkships, cashierships, and other responsible business situations are comprised in her sphere in modern France.

Whilst, on the other hand, the sphere of a Turkish or Egyptian lady extends scarcely beyond the walls of the harem. Who now will tell us what woman's sphere is? As the usages of mankind vary so much, let us hear how it is to be shown that the sphere *we* assign her is the true one – that the limits *we* have set to female activity are just the proper limits. Let us hear why on this point of our social polity we are exactly right, whilst we are wrong on so many others.

It is indeed said that the exercise of political power by women is repugnant to our sense of propriety – conflicts with our ideas of the feminine character – is altogether condemned by our feelings. Granted; but what then? The same plea has been urged in defence of a thousand absurdities, and if valid in one case is equally so in all others. Should a traveller in the East inquire of a Turk why women in his country conceal their faces, he would be told, that for them to go unveiled was indecent, would offend the *feelings* of the spectators. In Russia, female voices are never heard in church, women not being thought worthy 'to sing the praises of God in the presence of men'; and the disregard of this regulation would be censured as an outrage upon public *feeling*.

There was a time in France when men were so enamoured of ignorance that a lady who pronounced any but the commonest words, correctly, was blushed for by her companions; a tolerable proof that people's *feelings*, then blamed in a woman, that literateness which it is now thought a disgrace for her to be without.

In China, cramped feet are essential to female refinement; and so strong is the *feeling* in this matter, that a Chinese will not believe that an Englishwoman, who walks naturally, can be one of a superior class. It was once held infeminine for a lady to write a book, and no doubt those who thought so would have quoted *feelings* in support of their opinions.

Yet with facts like these on every side, people assume that the enfranchisement of women cannot be right, because it is repugnant to their feelings!

We have some feelings that are necessary and eternal; we have others that being the result of custom, are changeable and evanescent; and there is no way of distinguishing those feelings which are natural from those which are conventional, except by an appeal to first principles.

In Mr Thomas Hare's work *On Representation*, we find the following passage:

In all cases where a woman is *sui juris*, occupying a house or tenement, or possessed of a freehold, or is otherwise in a position which, in the case of a male would amount to a qualification, there is no sound reason for excluding her from the parliamentary franchise. The exclusion is probably a remnant of the feudal law, and is not in harmony with the other civil institutions of the country. There would be great propriety in celebrating a reign which has been productive of so much moral benefit, by the abolition of an anomaly which is so entirely without any justifiable foundation.

In *Thoughts upon Subjects connected with Parliamentary Reform*, by the late Serjeant Manning, we find this passage:

The exclusion of women, especially where a right of voting is annexed to the possession of property, seems to be a part of the *loi du plus fort*, a remnant of savage life, which the improvements of modern civilisation have not yet dealt with.

Political Rights of Women in Austria

By an English Gentleman, long resident in Austria

In the Crown lands of Austria, with the exception of Hungary (in which country, although qualified young men of twenty have the franchise, still women of all classes are expressly excluded from it), the following are the present laws as to the political rights of women:

1. In village communes (orts gemeinden) the right of voting must be exercised in person. But women are allowed to give their vote by proxy. Women, however, are not eligible for parish offices. Every woman has a 'virile' vote,[3] if she pays the sixth part of the direct taxes required from a commune. For instance, every commune has to pay 6,000 florins (circa £600), and every person belonging to it, without respect to sex, who pays 1,000 florins is a member of the commune[4] without election. In cases where women possess this 'virile' vote, they are likewise bound to exercise it by proxy.

2. In the circuit communes (bezirks-gemeinden), a more or less large union of villages, the same laws apply. Likewise in the representation of the circuits (bezirke), a woman, for instance, as owner of a so-called large landed estate (which pays yearly in direct taxes 100 florins), or of any mining, manufacturing, or commercial

business paying a like sum in direct taxes, possesses a 'virile' vote, which she, however, does not exercise in person.

3. In the country communes (land-gemeinden), are to be distinguished the representatives, *a* of the large landed proprietors, *b* of the towns, and *c* of the country communes.

As regards *a*, the census of direct taxes is 250 florins. Women are not excluded. The voting takes place in person, yet any owner of a large landed property, whether man or woman, is allowed to choose a proxy to give his vote for representation in the Diet. No woman of this class has yet appeared personally at the hustings.

As regards *b*, the election of deputies from the towns to the Diet; this takes place at a general assembly of all the members of the commune who pay at least 10 florins yearly direct taxes. Women are not excluded, and in many of the towns they have appeared in person, as the law does not allow of proxies.

As regards *c*, however, women are excluded from voting for members of the Diets, since these country communes have not the right of giving direct votes for such members, but must choose electors, literally electing men (wählmänner), but in the choice of these electing men, women have votes, though they do not give them in person; they exercise them by proxy.

There is great discontent in Bohemia and other Crown lands, in consequence of the country communes only possessing the *indirect* franchise, whilst the towns have it direct. The electoral laws are about to be revised, and, doubtless, qualified country women will then be able to exercise direct votes for representatives in the Diets as they do in the towns.[5]

Political Rights of Women in Sweden

From the Letter of a Swedish Lady

Women in Sweden have no direct vote in the election of members of the Diet; nevertheless, they have an indirect vote, yet only with respect to the Upper Chamber. The new form of Diet, which is only just now come into operation, is founded on the Communal Constitution of 1862, gives women precisely the same right of voting as men in the election of the communal landsting (provincial bodies) and the municipal bodies. Now it is precisely these two corporations, which are a kind of popularly chosen electors, who in their turn elect the members of the Upper Chamber.

Women may thus indirectly take part in the election of members of the Upper Chamber. On the other hand, all participation in voting for the Lower Chamber is denied them by the 14th section of the Statutes of the Diet.

Women have thus a direct right of voting only as regards the nomination of members of the communal administration, and this they seldom or never exercise personally at the ballot box. It is not allowed to send in voting papers, but they have the right to send their vote by a deputy, and this in most cases is the rule.

They have had, in the present form, the right of voting for the nomination of the communal administration since the year 1862, which right, as I have already said, extends, by the new constitution of the Diet, to an indirect share in the election of the Upper Chamber. Nevertheless, I believe that women in Sweden (at least those possessed of real property) had this right of voting at communal nominations before 1862, but of this I cannot give any distinct information.

To the question whether women exercise their right of voting, I wish I could answer decidedly, yes. But that, alas! is not the case. The thing is so new, and our women so unacquainted with citizen duties, that the greater number of them have not as yet awoke to the perception, either of the advantages or the responsibilities connected with the right of voting which has been accorded to them.

Yet it may be taken as a fact, that the greater number of ladies who pay taxes for real property, whether in town or country, make use of their electoral right. But this is not the case with married ladies whose husbands are alive; it is only so with the widows and unmarried. They, again, who pay taxes, either on income from capital or from work, and who, like the former, are possessed of the electoral right, have hitherto seldom or never availed themselves of it, partly in consequence of ignorance and indifference, partly also from the idea that one vote more or less makes no difference in the great whole. There is also some little excuse for this, owing to the defective communal laws, which, from an irrational scale of suffrage, favour the large landed proprietors and capitalists (amongst whom ladies are seldom found) at the expense of the lesser, and thereby renders them indifferent to the exercise of their franchise, which operates, in fact, also men placed in similar circumstances.

In order to give you some idea of the working of the system. I will mention that my mother, when she votes, as possessor of some property in the capital, for the municipal election, employs her son or some other male relative to vote in her behalf, after he has named to her, and she has approved of the person, to whom he wishes to give *his* vote. Every voter has, therefore, the right of voting by proxy.[6]

NOTES

1 If women do not wish for the suffrage it is unnecessary to maintain laws to prevent them from voting, as they would not exercise the right if they possessed it. Those who made the law to prevent women from voting, must have thought women would vote if not prevented. People do not take the trouble of blocking up a footpath, when they are certain no one wishes to go along it. A path is blocked up *because* passengers would go along it if left open.
2 If intelligence confers rights, then Mrs Somerville, Miss Martineau, Miss Herschel, and some others, ought to have more rights than average men of education; and average women of education more rights than uneducated men.
3 I.e. independent, for herself only, not as representing others.
4 Equivalent to our vestries, but more free from jobbing.
5 It appears to us that women in Austria have the same electoral rights as men, except that in some cases they are bound to vote by proxy instead of in person.
6 It is satisfactory to observe that the class of women to whom it is desired that the suffrage should be extended in England, viz., householders and freeholders, are the class who in Sweden generally make use of their electoral right.

Married ladies and the poorer classes of female voters do not appear to value the privilege, or at least make but little use of it.

A Conversation on the Enfranchisement of Female Freeholders and Householders

(reprinted from *The Englishwoman's Review*, April 1873)

Mr A (reading out loud):
> *The Humble Petition of the undersigned*

sheweth – That it having been expressly laid down by high authorities that the possession of property in this country carries with it the right to vote in the Election of Representatives in Parliament, it is an evident anomaly that some holders of property are allowed to use this right, while others, forming no less a constituent part of the nation and equally qualified by law to hold property, are not able to exercise this privilege.

That the participation of women in the Government is consistent with the principles of the British Constitution, inasmuch as women in these islands have always been held capable of sovereignty, and women are eligible for various public offices.

Your Petitioners therefore humbly pray your Honourable House to consider the expediency of providing for the representation of all householders without distinction of sex, who possess such property or rental qualification as your Honourable House may determine.

So you, Lady B. have signed this Petition? I am surprised, and really shocked!

Lady B. – You will not be surprised when you see the number of women who have signed; there are many of them your very particular friends, and you will be accustomed in a year to see ladies from all parts of England sending other petitions with the same prayer to the House of Commons – your surprise can't last long, but your reprobation may – so pray tell me why you are shocked.

Mr A. – It is because the moral elevation which I desire for your sex will be retarded rather than promoted by the possession of this right; on their intellectual development I do not see that it can have any special effect and on their social influence and position, as far as men are concerned, I think it will most likely act detrimentally.

Lady A. – A capital objection comprising three heads. First you would not have women voting because it might prevent or retard their moral elevation; why, it is as clear to me as daylight, that whatever will make women (one half of the community) consider the great social questions of the day which are moral questions as well as so-called political, must do good, and you cannot make women or men interested as a mass in questions which are decided entirely without their participation. I think men as a whole are the better for being citizens. Their intellectual development again, appears to me as certain a consequence as their moral elevation. You think voting detrimental to their influence and social position! You must remember that the prayer of the petitioners is that heads of families, spinsters, and widows, should have the franchise; having the property or rental qualification it seems to me this objection can only be answered by experience. Now, I know that many unmarried ladies of my acquaintance who are known as authoresses and in other ways distinguished, would utterly deny having any particular influence which would be lost if they voted; some have influence by writing, some by their friendship with the wives of electors and members of Parliament, and some by their acquaintance with men, but not one would admit they would lose influence if they voted. Do you know I think this is quite a man's view, but grant it for a moment, do you really consider men have a right to prevent women from abandoning this supposed subtle social influence, if women were willing, in exchange for the more solid advantage of a vote? It is not a question of forcing them to vote. But perhaps I misunderstood you, and you would not include politics in the proper sphere of women's influence at all.

Mr A. – Indeed, I do sincerely wish that women would take an interest in, and feel their responsibilities in respect to, public matters, but women are not more incorruptible than men, and the same circumstances which produce a lowering effect on the moral tone of the male sex, will produce it on that of the female sex, if it be equally exposed to them. Then why should you covet for women that direct participation in political life which we see has but too frequently a deteriorating influence on men?

Lady B. – I cannot believe but that the rights and duties of citizenship are elevating to men; probably you are thinking of the evil effects of 'treating', the meetings at public houses, and the drunkenness too often seen at elections; now it is curious, I have a letter from our cleverest opponent, Mr F. H., who says that 'an illiterate working man will be a very good voter because his habits of public meeting and discussing at Taverns, in work rooms, and in Trade societies, etc., give him practical instincts worth any reading'. You see, he thinks some of this rough sort of life which you think corrupting, essential to a good and useful voter; now, I think some of these frequenters of public places an essential ingredient in an election, but I am as certain that the quiet spinster sitting at home teaching her nephews and her nieces, or the hard-working widow woman who is carrying on her late husband's trade, the lodging-house keeper, or the rich Miss Bountiful of Philanthropic Lodge, would be also good ingredients in the elections of the men who are to govern the country. And again, to go back to your plea of loss of influence, I cannot see how any, who have social influence now, will lose it.

Mr A. – Oh Lady B., can you not see that their disinterestedness is the root of the influence! Standing aloof from political life, and placed beyond the reach of its temptations, women might bring to bear on politics the irresistible influence of pure and lofty minds obtaining their inspirations from sources far above personal ambition, party interests, or low considerations of expediency.

Lady B. – Really if it be the happy power of women to draw inspiration from such very pure springs, I do not see that being registered and voting in elections would deprive them of this power. I think they would remain as disinterested as they now are.

Mr A. – Why, if they descend into the arena and take part in the general scuffle . . .

Lady B. – Now, in plain language, going to facts, what is descending into the arena? Women would not go to the public house any more than at present and they certainly will not join in any street fights; just think for a moment what the women are who would have the franchise. They would be independent women, and having the right to give their voices in elections could not change their natures and make them into drunken men.

Mr A. – Yes, I think it would change their natures. I think it desirable that they should be uncontaminated by the practical, and that as long as the ideal transcends the real so long should they be kept apart.

Lady B. – Oh let us mix as much as we can the ideal and the real; it seems to me to be very desirable that women and men should mix their interests more and more. I do not like your way of keeping women apart. I do not quite understand the application of the ideal and real to this argument. You mean you fear this little change, for it is only a little change for English Women; they do now a great deal in public life. It will not really alter their position; to think so is a profound mistake: women will always be women and it is just that which makes one want their influence in the state for the sake of the country. I am sure it is a good education for women to have interests outside their homes. This, in point of fact, is the view which interests me most. I think the human being is ennobled by wide sympathies, and men and women who do not care how their country is governed, how the poor are cared for, how the criminals are treated, how the health of the nation is looked after, and all these great questions which fill our papers, are deficient in what makes them human. We have both the same end in view – the elevating men and women, but we disagree as to the means. You would not of course abolish, if you could, any of the liberties of English women. You would let them vote in Parish elections, for guardians of the poor and in election of the School board. You would let them vote as Governors of Hospitals, and as shareholders in all public Companies, and you adore your Queen, but you would draw a line just where it now is – would you not?

Mr A. – No, I would not draw the line where it is, I would go on farther and give women, married or single, more weight than they have in all Parish matters.

Lady B. – You would give! There it is; you would give just what you think would suit us, but you won't admit that women have any voice in choosing their own duties! It is strange to me you cannot let the principle of supremacy go at once. You need not fear that we should compromise our dignity or our delicacy. I really think you are still under the shade of barbaric times. Let me read you six lines from Sergeant Manning's 'Thoughts upon Subjects connected with Parliamentary Reform.' 'The exclusion of women, especially where a right of voting is annexed to the possession of property, seems to be a part of the *loi du plus fort*, a remnant of savage life which the improvements of modern civilisation have not yet dealt with.'

Mr A. – The whole question is begged there, I do not think it will be an improvement. I think women's activities should be exercised on their homes, the nursery, the schoolroom, the care of the sick, and on their parishes, and their practical power should radiate from these sources, without interfering with the political activities of men. But I concede so much that if I found all the educated women of my acquaintance wishing to have this particular privilege, I would do all in my power to help them to it. But I do not expect that. Perhaps the basis of my feeling of repugnance to the idea comes from the dread of wives having votes.

Lady B. – But remember, we only ask for female freeholders and householders, and we do not ask for a thing which has not some precedent. In England and France the heads of certain religious orders used to have votes, and in Austria, which is much more to the purpose, by the Imperial Patent of 1861 for the representations of classes and interests in the respective districts, one class represented is that of large landed proprietors, and in this class all females, whether of noble or citizen blood, if they possess the property qualification, have votes just the same as males. Women in their corporate character, as 'Stiftsdamen' or nuns, have the franchise too, if their revenues are derived from land. You see the change is hardly to be called a radical or liberal measure; in fact, in the Hungarian Constitution of 1848, when so many democratic changes were introduced, there is an express clause excluding women of any class of society from the franchise.

Mr A. – And I think in England you have not the reformers as a rule on your side. As you say, it is a matter of sentiment, and you find men for and against it in all political parties. I *feel* that women should be wives and mothers, and I really hardly like to give them any duties incompatible with these, or which would have to be abandoned if they married. I think of the absurdity of young female voters having to be struck off from the register of voters if engaged to be married. No! As there is one part of life during which a woman cannot vote, and that part the happiest and most complete, I do not think you should risk a struggle for the right which is only temporary.

Lady B. – In the first place, when you are accustomed to it you will not think it an absurdity, and just as men abandon their voting power if they go into the army or navy, so might women, when they marry, give up their votes. Now you are going into details, so will I, and let us consider the number of rich young single women above twenty-one. Are they not as a rule idle? I am quite certain that many fathers would be glad to give their daughters votes for educational reasons, and the independence of having a little property and its privileges would have a most beneficial influence on young women. There is a continually recurring injustice in the act of widows and single women not having votes; landlords dislike to let land unless a vote goes with it, and I have heard lately of seven ejections on one estate of widows, who if they could have voted would have been allowed to continue in their husbands' farms.

Mr A. – All these cases I grant, are hard, and it is hard to be a widow or a spinster! We cannot help natural misfortune by legislature.

Lady B. – And so you will not try to mitigate its hardness?

Mr A. – It seems to be the height of pedantry to legislate for very small classes.

Lady B. – The class comprises 170,000, but even were it smaller, it seems to me the height of civilisation to let small classes be heard. The very fact that women do not take the beer-shop view of questions is a very strong argument for their views being heard and attended to. Think of the mass of jointured widows and rich single women living at Bath; they could be bribed or intimidated! Why! I hear there are 700 female householders in Cheltenham. I should say all reason was on the side of giving them votes rather than their tradespeople; if you had to choose between the two classes, the ladies would be the most disinterested. And what influence have those 700 women which they would lose? To me it is inappreciable, certainly not to be balanced by the influence their 700 votes would have.

Mr A. – Yes, I give that up, it is evident. But I do not like women going to polling booths!

Lady B. – If it is disagreeable I should not like it, but it can now be made orderly, and it is, I am told, usually easier to vote than to go to the opera. I think you are driven hard for arguments when you descend to these details. The question is too serious to be despatched or evaded by trivialities; if there is a class of independent, duly qualified people who are disfranchised, you must very seriously consider why, and the more so, as these qualified persons are many of them highly educated and far above the great mass of existing electors in disinterestedness and in opportunities of unbiassed decision. It is a grave matter, and all I ask of you is that you will seriously consider the question.

Bessie Rayner Parkes

(1829–1925)

Little is known about the childhood and education of Bessie Rayner
Parkes except that she was the daughter of Joseph Parkes, a solicitor
with radical sympathies who was a friend of John Stuart Mill, and
close friend of Barbara Leigh Smith. She became the editor of *The
English Woman's Journal* in 1858 and for the next nine years
remained personally involved with all the activities and organisations which grew out of Langham Place, publishing her own
Essays on Women's Work (Alexander Strachan, London) in 1866.
Her growing interest in the work of the Irish Sisters of Mercy and
Sisters of Charity in the early 1860s eventually led her to convert
to Roman Catholicism. After the death of Adelaide Anne Procter
in 1864, who had been her close friend for many years, she became
quite ill. Convalescing in France with Barbara Leigh Smith
Bodichon in 1867, Bessie met Louis Belloc. He was an invalid and
her friends and family warned her against the relationship but, in
the September of that year, she and Louis Belloc were married.
When her husband died five years later, Bessie Rayner Parkes
returned to England with her two children and lived in Sussex.
Although she had no further active involvement with the women's
movement, her friendship with Barbara Bodichon survived. Apart
from her earlier feminist writing, Bessie Rayner Parkes published
two volumes of poems and several collections of essays and
memoirs. Significantly her reminiscences of Adelaide Procter,
published in a collection of essays entitled *In a Walled Garden* (Ward
and Bowney, London) in 1895, neglect to mention the latter's
contribution to the Langham Place activities.

The Market for Educated Female Labour*

(a paper read at the National Association for the Promotion of Social Science, October 1859 and reprinted in *The English Woman's Journal*, November 1859)

I have been asked to prepare a paper on the condition of women in England; and believing that their claims are so far advanced as to admit of being beneficially advocated in detail, I have resolved to confine my attention to the nature and extent of the Market for *Educated* Female Labour.

This is but a very small section of the whole; but since within its limits are comprised the highest intelligence and the purest morality, it must be regarded as of the utmost importance.

The proportion of the entire upper and middle classes to the lower is in itself but small; most people would be surprised to realise *how* small, for, taken together, the two first do not number half the latter, nor consequently a third of the whole population. It has been roughly calculated that the middle ranks are about three times as numerous as the aristocratic, and that the working classes are about three times as numerous as the middle ranks; or in other words, of thirteen units, *one* would represent the aristocracy, *three* the middle ranks, and the remaining *nine* stand for the 'masses'. So that four parts out of thirteen are all with which I now mean to deal; and of this proportion only the female members; and of these again only that section which has to gain its daily bread.

How large is that section? Let us inquire. Everybody here present will at once admit that the theory of civilised life in this and all other countries, not excluding the democratic States of America, is that the women of the upper and middle classes are supported by their male relatives: daughters by their fathers, wives by their husbands. If a lady has to work for her livelihood, it is

*I beg to acknowledge that in the preparation of this paper, I was greatly assisted by my friend Barbara Leigh Smith (Mrs Bodichon). B. R. P.

universally considered to be a misfortune, an exception to the ordinary rule. All good fathers wish to provide for their daughters; all good husbands think it their bounden duty to keep their wives. All our laws are framed strictly in accordance with this hypothesis; and all our social customs adhere to it more strictly still. We make no room in our social framework for any other idea, and in no moral or practical sphere do the exceptions more lamentably and thoroughly prove the rule. Women of the lower class may work, *must* work, in the house, if not out of it – too often out of it! But among us, it is judged best to carefully train the woman as the moraliser, the refiner, the spiritual element.

I will not here enter into any discussion of this theory. Nay, for my own part, I have little or nothing to urge against it, if it were practicable in action. It may be that the benefit conferred on society by a class of tender, refined, thoughtful women, secluded from its rougher paths and grosser problems, is inestimable. We can hardly imagine what a civilised country would be like without such a class of women, for they have existed in all ages, enriched by the higher forms of literature and art. I feel keenly that the benefit they confer does now largely exist in certain directions, and might under certain moral conditions be realised for the whole upper and middle classes, if the theory of a material provision for all educated women were humanly possible, *which it is not.*

It is not possible! Let us not forget this. Educated women must work. It is not my fault that I am obliged to assert this; nor your fault if you are compelled to believe it. Our theory and our practice are wide apart in this matter, and the cause of the discrepancy is as deep as the cause of strikes or commercial crises; nay, deeper still, as the cause of misfortune, improvidence, or crime in human nature.

The aristocracy are rich enough to make some invariable, though scanty, provision for their female members, but the middle class is at the mercy of a thousand accidents of commercial or professional life, and thousands and thousands of destitute, educated women have to earn their daily bread. I should only be tiring you if I entered into further details; besides, these very details are supplied by the actual cases in a printed report from which I intend to give you a few extracts. Probably every person present has a female relative or intimate friend whom trade-failures, the exigencies of a numerous household, or the early death of husband or father has compelled to this course; it is in the experience of every family.

Of course the first resource of these ladies is teaching; nothing else is obviously present to them. Now listen to the result. The reports of the Governesses' Benevolent Institution, one of the largest charities and most efficient organisations for the assistance of industry which exists in the kingdom, reckon fifteen thousand governesses as an item in our population! Fifteen thousand educated women, chiefly single or widowed, unsupported by their male relations, and in innumerable cases obliged to support *them*.

But it may be said, 'Well, fifteen thousand is a large number; but if an equivalent number of families require teachers, and can afford to pay good salaries, it is mere sentimentality to regret that these ladies are forced to work.'

We can soon answer this supposition; and here let me express hearty gratitude to the institution to which I have referred, for the admirable and ample information which its printed reports bestow. I am acquainted with no such mass of statistics, no such *resumé* of facts regarding any class of our country-women, as are therein given to the world. If any one wants to learn the truth about the condition of the educated working woman in England, let him consult the reports of the Governesses' Benevolent Institution. It is divided into several branches of usefulness. There is a Home for the disengaged at 66, Harley-street, London, and an elaborate system of Registration, by which last year fifteen hundred names were entered, and eleven hundred obtained situations. It may be recorded as a passing fact that the hall-book of the house, where Home and Register are jointly located, should record the visitors of one year as twenty-four thousand. There is a Provident Fund for the securing of annuities, of which we are told that the first payment, by a lady contracting for one of these annuities, was paid on the 20th of June, 1843, and that the amount now invested is £177,292 10s. 3d. There is also a fund out of which Elective Annuities are created, and a system of temporary assistance managed by a committee of ladies. The applications for this, in 1858, were eight hundred and thirty-eight, and the grants four hundred and ninety-three, to the extent of £1,346 8s. 8d. The total number of applications have been ten thousand three hundred and thirty-four; of grants, five thousand five hundred and seventy-one; and the total amount of gifts, £14,284 12s. 4d. Lastly, there is an Asylum for Aged Governesses at Kentish Town; it contains twenty-two apartments duly filled.

My hearers will consider these statistics as a somewhat astounding revelation of the need of assistance in which women stand. What should we think of educated men, who, after long lives of honest and industrious labour, sank into such depths of poverty that they required wholesale help by hundreds and thousands; for the total number of cases in nine years, to which the society has been useful, is twenty-six thousand five hundred and seventy-one.

Let us now see how and why these unhappy women endure such misery. We have roughly the means of ascertaining; for every May and every November an election occurs to the annuities, and I find one hundred and forty-five cases of candidates printed in the list for last May, of whom some three or four only could receive an annuity. I take the first ten cases, haphazard, of those who have in different years been elected; they read in this wise:

No. 1.   Miss S. M. A., aged fifty-nine. 1856. Father a colonel, in active service until Waterloo. Governess upon his death, and that of an only brother. Assisted relations to the utmost of her power. Frequent illnesses have consumed her savings; is now in very delicate health. Earned only £10 in the past year.

No. 2.   Miss S. A., aged sixty-eight. 1857. Father a large calico printer; her mother having impoverished herself to assist her son's speculations, she gave up the whole of her property to her and became a governess; and to the same purpose devoted all her earnings. Is now entirely dependent upon the kindness of friends.

No. 3.   Mrs A. A., aged sixty-six. 1858. Compelled to leave home by the embarrassment of her father, whom she assisted with nearly the whole of her salary. The foreclosure of a mortgage upon her property has rendered her entirely dependent upon two daughters who keep a small school. Is very deaf, has lost one eye, and suffers from great pain and weakness, arising from a threatening of an internal complaint.

No. 4.   Miss F. A., aged sixty-one. 1848. Engaged in tuition since nineteen, her father, a merchant, having left seven children unprovided for. Constantly assisted various members of her family, and still has a niece dependent upon her. Sight and hearing much impaired; only dependence a small day-school.

No. 5.   Miss M. A., aged seventy-four. 1848. Left home upon her father's failure. Fourteen years in one family. Devoted most of her salary to the support of an aged parent and an afflicted brother and sister. Supported afterwards an elder sister. Only income an annuity of £10 from a charitable institution.

No. 6.   Miss M. J. A., aged fifty-nine. 1852. One of sixteen children; left home in consequence at fifteen years of age. With two sisters, supported her father for many years, also an orphan niece. Impaired sight and infirm health have obliged her to subsist entirely upon a small legacy, now utterly exhausted. Mental derangement daily increases under the pressure of perfect destitution, having no means from any quarter.

No. 7. Miss E. A., aged fifty-eight. 1851. Her father died when she was very young; and her mother's second husband ruined the family. Greatly assisted her mother and sister. Being long crippled from a fall, and having some years since lost the use of her right arm and foot, is not only incapable of self-support, but entirely helpless.

No. 8. Mrs O. S. G. B., aged fifty-seven. 1858. Father a captain in the army. Her husband, a surgeon, died suddenly, having made no provision for her and two children. Assisted her mother for some years. She, suffering from chronic bronchitis and sciatica, and a daughter, also in very ill health, are without certain income, being dependent upon the letting of her apartments.

No. 9. Miss E. B., aged sixty-five. 1849. Left home, her father having become involved; supported him till 1846, and her aged and sick mother till 1834, and for the last nine years assisted in bringing up a niece. Sight and hearing both failing, and suffers from spasmodic affection of the heart. No income.

No. 10. Miss H. B., aged sixty-one. 1851. One of six daughters; left home, her parents' means being injured by mining speculations. Assisted them during twenty years, and educated some of her nieces when settled in a school, where her parents and a helpless invalid sister resided upon very slender means. In very delicate health, and has no income.

Here you see are ten cases of most deplorable destitution, arising from the most ordinary causes. Would to God there were any thing remarkable in them; but fathers fail and brothers speculate every day, and the orphan nephews and nieces are left to the unmarried as a legacy from the beloved dead; and in families of sixteen children all must work: there is nothing unusual here; and it is also amply proved that the savings of the average governess cannot support her in her old age. The very highest class of governess is highly paid, just because there are so few; if the number increased they would not command great salaries, and the pittance accorded to the average is an irrefragable fact.

Surely then in a country where the chances of provision for

women are so frightfully uncertain, parents in the middle classes ought –

Firstly, to train their daughters to some useful art, however humble:

Secondly, to repress all desire of forcing them into tuition, because it is more 'genteel':

Thirdly, to insure their lives when they cannot lay by money for their female children.

Let us consider more at length these three remedies. No class of men can compete with the governess in wretchedness; their misery being super-eminent is entitled to the profound consideration of all legislators, philanthropists, educators, and all who are in any way trying to benefit the condition of the people. It is the plague-spot in the condition of our prosperous and progressive country, and to find out the causes and suggest the remedies for different classes of female distress is one of the especial duties of the *ladies* assembled at this meeting.

As in natural sciences the discovery of great laws is constantly inaugurated by minute observation of particular facts, let us leave the census alone, and try to examine one family, the type of many thousands. The father, by his labour of head or hand gains sufficient to support his wife, and say three children, one of whom is a girl. The father will certainly send his two boys to school, whether it be to a twopenny, or to an expensive boarding-school: the girl will probably be sent also for a few years to one much inferior; but if there is work to be done at home she will be kept at home to do it. In the middle-class family we have taken as a type, she is much employed in making shirts for her two schoolboy brothers. We have heard of a case in which some young ladies, who were offered gratuitous instruction in one of the best ladies' colleges, were kept at home for that purpose. Her learning is not insisted on, while her brothers are urged forward, and every facility given for them to pursue their studies at home. When the girl is fourteen or fifteen, we shall certainly find her taken away from school, if not earlier; while the boys proceed to some higher place of instruction, or begin to learn a profession. But now that the daughter is permanently under his roof, perhaps the father, who depends entirely on his yearly income, may begin to have some little anxiety as to her future. Perhaps he may ardently wish for an instant that he could leave her an assured livelihood, or a means of gaining one. He balances in his mind the expense of training her as a first-rate governess; but the expense would be very great, and he has not courage or energy to look for any exceptional work for his young daughter; he would not make her a clerk or a nurse.

So he silences all anxiety for the future, by saying, 'She will marry: indeed it would be a very bad speculation, a very foolish outlay of money, to give her a trade or profession; she may never want it, and her brothers are sure to want all the money I can spare.' Plausible but fearful logic. It is true that the *chances* are on the side of her marrying, so it is not astonishing that an ordinary father trusts to them; yet the miseries which befall a penniless woman are so great, that if the opposing chance were but as one in a hundred, the parent should provide against it.

It is of this material that our forlorn single women are made: thousands utterly destitute save for charity; thousands more who, insufficiently provided for, eke out a miserable income by rigid and painful economy. We may lay it down as a primary social law, conceded by all political economists, that a father ought to provide for all his children, or give them the means of providing for themselves. For their sons they perform this duty with anxious care; but for their daughters they neglect it, because they hope and expect that someone else will do it for them. This is the plain state of the case; this *expectation* is in innumerable instances a daughter's *provision*.

But there is another reason why the father confides his daughter's future so wholly to her possible husband: women are so unused to have or to hold property, and the law throws the gifts or the earnings of a married woman so completely into her husband's power, that the father is little tempted to save up his money to give to another man; nor to train up his daughter expensively, when another man has legal power over the fruits of her education, and can take away any money she earns. Women have so little individuality in the eyes of most men, that when a parent has married his girl he feels to have washed his hands of all responsibility about her, and of course in her youth he looks forward to the chances of being able so to cast his burden on another. But surely in the present state of England, and even under the present state of the law in regard to the property and earnings of married women, there is a sort of madness in trusting to such a slender reed. The daughter may marry, but her husband may die, or fail, or be too poor to support her and her children; let her at least be trained beforehand to some possible way of getting her bread.

And suppose this girl, whom we took as a type, does not marry, and is left penniless and single by the death of her father. What can she do? She is untrained; she cannot be a good governess; she cannot undertake a national school; and her father taught her no business, and gave her no money to set up in one.

And here we come to our second proposition: that all ideas of the superior *gentility* of governesship should be discouraged. It is the overcrowding of the lower departments of that profession which causes such a frightful competition and depression of salaries. There will always be a fair demand and high pay for the very highest class of female teacher, who educates the daughters of the nobility and gentry, and fits them in manner and conversation for the station they will be called upon to fulfil. But why should tradespeople, housekeepers, and widows of all ranks, try and make their girls inferior, half-accomplished teachers, instead of honest, happy business women? Why should they drive them into an *unprogressive profession*, while even in a shop they would have more liberty and leisure and power of making way?

Of course, in urging parents not to make governesses of their daughters, if they can possibly help it, we must look out and try to open other paths. Why, if women must work, are they to be obliged to work only at the hardest, most ill paid, and unpleasant employments? Are they stronger, more hopeful, more persevering, that by social arrangements they are prevented from working in the progressive and more attractive employments, and thought to lose caste if they enter into business? It was once thought that a *gentleman* could only earn his bread as a soldier; yet even merchants and lawyers are now admitted under that exclusive name! It is but a small list, that of employments now possible; but it will widen every day. Let every father who has no money to leave his daughter see if he cannot educate and place her in some respectable work; telegraph clerk, book-keeper, woman of business, *quelconque*; surely in our commercial country it may be done. As to the arts and literature they must be left to individual capacities.

But the immense field of paid social labour, in schools, prisons, hospitals, workhouses, remains to be worked; and for this the woman's *ordinary* domestic training does in a great measure render her fit.

Thirdly. Every parent who can save money ought to insure his life for his daughters. It is lamentable to think how small a proportion of our population insures, when it is so cheap, so easy, so safe, and creates help for the women of a family just when, by the death of the helper, they would otherwise be left without resource. But the large subject of insurance in all its branches deserves far more than a passing allusion, and the principle could be applied in numerous ways to the benefit of women.

At the same time every effort should be made to aid in every way female education. The education of women of all classes is lamentably deficient; it is only necessary to read the Education Commissioners' reports to see how confessedly bad it is.

Girls are not taught so well, nor so many branches of knowledge, as boys, and there is a general indifference as to whether they make any progress or not. I earnestly desire to see benevolent effort directed into this channel. I wish to see the profession of the teacher elevated, and nothing would more surely conduce to it than opening the higher offices in the Educational Board to women. There is no reason why women should not be inspectors and examiners of girls' schools. I would also suggest that the middle-class examinations at Oxford, and other such examinations, be opened to women; and also that incalculable good might be accomplished by establishing examinations for volunteer lady teachers. There is much good done by corps of volunteer ladies assisting in the teaching of schools for the poor and middle classes, and there is no reason why this good should not be extended and increased. The examination should be in particular branches of education, and certificates given as to proficiency.

But the one conclusion which I desire to enforce is, that in all cases it is the *fathers* who are morally responsible for their daughter's welfare. Let each father consider how he can best provide, whether by giving her a special training, by saving money, or by insurance. One or the other he is bound to do; sacredly and morally bound. He has no right, in a country like England, to risk her future on the chances of marriage which may never be fulfilled.

What Can Educated Women Do? (I)

(reprinted from *The English Woman's Journal*, December 1859)

We should not omit to mention that the ordinary standard of female competency is not only not ignored in these speculations, but is actually regarded as of more immediate promise than talents of a higher kind. It is at this point, indeed, and this only, that the controversy we have been considering exhibits any symptom of radical innovation. Here, however, it has been asserted that, apart from all the contingent obligations of women, it is absolutely indispensable, as a measure of social reform, that woman's work should be called in and employed in certain departments of business. It is argued that women in workhouses, women in prisons, women in reformatories, and women in sickness, do imperatively require female attendance and supervision; that for lack of this superintendence rising female generations are viciously disposed, and that by excluding women from such places of trust and authority we not only deprive the sex of a remunerative occupation, but work infinite damage to the whole social body. We cannot enter into this argument more particularly at present. We do but allude to it not merely as indicating what has been called the 'great field of paid social labour', but as showing what opinions are at work upon the question besides those which are concerned simply with female employment. (From *The Times* of Nov. 17)

So much discussion has lately been called forth upon the destitute condition of educated women who have to earn their bread, that I think the wisest step now open to us is to discuss in detail the various possible distributions of their labour into new and more profitable channels, which I only alluded to last month.

The first point which strikes most thinkers is that remunerative labour, not only in our charitable institutions, but in those under the control of the Poor Law Board, is eminently needed from the heads and hands of educated women, for the sake of the inmates of those institutions themselves; and as it is also calculated to draft off from the labour market the best intellects, and the most reliable moral natures among women, such remunerative labour deserves our first consideration.

And here I must claim the indulgence of my readers, when I pass in review those social institutions of which I am necessarily ignorant as regards their practical working. I know nothing personally of hospitals, reformatories, or prisons, beyond the casual chances of inspection afforded to most ladies in the present time. Of the interior of workhouses I know a little more; but not very much. I must therefore appeal on these subjects to the judgments of women who *are* well informed, and who, by repeated visits, by diligent consultation of published works, and by active exertions within the walls of such institutions, are practically qualified to give a judgment on their condition. I allude to such thinkers and workers as Mrs Jameson, Miss Nightingale, Miss Twining, and Miss Carpenter, with other less known but most useful ladies.

These all declare, and have enforced their opinion through the press and by daily exertions, that our social institutions stand in the utmost need of the introduction of educated women in almost every department, working with and working under men, for we will not dispute about the exact position they are to assume, it is quite a minor detail. Therefore I shall support every assertion I make on these points, by quoting freely the words of those who are so much better fitted to judge than I am, and I should be thankful to see separate articles appear one by one on the details of each kind of superintendence, from the pens of practical workers.

In her 'Communion of Labour',[1] Mrs Jameson has classified our chief social institutions under these four heads: Sanitary, Educational, Reformatory, and Penal; and the first in order which she introduces is the subject of

Hospitals

I would ask anyone who doubts the efficacy of educated female labour in these abodes of pain and disease to read what is here said of some of those numerous institutions under the foreign Sisters of Charity. It is of course almost impossible to illustrate the subject in any other way except by referring to Catholic Sisters, or to Protestant Deaconesses such as those of Kaiserswerth, Berlin, and Paris, for hospitals have never been regularly tended by educated women who did not live in community. The ladies of St John's House, Westminster, are an example of Protestant action of this kind.

And as I am here discussing these topics, not from the benevolent, but from an *economical point of view*, I particularly wish my readers to take notice that communities relieve the labour market. It is very true that each individual worker is unpaid, and in that sense is a 'volunteer'; but it is equally true that as, wherever the system is really organised, all the workers are fed, clothed, and supported in old age from the funds of the institution, they actually constitute a very important part of the paid labour of the country. Those who are rich bring or leave fortunes to the community, but excellent and valuable workers are taken in without money, and thus (regarding the question on its purely economical side) they give their labour for a permanent maintenance. When, therefore, we hear from Mrs Jameson, of the Paris hospitals, including the Lariboissière, founded by a rich lady, and employing twenty-five Sisters of Charity; of the hospitals at Vienna; of the '*Spedale Maggiore*', at Milan, and the hospital of St John, at Vercelli, and another at Turin, all under the superintendence of Sisters, and all benefiting in the most undeniable manner by such care, insomuch that in one instance where they were expelled in 1848, they had to be recalled to save the hospital from almost cureless ruin, we must remember that there is an economical as well as a religious side to women's work in community, and that many of these Sisters represent a class equivalent to our wretched, superannuated governesses.

The same thing is true of the Lutheran Deaconesses. Miss Nightingale wrote many years ago a touching account of those first collected and trained by Pastor Fleidner, at Kaiserswerth on the Rhine. I have myself seen the vast hospital under their care at Berlin, and the smaller but most interesting establishment at Paris. The sources of information on these communities are cheap and accessible, and they may even be examined in practical illustration under the German Protestant Deaconesses at Dalston; therefore I will not refer to them more fully in this place, but proceed to

Prisons

Mrs Jameson tells us that an Act of Parliament, procured through Mrs Fry's influence, ordered the appointment of matrons and female officers in all our prisons; but that no provision has been made for their proper training, nor are the qualifications at all defined.[2] They do not, therefore, in general fulfil the requisites, nor produce the effects of educated labour; while in Piedmont we find the general Report on the Condition of the Prisons, addressed to the Minister of the Interior, stating that 'It is an indisputable fact that the prisons which are served by the Sisters are the best ordered, the most cleanly, and in all respects the best regulated in the country; hence it is to be desired that the number should be increased; and this is the more desirable, because where the Sisters are not established, the criminal women are under the charge of gaolers of the other sex, which ought not to be tolerated.' To this is added the testimony of the Minister himself. A prison is also mentioned which is actually *governed* 'chiefly by women, and the women, as well as the men who direct it, are responsible only to the government, and not merely subordinates like the female officers in our prisons'. This experiment at Neudorf had only had a three years' trial, but had so completely succeeded, that eleven other prisons were about to be organised on the same plan. It began by the efforts made by two humane ladies to found a reformatory for women. They sent to France for two Sisters, and after a while, government having noticed this small institution, it was 'taken in hand, officially enlarged, and organised as a prison as well as a penitentiary; the original plan being strictly adhered to, and the same management retained'. At the time of Mrs Jameson's visit 'the total number of criminals was more than two hundred, and others were expected the next day'.

'To manage these unhappy, disordered, perverted creatures, there were twelve women, assisted by three chaplains, a surgeon, and a physician: none of the men resided in the house, but visited it every day. The soldiers and police officers, who had been sent in the first instance as guards and gaolers, had been dismissed. The dignity, good sense, patience, and tenderness of this female board of management were extraordinary. The ventilation and the cleanliness were perfect; while the food, beds, and furniture were of the very coarsest kind. The medical supervision was important, where there was as much disease – of frightful physical disease – as there was of moral disease, crime, and misery. There was a surgeon and physician, who visited daily. There was a dispensary,

under the care of two Sisters, who acted as chief nurses and apothecaries. One of these was busy with the sick, the other went round
with me. She was a little, active woman, not more than two or
three and thirty, with a most cheerful face and bright, kind, dark
eyes. She had been two years in the prison, and had previously
received a careful training of five years; three years in the general
duties of her vocation, and two years of medical training. She
spoke with great intelligence of the differences of individual
temperament requiring a different medical and moral treatment.

We must bear in mind that here men and women were acting
together; that in all the regulations, religious and sanitary, there
was mutual aid; mutual respect, an interchange of experience; but
the women were subordinate only to the chief civil and ecclesiastical authority; the internal administration rested with them.

I hope it will be remembered here, and in other parts of this
essay, that I am not arguing for any particular system of administration, or discipline, or kind or degree of punishment; but merely
for this principle, that whatever be the system selected as the best,
it should be carried out by a due admixture of female influence
and management combined with the man's government.'

So much for the action of women in foreign prisons, and for
what might be expected from their introduction here. Also we
have testimony from the sister kingdom.

Captain Crofton, who organised the new system of secondary
punishment and prison discipline in Ireland, has made great use of
female officials, and has allowed that he could not have succeeded
without them; and Lord Carlisle in his speech at the Liverpool
meeting of the Association for the Promotion of Social Science, in
1858, bore the strongest testimony to the will and efficient working
òf these ladies.

Reformatories

I find the following passages in Miss Carpenter's works illustrative
of my position:

'A yet more striking fact is derivable from a paper delivered
into the Lords' Committee in 1847, by Mr Chalmers, Governor
of Aberdeen Prison. The percentage of female prisoners in all the
prisons of Scotland is nearly one-half; of juvenile female prisoners
under seventeen, between one-fifth and one-sixth; but the
percentage of *re-commitments of juvenile female prisoners is greater by
one-half* than that of males. This statistic fact would indicate that

young girls are generally much less prone to crime than boys of the same age, but that their tendency to it rapidly increases with their age, and that when they have once embarked in a criminal career, they become more thoroughly hardened than the other sex. The correctness of these painful results is proved by the testimony of the Bishop of Tasmania before the Lords.'

Now who is to stop young girls from embarking on a criminal career? Can men, however good and earnest, do all that is required, in the pulpit or the school-room; or must it be left to older and better educated members of their own sex? In Miss Carpenter's books, and in her various papers read before the Social Science Association, in different years, she makes constant appeal for help in the reformatory cause, one half of which help *must* obviously come from women; while in a paper sent by her in July, 1858, to this Journal, she puts this appeal in its more direct form. She calls on 'Christian women' to devote themselves to the work. She says that 'We must have in the school, a good matron, a good school-mistress, and a good industrial teacher'; adding, 'we have hitherto addressed women who have independent means, and who would gladly give voluntary and unpaid help. There may be, and doubt-less are, many who are compelled to labour for their maintenance, but who, while doing so, would gladly give in addition, a zeal and devotion which cannot be bought with gold, and which are most precious. They would willingly encounter difficulties and privations in this work of Christ's. Such might with great advan-tage enter reformatories as matrons, school-mistresses, industrial teachers. The greatest difficulty is at present to find fit persons for these offices; they will be gladly welcomed.'

I now come to the consideration of

Workhouses

and have applied to Miss Louisa Twining for the results of her large experience in what Mrs Jameson very naturally calls 'an institution peculiar to ourselves' as English people; adding that if 'ever the combination of female with masculine supervision were imperatively needed it is in an English parish workhouse'.

Miss Twining answers to my application by the following written statement:

'It has been asked in what way remunerative employment can be found for women in the management and superintendence of workhouses? There seem to be two ways in which both women and workhouses might be most materially benefited.

The first means for raising the standard for matrons would be to offer better salaries, so that such women as we find engaged in prisons would be induced to fill these posts. At present the salaries of matrons are far below those of masters; while one is sometimes eighty pounds, the other (in the same workhouse) is forty pounds per annum, and so on in this proportion, the matron always being considered subordinate to the master. Surely this is a very strange arrangement when we consider how large a proportion of inmates are women and children, and of the men the chief part are sick and infirm.[3] Yet, if the matron does her work conscientiously, her post is hard enough; indeed, to fulfil all its duties as they ought to be fulfilled is an impossibility. Another most fatal and monstrous evil in thus substituting man's work for woman's is the supervision of the younger women in workhouses by *men*, "labour" or "task-masters", *often* young, and *always* unsuited to the office (one, alas! requiring the utmost skill and judgment of experienced women). The utmost that can be expected of them is to keep the women at such work as hair or oakum picking by what means they can; the whole idea is revolting to common sense and judgment in every point of view. Were the *matron* made the chief person and head of the establishment, all this would be altered; a "labour-master" might of course be fitly kept to superintend such of the men as are able to work, and a clerk might be appointed to keep the accounts, the stores, etc., as in hospitals. If the present race of masters must continue as *heads*, no educated woman could of course act under them as subordinates. But no one *head*, whoever she might be, could be sufficient, and the question then arises, Will the guardians ever agree to pay as many persons as are required if our workhouses should become what they ought to be? There is then open the other way we alluded to by which women may be usefully and not ruinously employed in workhouses. This is by their being organised as bodies of workers, whether called deaconesses, or by any other name. Women of small means might club together and live in far greater comfort and economy than in separate lodgings; and such homes, in consideration of their usefulness, might lay claim to public support for the expenses necessary for maintaining a fund for pensions in sickness and old age, and for the support of those women who, though willing to work, would not be able to pay, etc., with as much right and reason as many of the present appeals for help and charity. These women might then be employed in workhouses, either as visitors or residents, without expense to the parish. Indeed the two plans we have suggested would be compatible, as the more highly paid and educated matron would of course be the most likely to welcome and co-operate with such fellow-workers.

Another opening for remunerative labour connected with work-houses, or at least *outdoor* poor, is the work of the relieving officer, why should not *some* women take a part of it? Women attend entirely to the administration of relief at the Bureau de Bienfaisance in Paris, and why should they not here do just as well for visiting the sick and poor in their own homes? It would in fact be merely the extension of district visitors' work, and a co-operation between them and parish authorities for their mutual benefit.'

Turning to

Educational Institutions

Our needs on this vast subject are perhaps more clearly recognised than in other departments of our social life. But the immediate effect has been to throw the education of great numbers of girls of the middle class into the hands of men, through the colleges established in London and in our provincial towns. It is impossible to regret this; the instruction of the good and learned men who have undertaken the part of professors to all these 'girl-graduates', is an invaluable gain to our generation. We have no women competent to instruct other women in the highest branches of knowledge, nor do I *ever* wish to see tuition handed over exclus-ively to our sex; it is a much better and more healthy thing that education should always continue to be a reciprocal thing: men teaching girls, and women teaching boys, in the departments in which the two sexes separately excel. But there are surely *some* parts of the great domain of education still closed to female teachers; in particular the office of inspector in girls' schools, and any share in the educational foundations, notably the grammar schools for the middle classes. Why should a distinguished poet, who also holds the office of school-inspector, be seen (as I have seen him) minutely examining the stitches in pocket-handkerchiefs and dusters? And why have we no grammar schools for our trades-men's daughters? Charity schools do not supply their place. Still I thankfully admit that the training schools for certified mistresses are an enormous step in the right direction.

Bessie Rayner Parkes

Factories

There is no subject on which I feel more deeply interested than in
the due superintendence to be exercised over the immense aggre-
gations of women now employed in factories. Without entering
into the merits or demerits of the factory system as regards women
– a system which some most intelligent thinkers earnestly deprecate
on sanitary and moral grounds – it is evident that, as thousands of
women and children *are* working within factory walls at this very
hour, it is most important that everything should be done, not
only to improve their condition, but to prevent their actual deterioration. Now this cannot be done by schools alone. To educate the
new generation aright is a great matter: but even for that which is
now acting or working on earth there is much to be done and the
mothers of the rising generation can be taught how to train their
little ones in all that concerns the bodily health and the spiritual
culture of the earliest years. A keen eye and a practised intellect
are invaluable when brought to bear on the needs of the artisan,
and in the thousand details of domestic life, a *woman's* eye, and a
woman's intellect, are indisputably more available than a man's.
Nobody, for instance, doubts that the clergyman's wife and the
district visitor have a very distinct and important part to play in a
parish; a part supplied in Catholic countries by the Sœurs de
Charité. To whom will the woman of the working class come to
tell a thousand petty troubles except to a woman? Who can judge
whether the meat has been made the most of, or the stuff 'cut to
waste', except a woman; and who is likely to be told of the
difficulties and disgraces which sooner or later touch every widely
connected household, except a woman? To whom will a mother
speak of her wandering daughter, or her scapegrace son, except a
woman? I do not deny that the clergyman and the minister may
do an immense work, nor that they combine many of the feminine
with the masculine virtues by reason of their special training. But
I think all my readers must acknowledge that a vast deal is still
left to the woman's peculiar province; and that where hundreds of
women are gathered together in any employ, it is very wise to
introduce among them the missionary labour of their own sex.
And though we all allow that 'Bible women', and Christian
workers of every class, however humble, may act beneficially on
the population, we have not enough of them, and it is still evident
to me, even with regard to them, that in no case is the superintending activity of educated women more urgently demanded.

I know of three cases in which it has been tried; perhaps my readers may be able to furnish other instances from their own memories. The first is at Halstead, in Essex, at the silk mill belonging to the Messrs Courtauld, where a lady has been employed for the last ten years in visiting the homes of the workers, and in exercising a general superintendence over the schools.[4]

The second was at Birmingham, under totally different and far more unfavourable conditions: men and women are mixed together in the workshops of that town; the trades are in many instances very rough and dirty, and the lady who attempted to organise a factory-home there seems to have felt her attempt almost a failure, and the conditions of factory labour destructive in soul and body to the gentler sex. Still, if this be true, all the more need for her presence and inspection! The *third* experiment was commenced this very year, in a mill near Cheadle, and promises to be most successful.

That every factory employing the labour of women and children should thus afford remunerative employment to the *highest class* of working English women, is a practical suggestion, the importance of which can only be truly felt by those, who, like myself, have seen its results in operation.

Emigration

Many other kinds of social work in which female workers might be most successfully started are suggested to my mind by the various letters which reach me, some of which will be found printed in another part of this Journal. Take for instance, the emigration system; why are there no women to take up and carry out Mrs Chisholm's work? There is a fearful disproportion of the sexes in our Australian colonies, which can only be redressed by persuading more women to emigrate from England. But it is not an easy thing for a single woman to emigrate; she is generally ignorant of business, she does not know where to go nor how to go, she is puzzled in what way to select a ship, and terrified at the unknown chances across the sea. A correspondent suggests that any two ladies who would devote themselves to seeking out female emigrants, and insuring a safe, comfortable, and reputable transit to one of our colonies, would confer great public benefit. Why cannot this be done on a regular plan, and in a professional way? Isolated charity alone will not succeed to any great extent. It seems to me that in all such work we must either employ paid agency or women living in some sort of community, otherwise we shall fail for want of organisation. This matter rests partly with government, and partly with emigration companies. Again, if we succeed in sending out any number of female emigrants, they should be accompanied on their voyage by a good matron, and met on the other side of the sea by a female superintendent, so that they may be taken first to respectable lodgings, and thence drafted out to different kinds of service. I am aware that I am suggesting arrangements which have in various instances been well carried out already, but I am sure that there is a need among women of all classes for further assistance towards emigration, and I think it rests with educated women to see how it can be wisely and kindly met.

Training

How we are to train the women who are so urgently needed in various departments of social labour is a question of considerable difficulty. Protestants object to setting apart any class of women who shall be morally bound to lead a life of celibacy devoted to good works; yet unless they are to remain at their posts, where is the good of giving them an elaborate training? To this I can only suggest two answers. Firstly, that the difficulty appears to have been turned or overcome in the case of teachers for certificated schools. They receive a competent training, they work for several years, and then they frequently marry; yet nobody argues that therefore it is foolish and expensive to train certificated female teachers. Secondly, the qualities required in the highest class of female superintendents are rather those which are matured by a life's experience than those which can be instilled into a woman by the efforts of others.

For the matron of a workhouse, or the superintendent of a factory, we do not want a clever girl, however well trained and certificated; we want a woman of mature age, whether single, married, or widowed; we want firmness, discretion, and experience of life. If a candidate possesses these she will soon learn the technicalities of her occupation; and if she do not possess them all technicalities will be but broken reeds. I am now speaking of the highest class of moral qualifications, of the rarest candidates for the most responsible social professions; for the subordinate branches of employment some similar system to the training school must be adopted, and certificates of ability bestowed. If these women marry (as it is to be hoped they will) they will carry into domestic life a very superior order of attainments and of qualities; as mothers of daughters they will exercise the best of influence over the next generation of their sex, and if they become widows, and if their husband's misfortunes (as in innumerable instances) compel them to work, they will form a sort of reserved fund for the filling of the highest posts of responsibility.

Upon the particular organisation of these necessary training institutions I do not feel competent to speak; while there are many ladies who possess all the requisite knowledge; but I consider it amply proved within the last half century that the want of the action of women in our English social institutions is a crying want of the age – it must be supplied, and the way to supply it will be found if we look for it.

When I read over what I have written, I see plainly that it will appear to convey only the merest truisms to those who have been long engaged in philanthropic labours. It has all been said over and over again in the last twenty years. But that is no reason why it should not be reiterated, for the beneficent effects of educated female employment in social institutions, is yet far enough from being a popular creed with the English people. An idea may be broached in books and pamphlets, and obtain great hold over a select class of minds, long before it penetrates familiarly into the columns of the newspapers, and becomes really incorporated with our national thought. Therefore, by systematically urging these things in a monthly periodical, it is to be hoped that a new range of readers will be touched. And we must not forget that it is absolutely necessary to convince the middle class before any of these reforms can be carried out and paid for. Who controls the workhouses? the guardians of each parish; chiefly tradesmen and shopkeepers. Who manages hospitals? Boards of officials who are little likely to have leisure for perusing the 'comparative physiology' of hospitals at home and abroad. Where does the power in our prisons ultimately rest, except in the persons of members of the government and members of parliament, who are too busy to digest blue-books which do not bear on their own particular bills. And how are the active merchants and masters of factories, who are the sinews of our commerce, to be convinced of the benefits of certain changes, unless they are presented to them in the newspaper which they read on the railway, or in the speech which they hear at a public meeting? Therefore it is that I hope to see these subjects brought up again and again, in every cheap and accessible form, till the thoughts they embody are thoroughly leavened through the homes of England, making the men willing to admit female co-operation in the institutions they control, and the women themselves ready and ardent to enter the new sphere.

I propose to consider next month those commercial avocations, trades, and mechanical arts, in which it is to be hoped that women can engage with prudence and a fair chance of success.

NOTES

1 'Sisters of Charity and the Communion of Labour.' Two lectures on the social employments of women, by Mrs Jameson; to which is added a prefatory letter to the Right Hon. Lord John Russell, on the present condition and requirements of the women of England. Longman. 2s.

2 In some instances superior women have been introduced; I hear of them at Wandsworth and Horsemonger Lane Gaol; while in her letter to Lord John Russell, Mrs Jameson says: 'The Female Prison at Brixton, containing, when I saw it, upwards of six hundred convicts, is managed entirely by a Lady-superintendent, her deputy, and forty matrons. There is, of course, a staff of chaplains and medical officers, but the government and discipline are carried out by trained women. The intermediate female prison at Fulham, into which the reformed convicts are drafted before their release, and in which they must pass the last two years of their term of imprisonment, is in the same manner under the control of an intelligent lady, assisted by a deputy and nine matrons. These innovations, which will appear extraordinary to many "practical" men, have been organised and carried out by Colonel Jebb.'

3 On the 1st of January, 1858, there were of *indoor* poor, 42,414 women, 53,551 children, while of males only 38,092.

4 See *Experience of Factory Life*, by M. M. Sold at the Office of *The English Woman's Journal*, price 6d.

What Can Educated Women Do? (II)

(reprinted from *The English Woman's Journal*, January 1860)

I concluded my last paper by proposing to consider in the current number of this Journal those 'commercial avocations, trades, and mechanical arts, in which it is to be hoped that women can engage with prudence and a fair chance of success'; but I have since learnt that a careful report on these several points is about to be prepared and published by the Committee appointed by the Social Science Association to report on the subject of Employment for Women; and as this report will contain matter collected from more numerous sources than I can hope to attain, I think it better not to attempt to anticipate its appearance, but on the other hand to confine myself this month to more general observations.

I believe it may be fairly taken for granted that the public opinion of this country sets strongly in favour of increased avenues of employment being opened to women; to judge by the articles which appeared simultaneously in the weekly periodicals, and by the vivid reflection of popular feeling flashed back from country papers, from Scotland and Ireland, one may reasonably conclude that comparatively few of those who think with or write for popular sympathies, doubt or deny the main propositions for which we have so earnestly contended in these pages. Let us therefore lay all argument wholly aside, and let us furthermore take for granted, what will easily be conceded, that, in answer to the question 'What can educated women do?' an able report will shortly point out many possible branches of employment; that to all situations of trust and responsibility in the care of the young, the sick, the criminal, or the insane, is added a wide list of occupations, such as printing, watchmaking, law copying, the applications of art to domestic purposes, and a dozen more of which we shall then hear in detail. There will yet remain two vital questions:

'*Why* do not educated women attempt these things?' and, '*How*, supposing them at last convinced, are they to set about them?'

Whatever efforts may be made by a small set of people, by a society, or by a knot collected round a periodical like this, it is very evident that they can only set the movement going. If it does not really create independent activity far and wide, the first impetus will be of little avail.

But it seems to me that this subject cannot be discussed in the manner of an essay, as if it were an impersonal affair; what we want to reach are the common thoughts and probable actions of women who are living and breathing at this moment in all parts of England. I will therefore speak with colloquial plainness and say that I have myself received at least a hundred letters during the past month, from ladies signing themselves by every Christian name in the alphabet, from Anne to Zora, all asking how they could get employment; and the lady who acts as secretary to the Society for Promoting the Employment of Women has *seen* at least a hundred similar applicants. We have both also been naturally brought into numerous anxious conversations respecting the wisest and the safest course to be pursued in the case of those intimately known to us and our friends; so that we ought at all events to have reached something like a fair and wholesome estimate of the real difficulties which beset a girl of the middle classes who wants to get a safe and paying employment. Two strike me as being of the most importance, and to create the greatest hindrance in their way: want of courage to face social opinion in a new path, and the want of a little money to start with.

I wish it were possible to drag these feelings of social caste fairly into the light of day. It is so very obvious that room *cannot* be made in the arts or in intellectual careers for the mass of unemployed women, and that they *must* resort to commerce and to trade if they wish to pass useful and happy lives; therefore the idea that a young lady cannot engage in business without losing caste must be conquered if any real way is to be made.

But even if any two young ladies personally known to us were at this moment to be anxious to start in some reputable business, an immediate barrier would arise in the want of capital. Girls never have any capital, they hardly know what it means; yet without it the very first move is impossible; they may *enter* a shop, but they cannot *own* one.

Consider the great difference between the position of young men and young women in this respect; the latter have only their pocket money, sometimes twenty pounds, sometimes thirty pounds a year; small sums varying according to the means of the middle-class parent, and to the number of his daughters. It is all they can do to dress upon this allowance; purchase a very few birthday presents, and buy writing paper and stamps for their limited correspondence. As to being able at any time to command a larger sum (even this being paid quarterly), it is a wild and impossible dream; and it is equally impossible to borrow, as they can give no security. Many and many a woman lives to middle age under her parents' roof with no more money in her purse at one given time than ten pounds.

But every respectable tradesman manages to start his son; it is an item in his life's expenditure for which he has all along calculated. He knew he must do it when the boy was born, and whether he pays to bind him as an apprentice, or helps him to a share in some business, or supports him during the first unproductive professional years, it comes home to him in the shape of money disbursed from his accumulated earnings – strictly capital – or set aside possibly in the latter case from his own regular income. As a little child, I used to hear of a certain legend of the last century, in which a thriving tradesman, finding no vacancy for his son in his native place, took him on a good horse with three hundred pounds of money to a fair town thirty miles distant, and there set him up as a mercer, to the great ultimate success of that youth. The substantial father, equipped after the fashion of 1750, trotting along with his boy and his bag of gold, is a picturesque type of what fathers do every day, though they go by railway now, and do not carry their capital in a leather bag. But I am very much afraid that that tradesman did not spend three pounds on his daughter; nor, as she could probably, in those days, bake, and wash, and brew, and make all her own garments, was her case a lamentable one as it might be now. Probably the going out as a governess was the very last thing that would have entered her head in 1750, and she either married some comfortable tradesman in her native place, and entered into all his household necessities, or she lived actively at home, very little troubled by ideas of gentility and the deprivations they entail. The arrangements of society answered pretty well for her then; but discrepancies have grown up and they do not answer now. She will suffer cruelly if she cannot make a little money to live upon, and she cannot make money without a little capital to start with: and, therefore, her chances of marriage being really diminished, she must work for wages as teacher or shop-woman with no hope of setting up on her own account.

It seems, therefore, as if no extensive relief of our suffering class of educated women could be achieved until fathers are won over to see the matter in its true light. But it may be said that fathers cannot afford to give capital, of however small an amount, to their sons and daughters too, But I submit that they are equally bound to their children of either sex, and that in very many cases where they bring their sons up to *professions* and leave their daughters *portionless*, they ought in justice to give the sons a lower and less expensive start in life, and keep some money laid by for their girls.

Moreover, fathers would then gain greatly in the relief of part of their present anxiety, for they certainly love their daughters, and often suffer greatly from fears for their future, though they may not have the courage to break through the social chains which cause those fears. If a girl were taught how to make capital reproductive, instead of merely how to live upon its *interest*, a much less sum would suffice her; and the father who gave or left her a thousand pounds would bestow upon her a benefit of which he could not calculate the results, instead of a miserable pittance of thirty or at most fifty pounds *per annum*.

In France it is considered morally incumbent on every parent to settle his daughter in life, and as a *dot* is an essential part of the matrimonial contract, every father in a respectable profession or trade considers himself bound to find a portion for his girl in relative measure to his position in life. We may complain with justice that thus to constrain the deepest affections is a great wrong to young French women, and that the wrong doing must bring a host of moral evils in its train; still we ought to confess that, according to his light, the French father does his best for the worldly welfare of his daughter: he feeds, clothes, and educates her in childhood, and when she grows up he settles her in life in that particular line of business which is considered best (a line of business which the *Saturday Review* affirms to be emphatically her own and her only true career), and he allots to her a certain sum as capital, in order that she may conduct that domestic business of household economy in the marriage life on terms of mutual respect and obligation. He does not ask any man to take her in as 'junior partner', on terms equivalent to board and lodging, and no salary required; he does not allow it to be an open, and in some households a constantly irritating question, whether her usefulness balances the substantial benefits she receives at his hands. She enters on equal terms in her woman's capacity, taking her little fortune and her household management, just as he takes his money and his work in the external world to constitute the double fund out of which they create their well-being. English readers will shrink from thus regarding marriage as a commercial firm; they will say that a husband and wife are one, and that he must not weigh what he gives her against what she gives him; that such a state of feeling is monstrous, and destructive to all the best and holiest interests of married life; and I quite agree with them, I think that marriage should be wholly independent of these considerations, that no woman should look to it as a maintenance. But nobody can deny that it is very generally considered in that light, even by the best people; there is a confusion in their minds between the Christian theory of the union of husband and wife, and the political economy which would throw the livelihold of all wives upon the earnings of all husbands. They want to reconcile the two things together, and it is only when they are startled by some very broad assertions, such as that made by the *Saturday Review* that all women who fail to marry may be considered as having 'failed in business', that they are roused up to declare that such a theory of marriage is abominable among a Christian people.

Therefore I would ask all my readers to settle this question quite fairly in their own minds. Is marriage a business relation, or is it not a business relation; or is it, as most people in the depth of their hearts consider it, a judicious mixture of the two? Whichever way you decide you are on the horns of a dilemma. If it is in ever so small a degree a business, then the French father is quite right to take rigorous care that his daughter be honestly provided with her share of capital, and he is quite right also to try and choose a respectable partner who will not waste that capital and bring the firm to bankruptcy. If, on the other hand, it is *not* a business in ever so small a degree, then you must make women 'independent factors', so that they may not be tempted to go to the altar for the bread that perisheth.

I am quite aware that there is a third suggestion lying on the debatable ground between the two theories. It is this, that every woman's power of household management is her natural capital; that if her husband brings the money and she brings the domestic work, she contributes her fair share to a firm which is partly spiritual, partly material; that God himself created this allotment, and that it is the *real* theory of marriage.

I mean to allow immense weight to this suggestion, because it is eminently true for the lower classes, where the married woman ought not to be the actual bread-winner.[1] I also think it ought to be true for a much larger portion of the middle class than will condescend to accept it. I think it is absurd to keep servants and to bring daughters up to idleness and penury, unable to do household work, and disgusted at the idea of marrying in a rank where it would be necessary to do it. I think that the way in which all girls who can possibly be supported in idleness shrink from real active household work is a great mistake and a great misfortune; that it does not help their intellectual development the least in the world; that they would be a great deal cleverer and healthier and happier if they did it; and that if poor middle-class fathers would bring up their little daughters to do the house work, after the fashion of Mary in the 'Minister's Wooing', and pay the money they would otherwise give to a servant for wages and board, to an assurance office to secure their daughters dowries, it would be a great deal the better plan in innumerable cases, and that plenty of time would remain for mental cultivation, though less for shabby and showy accomplishments.

But such an idea is widely removed from anybody's thoughts or practice at present, and the actual fact staring us in the face is that young men do *not* seek portionless wives, and do *not* consider the present amount of domestic knowledge and practice owned by young women as equivalent to 'capital'. Therefore we are obliged to put aside this third suggestion as being of no real use in regard to those included as 'educated women'.

Since, therefore, such are exonerated by custom and by the altered habits of society from those active domestic habits which make a woman in the lower ranks an equal sharer in her husband's labours, and enable her in single life to make a little money go a long way, and since public opinion nominally condemns marriage for a maintenance, where is the practicable alternative, except to help her to become an 'independent factor' on a higher level. It is very easy to cast a dexterous colour of ridicule over people and things by a happy epithet, which seems to embody a new idea in words and to point out its absurdity; but let us just consider what an independent factor really is, and who come fairly under that designation. In the first place, all domestic servants, to the number of 664,467 (according to the census of 1851), the nurse, the cook, and the housemaid, without whom we are accustomed to think that we could not exist for a day, are women working on their own account and away from their own homes, yet we do not find that tradesmen consider them unlikely to make good wives. Again, all dressmakers, shopkeepers, charwomen, etc., earn an independent livelihood before marriage, and in many cases continue to do so afterwards, yet we never heard a word about the unfitness of their pursuits, or any tendency in these to separate them from the men of their own rank. The real truth is that very nearly three-fourths of the adult unmarried women of this country, above the age of twenty, *are* independent factors; that they marry easily and happily from this position, and continue their work or discontinue it according to their individual circumstances, the number of their children, and various considerations which cannot be reduced to any rule. Therefore we are arguing about a very small, though very important, proportion of the whole body of women, and it is absurd to deal with the question as if it were a desperate, hopeless, and anomalous hitch in our social welfare.

To hear the remarks made by very clever and very kind people about this subject, it would be easy to fancy that some *bouleversement* of the whole nature and duties of women had become a lamentable necessity. The more I think about it, the more sure I feel that this notion is an utter exaggeration. I believe that the evil we are now trying so earnestly to remove is the growth of modern times, and closely connected with the growth of the middle class. As civilisation has increased during the last century, a number of women have been uplifted by the labours of men into a sphere where considerable cultivation and a total abnegation of household work have become a custom and a creed, but no corresponding provision has been made for them of occupation in the higher and more intellectual fields of work. They share, through their male relatives, in all the vicissitudes to which individual members of the middle class are subject; and they are helplessly dependent on these turns of the tide, having been trained to no method of self-help. All that seems to me to be wanted is that the women of the middle classes, belonging to professional or to commercial families, should heartily accept the life of those classes, instead of aping the life of the aristocracy.

Daughters living idly at home while their parents cannot hope to leave them a maintenance, are in fact the *exceptions* in our busy, respectable, female population. Let them shrink from creating an exceptional class of paupers, and take up their lot with the rest of their sisters, finding such occupations as will call out and employ their better education. I cannot see why working ladies need be more unsexed than working housemaids, nor why that activity, which is deemed to make a woman eligible as a wife to a working man, should, when exercised on higher subjects, unfit and discredit her to be the wife of a working barrister or medical man.

But it is little use to argue against ideas of caste which are so deeply rooted in our middle classes, unless some wise and active measures are also taken to change the current.

This brings me to the third great want which seems to me to hinder women from possessing themselves of a fair share of the domain of business: the want of efficient female superintendence in all those trades and offices in which women might otherwise be employed. If lack of capital prevents grown up daughters from leaving home and starting for themselves, lack of what they consider due and proper protection certainly weighs heavily with parents against parting with young girls, allowing them to be apprenticed to a trade or hired as clerks. In the minds of many men, this is an objection never to be got over, and no-one who has any experience of life will wonder at it. It is evident that the conditions of business life can, therefore, never be identical for men and for women; no sane person will tolerate the notion of flinging girls into those very temptations and dangers which we lament and regret for boys, and those who rise from the ranks into the middle class show the change in no more marked manner than in the standard of decorum they require from the gentle sex. If mothers are often less stringent than fathers, it is rather because they know less of what external life is, than because they would shrink less from exposing their daughters to evil example. Therefore we may talk to the wind about the folly of bringing up girls to be governesses, unless we so arrange that every woman is protected in the exercise of her profession almost as well as she would be if teaching by some domestic hearth. Nor is it any answer to say that some women, ten, twenty, or a hundred, have struggled nobly with the toughest problems of outer life; that Rosa Bonheur and Elizabeth Blackwell and Harriet Hosmer studied their professions in the general arena is very true and very inspiring, and makes one think well of one's kind, both men and women, but even their stories will never persuade the ordinary father to send his ordinary daughter out unprotected into the world of competition; and I think it very well that it is so. We must, therefore, exercise a little common sense in arranging all those workshops and offices in which girls work, and we must invariably associate them with older women; they must in all cases work in companies together and not intermixed with men, and so long as they are young they must be under some definite charge. This has been managed in the collegiate institutions now so generally in vogue for education; and I believe it rests with the women of the upper ranks to carry the principle down in minute ramifications into every department of woman's work. Let those who have birth, and leisure and means at disposal, set themselves to consider how they can make trade and professional life safe and respectable for young girls, and I am sure they will not find it a very difficult task. I may be reproached for not being willing to leave this matter to the natural action of society; but I confess I do think it requires at first a little 'benevolent' consideration from those who do not work for their livelihood. The prejudice to be got over in the minds of parents is so deeply rooted, and their fears so well founded, that I think the active interest of women of high social rank would smooth the way very much sooner than anything else. Many of them are deeply in earnest about charities for their own sex, and will spend time and trouble and money over schemes of less practical import. If they would but give direct countenance to all such new classes and workshops, as are opened for those who would otherwise be governesses, it would go a long way to legalise the change in the minds of men.

From the first days in which political economy rose from the region of empirics into those of science a covert war has been waged as to how far it expressed the whole truth in regard to social well-being. The great laws which it defines stand up like rocks amidst the wild waves of theory and compel them to retire, yet natures in whom love and reverence predominate insist on supplementing their shortcomings by a higher principle. Nowhere is this tendency more clearly to be discerned than in the writings of John Stuart Mill himself: indeed he occasionally retreats upon the moral intuitions of the human heart in a way that exposes him to censure from those who are willing to push intellectual conclusions to their farthest limits. The efforts made by the Christian socialist party are striking examples of attempts to interweave religious and economical law; and the necessity of allowing other considerations than those of science to rule our actions is shown with peculiar clearness by the social phenomena which accompany the introduction of machinery into any trade previously worked by hand. In the long run every such trade ends by employing many more hands at increased wages, but the immediate effect is to throw numbers of the old workers out of employ; and as human beings do not easily migrate from county to county, much less from country to country, and as moreover the grown man and woman cannot easily learn a new trade, even though such may be actually waiting for them in a fresh place, the immediate and invariable result of the introduction of machinery is a large amount of human distress, including hunger and cold and other very real griefs. Therefore, no manufacturer who is not influenced by selfish greed will introduce machinery where it was not previously in use, without taking pains to ease the transition to his workpeople. In like manner every effort ought just now to be made in aid of female emigration; for the sewing machine is destroying daily the wretched profession of the seamstress, to the great future benefit of the sex, but to the immediate anguish and destitution of the lowest class of worker.

And so I believe that though the opening of new paths to educated women will be a very great economical benefit, I see plainly that we have great moral interests also at stake which

171

require to be jealously guarded, that we may not look to the political economy of the question only, but must take anxious care to build up the new theory in connection with the old reverence for all that makes a woman estimable: in gaining somewhat we must not lose more. Therefore let us call on English women of social station to impart to this movement just that element of moral repute which it will eminently require to insure it from failure; let them weigh well the precious material out of which working women are to be made, and not leave the introduction of educated girls into business to the chances of the business world alone. Almost everything depends on the moral tone communicated from the headquarters of each separate sphere of employment; just as in the beginning of this century fiction was redeemed from its coarseness and absurdity by Sir Walter Scott and Miss Edgeworth, and a small contemporaneous knot of writers, so the professions, art, and literature receive in every age the powerful stamp of a few leading minds. On the ten or twenty women in England, who during the next dozen years may rise into eminence in any new sphere for their sex, will depend an incalculable amount of good or evil to our whole class of youthful educated workers. If such twenty maintain their position in all that is 'fair and lovely and of good report', and if they be well supported by those of their own sex whose names are an assured guarantee to the whole kingdom; if ladies who are exempt from the necessity of working will associate on terms of equality with ladies who are *not*, just as a baronet and a barrister are now for all conventional purposes of equal rank, then we shall see this 'new theory', as its opposers like to call it, carried triumphantly over every rock and shoal. It will become a respectable and desirable thing for a woman to become a good poet, novelist, or artist. In fine, it will no longer be half a disgrace for a lady to become an 'independent factor' in any other post but that of a governess.

If such hearty and generous pains be not taken, then the economical change (being of itself inevitable) will be worked out with peril and difficulty to the happiness of the community. But of this there is little fear. I rejoice to feel, from daily experience, how wide and warm is the sympathy of women with women, when once excited. I believe that all honour from their own sex awaits those who achieve distinction in any branch of work, and that those who make up their minds to seize the first opportunity that opens to them of pursuing any avocation, however humble, will find in future that their social *caste* is dependent on what they are, and not on the occupation on which they may happen to be engaged.

NOTE

1 Although not strictly incidental to the subject, I should like to observe in passing that no wise thinkers, however anxious to extend the spheres of employment for women, are satisfied with the state of things among the working classes which tempts the mothers of families away from their homes; and this on the plain and simple principle that a person who undertakes a responsible duty to another human being and to society at large, is bound to fulfil it. It is a matter of moral honesty, rather than of sentiment, and it would be very wholesome if it were so judged. The various degrees of external occupation which a mother can undertake ought likewise to be measured by the same standard. A great singer, an artist, or an author, who keeps good servants, may righteously afford the number of hours necessary to fulfil her profession, without any sacrifice of the welfare of her children, and there are innumerable excellent women who have combined these avocations and duties with irreproachable exactitude; but in the working class, where the mother is also nurse and house-servant, where all the cleanliness, economy, and comfort of a home depend on her actual and constant superintendence, her absence at any trade is as bad in a money as in a moral point of view. The frightful mortality among children who are left to the care of youthful, inefficient nurses, the accidents by fire and water and dangerous falls, sufficiently indicate the sanitary evils connected with the mother's absence. I was told the other day of an abominable practice occasionally pursued by ignorant mothers when leaving their children for the day; namely, tying a bit of sponge which had been previously dipped in some narcotic into an infant's mouth for it to suck! A very certain method of keeping the poor little thing quiet during its hours of loneliness. As regards economy, it is insisted upon by those who have most thoroughly studied the application of working men's wages, that if the husband is in full work, the wife's absence from home causes an actual loss, for which her earnings by no means compensate; in other words that the 'penny saved' in her household management, is actually *more* than the 'penny gained' by her labour. It is easy to believe this, but even if it were not true, the moral disorganisation caused by the housewife's absence from the working man's home, the discomfort, hurry, and ill-prepared meals, are more than sufficient reasons why every woman who has deliberately chosen to take upon herself certain heavy moral obligations, should fulfil them scrupulously to the exclusion of all temptations in other directions.

Statistics as to the Employment of the Female Population of Great Britain

(reprinted from *The English Woman's Journal*, March 1860)

As an important controversy has recently been raised, and is still much agitated, respecting the industrial employment of females – involving the questions (1) whether any such employment at all is desirable, and (2) to what extent, if desirable at all, and in what direction, a demand for such employment should be satisfied – it may be rendering some service to the disputants if, without taking any side in the dispute, we endeavour to present, in a concentrated shape, a few facts and figures relating to the subject.

Our statistics, it is true, are neither novel nor recent, being in fact but a reproduction of the information collected at the census of 1851; but it may nevertheless be instructive at the present time to have this information placed before us in a separate and special form, together with certain inferences and conjectures which the figures, when viewed in relation to existing controversies, naturally suggest.

Let us first obtain a view of the entire subject matter of the inquiry, by ascertaining the total number of persons affected by it.

In 1851, the total number of females, of all ages, living in Great Britain (Ireland therefore not being included) was 10,735,919. Of these about a third, viz. 3,692,218, were under fifteen years of age; and about three-sevenths, or 4,737,535, were under twenty years of age.

Now, it is argued by one of the parties in the controversy alluded to, that, as there are many kinds of remunerative occupation for which females are not physically disqualified, it is both proper and desirable that such occupations should be followed, if possible, by at least all those who have no independent means of support. On the other hand, the opposing party in the controversy

174

assert that, if females are not subject to a physical, they are subject to a natural, disqualification for industrial labour, inasmuch as their proper and peculiar business, trade, and profession are – to get married and manage a house and family; all who fail in this enterprise being in the position of bankrupt traders who fail in their respective pursuits. It is therefore urged that all married females should confine themselves to the domestic duties which constitute their proper occupation, and that all unmarried females should employ themselves exclusively in preparing for marriage. It is further represented that women, if placed in a position of independence as to means of livelihood, will not be so disposed to marriage (which is a public benefit) as if they were compelled to regard that contingency as their only source of support.

It is no part of our present task to criticise the view of marriage, and the motives which lead to it, thus presented to our notice. We are now only dealing with the question as a matter of cold statistics, and of the way in which they bear upon rival theories.

The amount of acceptance which these rival theories as to the proper province of the female population have met with, may be gathered from the statement that in 1851 there were 2,846,097 females engaged in some description of remunerative labour; besides about 500,000 wives and daughters of persons engaged in trades and occupations of a nature to make it likely that they assisted in the business and did not restrict themselves exclusively to domestic affairs. We may therefore conclude that by upwards of three millions and a quarter of our female population, out of the total of 10,700,000, the latter theory of their proper province is at present repudiated; or, if we exclude from the comparison all children under fifteen years of age, the number of females employed in occupations other than domestic will be 3,107,791 out of a population of 7,043,701.

Of course the vast majority of these industrious three millions belong to the working class of society; but the argument against the employment of females for the reasons stated is necessarily general, and must, if valid at all, apply to the poorer as well as to the richer classes. Marriage is not more the business of one class than of another; the poorest wife has to discharge the same domestic duties as the most wealthy; and the female artisan is as able to gain independence by her exertions, and as liable to whatever influence such independence may exert upon matrimony, as her more educated sister-worker.

Existing practice, then, is not in accordance with the theory under consideration; for not only do unmarried females employ their time in industrial pursuits, instead of spending it wholly in the business of husband-hunting, but a great portion of our married female population find it consistent, or make it compatible, with the domestic engagements which are supposed to constitute their only proper occupation, to devote a considerable portion of their time to remunerative employment in the various trades and manufactures. The actual number of wives thus returned as employed in 1851, was, in round numbers, 780,000 out of 3,469,000 wives; and that no doubt was an understatement. Of course this fact does not prove the theory to be erroneous, as it may very easily be replied that society loses more by the ill-consequences to husbands and children, of the absence of domestic care and instruction, than it gains by the additional labour of so many wives and mothers. The wide prevalence, however, of the practice bears against the theory with whatever weight may be due to the assumption that a civilised community will generally organise itself without any serious violation of sound principle.

Besides wives and unmarried females, there were 795,590 widows living in 1851. It will be felt to be a question, not merely interesting but somewhat serious, whether to this class also is to be applied the theory that, unless left in independent circumstances, their proper daily business is to direct their efforts so as to secure a repetition of former successful speculations, to make other ventures, to take new contracts, and to enter into fresh partnerships. We should all of us probably feel inclined to pause and reflect upon the consequences before assenting to the doctrine that widows unprovided for are not to engage in ordinary industrial pursuits, but are to seek their only means of support in the home of second matrimony. *One* of such consequences is shown by these figures of the census tables; for we there discover that of these 795,590 widows, there were probably about 400,000 (excluding annuitants, pensioners, and proprietors of lands or houses) who obtained some, if not the principal part, of their income from their exertions in professions, trades, commerce, or manual labour. One consequence, therefore, if the doctrine in question were to be enforced, would be the introduction of 400,000 additional competitors into the marriage-market, already perhaps sufficiently overstocked.

This last expression leads to another point. It is urged in support of the proposition that women should be taught to look exclusively to marriage as their calling, that Nature herself teaches this lesson by providing a numerical equality of the sexes. But what are the statistics upon this point? It is quite true that, as far as the number of births is concerned. Nature provides, in this country as well as generally throughout the world, an adequate proportion of each sex. Indeed, in Great Britain the number of males born constantly exceeds the number of females born; so that there would seem to be an adequate provision of husbands for all the females who might grow up to womanhood. But there is this peculiarity in the circumstances of this country, that the equality of the sexes, which exists at birth and continues up to the age of eighteen, then ceases. After that age there is a disparity in the numbers, which disparity steadily increases; so that the persons resident in Great Britain in 1851 of twenty years of age and upwards, were divided into 5,459,000 males and 5,998,000 females; showing an excess of the latter sex (if such an expression be allowable) to the extent of 539,000. This excess would be reduced by about 100,000 if the army and navy and other residents abroad were taken into the account; but these classes are clearly subject to such virtual disqualifications ⅰ. respect of marriage that it would not be proper to make any considerable deduction on this account. We may therefore assume that the number of females of a marriageable age, in Great Britain, will always exceed the number of males of the same age to the extent of about half a million; and the question is, How are we to deal with the half million (or rather, upwards of half a million) young women who, by the very ordinance of Nature, must necessarily, in a monogamic society, be unable to obtain husbands? If we are to admit the proposed doctrine that 'married life is woman's profession', and that all that can be said for those who do not get husbands is that 'they have failed in business' like any other insolvent tradesman, it is at all events a melancholy anomaly, which has no parallel in the commercial world, that 500,000 persons should be obliged to educate themselves for a profession in which it is known beforehand that, whatever their abilities, they cannot possibly succeed! Would not society, in adopting such a theory, be somewhat like the benchers of an inn of court if they were to allure a host of young men to become members, allow them to spend their three years in attending lectures, passing examinations, and otherwise qualifying themselves for the profession, and then refuse to call them to the bar because (as the said benchers had all along well known) the number of barristers was already quite complete and perhaps excessive?

We trust we are dealing with the question statistically. We only want to point out what seems to us to be a difficulty arising entirely out of the figures, leaving the difficulty itself to be dealt with by others, and merely suggesting whether, if an exception to the doctrine is to be admitted to the extent of half a million females, such an exception would not destroy the rule, inasmuch as it would be impossible to define beforehand the particular half million in whose favour the exception should be allowed to operate. It would doubtless be very rash to assume that the 500,000 young women in Great Britain who are destined to remain single all their lives, foresee that destiny in time to avail themselves of an exceptional liberty to earn the means of their support in other ways. If, then, it would be impossible to set apart any particular individuals as necessarily belonging to the half million of celibates, does not the allowance of a limited exception involve the allowance of a general exception in favour of all who may deem their chance of meeting the appropriate prince sufficiently doubtful to make it prudent for them to provide a resource in some remunerative occupation?

There is another point in connection with this subject, upon which statistical facts have a certain bearing. Another of the reasons put forward against the industrial employment of women is that if they are allowed or encouraged to acquire sufficient means to maintain themselves in independence, however moderate, they will become indisposed to benefit society by marrying. It is impossible of course to say how potent may be the natural distaste which is thus assumed to exist on the part of the fair sex for marriage viewed in any other aspect than that of a commercial bargain; but, unless that distaste be very powerful indeed, it might be thought that the possession of a certain independence, or of the abilities requisite to insure it, would by making the possessor more eligible as a commercial property, attract more offers of partnership than would otherwise be made from the other sex, and thus lead to an increased, rather than a diminished, number of marriage contracts. But it is not our wish to enter upon this question further, except under the guidance of figures; and we want to place the following figures before our readers, in order that their value as an indication of the extent of the repugnance supposed may be tested and determined.

The number of unmarried females industrially employed at the age of twenty years and upwards, in 1851, was 1,210,663. Now, as a test upon the point in question, let us see the number thus employed at the age of forty years and upwards. If the mere ability to live unmarried is as influential as is supposed in deterring from marriage, this 1,200,000 ought in twenty years to have diminished only by the number of deaths occurring amongst them in that period. According to the usual rate of mortality prevailing at that period, and allowing for an increasing population, the diminution would be from 1,200,000 to 664,000, as the number surviving at the age of forty and upwards. But the actual number found by the census was only 126,551. What then could have become of the 537,000 not accounted for by deaths? Is there any answer so plausible as that they ceased to be unmarried because they became married? I am aware that another solution may be suggested, viz., that they remained unmarried but ceased to be employed. But the figures show that the *total* number of unmarried females, employed or not employed, of the age of forty and upwards, was only 360,000, and that the whole number of unmarried females not employed was but 233,000. All that is proved positively by this is that a considerable number of the employed single women of the age of twenty to forty must have married before they arrived at the latter age, and that a considerable number more must either have married or, remaining single, have been transferred to the ranks of the unemployed. But although positive proof carries us no further than this, may we not, from the probabilities of the case, fairly infer something more? For instance, it is probably more reasonable to assume that the unemployed single women at forty were unemployed single women at twenty, than to assume that the employed single women at twenty had become unemployed at forty; and if it would be justifiable thus to suppose that the two classes of single women – the employed and unemployed – remained distinct, or at least without any important migration from one class to another, then it would become manifest that the employed single women obtained husbands in much greater proportion than the unemployed, and the theory under consideration would appear to be untenable. For, the number of unemployed single women of the age of twenty and upwards being 556,000, and the number of the age of forty and upwards being 233,000, the latter number is only about 75,000 less than the number (308,000) which the ordinary mortality of the twenty years would leave alive at the end of that interval. So that only about 24 per cent of the survivors could have married; whereas the proportion of marriages amongst the *employed* single women would be as high as 81 per cent.

Of course these calculations cannot be relied upon as furnishing accurate representations of the precise state of the case. They are only given as indicating perhaps to some extent the direction in which the statistics of the subject point.

A Year's Experience in Woman's Work

(a paper read at the National Association for the
Promotion of Social Science, August 1860 and reprinted
in *The English Woman's Journal*, October 1860)

Nearly a year has now passed since, through the means of the last
meeting of the Association for the Promotion of Social Science,
public attention in England was largely drawn to the subject of
female industry. Nor was it in England alone that this vexed
question came under discussion; France also contributed her
thoughts; and two elaborate articles in the *Revue des deux Mondes*,
and other papers in less important periodicals, testified that our
difficulties are also felt, although under somewhat modified
conditions, on the other side of the Channel.

My title to again introduce this topic to the notice of the Association is simple and direct – that of having experience to communicate in regard to remedial measures undertaken against the evils
which were deplored last year – experiments limited, it is true, to
one circle of people, and in the main, to one centre of action; yet
none the less valuable, because they afford us certain definite
lessons which a less concentrated sphere might less clearly bestow.

In November, 1859, *The English Woman's Journal* had already
been dealing with the various questions of woman's industry for
not quite two years. The Society for Promoting the Employment
of Women was as yet inchoate, but maturing its plans, and asking
for affiliation to this Association. A Reading-room for ladies, and
a Register for noting applications for the more intellectual and
responsible departments of female labour, had just been brought
into existence. Such was the beginning of our present organisation,
a year ago. Last winter every department received a great accession
of funds and of activity. The Journal greatly increased in circulation; the Society was absorbed into one created by and dependent
on this Association, with a committee of twelve ladies and twelve
gentlemen, which immediately began to consider the formation of

model industrial classes; the Reading-room was removed to large and excellent premises in a central situation; and, as a natural consequence of these improvements, to which a wide publicity was given by the press, the Register was literally deluged with applicants. It is not my province here to give an account of these separate departments of exertion towards bettering the condition of women. The report of the Society will be read in due time and place, and details regarding the successful establishment of a law-copying business will be given therein; the Victoria Press will tell its own story of the introduction of women into the printing trade. That of which I desire to speak to you here is the action of the Register, to which I alluded above, not so much of the little it has been able to effect, as of the much it has taught us regarding the real supply of educated labour in England.

When first this Register was opened, it was merely intended to act in a limited way among the ladies at that time subscribing to *The English Woman's Journal*, who, in those days of its infancy, numbered a few hundreds. Many of these ladies were actively concerned in charity; and had founded, or supported, or visited, industrial schools, and small hospitals, homes for invalids, and refuges of different kinds – institutions, in fact, requiring female officers. We thought that by opening a register which should act merely among our subscribers, we might occasionally find opportunities of putting the right woman into the right place; that Mrs A. might recommend an excellent matron or school teacher, and Mrs B. hear of her through our simple plan, combining an entry in a register book and an advertisement in the Journal for the current month. If in this way we get two really good and well-trained officials placed in a month, it would compensate for the little extra trouble. Being thus, as it were, a plan private to the circulation of the Journal, it was not otherwise advertised, nor was any publicity then sought for it. But when the whole question started into life, the advertisements put forth by the Society appear to have aroused the attention of women in all parts of the country; and as the Society and the Journal now had contiguous offices in the same house, no practical distinction could be made, and the secretaries of either were literally deluged with applications for employment. We had no sooner explained to the ladies who came on Thursday that the formation by the Society of model classes or businesses for a select number did not imply an ability on our part to find remunerative work for indiscriminate applicants, than the same task had to be gone over again on Friday. Indeed, I remember one Friday, in the month of March, when twenty women applied at our counter for work whereby they could gain a livelihood –

all of them more or less educated – all of them with some claim to the title of a lady.

Although not professing personally to enter into these applications, the replies to which devolved on the secretaries, I was very constantly in the office of the Journal when they were made, and entered into conversation with the ladies; in many cases, indeed, they came with notes of introduction to me or to my co-editor, and I had to ask them what kind of work they wanted, and, indeed, a more important question, for what kind of work they were fitted. In this way we may certainly lay claim to have heard more of women's wants during the last year than any other people in the kingdom; and that, just because the demands were so indefinite – the ladies did *not* want to be governesses, they wanted to be something else, and we were to advise them. In this way I have conversed with ladies of all ages and conditions: with young girls of seventeen finding it necessary to start in life; with single women who found teaching unendurable as life advanced; with married ladies whose husbands were invalided or not forthcoming; with widows who had children to support; with tradesmen's daughters, and with people of condition fallen into low estate.

To find them work through the Journal Register was a sheer impossibility. Not only were they far more numerous than one had ever contemplated, but they were of a different class. I had hoped to hear of and to supply a few well-trained, picked women to places of trust among our subscribers; but here were literally hundreds of women neither well-trained nor picked, outnumbering any demand by 99 per cent. The Victoria Press and the Law-Copying Class got into work, and employed from ten to twenty girls and women each; but it stands to reason that more could not be drafted into either establishment during the first year of its existence, without ruining the enterprise; while some time must be allowed to elapse before the idea involved in these model experiments could be expected to be seized by the commercial public, and an entrance be effected by women into either trade at large.

Since, therefore, we possessed but small power to aid numbers through the medium of our own organisation, it remained to be seen whether we could form a link between our Register and, firstly, the semi-mechanical occupations to which women have acquired, or might acquire, a title; and, secondly, the benevolent institutions of the country; so as to supply workers to the one, and matrons and female officials to the other.

To this end we adopted an idea struck out by a friend, and

printed long slips for distribution, containing, besides the addresses of the Victoria Press and Law-Copying Class (in case any vacancy might occur, or more hands be wanted), the addresses of the two chief offices of the Electric Telegraph in London, in both of which women are largely employed; and also the addresses of the two chief institutions for training and employing nurses; also of Mrs Lushington's cooking school, etc., intending to add to the list whenever we heard of any new institutions which would be regarded as centres of women's work. At the bottom of this list we notified that we ourselves kept a limited register for really competent matrons, clerks, and secretaries.

Now, in regard to what I have termed semi-mechanical occupations, I will dismiss them with a few remarks, to which I earnestly request your consideration. I am in this paper considering the needs of educated women; – of women who have been born and bred ladies – it is a real distinction from which, even in America, the most earnest democrats cannot escape, and which in England, however much the strict edges of the lines of demarcation between class and class may be rubbing off, still exists in full force. Looking at it from one point of view, we are sometimes tempted to regret the false notions of gentility which prevent women working bravely at whatever comes nearest to hand; but, in considering a whole class at large, an honest observer must feel that there is something noble – something beyond a mere effort after 'gentility', in the struggle to preserve the habits, the dress, and the countless moral and material associations of the rank to which they were born. A good and a refined education is a very valuable thing; and if educated women are to work at all for money, and I see no escape for a certain number being obliged in our country to do so, that education ought to secure them something more than a mere pittance.

Now the semi-mechanical occupation of the telegraph, and I believe it will be found to be the same with all semi-mechanical occupations, does not (except in the department of overseers) supply the needs of an educated woman, unless she be quite alone in the world, having neither parent nor child to support; and even then the wages hardly allow her to 'look like a lady', much less to live like one. Say that a woman in such a business earns a pound, or possibly, though I imagine rarely, 30s. a week – in the one case £50, in the other £75 a year – such a salary may keep a young, single, and perfectly unencumbered woman of the rank of a lady in food, and decent dress and lodging; but it does not constitute a sufficiency for an older woman, for one who may have claims upon her, or who feels she must begin to lay by for old age. I am quite aware that there are daily governesses who go out for less than £50 a year; their proportion is roughly estimated by the matron of the Governesses' Benevolent Institution as about one-third of the whole number of daily governesses. But many of these are not what we mean by ladies; they belong to tradesmen's families, and teach in the same; others again are quite young, and living with their parents, can afford to go out and teach for any sum they fancy pays them, and at a much cheaper rate than they could do if they actually supported themselves on their earnings. Others again are inferior in education, and so are driven down to offer their services at a low rate from being destitute of accomplishments. Custom does not shield the governess as it shields the physician, with his definite standard of acquirement guaranteed by his diploma, and his one guinea as a fixed recognition thereof; and therefore women will be found classed under the general head of 'daily governesses' who are very unequal in their qualifications and in the amount of salary they require and receive.

But it is none the less true that really educated women, possessed of a certain skill in music, drawing, and in modern languages – ladies such as teach ladies in the professional and merchant classes – ask and get more than £50 a year as a general rule. The conclusion, therefore, to which I have come is that it is chiefly for young people living at home with their parents, and for single women not possessing a high stamp of education, and having only themselves to support, that the semi-mechanical arts – such as that of working the telegraph, printing, law-copying, managing sewing-machines, etc. are profitable, and will supply with bread and meat and clothes; and that it is highly desirable to extend and encourage such occupation in every way, taking great care in the formation of model classes, or new businesses, to harmonise them as much as possible with the physical and moral conditions of female workers. The Society for Promoting the Employment of Women devotes its energies to increasing this kind of occupation, and deserves the active support of the public for its exertions, so that it may gradually be enabled to extend them in new directions, and offer fresh examples of the introduction of women into hitherto unaccustomed businesses and trades.

But for older and for highly-educated women – for those whom the keeping up of a social position has become a moral necessity, and for those who have others dependent on them – we surely ought to seek some employment which will secure them a fair income, and not consign them to simple trades, which, let them be ever so extended over numbers, cannot be parallel to the

professions which gentlemen require, or to the commercial enterprise which they carry on on a large scale.

Now there is work which really clever and energetic women are
wanted to perform, and which people are everywhere beginning to
say they ought to perform; all work involving *moral superintendence*
over women, and physical care of the sick and infirm of both
sexes. Mrs Jameson dwelt constantly of late years on this whole
subject, in her writings and in her private conversation; and Miss
Nightingale has begun to organise the training of women for the
latter purpose, and nurses are also educated at several institutions
under lay or Church influence. But as to placing educated women
to act as officials in charitable, industrial, penal, or reformatory
establishments, I really think I may say that nothing is done or
doing. We keep reiterating the need of them in each and all; but I
do not see that we are nearer the realisation of our wish than we
were five years ago.

Now, why is this? – I can supply one part of the answer from
our own experience of the last year; because the women who from
natural ability might be disposed and competent to undertake such
posts with advantage to themselves and others, do not ask for
them, have little idea of the kind of work, and little desire for it,
and would probably fail in doing it if they tried; *because they have
had no training*.

Although I have seen many highly educated and refined women
in want of employment during the last year, I have not seen half
a dozen who were competent, by their own conviction, to take
the responsibility of management on a large scale; the matronship
of female emigrant ships, the control of a wild troop of reformatory girls, the overseership of female factory operatives, or the
female wards of a workhouse.

Now, Sisters of Charity abroad do all these things. The popular
notion of a Sister of Charity in England is, that she is always
nursing the sick, or searching on a field of battle for wounded men
with a vestige of life in them, or visiting the poor at their own
houses – poetical and somewhat shadowy Evangelines, with
baskets on their arms. But, in good truth, these are but a small
part of their multifarious duties. They get through in separate
divisions nearly all the work performed (or unperformed) in our
workhouses; they take, feed, clothe, and teach orphan and destitute
children, and bring up the girls for service; they take bodily
possession of the old people and the cripples, and tend them in
other establishments; they distribute medicines, and manage most
of the casual relief funds of foreign cities. They also – and let me
particularly draw your attention to this point – undertake the care

of criminal and vagrant children. I saw in the month of April last the great Reformatory in the Rue de Vanguard, in Paris, where 100 girls of the lowest class – the majority actually prisoners and consigned there by Government – are under the care of the Sisters of Marie-Joseph. This establishment was founded partly in consequence of the exertions of Madame de Lamartine, and it was shown to me by Madame Lechevalier, who actually holds the salaried post of Government inspectress of the female prisons of France. Why have not we also an inspectress for our female prisons? Madame Lechevalier has often knocked up a prison at eleven o'clock at night when she suspected anything wrong; and I saw enough of her power of character, even during the few hours I spent with her, to convince me that she was a woman to hold a legion of female prisoners in awe.

Sisters of Charity are also now in France trying to make head against the evils of the factory system. I had not time, when in Lyons last year, to travel forty miles by railway to see M. Bonnart's factory, where they superintend the female workers; but in the *Revue des deux Mondes* for last February is to be found a very interesting account of three establishments where the young girls are engaged in manufactures under the care of sisters; one at Jujurieux, for taffetas; another at Tatare, for plush; and the third at La Seauve, for ribbons. Young girls on entering sign an engagement for three years, and a month's trial is also required. Workwomen are also received, who enter into an engagement for eighteen months.

But all these duties require something more for their wise fulfilment than love and patience; they require energy, foresight, prudence, economy, the habit of working in concert and subordination; and accordingly we find the women who are to fulfil them subjected to a severe and methodical training. The *Maison Mère* of the Sisters of Charity of St Vincent de Paul, in the Rue de Bac at Paris, sends out five hundred trained women every year to all parts of the world.

And we, if we wish to employ women successfully in works of benevolence and social economy, must find some way of training them for their duties, or we shall never achieve our wished-for results. Here and there we may find one specially gifted, to whom order and activity come by right divine; but if you take the few women who are *even now* filling marked positions of public importance, you will generally find they have received regular training in some way. Every one knows the severity of Miss Nightingale's preliminary studies, and the ordeal she passed through in hospitals abroad. Miss Carpenter had concluded a long and honored career as a teacher before she devoted herself to criminal children. Elizabeth Blackwell is hardly a case in point, as her possession of a degree involved her career as a student; and (I believe) Miss Dix and Mrs Fry forced their way by unusual energy, graduated themselves, so to speak; but all the institutions for nurses presuppose preliminary training; Miss Dence, the mistress of one of the best private asylums in England, was regularly educated under the leading physician who has devoted himself to ameliorating the condition of the insane; and there are now several establishments under the direct sanction of the Church of England, in which ladies are conducting refuges for their own sex, each undergoing a certain probationary discipline.

Thus we find in every department of benevolent exertions the want of efficient machinery for teaching those who are to help others. And this knowledge is necessarily of two kinds – intellectual and practical. Books alone will not give it, nor will books and oral instruction combined suffice. Not only must the mind of the worker be furnished with all necessary knowledge, but the habits of the worker must be trained in activity, prudence, and control. Such workers can only be trained *in* the works they are eventually to perform, just as the swimmer can only be taught in water. In religious communities this is effected by receiving beginners into the life of community; among us it can only be effected by receiving female pupil-teachers, as it were, into all our institutions, and this can only be done by the consent and co-operation, in many cases of Government, in all cases of the men who control all our institutions in England.

The pressure may 'come from without'; it *has* come from without, and it only needs to give it a right direction. Moreover, almost all the best men who are working in philanthropic reform say that they want female help to carry out their purposes properly; but it will be of little good to ourselves, or to them, or to the poor, the ignorant, the sick, or the criminal objects of their solicitude, if it be desultory and untrained. We must appeal to men to give us the necessary opportunity of learning; in fact, to help us to help *them*.

On one more subject I desire to suggest attention.

In enumerating the women who have achieved useful careers, Mrs Chisholm must not be forgotten; and in this connection she is doubly to be remembered. While endeavouring to relieve the strain of female necessities, we must not forget that our colonies are eminently in want of women of every rank, and that they are the natural destination of the great surplus which exists in England. If it were possible to plant those who are suffering and struggling at home (with problems which at the best are very hard for most women to solve practically), in useful independence or happy marriage over the broad fields of Australia and New Zealand, who among us but would say that it was by far the best solution of our difficulty?

But before educated women will emigrate in any number, the way must be made safe and respectable. They must find shelter and assistance on the other side of the ocean; a regular organisation must be created, and competent female officials appointed to the emigrant ships in which they are to sail, and others be ready to receive them on landing. We have tried this year to induce several ladies to take advantage of the assisted passages granted to Canterbury, in New Zealand, the only place to which assisted passages are granted for educated women. But we found none willing to start, even of those who would otherwise have liked to emigrate, because of the vague uncertainty which awaited them on the other side; no committee to put them into decent lodgings and assist them in looking out for situations such as are described by residents as actually vacant; nobody to whom to apply in case of illness; nobody to do what Mrs Chisholm did, when she made herself the mother of the female emigrant of a lower class. In fact, no progress will be made in this most necessary exodus, until a few carefully selected women, trained in all the necessary knowledge, are sent out from England, with a small fund and the best introductions to our chief colonial ports, and there instructed how to form local committees and *dépôts* for the reception of governesses, or any other educated ladies who desire to try the fortunes of a new world. If such a plan were carefully inaugurated, I believe that a few years would see a very sensible diminution of the strain at home; and I believe that the Society for Promoting the Employment of Women might very wisely lay the foundation of such a plan by selecting, instructing, and sending out the first officers, if the necessary funds could be provided for that purpose.

I will sum up, in a few words, thus, the meaning of this paper, and the results of the past year's experience as it has affected my mind. All the semi-mechanical arts are eminently suited for young people, and it greatly behoves fathers to train their daughters to the possession of some such means of gaining independent bread, in the morning of life, while health and spirits are, or ought to be, strong, so that while living under the parental roof they may secure themselves against a rainy day, when it may no longer shelter them. But there are many, many women to whom, by reason of age, health, or social responsibilities, the semi-mechanical arts are not applicable; women also whose capacities deserve and require a wider field of intellectual and moral exertion than the compositor's case or the law-copyist's desk can afford; and seeing, as I do daily, how great is the comparative delicacy both in brain and in the bodily frames of women of the middle and upper class – of the bad effect upon many of them of long hours of sedentary toil, and the supreme difficulty of introducing them in great numbers into the fields of competitive employment, the more anxious I become to see the immense surplus of the sex in England lightened by judicious, well-conducted, and morally guarded emigration to our colonies, *where the disproportion is equally enormous, and where they are wanted in every social capacity*; and to see a large number of those that remain, the single or otherwise self-dependent women, who must exist in every highly civilised and thickly populated country like ours, well and carefully trained in all those functions of administrative benevolence, which are in fact but a development of household qualities; the larger, the more generous, and equally distinctive part of woman's work in the world.

The Condition of Working Women in England and France

(a paper read at the National Association for the Promotion of Social Science, August 1861 and reprinted in *The English Woman's Journal*, September 1861)

During the last two years we have seen a great public effort made towards relieving the difficulties of a special class of women – educated women who need a livelihood. And by dint of discussion the subject has been so thoroughly ventilated, and by dint of exertion so many plans have been tried with more or less success, that we may be fairly said to have attained to something like a reasonable hope of abolishing the evil in a due course of years, more particularly since public opinion is steadily directing itself to what is by far the truest remedy – a well-organised, widely-diffused, and persistent system of emigration.

Although, therefore, the necessity of action has not diminished, but still exists, and will do so for many years to come, we may consider the necessity for talking and writing in general terms about this particular class of the feminine community to be at an end. We must all work, but those who are willing to help, now know where and how to apply.

Leaving, therefore, this difficult and much-vexed question wholly on one side for the time, I ask you to consider with me one which is much wider – which may indeed be said to include the first, and which I believe to be the most important social question of modern times, inasmuch as turn where we will it meets the social reformer on every side – I mean the change which the last century has brought about in the condition of the working women of England and France. I couple the two countries together because they essentially represent all that is implied in modern civilisation, its benefits and its evils, in an almost equal degree; for if England was in some respects an advantage in the race, be sure that France is pursuing with giant strides, and that her capitalists and her workpeople are fast becoming the duplicates of our own.

Everyone agrees, to judge by the incessant reference to it in the newspapers, that there is a certain phase of European life, peculiar to our generation and that of our fathers, which is so distinctly marked that it is indeed modern civilisation. Some years ago, when Charles Mackay's songs were popular in the streets, it was generally said to be the dawn of something quite new and splendid in the earth's history, the immediate herald of 'the good time coming', but a strong reaction has taken place towards an appreciation of mediaeval times; Mr Ruskin, Mr Froude, and a host of lesser men, have done battle for the Dark Ages, and it is now generally conceded that Venice, Florence, and Holland, possessed in their palmy days a very respectable civilisation of their own.

Whether, however, it be a marked growth, or only a marked change, it is evident that our ways are not as their ways, and that an immense increase of products, and a striking uniformity in what we produce, together with a constantly extending diffusion of material and intellectual goods, are the characteristics of the age of steam. England and France show them in every department of their public and private life, and the treaty of commerce, when once it comes fairly into play, is destined to increase them greatly, by stimulating each country to enormous production of its own specialities, so that all France, unless it goes to bed by gaslight, will probably adopt Birmingham candlesticks, and our Queen's subjects will more than ever be ruled in their costume by the fiats of Lyons and Paris for the year.

Now the point to which I am coming is the *price* at which this great European change has been accomplished: the price which has been silently levied in every manufacturing town in both kingdoms, the great revolution which has been so little noticed amidst the noise of politics and the clash of war – the withdrawal of women from the life of the household, and the suction of them by hundreds of thousands within the vortex of industrial life.

Perhaps you will attach more importance to what I say if I observe that I have only very gradually become aware that this tendency pervades all the social economy of our time. Figures alone do not always impress the imagination; so many women in the cotton trade, so many in the woollen, the mind loses its track among the *oughts*, just as the savage gets bewildered beyond his own ten digits. But in thinking of governesses, and why there seemed to be such an inexplicable amount of suffering in that class, I have been brought face to face with these wider and deeper questions, and have seen that their actual destitution, though specially the result of overflowing numbers, is but part of a general tendency on the part of modern civilisation to cast on women the responsibility of being their own breadwinners, and to say to them with a thousand tongues, 'If thou wilt not work, neither shalt thou eat.'

Look at the present constitution of Lancashire life; suppose the American war hinders the supply of cotton to such an extent that, before we can reckon on supplies from our Indian Empire or elsewhere, the mill hands are thrown out of employ, *who* will be thrown out of employ? Who are at least a majority of the total of the workpeople? Women and girls. You know what it is in Lancashire: those miles upon miles of dusky red dwellings, those acres of huge factories, those endless rows of spinning and weaving machines, each with its patient industrious female 'hand'. If a catastrophe falls on Yorkshire, and the chimneys of Bradford or Halifax cease to smoke, who are they that come upon the poorrates or hunger at home? Women and girls. I was told in Manchester, by one of the most eminent and thoughtful women in England, that the outpouring of a mill in full work at the hour of dinner was such a torrent of living humanity that a lady could not walk against the stream: I was told the same thing at Bradford, by a female friend of my own. In both instances the quitting of the mill seemed to have struck their imaginations as a typical moment, and they spoke of it as something which once seen could not be forgotten.

At Nottingham and Leicester, which I have visited this spring, the women are so absorbed into the mills and warehouses that little is known of female destitution. In Birmingham, where vast numbers of women are employed in the lighter branches of the metal trade, they may be seen working in the button manufacture, in japanning, in pin and needle making. In Staffordshire they make nails, and unless you have seen them I cannot represent to your imagination the extraordinary figures they present – black with soot, muscular, brawny – undelightful to the last degree. In mines they are no longer allowed to work; but remember that they did work there not so long ago, taking with men an equal chance of fire-damp and drowning, even being sometimes harnessed to the carts if poor patient horses were too dear.

I read the other day of a whip makers' strike, which took place because women were being introduced into a branch of work for which men had hitherto been employed; but perhaps the most impressive thing which ever came to my immediate knowledge was the description in a small country paper of a factory strike, in which a prolonged irritation existed between the hands and the very excellent firm owning the works. There were letters and speeches to and fro; placards on the walls, and a liberal expenditure of forcible Saxon language. Now who were these hands 'out on strike'? These people who made speeches, gathered together in angry knots at the corners of the streets? – Women!

After this, may I not say, that on no small body of ladies in London, on no committees or societies trying to struggle with the wants of the time, can rest the charge of unsexing women by advising them to follow new paths, away from household shelter and natural duties, when a mighty and all-pervading power, the power of trade, renders the workman's home empty of the house-mother's presence for ten hours a day, and teaches English women the advantage of being 'out on strike'.

For it is clear, that, since modern society will have it so, women must work: 'weeping', which Mr Kingsley regards as their appro-priate employment, in fishing villages and elsewhere, being no longer to the purpose. I do not say that these myriads are, on the whole, ill paid, ill fed, sickly, or immoral; I only wish to point to the fact that they are actually working, and, for the most part, in non-domestic labour, a labour which cannot be carried on under a husband or a father's roof. And recognising this apparently hope-less necessity, I believe it to be just and advisable that printing and all such trades be fairly thrown open to them; for we have to do with hunger and thirst and cold; with an imperious need of meat and drink, and fire and clothing; and, moreover, as trade uses women up so freely whenever it finds them cheaper than men, they themselves have a just claim to the good along with the evil, and, being forced into industrial life, it is for them to choose, if possible, any work for which their tenderer, feebler, physical powers seem particularly adapted.

Let us now turn to France. It is two years since I was in Lyons, and with the introductions of M. Arles Dufours, one of the leading merchants and most enlightened economists of France, visited several of the *ateliers* (workshops) where not more than six women are employed in the silk-weaving, under a mistress, or where sometimes the family only work among themselves. The conditions of this manufacture are very peculiar, the silk being bought by the merchants and allotted to the weavers, who bring it to the warehouse in a finished state, so that there is a singular absence of the bustle of English trade; there is comparatively little speculation, and in many ways the work is conducted in a mode rendering it easy for the female workers.

Little by little there, rises, however, a tendency to an industrial change. This subject is amply and eloquently discussed in those remarkable articles, from the pen of M. Jules Simon, which appeared in the *Revue des Deux Mondes*, and which are now gathered into a volume entitled. *L'Ouvrière*, the workwoman. He believes that the greater production which steam power creates will gradually tempt the Lyonese merchants to turn into master manufacturers, destroying the *ateliers* and the family work in common. At the time of my visit I only heard of one establishment actually in work on a large scale, and that was some miles out of the town, and had been created chiefly on a religious and charitable basis, that is to say, the young female apprentices are bound for three years, and are under charge of a community of religious women; but M. Simon mentions three principal houses of this kind, and alludes to others. Adult workmen are also received, being bound for eighteen months. The moral advantages of the surveillance exercised over the girls is apparent in the fact that they are more readily sought in marriage by respectable workmen than girls apprenticed in Lyons; yet the gathering together of numbers is surely, in itself, to be regretted, as paving the way for the adoption of the same principle for the mere sake of economical advantage. While families, however, eagerly seek the shelter for their daughters, the masters make no profits, because they are conducting business in a manner at variance with the habits of the surrounding trade; which instantly retrenches in an unfavourable season in a way which is impossible to a great establishment with an expensive plant.

The very same idea is being in this year of 1861 carried out in the French colony of Algiers for the first time. As I was an eye-witness of its commencement, in the month of January last, it may be of use for me to relate in what way – half-economical, half-charitable – the germ of a vast system of female industry may spring up. About three miles from the town of Algiers is a ravine of the most beautiful and romantic description, called from some local tradition *La Femme Sauvage*. It winds about among the steep hills, its sides clothed with the pine, the ilex, the olive, and with an underwood of infinite variety and loveliness. Wild flowers grow there in rich profusion, and under the bright blue sky of that almost tropical climate it seems as if anything so artificial and unnatural as our systems of industry could hardly exist for shame; yet in that very valley young female children are at this very moment, while I speak and you listen, winding silk for twelve clear hours a day!

The conditions of the case are as follows: Considerably nearer the town is a large orphanage, containing about four hundred children, under the care of the sisters of St Vincent de Paul. Many of them are half-castes, others the poorest dregs as it were of the French population; and they are exactly the same material as in

England or Ireland would be drifted into workhouses. Of course, in a place like Algiers, of limited colonial population and resources, it is no easy matter to find a profitable occupation for four hundred orphan girls, and therefore when M. R—— (the very same gentleman who had organised M. B——'s factory near Lyons) set up a silk-winding mill in *La Femme Sauvage*, the Algerine Government, which pays a considerable sum towards the support of the orphanage, were glad to apprentice thirty girls to M. R——, to be bound from the age of thirteen to that of twenty-one and to work, according to the usual conditions of French industry, twelve hours a day. The work consisted of winding the raw silk from the cocoon, by hand, aided by a slight machinery, and then in another part of the factory spinning it by means of the ordinary apparatus into skeins of silk ready for the market of the Lyons weavers. Three Sisters of Charity accompanied the children, and were to superintend them at all times, in the dormitory, the dining-room, and on Sundays, their only day of recreation. When the thirty apprentices were duly trained, M. R—— was prepared to take seventy more, who were also to be accompanied by their devoted superintendents; so that if not at this moment, at all events before long, there will be one hundred girls steadily training in that secluded valley, a thousand miles from here, the forerunners of a social change which may gradually develop Algiers into a manufacturing country, and absorb the lives of an untold number of women. I attended the little fête of installation, when a high ecclesiastical dignitary of Algiers came to perform divine service at the little chapel on the premises; he was accompanied by several of the civic functionaries of the town, whose carriages stood in the ravine, making quite a festive bustle. The two partners were gay and smiling – indeed, I believe them to have been good men, delighted not merely with the business aspects but with the benevolent side of their scheme; the sisters were radiantly pleased with the prospects of their charges; the dormitories were airy and wholesome, the dining-room and kitchen clean and commodious. The hundred girls, after being taught a respectable trade and enjoying careful moral superintendence during their youthful years, would be free at twenty-one, and would probably find respectable marriages without difficulty. Things being as they are in this modern life of ours it was undoubtedly a good and kind scheme, well and carefully carried out; careful for the welfare of the children in this world and the next; and yet, perhaps, you will not wonder that I could not help thinking of those poor children at their eternal spinnings whenever in after spring days I walked over the wild hills and through the scented glens of Algiers; and that they brought home to me, from the vivid contrast of the untrammelled nature around me, what perhaps in Europe might never strike the heart with equal vividness, that our modern civilisation is in some respects a very singular thing when the kind hearts of a great nation can best show their kindness to orphan girls by shutting them up to spin silk at a machine for twelve hours a day from the age of thirteen to that of twenty-one.

Eight years of youthful girlhood with the smallest possibility during that time of sewing, cooking, sweeping, dusting, and with neither play nor instruction except the little they can pick up on Sunday. What will they be like in the year 1869!

So much for silk at Lyons and Algiers; and remembering that at Lyons the mode of industry is as yet very favourable to women, let us see how matters stand in regard to cotton and woollen at Rouen and at Lille, where, as a rule, the system of large factories already prevails. Referring to M. Simon's book we find that he starts on the first page of his preface with stating that he has passed more than a year in visiting the principal centres of industry in France, and that whereas the workman was once an intelligent force, he is now only an intelligence directing a force – that of steam; and that the immediate consequence of the change has been to replace men by women, because women are cheaper, and can direct the steam force with equal efficiency. 'A few years ago,' says he, 'we had very little mechanical weaving, and, so to speak, no spinning by machinery; now, France has definitely and gloriously taken her place among the countries of large production' (*la grande industrie*). He speaks of the men gathered together in regiments of labour presenting a firm and serried face to the powers of the State, no longer needing a rallying cry of opposition, since they are in mutual intercourse for twelve hours a day. 'And what,' he asks, 'shall we say of the women? Formerly isolated in their households, now herded together in manufactories. When Colbert, the Minister of Louis XIV, was seeking how to regenerate the agricultural and industrial resources of France, he wished to collect the women into workshops, foreseeing the pecuniary advantages of such a concentration, but even his all-powerful will failed to accomplish this end; and France, which loves to live under a system of rigid administration, makes an exception in favour of domestic life, and would fain feel itself independent within four walls. But that which Colbert failed to achieve, even with the help of Louis the Great, a far more powerful monarch has succeeded in bringing to pass. From the moment when steam appeared in the industrial world, the wheel, the spindle, and the distaff broke in the hand, and the spinsters and weavers, deprived of their ancient livelihood, fled to the shadow of the tall factory chimney.' 'The mothers,' says M. Simon, 'have left the hearth and the cradle, and the young girls and the little children themselves have run to offer their feeble arms; whole villages are silent, while huge brick buildings swallow up thousands of living humanity from dawn of day until twilight shades.'

Need I say more, except to point out that when once any new social or industrial principle has, so to speak, fairly set in, the last remains of the old system stand their ground with extreme difficulty against the advancing tide, and that trades by which solitary workers can earn a sufficient livelihood are every day decreasing in value, or being swept off into *la grande industrie*. Sewing will assuredly all be wrought in factories before long; the silk work, which formerly stretched down the valley of the Rhone as far as Avignon, has gradually drawn up to Lyons, leaving the city of the Popes empty and desolate within its vast walls. At Dijon, M. Maitre has gathered up the leather work of that ancient capital into his admirably organised *ateliers*, where he employs two hundred men and one hundred women, and binds prayer-books and photographic albums and *porte-monnaies* enough to supply an immense retail trade in Paris. In England it is the same: we gather our people together and together, we cheapen and cheapen that which we produce. Did you ever, when children, play with quick-silver, and watch the tiny glittering balls attracted in larger and larger globules until they all rolled together into one? Such is the law of modern industry in England and France, and in all other countries according as they follow the lead of these two nations in the theoretic principles of life which lead to those results which are at once the triumph and the dark side of modern civilisation.

Having thus pointed out the conditions under which so large a proportion of our national commercial prosperity is carried on, permit me to say a few words regarding the practical consequences and duties it entails. Nobody can doubt that so vast a social change must be gradually inducing an equally great moral change, and that some of the consequences must be bad. I am careful to limit my expressions, because it must not be forgotten that I have not spoken today of the poor or of the degraded, but of the bulk of the factory workpeople of England and France, and of large classes in Scotland and Ireland, who earn their bread by respectable industry and are often the main support of their families. It is true that I have heard and could tell grievous stories of the wild, half-savage state of the women and girls in some districts, in some factories, under some bad or careless masters; but that is not the side of things to which I wish to draw attention: it is rather to the *inevitable* results of non-domestic labour for women and to the special duties it imposes on those of a higher class. In the first place, there are the obvious results of the absence of married women from their homes, an absence which I believe we may fairly state, should, in the majority of instances, be discouraged by every possible moral means, since the workman must be very wretched indeed before his wife's absence can be a source of real gain. Then there is the utter want of domestic teaching and training during the most important years of youth. How to help this is no easy matter, since, whatever we may do in regard to married women, we certainly cannot prevent girls from being employed in factories, nor, in the present state of civilisation, provide other work for them if we could so prevent them; and lastly, there is what I believe to be the sure deterioration of health; we are as yet only in the second generation, but any one who has closely watched the effect of ten hours in England and twelve hours in France, of labour chiefly conducted in a standing posture amidst the noise and, in some cases, the necessary heat of factories, upon young growing girls, knows how the weakly ones are carried off by consumption, or any hereditary morbid tendency, and what the subtle nervous strain must be upon all.

Believe me, there is enough in the necessary, and what we have come to consider the natural, features of modern industry, to arouse the earnest conscientious attention of the wives and daughters of employers, and of all good women whom Providence has gifted with education and means. And the need is peculiar, and so must the help be. Except in some isolated cases we will hope and believe that it is not, strictly speaking, missionary work. It is not to teach the wholly uneducated, to reclaim the drunkard, to rouse the sinner; there is enough of that to be done in England and France, but it is not of that I am speaking. Help and teaching and friendliness are wanting for the respectable workwoman, such as have already been partly provided for the respectable workman. When Lord Brougham, Dr Birkbeck, and others, started the Mechanics' Institution, when classes, and lectures, and savings' banks, and co-operative societies were created, it was to help those who were willing and able to help themselves, if put in the way. The Christian ministers of all churches and persuasions have generally of late years entered with warmth into these secular plans for the advantage of their flocks; and it is just such an intelligent effort, carried out by earnest and intellectual women, which is required wherever numbers of their own sex are gathered together to labour. I do not mean that the plans should be identical, but that the level of effort and of sympathy should be the same. I would see every large factory sustained in its moral advancement by female teachers capable of entering into the moral and physical life of the people; I would see evening classes, co-operative societies; and mothers' meetings of an upper sort, vigorously set on foot. I would have the amusements of the younger people guided, restrained, and elevated; and those women of the middle classes who crave for more activity, yet do not feel that they possess the peculiar characteristics needed to visit the very poor, to nurse the very sick, or to reform the very degraded, remember that there is an immense, an inspiriting field of exertion, one demanding intellect, study, and sympathetic apprehension of the social forces now at work in England and France, which calls for their religious endeavour and intelligent will.

The Balance of Public Opinion in Regard to Woman's Work

(reprinted from *The English Woman's Journal*, July 1862)

I should not this year have brought before the Social Economy Section a subject which has already received such ample ventilation in the columns of the public press, but for a sense of the responsibility under which it appears to me that we all labour in regard to what has been termed the movement in favour of woman's work, which makes me anxious to take this opportunity of stating my individual opinion, based upon the varied experience of five years.

I had at first intended to entitle this short paper the Progress of Public Opinion in Regard to Woman's Work, but in reconsidering the matter, I thought that the *Balance* of Public Opinion was a better name, inasmuch as the extreme complication of the question renders mere progression in any direction a dangerous matter, unless careful limitations are specified.

And here let me say that I think of all the many classes whose interests have received benefit from fair discussions at the five meetings hitherto held of the Association for the Promotion of Social Science, women owe the deepest debt of gratitude to those gentlemen who organised the Association.

From the first semi-private meeting at Lord Brougham's house, to which he referred in his Address last Thursday, and at which Mrs Jameson, Mrs Austin and Mrs Howitt were present, down to the present time; Lord Brougham and Mr George Hastings, and all the numerous gentlemen who have been brought in contact with the question, of whom I would specially name Lord Shaftesbury as President of our Society, have shown the utmost desire to give women fair play; and not only fair play, for they have so managed the meetings and discussions as to enable them to be carried on with perfect ease and propriety by all ladies desirous of taking part in any of the sections. I believe I may truly affirm that never before in the world's history have women met with such equal courtesy and true deference as that which has been shown them here.

For this reason, among many others, I feel that it peculiarly behoves women to show that they can appreciate and respond to this loyal justice on the part of men. To show that, being under no restraint and no repression, they can discuss the great question of social welfare, on which the ultimate fate of the nation in its corporate and its domestic life chiefly depends, with moderation and honest impartiality. And I do believe that, on referring to the newspaper reports, or examining the *Transactions* of the last five years, every one will admit that our sex fully deserved the noble confidence resposed in them by the gentlemen of this Association; that they have neither wasted its time in frivolities, nor offended it by one unwomanly word.

During this period an immense progress has in one sense been made in public opinion. The importance of all questions relating to the female population of the country has been admitted by the press and by the people. Nay, I believe that any Bill affecting the welfare of women would now receive more attention in Parliament than it would have done five years ago; and that many men would now feel doubly bound to plead the interests of those who could not there plead for themselves.

Since, therefore, there is no longer any occasion to strive to obtain a hearing, sure to be granted to us for every reasonable or practical purpose, I am doubly anxious that any discussion we may carry on this year should be marked by a desire to see and admit all sides of our question, and that we should each of us carefully state that which we believe to be truth.

Now, in summing up the papers, articles and speeches which have been everywhere promulgated on the question of woman's work, we find that at the threshold of the question we are met by two distinct theories, upon neither of which is it possible to speak or act exclusively, and yet it will make a great difference to our speech and to our action whether in the depths of intellectual and moral conviction we abide by the one or by the other theory. I will put it as simply and as shortly as possible: Do we *wish* to see the majority of women getting their own livelihood, or do we wish to see it provided for them by men? Are we trying to assist the female population of this country over a time of difficulty; or, are we seeking to develop a new state of social life?

I feel bound to say that I regard the question from a temporary point of view, and that I should greatly regret any change in the public opinion of all classes which would tend to make the men of this country more unmindful of the material welfare of the female members of their families.

When I brought up this question nearly three years ago at Bradford, I confined my observations to the surplus in the profession of the teacher. I took the statistics of the Governesses' Benevolent Institution in Harley Street, and urged as remedies for the terrible destitution endured by aged ladies, that parents of the middle class should either train their daughters to some useful art, however humble, or consider it their primary duty to insure their lives if they could not afford to lay by money for their female children. I showed that in a country like England, whose wealth is chiefly derived from commerce, the fluctuations of trade fall with peculiar hardship upon the defenceless sex. That not only do merchants fail, but banks also break, and that a horrible amount of real hunger and cold is undergone by many who have been ladies born and bred; while a larger proportion, though they may never know actual physical want, are forced into one overcrowded and perhaps distasteful profession, in which they spend their lives working for small salaries.

But I never wished or contemplated the mass of women becoming breadwinners. So far from being willing to see such a system encouraged, I think it is actually obtaining among us, through the operations of modern trade, to an injurious extent. With the greatest esteem for, and even gratitude to, many masters for the pains which they take for the instruction and moralisation of their workwomen, I do not believe our English factory system to be natural, and more especially the employment of married women away from their homes. I know all that may be said upon the other side; I know that any legislation on this topic would result in practical cruelty; that even rules imposed by the master of the factory would bear with harshness on the woman who may have a family to support, and a drunken or incapable husband. I believe that it is a point upon which we must allow free trade or that we shall fall into worse evils than those from which we now suffer. Nevertheless, the fact remains clear to my mind, that we are passing through a stage of civilisation which is to be regretted, and that her house and not the factory is a woman's happy and healthful sphere.

It is not possible to treat a subject like this in a scientific way. Philosophers who argue upon the laws which govern the development of men are almost always destined to see their theories pass away or fade into comparative oblivion before the century which gave them birth is gone. Rousseau is seldom heard of now; Fourier exists only as the prophet of a school; even the Political Economists no longer reign over the intellectual world as they did thirty years ago, when the Poor Law achieved the practical experiment of some of their principles. If, then, theories respecting masses of men are continually being broken to pieces, how much more impossible is it to argue from abstractions upon the nature of women; for a woman's life is certainly more individual, more centered in one house and one circle; and so it must be until the constitution of this world is changed. I can therefore only speak of women as I have seen and known them in different towns of this our country: in Birmingham, in Nottingham, in Edinburgh, in Dublin, in Leicester, in Hastings, in Glasgow. I speak of what I have seen of the lower classes, and of what I have heard from innumerable ladies, wives and daughters of squires, clergymen, doctors, lawyers, merchants. My opinions have been formed from these sources of information; and though I have found such ladies always willing and anxious in any plan for getting employment for their destitute sisters, I have always heard them lament when, from any circumstances, the family life of a district has suffered by the withdrawal of any large number of women from the home.

It may be asked, however, on what ground I have helped and sympathised with such a business as that conducted at the Victoria Press; a business which has commanded an extraordinary amount of popular sympathy for two years. I would answer that the reason why I was so glad to see it established and successful was not so much that women are employed in it, as that it is superintended by a woman. Since non-domestic labour is the rule for our present stage of national civilisation, it is exceedingly difficult to earn an honest livelihood in any other way, and if girls are allowed to spend ten hours a day spinning in a factory, they should also be allowed to spend them in printing, if that be a more remunerative occupation. But our *moral* sympathy is chiefly due to the Press on the score of Miss Faithfull's superintendence.

Were I asked if I should wish to see a regiment of women working in common printing offices under male supervision, I should answer No; or at least I should accept the idea with regret, and only on the principle that women must earn bread and butter. But were I asked whether I should be willing to see young women gathered together in printing offices or in the workshops of any mechanical trade, under efficient female supervision, then I should say that for the unmarried women it was, in the present state of the country, the one thing to be desired.

Before concluding this paper there is one point on which I wish to touch, because it is at the very root of the matter, and there is little good in our repeating year after year the old arguments on woman's work unless we are all content to face the serious questions which touch it on all sides. I allude to the difficulties imposed by the question of marriage. You have probably all seen and read the leading article which appeared in *The Times* of Monday the 9th; an article in which I entirely coincided, and upon which I should like to say a few words. The writer of that article expressed a considerable sympathy with woman's work, and made several observations which appeared to me marked by good taste and good feeling. But he stated that, after all, the question, though important, was a partial one, since the majority of women looked to married life as their happiest sphere, and that in the upper and middle ranks their entering married life would withdraw them from non-domestic labour.

This is to my mind a self-evident proposition, and I should like to place it in a light which, so far as I am aware, has never been cast upon it in any of the discussions; and which I believe would go far to clear it up to the satisfaction of all parties if my meaning were thoroughly understood.

When men who are good and sympathetic, and who, as we have every reason to believe, really wish well to their mothers, sisters, wives, and daughters, urge the claims of married life, in regard to the question of woman's work, what is it they mean?

What does married life mean in this Christian country, which professes and really does try and intend to carry out Bible maxims? I am not overstating the case; for the overwhelming majority of this kingdom, Protestants and Catholics, and even those who may be neither, are agreed in wishing to see Christian morality carried out in political and social life. Our schools, our reformatories, our teetotal societies, all prove this; and a book which preached pagan principles on any topic would have a bad chance of being circulated by Mr Mudie.

Now the household life in a Christian country has this very marked characteristic, that it is the primary unit in social organisation. The man alone, or the woman alone, is not strictly speaking that primary unit. With marriage and family life begins the great social chain which ascends from the house to the street, from the street to the parish, from the parish to the town, from the town to the country, and ends in the Government and in the Church.

The wife, in our civilisation, is the centre of domestic but also of social life. She is the mistress of a social circle and of a group of children and of servants. When sensible men say that the vast majority of women are destined to marriage, what they mean, the idea which really lies at the bottom of their minds, is, that were it otherwise the whole constitution of modern society would literally go to pieces. We should be like a house built without mortar, ready to be blown down in every high wind.

As I believe, therefore, firmly, that the married household is the first constituent element in national life, so I consequently believe that the immense majority of women are, and ought to be, employed in the noble duties which go to make up the Christian household; and while I fully admit the principle of vocations to religious and also to intellectual and practical life apart from marriage, I think that people are quite right who say that these will ever be, and ought ever to be, in the minority.

Female Life in Prison

(reprinted from *The English Woman's Journal*, September 1862)

A remarkable book has lately been running the round of the public press, which reads like a series of illustrations of *La Folie Lucide*. It is so fresh and lifelike, so full of the delicate painting which alone can do justice to the complexity of the feminine organisation, even when set all astray, that we believe conclusions may be as honestly drawn from its pages as from observations at first hand; for the Prison Matron has been trained by long experience, and her powers are enriched by comparison, until both observation and deduction are extraordinarily acute.

The author, whose name is not given, says on the first pages that she wishes it 'to be clearly understood that these are the honest reminiscences of one retired from Government service – that many years of prison experience enable her to offer her readers a fair statement of life and adventure at Brixton and Millbank prisons, and afford her the opportunity of attempting to convey some faint impression of the strange hearts that beat – perhaps break, a few of them – within the high walls between them and general society.' Thus the stories she tells are revelations of what passes within those dismal walls, whose secrets are so seldom told; the sequels, be it remembered, to the stories of the police court and of the court of assize which people *do* read over their breakfast tables, and which usually end thus – 'The jury, after some deliberation, returned a verdict of guilty; White, or Jones, or Brown, was sentenced to six years' penal servitude'; or 'Mr Justice Byles, in addressing the prisoner, said her case was one of the worst possible character, and he should therefore inflict upon her the heaviest sentence which the law allowed. His lordship then sentenced the prisoner to ten years' penal servitude.' Sometimes, too, we read that the sentence of death to be inflicted for child murder, or for making away with an intolerable husband, is commuted, by the Queen's gracious pleasure, to 'penal servitude for life'. For us that is the end of the drama we have been following with sad and breathless interest; the great curtain of stone and brick drops down before the sinful victim who, after occupying public attention for a brief space, is seen and heard no more.

Yet do they live, and count as we do the days of the week and the days of the month. Breakfast and dinner and supper arrive and pass for this dreary population, and each knows that it is the 1st of September, 1862, as well as any reader who glances over these pages. For the date which to you means Magazine day, or bird-shooting day, day for idling on the seashore or sketching in a Welsh valley, to them means a certain notch in the stick, actual or imaginary, on which are reckoned the days of penal servitude.

Millbank is an immense ugly mass of brickwork near Vauxhall Bridge; one side of it extends close to the back of the handsome new houses in Victoria Street, Westminster. It is a startling thing to go to a dinner-party in one of these houses, and in ascending the stairs, if perchance the painted windows are open, to see the huge frowning walls, brooding like Nemesis over our gay and kindly social life. One asks where is the deep-seated flaw, when a handsome dinner table, with its silver, its glass, its flowers, its courteous travelled host, and even the devoted clergymen who frequent that board, have as immediate pendant that frightful dwelling and that dreary crew? Are they of the same humanity, that accomplished woman with the Etruscan ornaments, attending so sweetly to her husband's guests, and that female fiend who last week knocked down three men, smashed nine windows, broke her scanty furniture into little bits, tore up her sheets into strips, and coolly begged the scared officials to wait 'until she had finished her blanket'?

There are children too in that household, pretty curled darlings in white worked frocks and little fat bare legs and red shoes, who come down and sit by their Papa at dessert, and have figs and raisins, and a teaspoonful of port wine in spite of Mamma's fore-boding remonstrances. In Millbank, just at the back, is a female creature who made away with two children because their father deserted her, and she was going on a journey and she didn't know what to do with them, etc.

Millbank, when the writer was a child, occupied a large open space where it was possible to find daisies and buttercups, and always dimly represented a country walk. The ground-plan of the building resembles a wheel, the governor's house occupying a circle in the centre, from which radiate six piles of building, terminating externally in towers. The governor was supposed by the little London child who ran about picking the daisies, to sit permanently in the middle of this wheel, with eyes preternaturally enabled to look in six directions at once; to be a sort of monstrous man-spider in his web. The neighbourhood has been built over; social life, as has been described, creeps up nearer and nearer, perhaps not an unapt symbol of the more kindly theories which constantly increase as to the treatment of criminals; but the vast prison is there, stern and immobile as ever. It is said to have cost half a million sterling; and may well hold its own and decline to be packed up like a Crystal Palace, or the work of any amateur or virtuoso.

It is a prison for male and female convicts. In charge of the female compartment are assistant matrons on probation, assistant matrons, reception-matron, principal matrons, latterly a chief matron on whom the practical working of the prison really devolves. The sole superintendence is now vested in Mrs Gibson.

The arrival of female prisoners at Millbank, says our informant, is 'unfortunately almost an everyday occurrence – the great sea of crime is never still, and its waves are ever breaking against the grim front of our penitentiary. These prisoners are not arriving from the county gaols – from Gloucester, York, Stafford, etc. – they are coming direct from the Central Criminal Court, etc., with the sentence of the judge still ringing in their ears; or back from Fulham and Brixton prisons, where they have insulted officers, or set the rules of discipline at defiance, and so are returned to Millbank, where there is little association, a stricter silence, and work more hard.'

Of all the ceremonies of reception, that of hair-cutting appears to cause the most dismay. One will bear it with stoicism, but a second will weep passionately, a third will have a shivering fit over it, and a fourth will pray to be spared the indignity, and implore the matron on her knees to go to the lady-superintendent, and state her case for her. A story is given of one old woman of sixty, 'with about the same number of grey hairs to her head'. She was an old prison-bird, had spent two-thirds of her life in prison, and was as vain of her personal appearance as any girl of seventeen.

'No, Miss B.,' she said to the operator, after catching sight of the scissors, and drawing herself up with the haughtiness of a duchess – 'not this time, if you please, Miss B. It can't be done.' But Miss B. replied that it could be done, and was absolutely necessary to be done before the prisoner left the room. 'Things have altered a little, Miss B., since I saw you last, I can assure you. You've no power to touch a hair of my head, Mum.' 'How's that?' 'If you please, Mum, I'm married,' and the old woman regarded the matron with undisguised triumph. 'And what's that to do with it? – sit down – you really must sit down.' 'What's that to do with it?' shrieked the old woman indignantly, '*why, it's my husband's hair now*; and you daren't touch it according to law. It belongs to my husband, not to me, and you've no right to touch it. Lord bless you, the Queen of England daren't lay a finger on it now.'

When she found that this argument was unavailable with the operator, she demanded to see the governor: he knew the law of England of course; and after the cruel deed was performed she vowed to make a full statement to the directors on the next board meeting, and begged to have her name put down to see those directors at once. Such an infamous violation of the laws of her country she had never been witness to in her time!

It would appear that the discussions concerning the property of married women had been fully appreciated by the class from which our prisoners are chiefly drawn, and that the women had acuteness enough to draw a meagre though imaginary consolation from the disabilities under which they labour! It may well be conceived, however, that even kicking, scratching, and swearing, as sometimes occur, are of no avail; and that with 'a registry of name, shortening of hair, a tepid bath, a change of the dress in which they are received to the brown serge, blue check apron, and muslin cap of prison uniform, the key turned upon a cell in "the solitary ward", and "one more unfortunate" is added to the list.'

We will not take up our space with describing the prison routine, though the account given of it in this book is curious and interesting, but turn our attention to the two classes of inmates: the prison officials and the criminals. The matrons are supposed in each case to have attained the age of five or six and twenty years before entering the service, 'although the rule is not rigidly enforced in this respect, and occasionally young fair faces, that have not seen one and twenty summers, appear in the ranks, to grow aged and careworn before their natural time. The prisons are no place for such innocent and inexperienced youth, and within the last year, I believe, the directors have very wisely resolved to more strictly enforce the rule alluded to. . . . The advantages of a service of this kind to respectable young women are not to be lightly disregarded, notwithstanding that the services are arduous, and the prisoners not the most cheerful or refined society. An assistant matron enters the service at a salary of £35 per annum – from which salary is deducted 3s. 4d, a month for the uniform dress – and rises £1 a year. In case of promotion to matron, an event likely to occur in the course of three or four years' service, the salary is £40 per annum, with an increase of 25s. each year. And in the event of rising to the post of principal matron – far from an impossibility before ten years' service is concluded – the salary is £50 per annum, with a yearly increase thereto of £1 10s. Encouragement to persevere in their duties is freely offered to these Government servants, and a life pension awaits them at the end of ten years' service.'

These conditions are far more favourable than women usually secure in their work; on the other hand, the duties are heavy. The prison matron is at her post from 6 in the morning till 9 in the evening three days a week; and from 6 till 6 on the other three. There is a 'Sunday out' occasionally, and during the year there are fourteen days' holidays, from which are deducted those days of sick leave, which are unfortunately not few and far between, the hours being long and the service arduous. The author of the book appeals earnestly against the overtask of strength to which the matrons are subjected; the average work being fourteen hours a day, 'too much labour – and such labour! – for any women not blessed with an undue amount of robustness and muscular power'. We recommend this chapter on the Matrons to all our readers who may be interested in the organisation of the higher and more responsible kinds of female labour. Mrs Jameson mentions the Brixton and Fulham establishments, into which the convicts successively pass from Millbank, and gives several pages of her 'Letter to Lord John Russell' to the subject of the superintendence of female convicts. They should be re-read in connection with this book.

Of the prisoners, numerous biographical stories are told, and many of those whose names were once familiar in the newspapers reappear here under their own or assumed names. Among the former is Celestina Sommer, who stood her trial for the murder of her daughter in April, 1856. The 'circumstances of the murder were peculiarly bold and cruel, and the sentence of the court was death – a sentence that, to the surprise and dissatisfaction of the public, was commuted to penal servitude for life; and Celestina Sommer, in due course, became an inmate of Millbank Prison, Westminster'. She is described as being a pale-faced, fair-haired woman, of spare form, and below the middle height; a quiet, well-ordered prisoner, with a horror of the other women, and partial to her own cell, and her work therein. She behaved well, and after a time was draughted off to Brixton, where symptoms of insanity began to develop. The author does not believe she ever fretted much about the murder; 'it was the peculiar method in her madness to forget it, or if not to forget, at least to regard it as an event of no importance to her future welfare'. Her particular forte she considered to be singing, and used to inform the other invalids in the infirmary that she had been one of the opera chorus before her marriage.

The bulk of the prisoners, however, are not darkly mysterious beings of an intelligent or reflective order, but wild women, in whom a certain uproarious violence seems the uniform characteristic. A sort of incontrollable desire for excitement seizes them at intervals, which, as they cannot get spirits to drink, or indulge in fighting or merry-making, as they did in the world, results in 'breaking out', or 'smashing'. Many women, in defiance of a day or two's bread and water, will suddenly shout across the airing-yard, or from one cell to another, with a noise all the more vehement for the long restraint to which they have been subjected; and such a proceeding, if remonstrated with, is generally followed by a 'smashing of windows, and a tearing up of sheets and blankets, that will often affect half a ward with a similar example, if the delinquent is not speedily carried off to refractory quarters'. In fact, 'breaking out', or 'smashing', is a highly contagious disease, and flies like wildfire. So great is the need of excitement in these unregulated natures, that the prisoners are occasionally known to arrange beforehand, 'in a quiet, aggravating manner', for a systematic smashing of windows and tearing of sheets and blankets; such conversations as this occurring: 'Miss G., I'm going to break out tonight.' 'Oh, nonsense! You won't think of any such folly, I'm sure.' Persuasion is generally attempted first, as breakings out are exceedingly inconvenient. 'I'm sure I shall then.' 'What for?' 'Well, I've made up my mind, that's what for; I shall break out tonight, see if I don't!' 'Has anyone offended you?' 'N——no, but I *must* break out. It's so dull here, I'm sure to break out.' 'And then you'll go to the "dark." ' 'I want to go to the "dark," ' is the answer. And then the amiable promise is frequently kept, and the 'glass shatters out of the window frames, and strips of sheets and blankets are passed through, or left in a heap in the cells, and the guards are sent for, and there is a scuffling, and fighting, and scratching, and screaming, that Pandemonium might equal – nothing else.'

Considerable method is sometimes shown, as in one instance where two women contrived to lock up a matron in an empty cell, and then dashed down the ward, darting from one cell to another, all of which were at the moment in process of ventilation, and destroyed the windows successively, to the number of 350 panes of glass. One desperate woman, of the name of McDermot, after having smashed her windows, was caught in the usual act of destroying her blanket, by the men, who came sooner than she expected. 'Hollo,' was her salutation, 'you're in a hurry this morning! just wait, there's good fellows, till I've finished my blanket; I won't keep you more than half a minute.' And the blanket being finished, 'with promptitude and despatch', she went off quietly to the 'dark'.

The really contagious influence of this sort of thing upon the nerves is shown by the confession of a matron who has since left the service, who told the author of the book (in confidence, and with a comical expression of horror on her countenance) that she was afraid she should break out herself, the temptation appeared so irresistible. 'I have been used to so different a life – father, mother, brothers and sisters, all round me, light-hearted and happy – that it is like becoming a prisoner oneself to follow this tedious and incessant occupation. I assure you, Miss ——, that, when I hear the glass shattering, and the women screaming, my temples throb, my ears tingle, and I want to break something dreadfully!' This singular confession is a commentary on the whole question, and leads one to consider what could be devised as a safety valve, or whether these outbursts must be submitted to as part of the inevitable reaction against necessary punishment by sequestration of the individual from society. The daily walk by twos and twos round the prison yard, the prayers and sermon in chapel, do not sufficiently diversify the monotonous tenor of prison days, to carry off the nervous electricity of these diseased organisations.

Now and then the women become insane, but it is hard to say whether the seeds of madness lurked in them before or no. Celestina Sommer, condemned for a brutal murder of her child, after whom, however, she never seemed to fret, gradually weakened in intellect, and had finally to be sent to Fisherton Asylum. Even at the best of times, their tricks and their daring are on the verge of sanity. Imagine women, who, for the sake of being sent to the Infirmary ward, will coolly pound a piece of glass to powder and bring on internal haemorrhage; twist staylaces round their necks till respiration almost ceases, or deliberately hang themselves with an eye to the chance of being cut down in time! Ingenious to the last degree is this latter invention. The woman hangs herself to the inside of her door by passing her bit of rope or string through the ventilator, stands meanwhile on her pail full of water, which she kicks away from her, sending the water streaming underneath the door over the flagstones of the ward. The water catches the matron's eye; the door is attempted to be opened; 'a heavy swinging substance, to the matron's horror, is felt inside the door; extra assistance is called, the woman is cut down, and the doctor is hastily sent for.' The woman, half dead, or wholly unconscious, is sent to the infirmary – triumphant! In one instance, a prisoner named Eliza Burchall planned a scheme with another woman, whereby Burchall was to hang herself at a given moment, and the other was to bring a matron on some excuse to Burchall's cell. Burchall, 'hearing footsteps approaching a few minutes before the time appointed, leaped off as arranged, and the footsteps *passed the door and went on down the ward.*' When the confederate arrived with the matron, some three minutes later, Burchall was found hanging by the neck, to all appearance dead, and it was only by the unceasing exertions of the surgeon, Mr Rendle, that the wretched creature was brought back to life, after remaining unconscious three and forty hours!

The histories here given of separate prisoners are in the highest degree interesting as psychological studies. What can chivalric worshippers of 'angelic womanhood' say to Sarah Baker, a very young, delicate woman, 'who soon became distinguished from the mass as an obedient, even cheerful prisoner'. She was sentenced for having thrown her child down a pit-shaft! and who (lest the reader might excuse the deed on the plea of mortal anguish) is reported to have spoken about it to another female prisoner in words so cruelly coarse that they are unfit to be copied here. In July, 1863, Baker will probably obtain her liberty – life women standing a chance of freedom after ten years.

Mary May was a prisoner of a different stamp – only in for petty larceny; a little weak in the wits, but affecting a supreme contempt for the other prisoners. 'I can't speak to 'em, Miss,' she would say confidentially, 'they are such a set of rubbitch.' She was partial to flattery and telling fortunes, and would promise the matron that gold and a young man with dark eyes were awaiting her. 'I dreamt of him last night, Miss!' But fortune-telling did not answer. 'The matron's fortune was in locking and unlocking, keeping a strict watch on her prisoners, and rising one pound five a year!' Then there was Solomons, an educated and even refined Jewess, in for receiving stolen goods – whose friends used to come to see her in silks and satins. And Trent, who was such a good dressmaker that she was employed by the matrons to make their best dresses, but who objected strongly to common dresses, because it was 'exceedingly annoying to be troubled with bad materials. When you have a nice silk, I'll think about it.' Eight-pence a week had been the sum allowed to dressmakers before her time, and Trent struck for a shilling – and got it!

We have already said that from Millbank the quietly behaved women are in time transferred to Brixton; from Brixton the very best are draughted off to Fulham Refuge, which was established in 1856. It is designed as an intermediate condition of partial restraint mixed with industrial training; and the accommodation is naturally limited, the daily average during 1860 being 174. The principal employment is laundry-work. Lastly, there is the voluntary Prisoners' Aid Society, which already affords great help to the discharged, and which, by means of a Government grant, might be rendered more comprehensive, 'and should be the Fourth estate for *all* prisoners who hope to lead better lives'.

These few pages do scant justice to a most remarkable book. The anonymous 'Prison Matron' possesses sense, kindness, and humour: and her pages are fresh and true beyond the wont of books in these days. It is already in the hands of circulating-library readers all over England. It is our province to hope and to urge that its innumerable suggestive stories, and its ample details of a life secluded from public observation, may bear practical fruit in local efforts for education and local dealings with the criminal class, since this is nourished in the bosom of our town and country populations, and, after the few years of penal servitude, thither ordinarily returns. Since we are told that discharged prisoners are furnished with a railway ticket for the neighbourhood of their 'friends', it may fairly be held that their condition, past, present, and future, is a matter, not only of Christian charity, but of practical general concern.

A Review of the Last Six Years

(reprinted from *The English Woman's Journal*, February 1864)

Six years have now elapsed since *The English Woman's Journal* was started, and this number for February, 1864, being the last of the twelfth volume, I have thought that it might be useful to say a few words to our readers regarding the motives which led to its commencement, and the reasons which have induced those who started it to carry out their undertaking in one particular way. Numerous questions are constantly (and very naturally) asked by friends who come to the office, of those who conduct its practical business; observations are made as to the relative size and the special nature of the contents of the Journal, and many suggestions made in a kindly spirit for its supposed possible improvement. It is to the answering of these questions, observations, or suggestions that I would now address myself; and I do so individually, because until lately I possessed immediate control over the matter in hand; and because considerable sums of money have been, from first to last, practically confided to me for the purposes of our cause.

Ten years ago, although there was an earnest and active group of people, deeply interested in all that relates to female education and industry, and to the reform of the laws affecting the property of married women, and though efforts were being made in many directions for the bettering of the condition of the mass of single women in this country, there was no centre of meeting, nor any one work which could be said to draw together the names of the ladies so actively employed. But the separate exertions carried on were surely and solidly laying the foundations of what has now taken its place as one of the chief social 'movements' of the day. In Education, a great start was made by the erection of the 'Ladies' Colleges'. Both at the one located in Harley Street, and at the one carried on in Bedford Square, under the auspices of a most generous and indefatigable foundress, the girl pupils were brought in contact with the minds of several eminent professors of the day. The whole standard of female education in regard to history, the dead and living languages, mathematics, and musical science was changed. The pupils were made to understand what is knowledge and what is not, and to appreciate as well as to acquire.

In literature many women had achieved a solid reputation, among whom perhaps Miss Martineau took the first place, from the number and practical nature of her forcible writings; and one other mind, deep, thoughtful, and sincere, had been frequently attracted away from the more intellectual and artistic pursuits in which it was chiefly distinguished, towards the problems of woman's life and work: I refer to Mrs Jameson. The oftener I recur to those former years, and to the thoughts and plans current among the younger generation of my sex, the greater is, I feel, our debt of gratitude to her, for the influence she exerted, not only in her writings, but in her own person. She was ever ready to give time, thought, and her best judgment to the plans of her younger friends; and her long experience of life, and strong sense of religious and social morality, acted as a firm restraint against all antisocial theories, such as have occasionally been started, apropos of these questions, in other countries. She was thoroughly liberal, widely cultivated, not at all cowardly as to the trying of experiments (such as the medical career), but she always appeared to act from some inner law of womanhood, which it was impossible for her to infringe, and which imparted grace and consistency to everything she said and did.

The department of intellectual activity in which she naturally took most interest was that of the artist; and a group of young women, who pursued art in one or other of its various branches, were among her constant visitors during her sojourns in London. It was, however, to all the problems connected with the care of the sick and the relief of the poor that her thoughts chiefly turned, in those intervals of leisure left by her own works on historical art. Her pursuits had led her to a lengthened residence in various continental cities, and she had investigated with zeal and care the institutions which are there so deeply rooted, and which may be said to supply the place of our poor law. The result in her mind was a strong belief in the efficiency of sisterhoods; and she embodied her opinions in two admirable lectures, entitled 'Sisters of Charity', and 'The Communion of Labour', which were personally delivered in the drawing-rooms of two lady friends, and afterwards reprinted by Longman. To these were finally appended her admirable 'Letter to Lord John Russell', in which she touches on many wants suffered by her countrywomen, and devotes some pages to the consideration of the medical question. This letter is one of the most remarkable productions of Mrs Jameson's pen. It is characterised by a simplicity and dignity which reveal the aged and experienced woman, willing to come forward and stake her well-won reputation for the sake of those younger than herself; it is written alike without heat and without timidity, and is a noble example of that style of writing in which the moral character of the author penetrates every sentence, and infuses an authority to which mere eloquence could never attain.

The general movement had attained the level I have attempted to describe, when a bill was introduced into parliament for securing the earnings of married women to their own discretionary use. It was presented in the Upper House by Lord Brougham, and in the Lower by Sir Erskine Perry. The long list of signatures was headed by the names of Anna Jameson and Mary Howitt, followed by numerous signatures of eminent women, among them that of Elizabeth Barrett Browning. In its immediate object this effort failed. The bill was not carried; but it undoubtedly exercised a strong influence in that clause of the ensuing Divorce Bill, which secures to *deserted wives* the use of their own earnings for themselves and their families; and in so doing, helped to prevent the recurrence of all the worst cases of misfortune resulting from the law; for whatever may be considered the abstract justice of the case, it was in cases of desertion or cruelty, when the husband, returning, swept off at a blow, the hard-accumulated earnings of his wife for her family, that bitter injustice chiefly resulted. Such cases are now under legal protection.

But this, though fairly to be laid to its credit, was far from the only effect of the defeated bill. It induced, throughout the spring and early summer of 1856, a lively discussion in the newspapers; and though ridicule was, in some instances, poured on its supporters, much real, warm, lasting sympathy was elicited, and many men came forward to give their help. Even more important was it that, in the effort to obtain signatures, people interested in the question were brought into communication in all parts of the kingdom, and that the germs of an effective movement were scattered far and wide. It is an act of justice to recall that the first idea, and much of the subsequent working consequent on the introduction of this bill, were due to Miss Leigh Smith, now Madame Bodichon, a lady since her marriage absent from England during the greater part of each year, but who has been, from first to last, an unfailing friend to the cause.

It was some six months later, in October, 1856, that a stray number of a periodical, professing to be edited by ladies, caught my eye in the window of a small shop in Edinburgh. On making some enquiries at the office, I found it to be a paper of a very harmless but very inefficient sort, full of tales, poetry, and occasionally articles on charities. The proprietor, however, wished to improve it, and Miss Isa Craig and I wrote several articles for him; and when I, shortly after, left England to spend the winter and spring abroad, Miss Craig undertook to watch *The Waverley Journal* for me, as I had good hopes that it might eventually be pressed into our London work. When in Rome, in April, 1857, I received from Scotland what was in fact an offer of the entire control of this periodical; and then it was that I asked Mrs Jameson's advice as to the desirability of attempting to devote such a magazine to the special objects of woman's work. She entered into the point with her usual sympathetic kindness, and gave her advice in the affirmative. Thereupon, I wrote back to Scotland, that I would return in June, and take the control of *The Waverley Journal*, which I accordingly did; and Madame Bodichon placed in the hands of Mr George Hastings a considerable sum of money, to be applied to the improvement, and if desirable, the purchase of the magazine. Negotiations with the proprietor were entered into, which, however, proved unsatisfactory; and Mr Hastings advised us not to spend money and effort over a property which did not appear to be worth either, but to start afresh, with a new journal of our own, in London. It took some months to arrange our plans; but at the close of 1857, the editorship of *The Waverley Journal* was relinquished, and in March, 1858, *The English Woman's Journal* was commenced, Miss Hays and myself being joint editors; the necessary money having been collected from various good friends to the cause, in the form of shares in a limited liability company. Six years have elapsed since that time, during which seventy-two numbers have been issued, at a cost of anxiety and responsibility far beyond what any merely literary journal could entail, inasmuch as the subject matter of this particular periodical touched at all points upon the dearest interests and safeguards of civilised society, was partially connected with the religious views of various bodies of Christians, and presented in other directions a perfect pitfall of ridicule, ever ready to open beneath the feet of the conductors.

It now needs to be considered in what relation this journal could be expected to stand to the rest of the periodical press. Had it from the first any hope, any expectation, any *wish* to come forward in the same field with the able monthlies, which contained the best writing of the day? To this question an emphatic *no* must at once be given. Such an idea would have been perfectly hopeless and absurd, and indeed self-destructive; for a subject cannot be at once popular and unpopular, rich and poor, clothed in purple and fine linen, and undergoing incessant fear of a social martyrdom. If it had been wished to start a brilliant and successful magazine, some eminent publisher should have been secured and persuaded to undertake active pecuniary interest and risk; all the best-known female writers should have been engaged, 'regardless of expense'; *and then* – goodbye to the advocacy of any subject which would have entailed a breath of ridicule; goodbye to any thorough expression of opinion; goodbye to the humble but ceaseless struggle of all these years, and to the results which have sprung up around the small office where so many workers collected together, because the purpose and the plan were *honestly conceived and carried out.*

A few dates and details as to the different practical branches of the movement may not be out of place, in connection with this slight sketch of the history of the Journal. The first of those who joined the early work was Miss Maria Rye. At the time of the proposed introduction of a bill on the property of married women, our attention was attracted by an excellent article on the subject in the *English Woman's Domestic Magazine*, signed 'M. S. R.'. An enquiry made of the editor was answered by a visit from the young writer, then living near London with her family, and devoting her leisure to literature. From that time she became the fast friend of her fellow-workers; and when it became necessary to engage a secretary to manage the large amount of correspondence which the bill entailed, Miss Rye became that secretary, and was immediately brought in contact with its supporters, many of whom were men of eminence. In the summer of 1857, Miss Craig first came from Edinburgh, and became assistant secretary to the National Association for the Promotion of Social Science, then in the course of formation. A year and a half later, in November, 1858, Miss Faithfull was first introduced at the office of *The English Woman's Journal*, with the work of which, for some months, she was more or less connected. In June, 1859, Miss Boucherett came to London, desirous of organising the Society for Promoting the Employment of Women, and found in the same office many friends and helpers; and for a few months Miss Sarah Lewin, and afterwards Miss Faithfull, were secretaries to the infant society, which was finally organised in connection with the Social Science Association.

It was now, in the winter of 1859–60, that the group of works, which have since been frequently reviewed by the press, took their rise – all of them in a certain way linked to Miss Boucherett's society, except the Victoria Press, which Miss Faithfull undertook, on a separate basis, in connection with a gentleman, who had for many years desired to see women employed in printing. At the same time the Law-copying Office was started by the society, and Miss Rye installed as manager; and Miss Boucherett herself undertook the direct superintendence of the Middle-class School, intended to fit young women for taking situations as book-keepers, cashiers, and clerks.

A Register was likewise formally opened at the office of the society, and absorbed into itself a small register previously kept in the office of the Journal; but as the two offices were at this time brought under one roof, at 19, Langham Place, the register work has since been carried on almost without distinction in either room.

The Reading Room, which had been started over the little office which the Journal originally inhabited in Prince's Street, Cavendish Square, was at the same time moved into the same large house, secured by the munificence of one lady for the three institutions, and where they have now remained for four years.

The Emigration movement, in which Miss Rye's name has lately become prominent, grew naturally and imperceptibly out of the work of the Law-copying Office. So many women applied for employment, to whom it was impossible to give it, that Miss Rye tried to assist some of them to emigrate. One by one was thus helped with a little money, lent by friends for the purpose, and furnished with letters of introduction. Little by little her time became absorbed by constant claims of the kind. The law-copying business was carried on under a forewoman, and Miss Rye gave herself up to the assisting of emigrants, and at last determined on taking a voyage to our colonies in one of the emigration ships, that she might herself investigate the condition of the labour market, and the best means for supplying needs at home and abroad. Miss Jane Lewin has been Miss Rye's associate in the work from the first, and now superintends the Middle-class Emigration Society at 12, Portugal Street, W.C.

The last point of interest in the movement is the experimental examination of girls, conducted by the examiners of the University of Cambridge, which took place the first week of December last, at which upwards of ninety students presented themselves, and which may ultimately lead to the full opening of the examinations of both universities. The consent of the Cambridge authorities was obtained chiefly through the indefatigable exertions of Miss Emily Davies.

I must not omit to add that the present editor of the Journal is also one of its oldest contributors, under the signature of 'Asterisk', and 'E'. Her first connection with the office arose more than six years ago, when she actively interested herself in the setting aside of one of the great London swimming baths for the use of ladies on one day of the week. A recent shipwreck had roused public attention to the desirability of teaching women to swim; and Miss Martineau, in particular, had written a very forcible article in one of the periodicals. Chiefly by the exertions of 'Asterisk', the Marylebone swimming bath was made available, and a teacher engaged; and I believe there is now an excellent establishment at Brighton similar to those on the French coast. Our constant secretary, Miss Sarah Lewin, occupies her old post, most of her time being devoted to the society's register.

In this general outline no mention has been made of the many many kind friends and helpers who have encircled us with help and sympathy from the first, and who have been the main stay of those whose names happened to become more prominent. One lady, who has often signed herself as 'A Clergyman's Wife', in the pages of our 'Open Council', has been indefatigable, particularly in the department of emigration. The society's office has received constant assistance from members of the committee; and a young friend has lately undertaken a large share of the regular duty, during the temporary absence on the continent of the lady who has for nearly four years occupied the post of secretary – Miss Crowe. There is no possibility of recording the manifold acts of help and kindness which have taken place on all sides; and when I look back over these years, and compare the measure of our success with the plans which floated before our inexperienced eyes at the beginning, I am doubly impressed with the power of individual character and individual effort. In this sort of work, as in commercial barter, an adequate price must be paid down for every result. 'Though the mills of God grind slowly, yet they grind exceeding small,' says Longfellow, translating from a German poet; and whoso wishes to achieve any lasting good, however small in quantity or humble in kind, must pay down true coin, of motive and practice, of outline and of detail.

This is the more imperative, because, in any purely secular work, it is next to impossible to secure those peculiar benefits which spring from thorough organisation, by which the weak are sustained, the idle stimulated, the unsteady held in check. Any twenty people will obey a common religious authority, and they will obey the law of the land, when it enforces measures for its own defence (as in the army and navy), or when it enforces the fulfilment of contracts, as in the different relations of master and workman. But when simple benevolent work is in question, which is carried on, neither by the direct authority of a religious body, nor by the principle of pecuniary contracts, it is next to impossible to combine a number of people in any reasonably permanent or satisfactory manner. There is a want of organic coherence in the elements of human character, and this is why the best workers are apt to lament the difficulties of working through committees, even when these committees are formed of really sympathising people. Then it is that the personal worth of every individual tells conspicuously upon the matter in hand; or rather we may say that, *without* personal worthiness, there is really no achievement at all. Societies and committees have no inherent aptitude in getting through work; indeed, it may be doubted whether some of the *momentum* is not actually lost in the friction they entail. Their great use is in offering a guarantee for the funds subscribed by the public; the wisdom of the redistribution is purely according to the honesty and the energy of the individual members to whom any branch is committed. A flaw in the instrument is a flaw in the result, to a much greater extent than in the working out of a system. Among the hundreds of thousands of Wesleyan Methodists, all backing each other up by that mighty power of religious communion, the inferior capacity – the slacker zeal of some members, are hardly visible, being so intimately blended with the common stock. But let none argue thus in choosing helpers for a secular work; such work lacks the fusing element, and each atom stands out, hard or soft, round or square, crooked or straight, as the case may be. Even worth will hardly save weakness, and strength carries its own ends in lower spheres. To those who watch with yearning anxiety the progress of a movement like ours, the great source of hope and cheerfulness lies in the attainment of a thorough conviction that, however much it may fail in rounded unity of action, no effort, no thought, no single, true, unselfish exertion of one for another, amidst all the many people gathered together in its progress, has been in vain.

Jessie Boucherett

(1825–1905)

Jessie Boucherett was the youngest daughter of Louisa Pigou and Ayscogne Boucherett, the High Sheriff of Lincolnshire. After completing her education at a boarding school in Stratford-upon-Avon, she helped to run a dispensary and cottage hospital in Market Rasen. Her elder sister, Louisa, was a pioneer in the movement to board out pauper children and it was this sort of philanthropic work which was considered to be a suitable occupation for the daughters of a country squire. But Jessie Boucherett turned her attention to feminist reform after reading a copy of *The English Woman's Journal* and, shortly after establishing herself at Langham Place, founded the Society for Promoting the Employment of Women. In 1863 she published *Hints on Self-Help: A Book for Young Women* in which she urged them to develop new skills in order to achieve financial independence. A member of the Kensington Society, she drafted the suffrage petition, with Barbara Bodichon and Emily Davies, which was presented to Parliament in 1866. In 1865, she revived *The English Woman's Journal*, which had ceased publication partly due to Bessie Rayner Parkes' ill health, changing its name to *The Englishwoman's Review* and remained the editor for the next six years. During this time she was active in the campaign for women's higher education and involved in the foundation of Girton College. In 1869 she contributed a chapter, entitled 'Provisions for Superfluous Women', to Josephine Butler's volume of essays, *Woman's Work and Woman's Culture* (London, 1869); in 1884, she contributed an essay, entitled 'The Industrial Movement', to *The Woman Question in Europe* edited by Theodore Stanton (New York, 1884); finally, in collaboration with Helen Blackburn, she wrote *The Condition of Working Women and the Factory Acts* (London) in 1896.

On the Obstacles to the Employment of Women

(reprinted from *The English Woman's Journal*, February 1860)

The fact revealed in the census of 1851, and brought into notice by the article on female employment in *The Edinburgh Review* for April, 1859, that two millions of our countrywomen are unmarried and have to maintain themselves, startled every thinking mind in the kingdom, and has done much to effect a change in public opinion, with regard to the expediency of opening fresh fields of labour to the industry of the weaker sex. Until that circumstance became known, benevolent persons were generally of opinion that as married life is the happiest lot for women, so all public plans and arrangements in relation to them should be made solely with a view to their occupying that position, for though it was always apparent that a considerable number of single women existed, and that some experienced difficulty in earning a livelihood, the greatness of their numbers was never suspected, nor was the cause of their difficulties understood. When, however, it was shown that one-third of the women of Great Britain were unmarried and unprovided for, except by such means as their own exertions might procure, it was at once perceived that to make all social arrangements on the supposition that women were almost invariably married, and supported by their husbands, was to build on a fallacy, and that these two millions of independent workers, if considered at all, must be regarded as their own 'bread-winners'.

Frightful accounts of their sufferings were almost at the same time made public. Stores in the newspapers revealed the lowness of the wages paid to needlewomen, and the cruel sufferings from overwork inflicted on milliners' apprentices. Workhouses were found to be overcrowded with able-bodied females, while charities were besieged by women praying to be provided either with employment or bread.

Thus roused, the public feeling began to show itself, and during the last few months many newspapers and periodicals have raised their voices to complain of the overcrowded condition of the few employments open to women, to plead for the enlargement of their sphere of industry, and to urge that every facility ought to be given to enable them to support themselves.

At last the leading journal itself was touched, and thus gave its fiat.

'We sincerely hope that a new system may be instituted at once, and that we may no longer see women who, like men, must needs turn often to labour for their bread, condemned, unlike men, to the ranks of one miserable and hopeless calling, or left with the single alternative of becoming, according to their positions, either distressed needlewomen or distressed governesses.' – *Times*, November 8th, 1859. The point, therefore, may be considered as decided that there is a deficiency of employment for women; that this deficiency is a serious evil; and that it is desirable to institute a new system by which the evil may be remedied.

The points, then, which it now concerns us to consider, are, in what the impediments consist which oppose themselves to the more general employment of women, and in what manner they can be the most expeditiously and effectually overcome. For this object the best plan will, perhaps, be to take each department of industry upon which women are now endeavouring to enter, by itself, and discuss the obstacles that lie in their path. We will begin with such employments as are interesting to the class of workers who stand highest in the social scale, and to whose fate attention has lately been drawn by the paper read at Bradford by Miss Bessie Parkes, and afterwards published and favorably commented on by *The Times* and various other newspapers. The ranks of the army of governesses are generally recruited from the upper division of the middle classes of society, though many belong to an inferior grade. Ladies who enter upon this occupation are not unfrequently the daughters of professional men, naval officers, and poor clergymen, but a very considerable number are also the daughters of tradesmen. Neither is there any doubt that far too many enter on the profession; that they compete with each other, undersell each other, and thus bring down their own value, till the salaries are reduced to a rate which renders it quite impossible for a person receiving only average pay to dress herself neatly, and at the same time lay by a provision for her old age. The only remedy for this state of things is to find some fresh occupation for the numbers of middle-class women who are obliged to earn their bread, and the occupation must be of a nature requiring intelligence rather than bodily strength.

The employments which most readily suggest themselves are

clerkships of various kinds. Women might be copying clerks in law offices, and clerks in banks; post-office clerks they sometimes are, but they might be thus employed far more frequently than is now the case. There is also another employment for which women would be eminently suitable. Many of the smaller shopkeepers in London, and probably in the country also, are unable to manage their own accounts or keep their books, the money they receive and expend is roughly written down, and once a month a regular accountant comes who examines into the details, strikes the balance, and sets everything to rights. Now, this is a profession that women could enter without the smallest inconvenience, and by which a considerable number could be comfortably supported.

When a tradesman has no son, it would surely be far better that he should bring up his daughters to succeed him in the business, than train them to the hopeless profession of a governess; for the large millinery establishments carried on by women show that, when properly taught, they are capable of conducting mercantile affairs. The obstacles to this social change are of two kinds; imaginary ones proceeding from prejudice, and those which are of a solid nature. An imaginary one is the impression that no profession is genteel but that of teaching, and that a woman would lose caste who employed herself in any other manner. Small account should be made of this however; for prejudices will never long withstand the money test. If women found they could gain a comfortable subsistence in an ungenteel manner, they would soon abandon their fanciful gentility.

Another obstacle is the impression that women are so intellectually inferior to men that they would be incapable of performing the duties of such offices in a satisfactory manner. Now this prejudice, like the former, would not long withstand the money test. If employers found that they could get female clerks to do their work as well as men, and at a cheaper rate, they would soon employ them in preference.

But the question is, could women be found who could fulfil these duties in a satisfactory manner, and if not, what is the reason? Does it proceed from the hopeless and irremediable cause of natural stupidity, or is it the badness of their education which occasions their incapacity? It is my belief that only a very few and exceptional women could *at present* be found who would be capable of performing the ordinary duties of a clerk. A gentleman who spoke on this subject at the meeting of the National Association for Promoting Social Science, at Bradford, stated that being anxious to make his daughters good arithmeticians, he directed their governesses to instruct them in the science, but received an answer from several in succession that, if he wished the young ladies to learn the rule of three, he must employ a tutor. None of these teachers, therefore, could have given satisfaction as accountants. In ladies' schools a master is invariably employed to instruct the pupils in arithmetic; now why should the schoolmistress put herself to this extra expense if it were not for the fact that none of the female teachers in the house understand it? It appears from these facts that although a few women of the middle ranks might now doubtless be found capable of acting as accountants, yet that the number of them is very small. The deficiency in point of grammar is almost as great as in regard to arithmetic. The writer knows a person who had passed two years as teacher in a school intended to prepare girls for governesses, who yet could not be trusted to write an ordinary business letter, on account of the frequent grammatical errors she committed; and as it is reasonable to suppose that her pupils were no better instructed than herself, we may conclude that none of them could take a situation as corresponding clerk. It is easy, however, to find a test by which this last point may be ascertained. Let any good grammarian request his children's governess to parse a sentence out of a book, and her manner of doing it will at once prove her capabilities.

Let us now examine whether this ignorance proceeds from imbecility, or is the result of inferior instruction. It is the general opinion of schoolmasters who teach boys and girls in classes together that the girls are the quickest at calculation, which does not look like natural inferiority; and abroad, both in France and parts of Germany, women are commonly employed as cashiers in shops, and as ticket clerks at small railway stations. French governesses, too, will almost always be found capable of explaining the rules of their own language, thus surely showing that there is no peculiar inaptitude in the female mind for understanding grammar and accounts, but simply that English women are not taught them properly. We think, then, that it may be fairly concluded that the one great and serious impediment to the general employment of women in situations requiring education and intelligence, is the general inferiority of the instruction they receive. Their great misfortune is that they are given no special training. This is not the case with men. If a boy has to earn his own living, he is educated for a profession or a trade. At fourteen a lad must decide whether he will be a sailor or an artilleryman, that he may receive the requisite instruction. A man who intends to enter the medical profession must study for three years. Very few men who have been educated for one profession are capable of turning to any other. A few of remarkable energy and talent have done so; but, as a general rule, a man must go on as he has begun. A man who has been educated for the church would not make a good merchant's clerk, and a first-rate lawyer would be puzzled to explain the accounts of a bank; while those who have received what is called a general education are usually found incapable of any profession or employment whatever.

Now this kind of teaching, which with men is the exception, is with women the rule. The education they receive is *invariably general*. With regard to the daughters of the aristocracy and of the more wealthy portion of the middle classes, it is perfectly just and reasonable that it should be so; for they are provided for, and will never have to struggle for bread. The object of their education is, as it ought to be, to render them agreeable and intelligent members of society, and a slight acquaintance with several subjects will tend to produce this effect far more than a thorough knowledge of a few. But a rule which is perfectly right applied to one class becomes injudicious, and even cruel, when extended to all.

We dwell on this point because we fear the anxiety to employ women is now so great, that benevolent men will give them occupation under the impression that persons who have received the ordinary education of a governess, and are considered qualified to teach, will be capable of any other employment which requires intelligence. The experiment thus tried is sure to fail: then the reaction will come, and we shall be told that attempts have been made to employ them, but that they proved unequal to their duties, and that, in fact, the female mind is so volatile, or so obtuse, or so something or other, as to be totally incapable of performing ordinary business transactions: and thus the very impression we seek to diminish will be strengthened tenfold.

There certainly now exist a small number of women who are capable of transacting business, a few have been fortunate enough to receive by some accident a boy's education, and some women of ability have taught themselves a considerable amount of practical knowledge; and if an employer be lucky enough to light on one of these, she will be sure to give satisfaction. But the great mass of women are not of this description; and if, by mistake, employment should be given to one who has received only the ordinary amount of education bestowed on governesses, let her employer on dismissing her say to himself, not that she has failed because she is a woman, but that unpractically educated people are incapable of practical work. If we would lessen the numbers now pressing into the already overcrowded profession of teaching, and enable women of the middle ranks to engage in other spheres of remunerative employment, our first step must be to provide them with a more practical education.

If we seek to discover the best means of so doing, we cannot do better than observe the method pursued to afford their brothers the means of earning their livelihood, and follow the same plan. There is scarcely a considerable town in England which does not possess its endowed school, where the sons of little tradespeople are provided with an excellent education at a rate considerably below cost price. In one which is about to be built, day scholars will be taught 'the principles of the Christian religion, reading, writing, arithmetic, book-keeping, geography, history, English literature and composition, the Latin, Greek, and French languages, the principles of natural philosophy, mathematics and algebra, and also such other arts and sciences as may seem from time to time expedient to the trustees' for four pounds a year, and boarders from a distance will be received for twenty pounds; and the whole country is full of other institutions of a similar description. These schools have a double effect; not only are the boys taught in them well educated, but they tend to raise the tone of education generally. The master of a private school must be able to offer yet greater advantages if he hope to compete against the good teaching and low price of these foundation schools.

With girls' schools there is no competition of this sort, nothing to raise the level of education. The only choice offered to parents of the same class for the education of their daughters lies between Miss Jones's establishment, where the course of education consists in playing on the pianoforte, working in worsteds and doing crochet, and the seminary for young ladies kept by Miss Robinson, where dancing, deportment, and flower painting are the order of the day.

Endowed middle-class schools for girls, under proper inspection, ought to be established in every large town in England. Their absence is one of the great deficiencies of the age. Of course, the founding of them must be a work of time, expense, and individual effort; but what great work was ever executed without an outlay of time, money, and individual effort?

There is a means, however, by which perhaps large sums of money might be procured for the purpose, which should not be neglected. It often happens that when charities are reformed a large amount of property falls into the hands of the Charity Commissioners, who, with the consent of the Court of Chancery, may dispose of it as they think proper. At present these funds are frequently employed in founding middle-class schools for boys only, but perhaps if public attention were called to the subject half the money might be procured for the girls; indeed, if the rules of justice were observed, the whole of the funds thus produced in the next twenty years would be bestowed on them exclusively, to make up for the undue partiality hitherto shown to boys.

Schools of this sort once established, the instruction given in them ought to be of such a character as would fit the pupils for future life. Those who have any talent for music should be trained as organists, a profession well suited to women: some should be taught French, often useful in commercial transactions; all ought to receive a solid English education, and be especially taught arithmetic, book-keeping, and every branch of accounts. They should also be taught, as much as possible, the meaning of business terms, be shown the proper forms of letter writing, and be given every kind of useful, practical knowledge of that sort. By this description of teaching, the character of girls of the middle class would be changed. They are now taught accomplishments, and told that the great object in life is to please; they therefore naturally grow up vain, and often think of little else than how to make themselves attractive by means of smart clothes and an affectation of fine lady manners.

But set before them that the great object in life is to earn their own living, that many among them will not marry, and must either work or trust to charity for bread; teach them above all, that it is more honourable to depend on their own exertions than to marry for the sake of a maintenance, and then a different spirit will arise among them.

Women thus educated will be able to find ample employment if they remain single, and if they marry will become real helpmates to their husbands instead of the heavy useless burdens they now too often are, unable to keep the accounts of their husbands' shops, or even of their own households, and not possessing sufficient intelligence to find pleasure in anything, but buying and exhibiting their handsome dresses.

If young women of the trading classes were thus enabled to become clerks and accountants, and to take part in commercial business, the number of candidates for places as governesses would be much diminished, and would consist principally of ladies who had known better days, and of the daughters of the clergy and professional men left without fortunes; and as the competition would diminish with the numbers seeking engagements, these could ask sufficiently high salaries to enable them to live in tolerable comfort during their old age, without being beholden to charity; and being principally gentlewomen by birth and manners, the unfavourable impressions now existing against governesses would gradually fade away. The profession would rise in public estimation, and those following it would receive the respect and consideration due to them.

We will now proceed to the next branch of our subject, the overworked dressmaker and distressed needlewoman.

Gentlemen sometimes wonder why women submit so quietly to the ill-usage inflicted on them by their employers, and why, when they find they are required to sit for sixteen or eighteen hours a day at their needles, they do not leave their service, and go and seek for work elsewhere.

The reason is simply that if they did so they could not find it. It is the old story; the supply of labour is greater than the demand, and therefore the employed are at the mercy of the employer. The milliner, outfitter, or slopseller, who the most grinds down his workwomen, can afford to undersell the others, and so makes a fortune.

It is a competitive school for cruelty on a grand scale: the most cruel wins the prize, and grows rich first; the most merciful is undersold and ruined. The only hope of protecting the employed from the effects of this system is to provide those who want work with other occupations, so as to cause the value of female labour to rise in the market. The question then is, Are there any employments suitable to women of the lower classes from which they are now debarred by ignorance, prejudice, and other causes? There are many. Thousands of women might be employed to wait in shops where light articles of female attire are sold; and there are departments of industry, such as clerkships in post-offices, savingsbanks, railway-ticket offices, and others too numerous to mention, for which nothing is required to fit hundreds of them but a moderate amount of education. Thousands more might be employed as watchmakers, workers in jewellery, and painters of porcelain, if they were not prevented by causes to which we will refer hereafter.

Let us consider separately the impediments to each sphere of industry.

The employment which presents the widest prospect of remunerative occupation for women is perhaps that of saleswomen in shops; for it was remarked by Lord Shaftesbury, at Bradford, that no less than thirty thousand men are employed in the sale of various articles of millinery. The principal objections urged against the substitution of women are:

First, that they cannot stand the requisite number of hours; the answer to which is that thousands of them now stand working in manufactories for ten hours a day.

Second, that ladies dislike being waited on by women. The proverbial difficulty of proving a negative renders it almost impossible to show that this impression is a delusion. Ladies, however, know that provided they are well attended to, they are generally indifferent to who waits on them; and that though some may prefer the services of men, yet their numbers are more than counterbalanced by those who have a special dislike to them. Let every man inquire of his own family and acquaintance what the feeling on this subject is, and draw his own conclusions from the answers he receives.

The third objection is that in the fashionable parts of the town it would be impossible for shopkeepers to provide lodging-houses for their saleswomen sufficiently near their establishments, and that these, if left to seek their own lodgings, would be so little under control that it would be difficult to insure the respectability of their conduct. There is some show of reason in this objection, though we do not think it a really solid one; for the question is not whether a saleswoman is absolutely and positively certain to be respectable, but whether a girl who is provided with her meals and receives thirty or forty pounds a year salary, but has to seek her own lodgings and is under little supervision, is more or less likely to conduct herself well, than the same girl receiving fivepence a day as needlewoman, and having equally to provide her own lodgings, and be under no supervision at all?

The girls already exist and lodge somewhere; and who can doubt that they are more likely to behave well and steadily if provided with remunerative employment than if left to pine on a wretched pittance that will barely maintain life. The same reasoning applies to every department of industry for women; in every path there is danger, but the greatest danger of all lies in extreme poverty.

The real impediment to their employment in shops is their ignorance of accounts. Few women of the lower classes can do accounts quickly and accurately. In many schools girls are made to sit down to their needles while the boys learn arithmetic. In others, where the funds will not allow of the employment of both a certificated master and mistress, a master only is engaged; and as there is no rule of the Council of Education compelling the managers of schools thus situated to teach the girls together with the boys, the former are frequently made over to some poor creature who can be had cheap, and who can read, write, and sew; or whose arithmetic, if she profess to teach it, is so imperfect as to be merely nominal. The natural result of this plan is, that thirty thousand men are employed to sell ribbons, laces, and other articles of millinery, while our streets are full of starving women who cannot find employment, and so long as this sytem of education is pursued the same results must inevitably ensue.

Last winter, a district visitor in a London parish found a respectable girl just recovering from illness in a lodging-house: she had been a seamstress, had caught a fever, and spent all her money. The mistress of the lodgings had kept her as long as she could afford, but was now about to turn her out. The visitor asked the girl what she meant to do; would she return to her old life of sewing? 'No,' she replied, 'it had made her ill; if she returned to it she must die.' Well, had she any plans; how did she mean to live? After a pause, the girl said she thought she should beg in the streets. The visitor took care of her, and got her a place in a shop. She was slow and ignorant at first; but the people of the shop were patient and merciful, and she is now doing well. It cannot be expected, however, that many tradesmen will be equally benevolent, and risk injuring their custom by employing incompetent persons to wait; therefore, if we wish women to be employed behind the counter, we must establish in every quarter of London, and in all country towns, evening classes for young women and girls, where they may learn arithmetic and book-keeping, and where those pupils who become proficient may procure certificates of competency. If this is done they will be enabled when their sewing trade fails, as fail it shortly will, not only to become saleswomen and cashiers, but to engage in other occupations enumerated before, where intelligence is required rather than strength.[1] We have said that the sewing trade will shortly fail, bad as it is now, it will soon be worse. In fact, ere long it will cease to be a trade at all, for everywhere the sewing machine is superseding human fingers; the few seamstresses who will retain their places will be kept to tend the machine, not to do the sewing. These machines can execute every kind of work, except perhaps elaborate trimmings, not only as well, but far better than women; they can sew shoes, gloves, gown bodies, and shirts, and make every description of under-clothing with wonderful despatch and neatness. We have seen a small one doing in two minutes as much work as an expert needlewoman could execute in ten: it is said that some larger ones can perform the work of twelve seamstresses. Let us suppose, however, that an average machine can do the work of five only, then four will be thrown out of work when their use becomes general. It is said, however, that as the cost of making clothes will be lessened by the use of the machine more will be bought, so that the same number of people will in the end be employed; and the example of the power-loom (which threw large numbers of weavers out of work at first, but which was the ultimate cause of many more being employed) is quoted to show that the distress occasioned by the sewing machine will only be temporary. The cases, however, are widely different. A great part of the value of woven manufactures consisted in the labour bestowed on them, so that by diminishing the expense in that particular the price was materially reduced, and people were enabled to purchase a much larger quantity. But in the present instance this is not so. A *very* small part of the expense of a silk dress consists in the labour of making it up. Perhaps the wages of the milliner's girl who makes up a dress worth five pounds may be five shillings. Now let this be deducted from the total of the account, so that the work shall cost absolutely nothing; yet it will not encourage ladies to buy more gowns, for the diminution of price is fractional. Neither in coarser materials will any considerable saving in price be effected; yet, unless the reduction be so great as to induce the entire population to buy five times as much clothing as they do at present, numbers of women must be permanently deprived of employment.

And this calculation is founded on the supposition that the machines will never improve, but will remain doing on an average the work of five women a day; though in reality it is probable they will soon work at a much faster rate. The distress thus caused will spread into the country. In many small towns five or six dressmakers have contrived to earn a living; but now the first one among them who can collect capital enough to buy a machine will be able not only to undersell the others, but to excel them in the beauty of the work done; and thus collecting the whole of their custom to herself, can drive them out of the trade. Then unless they are sufficiently educated to turn to some other profession they must either become domestic servants, for which their previous life has unfitted them, or take refuge in the workhouse. We wish to attract attention to these points, because we fear that much valuable time is now often spent in schools in teaching a trade which will shortly become obsolete.

It will always be useful to women to know how to sew, that they may make and mend their own and their children's clothes; but one hour's teaching a day, or two hours three times a week, continued for two or three years, would give them sufficient skill for the purpose. It was perfectly right when sewing was an art by which women could earn a comfortable living, that girls should pass two or three hours a day in learning it; but now the time so spent would be much more usefully employed in training some to be domestic servants, and in perfecting others in writing, arithmetic, and book-keeping, so as to enable them hereafter to engage in remunerative occupations.[2]

Another employment which women are now endeavouring to enter is the management of the telegraph. Here they do the business better than men, because of the more undivided attention which they pay to their duties; but considerable inconvenience is found to result from their ignorance of business terms, which causes them to make mistakes in the messages sent. However, a short course of previous instruction easily overcomes this impediment.

The obstacles to their employment in the watch-making and china-painting departments of industry are of quite another nature from those hitherto spoken of. No education is required for these occupations, only manual skill to be acquired by practice. At Geneva, women are employed in watch-making, in preference to men, both on account of the superior delicacy of their touch, and the greater cheapness of their labour, which occasions Swiss watches to be so much less expensive than English ones that several thousands are imported into this country every year. Women, however, cannot be employed in England in this manner, because of the jealousy of their fellow-workmen. If a master were to employ women in any part of the business, the whole of his workmen would strike at once; and as only a very few women are as yet sufficiently skilful to be of use, he could not trust to their services alone, but would be compelled to yield the point and dismiss them. It is hoped that in course of time, by patience and perseverance, this difficulty may be overcome, but it will, probably, be some years before watch-making can be looked upon as a branch of industry open to English women.[3]

The impediments to their employment in china-painting in the potteries are somewhat of the same kind. It appears that both men and women are employed in this art, but that the women having excited the jealousy of the men by surpassing them in skilful execution, and consequently earning better wages, were by them forcibly deprived of the maulsticks on which it is necessary to rest the wrist while painting. Thus the women are at once rendered incapable of any fine work, and can only be employed in the coarser kinds of painting. The masters submit to this tyranny, though to their own disadvantage, being probably afraid of a strike or riot if they resist, and the women are forced to yield from the fear of personal violence from their less skilful but heavier-fisted rivals. This story appeared in *The Edinburgh Review* for April, 1859, and it is surprising it did not excite more general indignation.

It certainly appears that a strong body of police and an energetic magistrate are all that is required to remedy this glaring injustice. If two or three dozen of the ruffians were sent to prison for six months with hard labour for assaulting the women, the tyranny would probably be put an end to at once.

But the chief obstacle, the monster impediment, to the more general employment of women, in branches of industry which require either skill or education, is the impression that their employment would throw men out of work, and deprive them of their livelihood. From this fear a few benevolent persons, and many who are not benevolent, are induced to oppose themselves to any improvement in the education of girls, and to all measures that might tend to enlarge the sphere of female industry. I shall therefore do my best to answer this objection fully. With regard to educated women, their increased employment need not and would not have the effect of throwing men out of work, because the progress of civilisation is continually opening *fresh* occupations to educated persons; great numbers of women could therefore find employment if they were properly instructed, without displacing one solitary man. To give an instance, a scheme is at this moment under consideration, which if carried out will give remunerative occupation, requiring the smallest possible amount of physical strength, to some hundreds of good accountants. Mr Sikes, of Huddersfield, has drawn up a plan for increasing the number of government savings' banks. He proposes to establish one in connection with every money-order office throughout the kingdom; and it appears that the number of these is two thousand three hundred and sixty. These banks are to receive the smallest sums, and to be open every day, in order to afford the greatest possible facilities for the formation of provident and saving habits.

In places where the post-office clerk is not already fully occupied he will be able to attend to the bank as well as to his other duties; but in many instances this will not be the case, and a new clerk will be required. Now why should not this clerk be a woman?

The objection commonly raised against employing women in any but the most unremunerative offices, viz., that they deprive men of employment, could not be raised here; no man would be turned out of work by the admittance of women to this department of labour, as all these offices will be freshly created.

If the report be true that Mr Sikes' scheme has been approved of by the post-office authorities, there can be little doubt that it will be carried through Parliament during the next session, and put into execution shortly afterwards; thus affording a good livelihood to perhaps more than a thousand women, without exposing even one man to the smallest inconvenience.

If women were qualified to fill clerkships and other similar situations the effect would be not to diminish the number of men now employed, but merely to prevent male clerks from becoming still more numerous. A father, instead of bringing up both his sons to be clerks and both his daughters to be dressmakers, would train one son and one daughter as clerks, one daughter as dressmaker or governess, and the remaining son would be a carpenter or builder, and perhaps go to the colonies, where workmen of this class are in great demand. Fifty years hence, if England's prosperity continue, there will be twice as many people employed in work which requires intelligence as there are now. Half of these, if the proposed system of education were carried out, would be women, instead of the whole being men as must be the case if the present system of education be maintained; yet no man would have been turned out of work to make place for them. Nor would the number of marriages be at all reduced by this arrangement, as some people fear; for the higher clerkships, to which good salaries are attached, would still be filled by men, as their superior health and strength must always make them preferred and give them the advantage over women, who would only be employed in places where economy was an object and where the clerks do not receive sufficiently high salaries to enable them to marry; for these men either are, or fancy they are, obliged to dress and live like gentlemen, though by birth they have no pretensions to consider themselves such. Thus great numbers of them cannot afford to marry, but remain single all their lives: whereas, if they had been brought up to a manual trade, and had either stayed in England or gone abroad, they would have been able to marry and live comfortably on their wages; for though a carpenter may earn no more than a clerk, yet, not being obliged to live like a gentleman, his money goes much further. He would thereby provide for two women, the wife he married and the female who would occupy his post as clerk, while he himself would lead a happier life, and add to the wealth of the country by his reproductive labour in some handicraft.

There is but one occupation for men which would be swept away, viz., the sale of light articles of female attire in shops, an employment which all will agree is more appropriate to women. Yet even in this instance the men now employed would continue at their posts all their lives, only large numbers of fresh young men would no longer enter the profession every year as at present; none would enter but those learning the trade with the intention of hereafter keeping a shop themselves. The new shop-assistants in silk-mercers', haberdashers', and lacemen's establishments would therefore be almost exclusively women, so that when the present race of men milliners had died out the genus would have become extinct, without the infliction of the slightest privation on one individual now employed, and with no worse result to the rising male generation than that of compelling them to take a share of those hardships which are now the exclusive portion of their sisters; hardships which, perhaps, would render them less unwilling to enter the service of their country, since, as Sir Archibald Alison observed at the meeting at Glasgow for raising a volunteer corps, 'the enlistment of soldiers and sailors is a mere money question'. If men can obtain plenty of easy remunerative labour elsewhere they will not enlist, unless the government can afford to pay them higher than private employers.

When a man can choose between selling lace in a comfortable shop and having to endure the hardships of a soldier's or a sailor's life, he naturally prefers the shop. Therefore thirty thousand men milliners exist in England, while their thirty thousand sisters encumber the workhouses! Nor are they to be blamed for this; it is the system that is in fault, not the individuals.

But change our present plan, grant to women the means of a special education, and so raise them to an intellectual equality with men, and give them, as much as the difference in their strength allows, an equal chance of earning their bread, and at once their position will be infinitely improved. If, in addition to this, the powerful protection of the law were extended to those women who are either deprived of their tools or forcibly prevented from working by their male competitors, immense benefit would be conferred on the two millions of our countrywomen who, as the census tells us, are unmarried and have to maintain themselves by their labour, while men would be subjected to no more inconvenience than is necessary to enable us to maintain our national defences without having recourse to the aid of foreign mercenaries.

Granting, however, that this was not the case. Supposing even that there was such a general want of employment both for men and women that whatever was added to the prosperity of one sex must be deducted from that of the other, still the advocates of the 'woman's question' would not abandon their ground. They would maintain that it was not just to cast the whole of the suffering thus occasioned on the weaker half of humanity, and that men ought not to shrink from taking their share of the misery. Listen to the exposition of the duty of men towards women given by Mrs Beecher Stowe, and judge if it be not the true one: 'I take it, wherever there is a cross or burden to be borne by one or the other, that the man who is made in the image of God as to strength and endurance should take it upon himself and not lay it upon her who is weaker; for he is therefore strong, not that he may tyrannise over the weak, but bear their burdens for them.' How great a contrast is there between the spirit of Christianity and the course of conduct too frequently pursued in this our country! 'He looked for judgment, but behold oppression; for righteousness, but behold a cry.'

Believing, as we do, that a selfish disregard of the interests of women and a cruel indifference to their sufferings is the great national sin of England, and that all national sins, if unrepented, meet with their punishment sooner or later, I conclude these pages with the expression of an earnest hope that we may repent in time, and that before many years are past our practice in this respect may be found in accordance with the precepts of the religion we profess to obey.

NOTES

1 A society whose object is the establishment of such classes has recently been formed, in connection with the National Association for the Promotion of Social Science, the office of which, where further particulars may be ascertained, is at 19, Langham Place.
2 It would be useless to give this high education in workhouse schools as no-one can be employed in shops or situations of a like nature, unless they can deposit a small sum of money as a security for honesty, which of course would be impossible for pauper girls, who should therefore be trained to domestic service.
3 We have read since writing the above, in *The English Woman's Journal* for December, 1859, page 278, that there is a manufactory at Christchurch, where five hundred women are employed in making the interior chains for chronometers, they are preferred to men on account of their being naturally more dexterous with their fingers, and therefore being found to require less training.

This manufactory has been established more than fifty years, and shows that as women can perform that part of watch-making which is the most difficult, and on the perfection of which the lives of thousands of sailors and passengers depend, that the only impediment to their employment in its other departments is the opposition offered by the workmen, and it also affords a useful hint to watchmakers to set up any future manufactories where they may wish to employ women, *in the country*, where the spirit of combination is less strong.

On the Education of Girls with Reference to their Future Position

(a paper read at the National Association for the Promotion of Social Science, August 1860 and reprinted in *The English Woman's Journal*, December 1860)

It is encouraging to those who take interest in the improvement of the female portion of the community, to observe that in the educational department of this Society no less than four papers on the education of girls were read last year, and that the topic was also referred to incidentally in several others.

This will not perhaps appear a large proportion, when it is considered that the number of papers read altogether in that department amounted to forty, but it is so much greater a share of attention than is usually bestowed on the subject that it must be regarded as a gratifying circumstance.

It is difficult to say why the education of girls should be considered as of so much less importance than that of boys, but such is certainly the case. 'Why is it,' says the Rev. J. P. Norris, in his report to the Committee of Council of Education, 'that where you find three or four good boys' schools you will find barely one efficient girls' school? Why is it that in pamphlets, speeches, and schemes of so-called National Education, they are almost universally ignored? And what is the result? For want of good schools, three out of four of the girls in my district are sent to miserable private schools, where they have no religious instruction, no discipline, no industrial training.' Also Mr H. Chester, President of the Society of Arts, observes, 'The education of women of every class among us is in urgent need of improvement.' . . . 'Much less has been done for girls' than for boys' schools.' And this indifference continues to prevail, although several gentlemen, who have good opportunities of judging, have given it as their opinion, that as the training of children of both sexes during their early and more impressionable years must necessarily be in the hands of women, their education is in truth more important than that of men. But setting this part of the question aside, let me observe that there is no doubt that a good education is an excellent preparation for the journey of life, and that it enables those who possess it to avoid dangers and to surmount difficulties which are not unlikely to prove fatal to those who start unprovided with this support.

Now what should we say to a parent who on sending his two children out on a voyage took pains to furnish the stronger with every necessary, but left the weaker comparatively uncared for? Should we not say that such conduct was cruel and unnatural? Yet it is what we ourselves are guilty of every day – for the public must be considered collectively as the parent of the rising generation, and everywhere do we see signs of the pains taken to prepare boys by education to pass happily and honourably through their lives, while the attention and forethought which are bestowed on their sisters' future well-being are comparatively of a trifling description. But perhaps it will be said that women do not require so much preparation as men, because they will marry, and will thus be relieved from the burden of supporting themselves. To a certain extent this is true, yet it is a question whether married women have not serious difficulties of another kind actually thrown in their way by the inferiority of the education they receive. To place a woman on a much lower intellectual level than her husband cannot tend to make her position an easier one or to increase her chances of domestic happiness. Her troubles may not be those of a bread-winner, yet they may be very painful and make her life a miserable one. Without dwelling further on this point, however, I must observe that the argument here used does not apply to one-third of the women of Great Britain, for out of six millions of the weaker sex, two earn their bread as single women. How many more unmarried there may be who are supported by provision left them by their parents I cannot tell, neither does it affect the case; but it is a fact recorded in the last census, that out of every three women existing in this land, one is now not only walking alone through the journey of life, but providing for herself by the way. One out of every three of the young girls we bring up will have to fight the great battle for bread. At present they enter on the contest ill-taught, untrained, and most insufficiently prepared. Is it surprising that many fail to win their daily bread? Is it wonderful that every employment suitable to ill-instructed persons should be overcrowded with female applicants praying for work, and beating down each other's wages by competition to starvation point? Need we marvel that our workhouses should be encumbered with able-bodied women? Is it not rather the natural result of the system pursued?

It was stated at the public meeting of the refuges in London that numbers of women of unblemished character wander every night through the streets without the means of procuring shelter or food, resting on door-steps or sleeping under archways. And this state of things must continue, and indeed cannot fail to grow worse and worse, unless far greater efforts are made to prevent it than are now in action or even in contemplation.

Any attempt to enter on the whole subject, and show how the condition of these two millions of working women might be improved, would far exceed my powers or the limits of this paper; I shall therefore confine myself to one branch, and will endeavour to point out the deficiencies in the education given to girls belonging to the middle classes and the evil consequences which this deficiency entails on them in after life.

It would be curious and instructive to mark the difference between the numbers of endowed middle-class schools for boys and those for girls all over the kingdom, and I regret that I have been unable to procure such an account. In one small district, however, I have been able to obtain this information, and it must serve as a specimen of the whole.

I find in a history published in the year 1828, of that part of Lincolnshire which is called Lindsey, and consists of about one-half of the county, that it contains ten endowed grammar or middle-class schools for boys; some of which are free, and all very cheap, and are made use of, for their sons, by tradesmen and farmers, and even occasionally by the clergy and professional men; but for girls of the same rank there is no endowed school at all. Besides these, there are for the labouring class several partly endowed schools for boys, and a few mixed ones, but for the daughters of the middle class there is no educational provision whatever, though so much has been done for their brothers. I do not select this particular district because it is especially favourable to my views, but merely because I could here find the information which I could not readily obtain elsewhere, and I am not aware that it is at all different from the rest of England. It is probable that when the greater part of these schools were founded, two or three centuries ago, there were very few single women of this class who had to provide for themselves, therefore the education of the girls was of comparatively little importance, and of course I do not suggest or desire that any alteration should be made in the state of these existing schools, I only wish to point out that any future endowments ought to be for girls' schools, and that any money which may hereafter fall into the Court of Chancery or the hands of the Charity Commissioners ought in fairness to be expended, not for the benefit of boys, who are more than tolerably well provided for already, but for the girls, for whom no provision at all exists, and who have no means of education within their reach, except such as are offered in private schools, where the instruction is necessarily expensive and which have not the advantage enjoyed by endowed establishments of being supervised by educated persons of station.

The efficiency of the education given in these private schools may be ascertained by any one who will take the trouble of questioning a pupil from 'a seminary for young ladies'. But he must not only inquire what the course of study has been, he must also ascertain whether the pupil has really learnt any one of the things professed to be taught. Let him, as a test, request her to work a sum and to write a letter, when her deficiencies will at once become apparent. It is of course possible that a few good private schools may be found, but as a general rule the result of an examination will be unsatisfactory in the extreme. I have known a grown-up girl who had gone as far as practice in one of these establishments who yet could not do a sum in multiplication, and a younger one, from another school, who had been a considerable time at long division yet could not add correctly.

In short, the object of the managers of these schools is, naturally enough, less to give a good education to the scholars than to make money for themselves. This is effected by advertising showy accomplishments, which, compared to useful instruction, are easy to teach and easy to learn, and which are therefore popular with the pupils themselves; and they trust that the superficial character of what little solid teaching they profess to give will not be discovered by the parents, a confidence which is usually perfectly well placed, for the fathers are generally too busy to attend to their daughters' education, and the mothers, having been no better taught themselves, are incapable of finding out deficiencies.

It is probable that the education given in private boys' schools of the same class would be equally bad if they were not held in check by the number of endowed schools which exist all over the country. Thus these schools are useful, not only from the good education they afford in themselves, but also in compelling the private ones to keep up to their mark to a considerable extent.

Now this is an advantage girls do not possess, and it is to this I believe that the inferiority of the instruction they receive is owing, there being nothing by which to test whether it is good or worthless. The pupils from Miss Brown's may perhaps be compared to the pupils from Miss Jones's, but as they are probably about equally ill taught nothing is elicited by the comparison. What is required in every town is a good female middle-class school, endowed if possible, but at any rate under the management of educated persons of the higher ranks, the object of which should be not to make money, but to afford an education which would be of practical use to the pupils in after life.

Such a school would be most valuable in itself, but the greatest benefit conferred by it would be to serve as a standard by which to measure the education given in private schools, thus compelling an improvement in the instruction. It need not cost more than £40 to set up a school on this principle – if the rooms were hired only, not built – and in a few months it would probably, if well managed, become self-supporting.

As prevention is better than cure, money given for this purpose would be at least as well bestowed as that which is spent in relieving the distress or mitigating the evils which the want of such educational establishments has occasioned.

The education provided should be, for the younger children, of a general nature, and more for the purpose of developing the reasoning and thinking powers than for that of filling the memory. The elder girls should receive such instruction as would qualify them to engage in business and earn their own living hereafter. For this object, arithmetic and book-keeping should be particularly attended to. Arithmetic will not, unless followed up by book-keeping, be of much service in procuring well remunerated situations, but great numbers of these would be open to women who thoroughly understood this branch of business. For instance, every large shop has its cashier, and the duties of this office might be perfectly well performed by a woman, as indeed they very generally are in France.

Again, small shops do not possess cashiers, the books being kept in a rough way by the owner; but every three months an accountant comes round who looks over them, strikes the balance, and sets all mistakes to rights; now why should not this accountant be a woman?

Another wide field of employment of the same kind will probably be opened shortly. Mr Syke's plan for forming savings' banks in connection with money order offices can scarcely fail to be put into execution before many months have elapsed, and this will occasion a demand for a large number of clerks, who must understand accounts well, be thoroughly honest, and yet not require a very large salary; a combination much more likely to be found in women than men, if they were only properly instructed; and a staff of sober, well-conducted clerks, requiring only moderate pay, would do real service to the country in this situation.

An objection to the teaching of book-keeping in schools has sometimes been raised on the ground that the systems of keeping accounts are so numerous in trade that almost every shop or office adopts a different plan; but in fact, the differences between the systems are only like those to be observed in books of grammar, and a person who in learning a foreign language had made himself master of the system pursued in one grammar would find little difficulty in comprehending the plan adopted in another by a different author. But the best argument for teaching girls book-keeping is, that it is frequently taught at boys' schools, which would not be done if it were found to be of no use afterwards.

A register ought also to be kept at the school for the convenience of employers who might want female book-keepers, clerks, or saleswomen.

A good knowledge of arithmetic short of book-keeping, especially mental arithmetic, would enable girls to become saleswomen in shops. It has been frequently stated that 30,000 men are employed in England in the sale of articles of female attire. Now no one can wish to see a fresh generation of boys brought up and sacrificed to this feminine occupation, yet this must happen unless a sufficient number of girls are educated to undertake the work in their stead. The ribbons and laces must be sold, and if women are not well enough taught to act as saleswomen without occasioning delays and inconvenience to the customers by their want of quickness, men will assuredly be employed for the purpose. The good instruction given in National Schools is of little use in fitting girls to take these situations, for as the scholars generally belong to the class of labouring poor, they rarely possess the requisite manners and appearance, nor can they make any money deposit as a security for honesty, which is not unfrequently required.

It is a curious anomaly, that girls of the lower orders are provided with a superior education, of which, for the above reasons, they can make little use, while nothing of the kind is within the reach of the poorer division of the middle classes, to whom good instruction would be of such inestimable value.

There are several other branches of practical education, besides arithmetic and book-keeping, which might be taught in middle-class schools with great advantage, but it would take too much space to enumerate them. Perhaps, however, it may be said, that as there are already complaints that the market for educated women is overstocked, it would be worse than useless to train others to enter it, but everything depends on the kind of instruction given.

Of practically and specially educated women there is an actual scarcity, there being for instance, at this moment, a great demand for them as matrons of charitable institutions, a demand that cannot be supplied, as women of the working classes, though often well educated, are unsuitable in other respects, while middle-class women are too ignorant. But it is perfectly true that there is a great surplus of unpractically educated, accomplished women, as is shown by the numbers who become governesses, and by the low rate of remuneration they receive. It is shown also by the crowds of those who, too ill-taught even to be teachers, still call themselves educated women, and are anxiously, and of course vainly, seeking for some employment by which bodily weakness and mental ignorance combined may be enabled to earn a livelihood.

These are the very people produced by the private schools, of which we have been speaking, whose sufferings are so much to be deplored, and whose numbers we seek to diminish by means of special and practical instruction. At present the evil has an inclination to multiply itself; for as practically and specially educated women can obtain well remunerated work, they do not care to teach, and consequently useful learning is expensive, while the number of persons who try to live by teaching accomplishments, makes accomplishments cheap to learn, and people learn them as they buy bargains, purchasing what is of no use because it is cheaper than what would really be of service.

The only way to check this is to provide useful instruction at a cheap rate.

If any one is afraid that by enabling women to engage in remunerative occupations, young men entering life may be inconvenienced and compelled to turn to rougher, harder work than is agreeable to them, I refer to the article in the *Quarterly Review*, of June last, on 'Workmen's Earnings and Savings', where they will see that no man with ordinary health and strength need suffer privation, if willing to work, and not recklessly extravagant. If more girls were trained to employments requiring intelligence, more boys would be trained to those requiring strength. If there were fewer shopmen, there would be more mechanics, soldiers, sailors, and workmen of all kinds, but not more male inmates of the workhouse, or dependents on charity.

In speaking of the advantages to be derived from a higher, sounder, more practical and religious education for girls, I have said nothing of the advantage men would derive by being provided with more intelligent and companionable wives; nothing of the benefits to be conferred on children; nothing of the increased

247

chances of domestic happiness which must result from increased freedom of choice in marriage, for a woman cannot be said to be free when the option offered is to marry or to starve; nor have I referred to the higher tone of feeling such an education would infuse among the girls themselves, now but too justly accused of caring for little save vanity and dress. I have dwelt entirely on what appears to me the chief point of importance, viz., the removal of the sufferings now entailed by ignorance on those single women who have to earn their own bread, but it should not be forgotten that these other advantages would be secured also.

That women who are left unprovided for and find themselves forced, perhaps when no longer young, to trust to their own exertions for subsistence do suffer, and suffer most severely, may be seen by any one who will spend a few mornings at the office of the 'Society for Promoting the Employment of Women'.

The plate on the door attracts numbers, many of whom belong to the class we have been discussing; they frequently describe themselves as 'educated women', but when asked what they can do towards earning a livelihood, it appears they can do nothing. Sometimes they say they should be glad to learn anything that would enable them to live, but add piteously, that it must be something which can be learnt very quickly, as their means are nearly exhausted. As no remunerative employment can be learnt quickly, it is unnecessary to say that assistance can seldom be given to these poor creatures, whose melancholy fate it must be either to join the crowd of needlewomen and help to beat down still lower the wages of that miserable profession, or else to retire into the workhouse, there to spend the rest of their lives, for women who have been brought up in a superior station have neither strength nor skill to become domestic servants, the only employment open to ill-educated women without capital.

I cannot but think that there exists a confusion in the minds of many persons on this subject amounting almost to a feeling that it is wrong to teach women anything practically useful. But our ideas would grow clearer if we would steadily bear in mind that one-third of our female population must either work, beg, or starve. If whenever we meet a string of schoolgirls not belonging to the wealthy classes, or see a merry group at play, we would remind ourselves that one out of every three will have to earn her own bread in future life, we should surely feel some interest in ascertaining that their education is calculated to assist them in so doing.

I conclude with some short extracts from a letter addressed by Mr Harry Chester to the Editors of *The English Woman's Journal*, and regret that my space forbids me to give the whole. 'The question you propose to deal with is I think simply a question of education, *i.e.*, if you can improve the education of females, but not otherwise, you can improve the market for female labour; and one of the great wants of female education is, I think, the want of some external standard such as the Society of Arts now supplies. A woman who had obtained from the Society of Arts a certificate of the first or second class in book-keeping could scarcely fail to obtain employment as a book-keeper, and one cannot see why the wives, sisters, and daughters of commercial men should not act as their book-keepers.' . . . 'I regard the question you desire to solve as simply and remarkably a question of the improved education of women; as shall be the education of women, so shall be the remuneration of those women who labour to live. You may think lightly of the objection taken by the *Saturday Review*, that if you increase woman's power of gaining her own livelihood you diminish the number of marriages, and so injure society, for you may rely that such a power, making her more valuable in a pecuniary sense as a wife, increases her opportunities of marriage, and it is neither for her own good nor that of society that she should marry for hunger, instead of for love and esteem.' . . . 'You might establish classes for the special instruction of young women, who have left school, with a view of qualifying them to act as book-keepers, clerks, etc. You may be sure that well qualified women would immediately obtain employment.'

A school and classes on this principle have been opened in London, but as the first quarter is not yet concluded, I cannot speak of its success, though I trust to do so next year. Prospectuses can be obtained at the Office of *The English Woman's Journal*.

Local Societies

(a paper read at the National Association for the Promotion of Social Science, August 1861 and reprinted in *The English Woman's Journal*, December 1861)

The success of the movement for increasing the number of employments open to women must depend, in great measure, on the extent to which the ideas and plans of the Central Society are taken up and carried out in the country.

The use of the London Society is to make experiments in order to ascertain practically what employments are suitable to women and what are not. There are many different theories and opinions on the subject, the truth of which can be proved by experience only. Each experiment is expensive, as first attempts must necessarily be, and in some instances costs more than it is worth, if the number of women employed at that one place be taken alone into consideration, but not more than it is worth if the value of the knowledge obtained be considered. This knowledge will enable local societies or private benevolence to carry out the same plans in other towns at a small expense, and thus will indirectly provide a large number of women with a respectable means of earning a good livelihood.

The object of this paper is to show which of the experiments of the Central Society are the most successful, and to suggest the means by which they may be carried out in other places.

The most successful experiment is, without doubt, the printing establishment called the Victoria Press. Strictly speaking, this establishment ought not perhaps to be reckoned among the Society's efforts, as it was not set up by the Committee, but was a private undertaking. The Society spent £50 in apprenticing five young women, and the Press is therefore generally considered to form a part of the whole undertaking. Here twenty young women and girls find employment, at as good wages as lads in the same position usually earn, and at work easy in comparison of that required from milliners' apprentices, the hours of labour being only eight a day, with occasional overtime of a couple of hours. The business at the Victoria Press has increased so rapidly that at the end of a year and a half the premises in Great Coram Street are hardly sufficient for the necessities of the Office.

But successful as this experiment has proved in a benevolent point of view, and promising though it be in a commercial one, it is still an enterprise that would not be easily carried out in the provinces, as a printing press requires a large capital to begin with, and if not thoroughly well managed might prove a losing concern.

The Law-Copying Office established by the Society in Portugal Street would be much easier to imitate and have a greater probability of success. How often it happens in country towns that a professional or commercial family is suddenly, by the imprudence or death of its head, deprived of the means of support, and is forced to appeal to the charity and good feeling of its fellow-townsmen and country neighbours for assistance? And very much perplexed the neighbours and townsmen are with their charge, by the daughters of the family especially. The only profession open to them is teaching; but if ill-prepared or unwilling to become governesses, it is exceedingly difficult to know what to do.

The obvious thing is, of course, to subscribe to pension them, but why should women in the prime of life be pensioned? Probably they would be only too glad to work, if some means of earning a livelihood were offered, and this means the Law-Copying Office presents. The first step towards the establishment of one is to secure the patronage of the solicitors of the town, to induce them to promise that, as soon as the daughter of their ruined fellow-townsman is well-qualified, they will give her a share of their custom. The next step is to send her to town to learn the business under Miss Rye's instruction, at 12, Portugal Street. Miss Rye would charge £5; and as she might board and lodge at the Ladies' Home, 51, Charlotte Street, for ten shillings a week, the expense would not be great, as the business can be thoroughly well learnt in six months. When qualified to commence business, little or no capital would be required (for she must lodge somewhere, and the office would serve as her sitting-room); a desk, some pens, and a small supply of parchments and paper would suffice. She would be paid at the regular rate of law stationer's charges, and if the solicitors were friendly towards her, and she did the work well, she would be able to live, and by degrees, as the custom increased, could take a female clerk under her – perhaps, in time, two or three – and so gradually work her way up till she earned a good maintenance.

A far better position, surely, than dependence on charity or becoming a teacher with no taste for the profession! An educated and energetic person, with £30 or £40 to begin with, might, if secure of a solicitor's patronage, start herself in this business without being under obligation to any one. Miss Rye has authorised me to say that there is a favourable opening for female law stationers in two great towns, and that it is her belief the business will be found to answer very well.

Another branch of employment might be widened, if not opened, by the efforts of a local society. It may be seen, by glancing at the advertising columns of *The Times*, that there is already a small demand for women as book-keepers, and it is probable that this demand would increase if the supply were of better quality; but as book-keeping is never taught in girls' schools, or in places of adult education for young women, it is exceedingly difficult for a girl to become acquainted with the business. She can only acquire a knowledge of it by chance, or by picking up stray pieces of information from her male relations. If, therefore, local societies were to subscribe to engage the services of a good commercial master to teach a class of girls of the rank of small tradesmen's daughters accounts and book-keeping, they would probably enable many of them to engage in an occupation which, compared to those usually followed by women, is remarkably easy and agreeable.

The hours in a shop seldom exceed ten, with an interval for dinner and tea, and a book-keeper would be seated during a great part of the time.

No young person should be recommended to a situation till the master had given her a certificate of competency, and no certificate should be granted till she was thoroughly well-instructed in arithmetic as well as book-keeping. She ought to be able to do the first four rules in arithmetic, bills of parcels and practice, quickly and correctly, and to reckon rapidly questions on the prices of articles without a slate. Above all, neat handwriting and a knowledge of spelling are essential.

If she knows less than this, she is not fit to take a situation; and every incompetent girl who gets a place does great injury to the cause of the employment of women, as her failure tends to strengthen the too prevalent impression that they are by nature unfit for any occupation that requires intelligence.

Where the means for paying a commercial teacher are not forthcoming, any lady with a good knowledge of arithmetic might easily prepare herself for the post of volunteer teacher by studying book-keeping by single entry (Chambers' system is, perhaps, the easiest; Haddon's the shortest and most comprehensive), but it would be rash for an amateur lady teacher to take upon herself to grant the certificates; the services of a professional gentleman should always be engaged for this purpose, as only those who practically understand the business can know exactly what is wanted. I must remark, however, that the instruction given to adults is seldom satisfactory unless there is some little foundation of sound education to begin upon. It often happens that a girl of seventeen or eighteen comes to the classes in London deficient in spelling and handwriting, and unable to multiply correctly, though she may have attended a genteel private school for years, and have gone as far as practice in the arithmetic book. Six months of good teaching will effect a great improvement in her acquirements, but even that is a poor substitute for really sound instruction in child-hood, as the knowledge so hastily attained can only be superficial, and habits of industry and perseverance cannot be formed in so short a space of time. Still, necessarily imperfect as adult instruction must always be, it is much valued by those for whom it is intended.

The average attendance in the afternoon at the classes established in London, to which the Central Society gives an annual grant, is fifteen, and in the evening eight – in all twenty-three; but as several pupils are prevented by duties at home from attending more than once or twice a week, the total number of young persons to whom instruction is given is considerably larger than the attendance on any one day. They pay for writing, arithmetic, and book-keeping 4s. 6d. a term, consisting of fourteen or fifteen weeks. This is very cheap, but as they have to pay out of their own pocket-money they could probably not give much more. A shilling a week was asked at first, but the number of pupils only amounted to seven.

Whenever it is necessary, in order to establish adult classes, to hire a room and buy benches and desks, I believe that a school for children may be set up at little or no expense. In making this statement, I speak from experience. It was found in London that the grown-up women preferred coming in the afternoon. During the whole day, therefore, till three o'clock, the room stood empty and useless. I was induced consequently to speculate in a child's school, and I do not regret it, as, since Christmas last, the extra expenses entailed by it have only amounted to £54 11s. 6d., while the receipts have been £43 16s. I am supposing, however, that the parents in every case pay, and that there are no defalcations, which at present is not quite certain, as part of the £43 16s. is still owing.

I should recommend, therefore, in case this idea should be carried out in other places, that payments be either required in advance or else by the month. The price asked at this school, of which I am Hon. Sec., is £1 1s. a term for girls above ten, and somewhat less for those under. We began after Christmas with twelve children, and ended the July term with twenty-four; and I have no doubt that next year it will be numerous enough to be self-supporting, and very probably after that it may be profitable and serve to pay the expenses of the adult classes, which was one of my objects in establishing it.

The instruction given is of a more practical nature than usual, much attention being paid to arithmetic, and book-keeping is taught to the elder girls. In this they take interest, and are glad to learn it, which is surprising when the dryness of the study is remembered; but children like the idea of being useful, and are pleased with the prospect of helping their father to keep his accounts when they grow up. Book-keeping need not, therefore, be omitted in schools from the idea of its being distasteful to the pupils.

I am very far from holding up this school in London as a model one – I know several others quite as good and some much better – I only mention it to show that where the rent is secured a middle-class school may be established very cheaply, and that useful instruction does not repel parents or children; and when we consider that the inferiority of their education is one of the principal causes of the difficulty in finding suitable employments for women of the lower middle class, I think that the opening of good useful schools for children of that rank may well come within the scope of local societies for promoting the employment of women.

In starting this school a clergyman who had considerable local influence gave great assistance by getting pupils; and I would venture to recommend that, when practicable, the co-operation of the clergy should be sought.

No difficulties with regard to religion have arisen: when the parents wish it, the children learn the Catechism of the Church of England; when this is not the case, they learn a portion of Scripture instead.

There is another way in which local societies might perhaps do good service to the cause.

There often appear in newspapers advertisements to the effect that 'an apprentice is wanted' to the wood engraving business, or the hair-dressing or photographic trades – 'a premium required' is frequently added. In many instances a clever girl who had a taste for the business would be preferred to a boy; and when the advertiser was known to be a person of respectability the Society might advantageously pay the premium, and so secure a fair start in life to a deserving young woman.

This plan has been tried to a small extent by the London Society, and promises well, though hardly sufficient time has passed to render its success as an experiment certain. Several other trades besides the three mentioned would afford a good opening to a clever girl.

In every part of the kingdom, and in various ranks of life, women are suffering from a scarcity of unemployment. Restricted to a few occupations, for which their numbers are too large, the value of their labour is unduly depreciated by competition, so that they are not paid what their work is worth to the employer, as men are, but receive only a small portion of its value. Thus we see women in the fields doing far more than half a man's work, and receiving far less than half a man's wages. In large towns we see them working fourteen hours a day as needlewomen for 4d. In a higher rank they go out as governesses at salaries so low as to make it impossible for them to save anything for their old age. Everywhere they are suffering from an unnatural and artificial depression of wages, being excluded either by prejudice, bad education, or sometimes by combinations among workmen, from occupations that are really suitable to them. Everywhere, therefore, are local societies required. Every town, and even village, would be the better for one, which should devote itself to watching over the interests of the weaker sex, and protecting them from oppression. It should assist with money, if necessary, any energetic woman who might attempt to enter on a new occupation, and, at all events, its members should afford her the valuable moral support of approbation.

There are probably few towns in which two or three hearts are not interested in the condition of women, but being so few they think they can do no good, and are unwilling to come forward and form plans for its amelioration. But I would beg these friends to the cause not to be discouraged. Let them remember that the sufferings of women from the overcrowding at their narrow labour-market is no imaginary grievance, but a sad reality, which none but the thoughtless can overlook. When, therefore, attention is called to the subject many who were indifferent will become interested; and even some of those who at first may oppose the movement will be led to look into the facts of the case more closely, and, perceiving the truth of the hardships complained of, will perhaps be induced to join it at last.

We must not despise the day of small things. If only half-a-dozen persons, or fewer, agree on this subject, let them form themselves into a committee, and if the funds are only large enough to apprentice one girl to a new trade, let a suitable young person be sought out and apprenticed; for if she gives satisfaction to her employer she will pave the way for others to follow. If only three or four young women wish to be taught arithmetic and book-keeping they should be formed into a class, for if the teaching is good others will certainly soon join them.

Whenever it is possible, a practical beginning, however small, should be made, trusting that the real goodness of the undertaking and the usefulness of the work done will gradually gain support and enable the operations to be extended.

There is a point to which I am anxious to call the attention of all who are interested in this cause, for I think that a new and very formidable danger to it has arisen. It has been proposed, to put an end to strikes and to the disputes that are so frequently occurring between employers and workmen, to establish boards of arbitration composed half of employers and half of delegates elected by the workmen, which board shall have the power to decide any differences arising between the two parties. This seems a very sensible plan, but in trades and manufactures in which both men and women are employed, it is also proposed to exclude women from all share in the election of the delegates. At first sight this appears a trifle – more perhaps an affront than an injury – but it should be remembered that when men and women are employed together, it is the almost invariable desire of the men, either to turn the women out of work altogether, or else to restrict them to only the least remunerative branches of the business. Thus women are altogether excluded from the printing and watch-making trades by combinations among the workmen. In the potteries they are confined to the coarser parts of the china painting. In Coventry and its neighbourhood, during the war with France, when the ribbon trade was flourishing and the workmen could dictate terms to the manufacturers, they were restricted to only one kind of weaving, which was peculiarly ill-paid. In Birmingham, only a few weeks ago, the whipmakers struck because a part of the masters had employed women in some of the well-paid departments of the manufacture. These examples show that nothing is to be expected from the generosity or good feeling of their fellow-workmen. If the women now employed in the numerous kinds of manufacture in which both sexes work together are prevented from voting for the delegates to boards of arbitration, they will be thereby rendered totally defenceless, and placed in a far worse position than before boards of arbitration came into existence; and it is much to be feared that before long they would find themselves turned out of every trade altogether, or confined to the least remunerative portions of it. These boards of arbitration are likely to become important elements in the government of the manufacturing districts. It was, I believe, proposed in Parliament to give them legal authority; and though the measure was rejected, they can hardly fail to obtain immense moral weight and influence. It is therefore of the utmost importance that they should be fairly and justly constituted, and rendered incapable of becoming instruments in the hands of the oppressor. But perhaps it may be said, that if women had votes, the men would not allow them to use them; and this would doubtless be the case if they voted together, but an arrangement to prevent any interference might be made. The proportion of women to men engaged in the manufacture could be ascertained from the masters, and consequently the number of delegates to which they would be entitled. These they might elect away from the men, and under the protection of the police, no men except candidates for election being allowed to go among them, lest they should use violence. By this means the women would be represented at the board, and it would become a matter of impossibility to oppress them to any considerable extent. I beg to lay this suggestion before the consideration of any local society that may arise in a manufacturing district, in hopes that by their calling the attention of the influential gentlemen of the neighbourhood to this point the threatened evil may be averted. It is no easy task to abolish an old-established abuse or injustice, but it ought not to be difficult in these days to prevent the erection of a new one.

On the Choice of a Business

(reprinted from *The English Woman's Journal*, November 1862)

The choice of the employment to be followed must mainly depend on the social position, education, and opportunities of each individual, but some hints may be useful as applying generally to all.

Those professions should be avoided which are already overcrowded and consequently underpaid.

This is a truism, yet, strange to say, this plain rule is little considered by young women starting in life; for though it is obviously bad policy to embark in an underpaid employment, it is also difficult to get out of the beaten track.

Thus, though every one knows that there are already far too many governesses and dressmakers, girls of the middle class beginning life seldom think of becoming anything else; they hope to succeed better than others; a few do well they think, and why should they not be among the few? Now if a young person has no choice but to become a dressmaker or a governess, she is right enough to enter on her work in a cheerful spirit, and to hope for the best; but if she can avoid entering these employments, it is her *duty* to do so as well as her interest. It is her duty, because as the numbers are already too great, her success can only be purchased by another person's failure. There is bread to be won for only a limited number, and if she succeeds in winning her loaf someone else must go without. If, therefore, any other opening presents itself, she should eagerly avail herself of it, not only on her own account, but out of consideration for the general good. Perhaps it may be said that every department of labour in England is overcrowded, and that she cannot enter any without occasioning inconvenience to those who are already there. In many departments, though not in all, this is true; but to occasion inconvenience is very different from causing starvation.

To compel a strong and healthy man or woman to emigrate to the colonies, where every kind of working man, and some kinds of working women are in demand, is to occasion inconvenience. To compel a stout lad who had intended to engage in some easy handicraft requiring no exertion, to change his plans, and embark in some manly and laborious trade, is to occasion inconvenience. But to take the work from those who have it not in their power to turn to any other kind of employment, and who could not earn their bread in the colonies any better than in England, the market for them being overstocked there as here, is to cause starvation. For the active and strong to engage, without necessity, in employments fitted for the weak, is an act of blameworthy selfishness.

Needlework, being a sedentary employment requiring little strength, is peculiarly well suited to the feeble, and is injurious to the muscularly strong, who require active exercise. Nature here, as in many other instances, has pointed out the proper division of labour, and punishes those who infringe her rules by destroying their health.

Teaching is not injurious to the strong, though in some respects suited to the weak also, but those who have another opening, and are blessed with health and strength, should avail themselves of it, for numbers of persons have no other opening and must teach or beg; those therefore who can obtain equally remunerative employment in another direction, should not fail to do so; and this not only on the low ground that it will in the end prove advantageous to themselves, but on the high ground that so to act will be for the benefit of all. There are, however, exceptions to this rule in the case of teachers.

One great cause of the want of employment for women is the inferiority of their education. A really superior, well-qualified person is therefore a benefactor to her sex when she becomes a teacher; because, by the instruction she affords her pupils, she will enable them to earn a good livelihood hereafter, which they would not have been able to do had they been ill taught. On this account ill-qualified women are doubly bound not to become teachers, as they will infallibly injure the prospects of their unfortunate pupils.

It will, perhaps, be well to mention some other employments for women.

Professions connected with literature and the arts need not be spoken of, as all who possess sufficient taste and talent will be sure to enter on these agreeable avocations, but I may observe that a new though humble branch of art is being opened to women – that of house decorators. They paint the doors, shutters, and other woodwork with various kinds of designs, coats of arms, etc., chiefly in oil colours. A lady of my acquaintance has had part of the woodwork of her house thus decorated with coats of arms and mottoes connected with her husband's family.

Another good employment is the tinting of photographs. Any woman with an ordinary knowledge of painting in water-colours, whether portraits or flowers, could do it with a little practice. To make the photograph take the paint, it must first be washed over with gum-water, or silica, which is better, and left to dry. The flaws must be covered with white paint. Moist colours should be used. Some knowledge of art is required, to choose harmonious colours for the dresses and backgrounds, and of course the better the artist, the more highly finished and the prettier the picture will be, but many women have sufficient knowledge and skill to attain to the art, if they would buy a dozen common photographs to practise upon. It is an easy accomplishment, and as most people are discontented with their own photographs and would like to have them improved, an artist of this kind would probably find plenty of customers.

Nurses for the sick are scarce, many women of doubtfully sober habits being employed in that capacity through the difficulty of obtaining better. Respectable women are trained to be nurses and are taught midwifery at King's College Hospital, in Portugal Street, W.C. But this noble profession is suited only to persons possessing strong nerves and superior intelligence, as well as good health, and requires a peculiar cast of mind, combining force of character, good temper, and the power of being contented with little gaiety and amusement. Only a select few can therefore be fitted for it; but those who feel themselves suited for this employment could not engage in a more useful and honourable career.

The copying of law papers, or law stationery as it is usually called, is a very good profession for women who unite a tolerable education to natural intelligence. Persons now engaged in this trade who were once daily governesses, have expressed a decided preference for their present employment. The average earnings, when in full work, are £1 a week, but very skilful hands can make more. Those wishing to learn the trade can be taught in several offices; but it would be useless for anyone to try to set up for herself unless she was assured of the patronage of several solicitors. Probably, however, solicitors have poor female relatives, like other people, and would be glad to provide for them in such a creditable and ladylike manner. The head of one of the establishments is the daughter of a solicitor.

It is needless to speak of clerkships in telegraph offices as these situations are so sought after that there are far more candidates than vacancies. The kindhearted gentleman, J. Lewis Ricardo, Esq., M.P., who first caused girls to be taught this trade, is recently dead, and women may well mourn his death, for in him they have lost a most efficient friend.

A good many young women are employed as assistant clerks in Post offices, and sometimes in private business offices to copy letters, etc. A good handwriting is the chief requisite; the power of making money calculations quickly and correctly is also needed, a point in which women almost always fail, owing to their superficial and inaccurate education, and which, if they are wise, they will remedy by self-teaching, or by taking lessons in arithmetic, before they attempt to take a situation of the kind. Sometimes they are employed as book-keepers in shops; these situations are tolerably well paid but are not easy to obtain.

Saleswomen in shops are generally well paid; it is a position that requires much bodily strength because of the number of hours they have to stand; a good knowledge of arithmetic is also necessary, as indeed it is in almost all employments but those of ill-paid drudgery. A good temper, or at least the power of self-control, is also requisite, to secure invariable courtesy towards the customers. The slightest want of politeness towards customers, even if they are themselves unreasonable and rude, is a breach of honesty towards the owner of the establishment; for if customers are offended they are likely enough to withdraw to some other shop. No-one therefore should enter on this employment who does not possess entire self-command.

In all cases where a father with daughters keeps a shop, they should learn to serve in it, unless indeed he has already made his fortune and can leave them comfortable independent incomes; for a daughter thus trained will always be able to earn her bread, and if she have no brother, or if he enters some other profession, she will then be able to succeed her father in the business, and will know how to carry it on. This is sometimes done, but not so often as it ought to be, and the custom seems to be confined to some particular trades, for which there appears to be no reason. If women have commercial ability enough to carry on the trade of bookseller and baker, why should they not also be grocers, drapers, silk mercers, hairdressers, etc.? One trade is probably not much more difficult to learn than another, and the bookselling trade, which women often engage in, is perhaps as difficult and complicated as any. It is to be feared that this arrangement would be objected to by the daughters themselves, partly from a love of idleness, and partly because there is a foolish idea that to become a tradeswoman is less genteel than to be a governess; the silly girls not perceiving that an independent position is in fact quite as dignified, and much more comfortable than that of a teacher, and that whatever advantages a governess may have in point of gentility, are more than counterbalanced by the solid comforts on the other side.

If girls would learn their father's business, it might then, in cases where there is one son and one daughter, be left to them as joint-partners, as is often done when there are two brothers. But whether this was done or not, the knowledge acquired behind her father's counter would enable her to get good situations in other shops. A girl should always consider it a great advantage to be taught her father's trade, as she then learns under his protection, is sure to be well taken care of if ill, and not to be overworked. A photographic artist at Brighton has brought up his four daughters to his own business, and it is said the whole family are prospering. Such examples should be more frequently followed. The daughters are thus provided with a comfortable maintenance, and their father on his deathbed will have the comfort of reflecting that he has secured them from the evils and dangers of poverty.

There are several other handicrafts requiring skill rather than strength in which women might very well engage, though they seldom do, and which they should beg their fathers as a favour to teach them.

From whatever cause it may proceed, it is certain that a lack of spirit and energy is often to be seen in women; they seem to be willingly helpless and contentedly inferior, as if they thought that God had made them so, and it was not their own fault. For example, I once went into a shop kept by a widow in which there stood a weighing-machine where people were in the habit of getting weighed. I told the mistress I wanted to be weighed; she replied she did not understand the machine herself, but her 'young man' would soon be back. Now the woman could have learnt the use of the machine by half an hour's study, but would not take the trouble, and thus left herself at the mercy of her assistant, for as all the heavy packages of groceries were weighed by it, it was perfectly in his power to cheat her.

This quiet acquiescence in ignorance and helplessness is melancholy to observe, and unhappily such instances are not uncommon.

In France women have far more energy, and constantly undertake the whole management of shops.

At Dieppe they carve ivory brooches and other ornaments, and send them to England, where great numbers are sold, by which they must reap a little harvest.[1] Why should not English women pursue this easy and pleasant trade?

Great quantities of ladies' shoes are also imported from France, said to be made by women, and sold at a very low price. English shoemakers should teach their sisters and daughters the handicraft, for why should foreigners enrich themselves while our own women starve?

For persons who have not had a superior education, and who have no chance of learning a handicraft, cooking is by no means a contemptible employment.

Formerly women could only become cooks by first becoming scullery and kitchenmaids and working up through a long course of drudgery; but now, by means of the various cooking schools established in London, a person can at once begin at the top of the profession, and thus cooking becomes a trade fitted to a much higher class of persons than it used to be.

Cooks' wages are never low and are sometimes very high; they may be said to range from £16 a year to £60, according to the skill of the performer. These cooking schools will also be useful to women who belong strictly to what are called the labouring classes, for many of them have not sufficient strength to go through the apprenticeship otherwise necessary in farm-houses and such-like hardworking places to prepare them for service in gentlemen's houses, but now, by paying a fee, they can be taught to cook and can at once be made capable of taking good places.

There is another plan by which this useful profession might be made accessible to numbers now excluded from it. At present families are generally supplied with cooks from the kitchens of people who keep larger establishments than they do; thus the duke's kitchenmaid goes to the squire as cook, and the squire's kitchenmaid becomes cook to the village doctor or clergyman. But as there are many more small than large establishments, the supply is insufficient, and though nobody goes without cooks, women who know very little about cooking are often engaged, and ill-dressed dinners are the consequence.

This might be remedied by introducing the apprentice system common on the Continent. It now often happens that a cook does not choose to teach her kitchenmaid much. Perhaps she is afraid that she might be engaged in her own stead if she grew skilful, o perhaps she is simply ill-natured and does not choose to take the trouble and so the poor maid gets little instruction. But if the cook was allowed to take an apprentice and to receive a fee for teaching her, she would take pains to teach, and at the end of the year would send her out an accomplished cook. This system works well abroad, and there does not seem to be any reason why it should not in England. It would cost the mistress of the house nothing but the food of the apprentice, and the use of an extra hand in the kitchen would be worth that. The cook would be glad to receive a fee, the apprentice would be glad to learn, the kitchenmaid would hear the instructions the cook was giving the other girl and pick up a little knowledge by this means. Thus all parties would be benefited and the race of cooks multiplied and improved. Two grades of cooks would then exist; those who began as scullerymaids and gradually worked up from the lowest ranks, and those who became cooks by purchase, paying a fee to learn. These latter would belong to a higher class than the former, and be more fit to become housekeepers.

Industrial schools will be of use in enabling many girls to become servants who would otherwise have found it impossible, for gentlefolks will not engage untrained girls; they must therefore get their training either in industrial schools, or in hard places where the work is severe and the pay only just enough to supply them with clothes.

Parents hardly seem sufficiently aware what a benefit these schools will confer on their daughters, by enabling them to avoid these hard places. If a young creature, whether a horse or a human being, is overworked in its youth, it cannot recover entirely, and never becomes as strong and healthy as it would otherwise have been. Horse-flesh is so very valuable that no-one would think of setting a two-year-old to pull a cart, because of the injury that would be done it; but it is not thought necessary to take so much care of girls, who are sent out to work hard while still growing, to their great future injury.

Some spirited ones, who will not give up soon enough, break down under it at once, and return home, perhaps to die, perhaps to be delicate for life, which for a working woman is the worst fate of the two. The very strong can stand this early hard work, but girls of average strength are hurt, and the weakly cannot bear it at all. But where industrial schools are established, this evil can be done away with, for girls taught in them will be able to get tolerably good places at once, and the knowledge of this will compel harsh mistresses to be more considerate to the poor young girls whom they employ; for if they treat them ill, they will be unable to get any servant at all, as the girls will go to the industrial school to learn their business, rather than take a place where there is danger of their being overworked; and in these schools they will learn much that is valuable besides. Habits of truthfulness and tidiness will be inculcated, and in many cases much that is evil in example may be avoided by keeping away from the wretched places to which girls are often compelled to go, to learn to be servants.

When once a girl has learnt enough of her business to be able to take a place in a gentleman's family, the life is far from disagreeable. There is plenty of companionship to promote cheerfulness, and, if a woman is careful, the wages are generally sufficient to enable her to save a competence for her old age. Some people complain that maids' wages are too high; a most unreasonable complaint, for surely a person who works hard has a right to earn enough to keep her out of the workhouse in her old age; and it does not appear to me possible that this should be done under £14 or £15 a year, and even then it can only be effected by great economy. So far then from maids' wages being too high, they are, in my opinion, almost lower than is right; and ladies who endeavour to force them down commit a great injustice. The wages of an ordinary woman with no particular skill ought to be sufficient to enable her to provide for her old age, and those who have skill besides, such as cooks and ladies' maids, ought to be paid for it over and above.

Still, compared to other employments for women, the profession of a servant is a good one. But some may, perhaps, think that a needlewoman's life would be freer, and prefer it on that account. It is true that it is freer in some ways, but the freedom is often dearly purchased. In dressmaking establishments the hours of work are fearfully long, frequently lasting from eight in the morning till eleven at night, with only the necessary interval for meals. No time for taking a walk on week days, and no holiday but Sunday. This discipline soon destroys the health, and a girl with a strong constitution is often the first to fall ill.

Those, however, who prefer this trade in spite of its drawbacks, should take care to sew pretty well before they are apprenticed, or they will not give satisfaction. Parents who intend their daughters to be dressmakers should send them to schools where needlework is made a great object, that they may start with every advantage. It is hard on the head of a dressmaking establishment to be provided with an apprentice who cannot sew tolerably, and such incapacity is likely to make her not a little severe towards the unfortunate girl.

Plain needlework done at home is so ill-paid that almost the worst kind of servant's place is preferable to this employment. The following is a list of the usual prices paid for needlework by the great shops and the contractors.

Ordinary gentlemen's shirts 10*d.* a piece (it takes twelve hours to make one); common men's shirts from 4½*d.* to 3*d.*, one firm gives only 2½*d*. (two shirts may be made in ten hours); for heavy corduroy trousers, 6*d*. (a pair can be made in twelve hours); great-coats, 7*d*. or 8*d*.

No class of needlework (except dressmaking) can be named which is not paid at the same inadequate rate, and 30,000 women live by this trade in London alone. Thus the better class of workers receive 10*d*. a day, the inferior 8*d*., and the lowest, 6*d*., out of which thread has to be found. Life on these terms is not life, but a slow death.

No-one can live long on the diet necessitated by a remuneration of 8*d*. or 6*d*. a day, when lodging, clothes, fire and candles have to be found as well. A strong person may perhaps exist for a year or two, then a cold or some slight ailment turns to consumption or low fever, and they die, and are entered on the death-rate as dying of these diseases, but the real cause of death was the previous low living and want of the comforts of life.

That women do so die instead of earning their living by wicked-ness is very wonderful, and much to their credit; that with the doors of a comfortable prison open to them if they steal, that they should not steal, speaks highly for their good principles; they are as truly martyrs as those who perish for their religion by the hand of the executioner; in truth, their trial is longer and more severe, for who would not find it easier to die a public and speedy death, supported by the admiration of friends and sympathisers, than to perish slowly and obscurely as these poor creatures do? That many fail in the ordeal is but to say that only a small percentage of the human race are fit for martyrdom.

All who are wise will avoid this profession; not that needlework is in itself a bad employment, on the contrary, it is a very good one, but because such numbers crowd into it, that the competition drives the payment down to a point below that at which life can for long be sustained.

All who have good feeling, all who love their neighbour as themselves, will, if they have a chance, turn to some other means of earning a livelihood, that their unhappy sisters who have no other opening, no way of escape, may have more room to struggle in, and a better chance of obtaining tolerable terms from their employers.

I believe the real, true cause of all this misery to be the neglect of parents to apprentice their daughters to some trade or handicraft as regularly as they do their sons. There is no reason why one sex should be more neglected than the other, and no father would think of declining to put his son to a trade because an uncle might perhaps leave him a fortune, neither ought he to think of not apprenticing his daughter, because she may perhaps marry; for, as the *Melbourne Argus* truly says, 'the number of marriageable educated women in the world, is out of all proportion to the number of educated men who are prepared to marry them'.

If women were quite positively certain to marry before their father's death, the present system would not be so bad; but as they are not, it is wicked and cruel, and based on a fallacy. Some day the contrary principle will be universally admitted. In course of time newspapers will take up the subject, leaders will be written, and lectures given on the duty of parents to their daughters; clergymen will preach about it, and tracts will be distributed, and then it will be recognised that a father who cannot leave his daughter a fortune ought to teach her a trade that she may be able to earn an honest livelihood, and the man who fails to do this will be thought less well of by his neighbours. Then the position of women will begin to improve, and this superfluity of helpless miserable creatures will gradually diminish, till it ceases to exist.

Meanwhile, the only advice I can offer to the already existing untrained women, who are too old to be apprenticed, is that those who are fitted for it should become sick nurses, and that those who are not, but possess health and strength, should learn cooking and go into service, either here or in the colonies. I fear they will consider this a degradation, but I do not see what else there is for them to turn to, and it is less degrading to live by honest work than to depend on charity. To those who have not strength for this, I can recommend nothing; but the British public should remember that they are worthy objects of benevolence, for they are suffering, and suffering severely, more from the fault of others than from their own, and they belong to a class to whom life in the workhouse is more than usually irksome and painful.

NOTE

1 Women in France also work as jewellers; polishing, setting, and imitating precious stones. This is probably the reason why French jewellery is so cheap and pretty. They are beginning to do mosaic work like the Florentines. In Switzerland women make watches, clocks, and spectacles.

On the Cause of the Distress prevalent among Single Women

(a paper read at the Social Science Congress and reprinted in *The English Woman's Journal*, February 1864)

There is a general impression that the difficulty of providing for our large numbers of single women is occasioned solely by an inequality in the numbers of the sexes; and that this inequality is something new, and the result of civilisation. I propose to show that it proceeds from some other cause, besides the inequality of numbers in the sexes, and also that both the difficulty and the inequality, far from being modern evils, are extremely ancient, and are felt in uncivilised as well as civilised communities.

In all ages, men, from their more exposed and adventurous lives, must have been killed off sooner than women; and in barbarous countries, where every man is a hunter and a warrior, and where fighting and the chase are everyday occupations, the mortality among the men of the community must greatly exceed that among the women. We see that it is so to this day among savages. Polygamy is the usual and ancient method of providing for the surplus of women thus produced. We have all laughed at the story of the New Zealander, who on being asked how he had provided for his second wife, from whom he had parted at the recommendation of the missionary, replied, 'Me eat her.' It was but his way of getting over the usual difficulty, and solving the common problem of how to provide for superfluous women; unfortunately, his way, like that of many better instructed men than himself, had the objection of being unpleasant to the party chiefly concerned.

In the ancient empire of China, they evade the question altogether, by calculating how many women they shall want for wives, and drowning the rest as infants.

In the middle ages, and in some Roman Catholic countries at the present time, the plan adopted was that of shutting up superfluous women in convents, and supporting them there on lands left by the benevolent for the purpose. This plan, doubtless, mitigates the evil, yet is open to two great objections. First, that the persons shut up are not always contented with their position; and, second, that many are left out, who being very badly off, would be glad to get in, but cannot be received for want of means to support them. Besides this, the immuring of large numbers of able-bodied women who, under different circumstances, might have added to the wealth of the country, by their labour, appears to political economists a sad waste of material. This was one of the pleas on which Convents were abolished in France at the revolution; and in Italy, but a few months ago, several were suppressed on the same ground.

In our own country, the difficulty of providing for superfluous women seems to be an old one, for Lady Juliana Berners, an abbess, who lived in Edward the Third's reign, and wrote a book, speaks of 'a superfluity of nuns', and not long afterwards, I have read that a law was passed forbidding men the use of the distaff and spindle, in order that some profitable employment might be left to single women. A trace of this old law, which, perhaps, preserved spinning as an employment for women, remains in our language, in which an unmarried woman and a 'spinster' are synonymous terms.

We see, therefore, that the inequality of numbers between the sexes, and the difficulty of providing for superfluous women, are not facts of modern origin, and are not confined to highly-civilised communities. But though women have always been more numerous than men, and though the difficulty of providing for the former is nothing new, it is true that civilisation has increased the evil, by increasing the proportion of single men, and consequently that of single women. Civilisation means increased comfort, and few civilised men will marry until they have attained a position which will enable them to command the comforts they have been used to as bachelors; this to many does not occur till late in life, and to some it never occurs at all. Civilisation, too, requires a number of soldiers and sailors to defend it, and many merchant-seamen to bring it luxuries, and of these the greater part must necessarily be unmarried. Thus a large proportion of women cannot marry till they have been for some years dependent on their own exertions for support, and many can never marry at all. The employments open to them, teaching, domestic service, and needlework, cannot contain the numbers seeking means of subsistence, hence arise competition, low wages, and the distress of which we hear so much. In civilised countries, even where the men exceed the women in number, as in the United States and our own colony of Melbourne, the women still find it difficult to live. It is stated by Dr Channing (an American) that in New York alone, in 1860, there were found to be 534 women who could earn only a dollar (4s.) a week, and a very large number besides who could earn nothing at all. This shows clearly that the excess of women above that of men is not the sole or even chief cause of the existing distress, and that if we could equalise the number of men and women in Great Britain we should still not be out of our difficulty. This is an important point, because many people believe that to produce this equality would at once put an end to the distress. Such an equalisation would diminish the distress, but would certainly not put an end to it, as the example of the United States clearly shows. Since, however, it would diminish it, female emigration, under judicious regulations, ought to be encouraged by every means in our power.

The national plan at present adopted in England for providing for superfluous women is that of shutting them up in workhouses. It is not very unlike the mediaeval one of convents, and presents many of the same defects; many women requiring relief being excluded, while the condition of those admitted is one of unhappiness and uselessness, and the waste of good working material equally great in both cases. To me the first defect seems the worst. Often, in London, when the overcrowded wards are closed, women, sometimes a crowd of women, are shut out and left to spend the night on the stones of the street, and this happens even when snow is on the ground! I write with several instances before me, cut out from newspapers during the last few months. In one case, a respectable tradesman, who lives opposite a workhouse, complains to the magistrate in Lambeth Police Court that he is frequently distressed by seeing numbers of poor creatures refused admittance. On one bleak night, he saw four girls huddled up together on the ground in front of the workhouse, from which they were excluded. Truly, there is nothing to be proud of in our present plan. If a humane Chinaman were to pass by a workhouse at night, and to see one of these heaps of shivering humanity lying out in the wind, rain, or snow, he might well be excused for thinking the system pursued in his own country the least cruel of the two!

The number of adult women inhabiting workhouses in England and Wales in March, 1861, was 39,073, yet this does not represent the number of those requiring relief, for as we see, many are excluded who would be glad to get in. We must, therefore, confess that our present system, like those which preceded it, is not satisfactory, for while it imposes an enormous expense on the community, it is still inefficient, and leaves large numbers of poor women unrelieved to suffer cruel hardships.

Thus all the plans for providing for superfluous women hitherto tried, whether by civilised or uncivilised nations, have proved more or less objectionable or inefficient.

There remains, however, one other plan, a plan which has never been fully tried, but which, if successful, would have the effect of putting an end to superfluous women altogether, by converting them into useful members of society. This plan is to admit women freely into all employments suitable to their strength. Perhaps this is the plan intended by Providence all along, and it is from failing to fulfil it that we have fallen into such great difficulties. The supposition is probable, because we can scarcely believe that large numbers of women were created expressly to be starved to death or supported by charity. But though this plan may seem obviously the right one, though it may recommend itself alike to philanthropists and political economists, let it not be imagined that it is an easy one to carry out. The accomplishment of this plan requires no small amount of good feeling and generosity on the part of working men, for if women are to be admitted into all trades suitable for them, what is to become of the men who had intended to enter them? If a ladies' hairdresser brings up his daughter to succeed him instead of his son, what is the son to do? There is no room for more men in other trades, so he may be compelled to emigrate, and if he is not adventurous, if he loves ease, if he shrinks from leaving his friends and parents, he will prefer remaining at home. If, then, he is not generous, he will beg his father to let him succeed to the business, and leave his sister to take her chance, like other girls, and marry or starve, sink or swim, as fate may decree. The same principle applies to all easy trades and handicrafts; but I have selected the example of a ladies' hairdresser, because the arrangement of ladies' hair, the manufacture of wigs, and the making of hair bracelets and chains, are employments which can hardly fail to be considered appropriate to women, yet this is one of those trades which are zealously defended against them, and into which it is hardly possible to introduce them, as even if the master tradesman be willing to allow it, no workman will teach a woman the art of hair-cutting or working in hair, nor allow her, if she has learned elsewhere, to work with him in the same establishment.

It is from this system of exclusion which arise most of those evils that press so heavily on women all over the world, and the system does certainly not proceed from *over-civilisation*, but is rather a part of barbarism! If Chinesemen would admit women into their easy trades, there would be no necessity for drowning female infants, but then their introduction might lower wages, and would certainly compel men to emigrate, and as they are not inclined to submit to these hardships, perhaps the kindest thing they can do by women is to terminate their existence while still children. If the New Zealand chief would have allowed his discarded wife a house and land, she might have supported herself, and there would have been no necessity for eating her; but then he wanted all the land for himself, and, besides, he probably thought, that to give women land, and let them build houses, might raise up in them a dangerous spirit of independence, and would quite destroy their feminine charms and characteristics, so it seemed to him much better to eat her, according to the ancient and venerable custom of the country.

I have dwelt on the universality and antiquity of the difficulty experienced in disposing of superfluous women, because it is sometimes thought that the difficulty we now labour under is only temporary, and occasioned by a particular crisis in civilisation, which will presently pass away of its own accord, and, of course, if people think this, they are little likely to exert themselves to remove the evil. But, in truth, the 'woman question' as it is called, is pretty nearly as old as the world itself; the only new thing about it is the attempt now made to give it a rational and humane answer, and it is probable that the successful solving of the problem will be one of the highest triumphs of Christianity and civilisation.

In barbarous times and countries, the women were got rid of without regard to humanity, but when the light of Christianity spread over the world, a better spirit arose, and the convent system was instituted with the view of disposing of them without suffering. The convent system was, in fact, a kind of compromise between right and wrong. As bad people would not allow women to become industrious self-supporting members of society, good people took charge of them, and maintained them at their own expense. Our workhouses, refuges, penitentiaries, and other charities for women, are all in the same spirit of compromise, they are wretched substitutes for the means of earning an honest living, but are far better than nothing at all. Workhouses are in one respect superior to convents, as those who avail themselves of their shelter are free to leave it whenever the opportunity of employment offers itself; on another point, however, they are inferior, being made purposely uncomfortable to deter people from entering on the supposition that none lack work but the idle. Now, as far as regards women, this supposition is untrue, every employment open to them being overstocked, while many which they would be glad to enter are kept closed against them, and it is manifestly unjust to prevent women from getting employment yet to punish them for not working. If, as many persons think, it is to the advantage of the community that women should be excluded from easy handicrafts, for the sake of keeping up wages and retaining more men in the country, then the community who profit by their enforced idleness ought to maintain them in comfort.

It may, however, be easily shown that in some trades it is suicidal policy in the workmen to exclude women. When an article is capable of exportation, and is manufactured by women abroad, it is evident that unless Englishmen consent either to admit women or agree to work themselves as cheaply as women, they must be undersold and lose the trade. This has actually happened in the watch trade, as Mr Bennet in 1857 foretold it would. The writer of a tract, entitled 'Female Labour', issued by the Working Man's Social Science Committee, quotes the watch trade at Coventry as an example of the high rate of wages occasioned by the non-employment of women, to encourage workmen in other trades to keep them out. A different moral may now be drawn from the instance selected, as these watchmakers are now ruined and living on alms, their trade having gone to Neufchatel. The loss of this trade is a serious one to the whole country, for hundreds, perhaps thousands, of women might have been comfortably supported by it, who will now have to be maintained by the rates, or be forced to live by dishonest means.

One of the strongest objections to the introduction of women into trades, is the danger lest the consequent reduction of men's wages might render it necessary for married women to go out to work to increase the resources of the family, to the destruction of all home comfort, and the injury of the health of both mothers and children. But the fact is that the wives of well-paid workmen in trades from which women are carefully excluded, are even now frequently compelled to go out to work or else to take in washing at home, to aid in the support of their families, as so large a proportion of their husband's wages are spent at the alehouse, that the remainder is not enough to provide ordinary comforts without the assistance of the earnings of the wife. We need not, therefore, be afraid of incurring this evil, because it is already incurred. Moreover, the wages to which the men would be reduced would still be sufficient to maintain a family without the assistance of the wife if they would renounce the alehouse. French workmen, in trades open to women, earn from 2s. 6d. to 4s. 6d. a day, the average being about 3s. 6d.; there is no reason to suppose that

Englishmen would get less, and this is certainly enough to rear a family upon, as agricultural labourers in Lincolnshire will bring up large healthy families on 2s. 3d. a day with no assistance from their wives except in harvest-time. Where the payment is by piece-work, the women employed in these trades earn as much as the men; where they are paid by the day, they get from 1s. 3d. to 2s. 6d., which is quite enough for a single woman to live on in comfort.[1]

With regard to the men, we see that it is not a question of reducing them or their families to want, but of curtailing their means of enjoyment; the effect, however, of this curtailment of the means of enjoyment would be to deter numbers of young men and boys from entering these trades. Many would prefer the high wages offered in the Colonies to 15s. or 20s. a week in England. Thus, they would emigrate and leave their trade to their sisters, to the great benefit of both parties, for when the effort of leaving home is once made, it seems certain that men are happier when engaged in active out-of-doors work than when employed in sedentary labour, which being unnatural to men, almost invariably injures their health. The Colonies would be greatly benefited also by the change, their prosperity being checked by the want of male labour. One Colony (Queensland) is actually petitioning to be allowed to import negroes, so great is the want of labourers. If this petition is granted, the English nation will present a strange spectacle to the world; negroes doing Englishmen's work abroad; men doing women's work at home, and women starving, begging, and sinning, because they can get no honest employment!

But perhaps it may be asked, Why not export the superfluous women and leave the men at home to follow their trades in peace? The answer is easy. Because women can neither plough, cut down trees, dig for gold, nor perform any of the rough work wanted in a wild country.

If the civilised world has grown too small for the numbers inhabiting it, so that there is not work for all, it is in the power of men, and men only, to enlarge these limits. It is the bounden duty of England to send out as many women to the Colonies as are wanted to be wives, teachers, or servants; to send more would be a crime, because they would not find employment. When we read that in some Colonies there are hundreds or perhaps thousands of men more than women, we must not suppose that such a number of women is wanted as would make up the difference. Many of these men are gold diggers and squatters in the bush and backwoods, who are leading a wild rough life and do not wish to be encumbered with wives. In a few years they will settle down and marry, and be succeeded by a new set of diggers and squatters, who, like their predecessors, must be unmarried; thus, the number of men in a colony must always exceed that of the women. If the numbers were equalised, crowds of women would find themselves on a foreign shore without the means of living.

It has been shown that young men engaged in feminine avocations would be positive gainers by any change which should induce them to emigrate, yet it cannot be denied that middle-aged and married men, as they could not leave the country, would be exposed to inconvenience by the reduction of wages which the introduction of women into their trades would occasion. This inconvenience would be somewhat mitigated by their being relieved from the maintenance of their daughters; still men who were used to earning five or six shillings a day would, on being reduced to three or four, find themselves deprived of many luxuries and comforts, and that this should be the case is a cause of just regret. But the fact is that whenever a false step has been taken, some suffering must always be endured in retracing it, and in employing men in trades suited to women a false step has been taken. Mr Howson, the Professor of Political Economy at Dublin University, has remarked that to employ men to do work which can be as effectively performed by women is as bad policy as it would be to employ an engine of fifty-horse power, where one of forty would suffice.

The question now is whether we shall continue in the false course, or endeavour to retrace our way. It is but a choice of evils, and we must decide whether it is a greater evil for women to continue unable to earn an honest livelihood, or for the men in certain trades to be deprived of some accustomed enjoyments, though still retaining enough for the support of themselves and families in health and tolerable comfort.

It appears to me that our continuance on the present system can only be justified on the principle of the lady who said, 'It seems *natural* that *women* should suffer, but it is *sad* when *men* have to endure privation.' If we think it natural, and therefore not wrong or shocking that women should be unable to earn an honest livelihood, then let us make no change; but if we believe that God is no respecter of persons, and that the happiness of women is of as much importance in His eyes as that of men, we ought to endeavour to lay the burden of poverty as equally as possible on both, and not to place the chief weight on those who are the least able to bear it, so as to crush them to the earth.

We must remember, too, that the evils which would attend a fair readjustment of the labour market would be but temporary, while the benefits arising from it would be permanent. In the course of a generation the inconvenience occasioned by the introduction of women into easy trades would be over, while the advantage to society would last for centuries. If the change had been made a hundred years ago, comparatively few workmen would have suffered from it, while the distress into which our working women are now plunged would never have existed in its present extent. If the change was to take place at once, the number of workmen inconvenienced by it would be smaller than if it is delayed a century, while our women would be saved a century of suffering. In this, as in every other case, the longer the wrong course is pursued the more difficult it is to retrace our steps. It should be observed, too, that if the change is not made quickly, the trade in all articles which are capable of importation and can be made by women, will leave us, and be established instead in those countries where women are freely allowed to engage in them.

The employment of women in France is rapidly extending in all trades which require neatness, taste, or delicacy of touch. The law there forbids workmen to strike unless they can obtain leave from the government on shewing good grounds of complaint; and the government does not consider the introduction of women sufficient cause for a strike, nor will it permit of threats, violence, or combinations to exclude them. On the contrary, every thing is done to encourage the employment of women. For instance, the Empress causes the decoration of china to be taught in the girls' schools under her control, and personally bestows prizes on the best pupils in the art. A school, too, with workshops attached, has been established for the purpose of teaching girls various other trades well suited to them. It is evident, then, that unless we follow the example of our neighbours, and encourage the employment of women, every trade which can be affected by foreign competition must speedily be taken from us. Duty and an interest are therefore co-incident. It is our duty to obtain for women the means of earning an honest livelihood, and in the long run it will prove our interest also.

NOTE

1 The rates of wages in France is taken from the census of 1848, and also from a statement of the correspondent of the *Morning Post* of a few weeks ago. The French workmen are discontented with their rate of

payment, and are petitioning for leave to strike to turn the women out, a petition which is not likely to be granted. In some trades, the wages do not seem to be lowered by the introduction of women; for instance, in the decoration of porcelain, it is women who earn the highest wages. One woman gets 20 francs (16 shillings) a day, and no man in the trade gets as much. These cases are, however, exceptional; as a general rule, there can be little doubt, that the introduction of women has a tendency to lower wages.

Emily Faithfull
(1835–95)

The youngest daughter of a Surrey clergyman, Ferdinand Faithfull, Emily attended Kensington Boarding School and was presented to Court. During her twenties, she left the fashionable circle of her society friends and became involved with the activities of the Langham Place Group. She helped Jessie Boucherett to organise the Society for Promoting the Employment of Women and, after training as a typesetter, founded the Victoria Press in 1860. Three years later, she started *The Victoria Magazine* but the success of her publishing ventures was somewhat marred when she was cited in a highly publicised divorce case, between Admiral Henry Codrington and his wife, Helen Jane, and suspected of lesbianism.

In 1867, Emily Faithfull withdrew from the Victoria Press but continued to be active in other areas: she was the first woman to join the Women's Trade Union League, started by Emma Paterson in 1875, and was one of the founders of the Women's Printing Society. In 1877 she established the *West London Express* which was so successful that it soon became necessary to increase her staff of women compositors and introduce new steam machinery. During the 1870s she joined the staff of the *Ladies Pictorial* and founded the International Musical, Dramatic and Literary Association in order to secure better protection of copyright. Her travels to America are recorded in *Three Visits to America* (1884). She also wrote two novels: *Change Upon Change; A Love Story* (1868) and *A Reed Shaken With the Wind; A Love Story* (1873).

Victoria Press

(a paper read at the National Association for the Promotion of Social Science, August 1860 and reprinted in *The English Woman's Journal*, October 1860)

When we remember the impetus given to the question of female employment by the discussion which took place at the meeting of this Association, at Bradford, last year, it seems but natural to suppose that one of the practical results of that discussion will be a matter of great interest to the present audience, on which account I venture to bring before your notice the origin and progress of the Victoria Press.

It has often been urged against this Association that it does 'nothing but talk'; but those who fail to see the connection existing between the promotion of social science and the development of that science in spheres of practical exertion, must acknowledge that if all discussions led to as much action as followed that which took place upon the employment of women, the accusation would fall to the ground. A thorough ventilation of the question of the necessity for extending the field of woman's employment, was at that time imperatively needed. The April number of the *Edinburgh Review* for 1859 had contained a fuller account of the actual state of female industry in this country than perhaps had ever been previously brought before the notice of the public. The question had begun to weigh upon thoughtful minds, and even to force itself upon unwilling ones, and the notion that the destitution of women was a rare and exceptional phenomenon, was swept away, as *The Times* observed, when Miss Parkes, addressing this Association at Bradford, did not hesitate to ask whether there was a single man in the company who had not, at that moment, among his own connections, an instance of the distress to which her paper referred. The discussion which followed operated in a most beneficial manner; it forced the public to put prejudice aside, and to test the theory hitherto so jealously maintained, that women were, as a general rule, supported in comfort and independence by their male relatives. The press then took up the question, and, with but few exceptions, dealt by it with a zeal and honesty which aided considerably in the partial solution of a problem in which is bound up so much of the welfare and happiness of English homes during this and future generations.

One by one the arguments for and against female employment, apart from the domestic sphere, were brought forward and examined; and where objections arising from feeling could not be vanquished by argument, the simple fact of women being constantly thrown upon the world to get their daily bread by their own exertions, left the stoutest maintainers of the propriety of woman's entire pecuniary dependence upon man, without an answer.

In the November following the Bradford meeting, the council of this Association appointed a committee to consider and report on the best means which could be adopted for increasing the industrial employments of women; in the course of the investigation set on foot by this committee, of which I was a member, we received information of several attempts made to introduce women into the printing trade, and of the suitableness of the same as a branch of female industry. A small press, and type sufficient for an experiment, were purchased by Miss Parkes, who was anxious to test, by personal observation, the information thus received. This press was put up in a private room placed at her disposal by the kindness of a member of this Association. A printer consented to give her instruction, and she invited me to share in the trial. A short time sufficed to convince us that if women were properly trained, their physical powers would be singularly adapted to fit them for becoming compositors, though there were other parts of the printing trade – such as the lifting of the iron chases in which the pages are imposed, the carrying of the cases of weighty type from the rack to the frame, and the whole of the presswork (that is the actual striking off of the sheets), entailing, particularly in the latter department, an amount of continuous bodily exertion far beyond average female strength.

Having ascertained this, the next step was to open an office on a sufficiently large scale to give the experiment a fair opportunity of success. The machinery and type, and all that is involved in a printer's plant, are so expensive that the outlay would never be covered unless they were kept in constant use. The pressure of work, the sudden influx of which is often entirely beyond the printer's control, requires the possession of extra type in stock, these and other economical reasons which will be easily understood by all commercial men, necessitate the outlay of a considerable amount of capital on the part of anyone who wishes to turn out first-class printing. A gentleman, well known for his public efforts in promoting the social and industrial welfare of women, determined to embark with me in the enterprise of establishing a printing business in which female compositors should be employed. A house was taken in Great Coram Street, Russell Square, which, by judicious expenditure, was rendered fit for printing purposes; I name the locality because we were anxious it should be in a light and airy situation, and in a quiet respectable neighbourhood. We ventured to call it the Victoria Press, after the Sovereign to whose influence English women owe so large a debt of gratitude, and in the hope also that the name would prove a happy augury of victory. I have recently had the gratification of receiving an assurance of Her Majesty's interest in the office, and the kind expression of Her approbation of all such really useful and practical steps for the opening of new branches of industry for women. The opening of the office was accomplished on the 25th of last March. The Society for Promoting the Employment of Women apprenticed five girls to me at premiums of £10 each; others were apprenticed by relatives and friends, and we soon found ourselves in the thick of the struggle, for such I do not hesitate to call it; and when you remember that there was not one skilled compositor in the office, you will readily understand the difficulties we encountered. Work came in immediately, from the earliest day. In April we commenced our first book, and began practically to test all the difficulties of the trade. I had previously ascertained that in most printing offices the compositors work in companies of four and five, appointing one of the number to click for the rest, that is, to make up and impose the matter, and carry the forms to the press-room. The imposition requires more experience than strength, and no untrained compositor could attempt it, and I therefore engaged intelligent, respectable workmen, who undertook to perform this duty for the female compositors at the Victoria Press.

I have at this time sixteen female compositors, and their gradual reception into the office deserves some mention. In the month of April, when work was coming in freely, I was fortunate enough to secure a skilled hand from Limerick. She had been trained as a printer by her father, and had worked under him for twelve years. At his death she had carried on the office, which she was after some time obliged to relinquish, owing to domestic circumstances. Seeing in a country paper that an opening for female compositors had occurred in London, she determined on taking the long journey from Ireland to seek employment in a business for which she was well competent. She came straight to my office, bringing with her a letter from the editor of a Limerick paper, who assured me that I should find her a great assistance in my enterprise. I engaged her there and then; she came to work the very next day, and has proved herself most valuable.

I have now also three other hands who have received some measure of training in their fathers' offices, having been taught by them in order to afford help in any time of pressure, or in case any opening should present itself in the trade, of which a vague hope seemed present to their mind. From letters which I have received from various parts of the country, I find that the introduction of women into the trade has been contemplated by many printers. Intelligent workmen do not view this movement with distrust, they feel very strongly woman's cause is man's; and they anxiously look for some opening for the employment of those otherwise solely dependent on them.

Four of the other compositors are very young, being under fifteen years of age; of the remaining eight, some were apprenticed by the Society for Promoting the Employment of Women, having heard of the Victoria Press through the register kept at Langham Place; and others through private channels. They are of all ages, and have devoted themselves to their new occupation with great industry and perseverance, and have accomplished an amount of work which I did not expect untrained hands could perform in the time. I was also induced to try the experiment of training a little deaf and dumb girl, one of the youngest above mentioned; she was apprenticed to me by the Asylum for the Deaf and Dumb, in the Old Kent Road, at the instance of a blind gentleman, Mr John Bird, who called on me soon after the office was opened. This child will make a very good compositor in time, her attention being naturally undistracted from her work, though the difficulty of teaching her is very considerable, and the process of learning takes a longer time.

Having given you a general description of my compositors, I will only add that the hours of work are from nine till one and from two till six. Those who live near, go home to dinner between one and two; others have the use of a room in the house, some bringing their own dinners ready cooked, and some preparing it on the spot. When they work overtime, as is occasionally unavoidable, for which of course they receive extra pay per hour, they have tea at half-past five, so as to break the time.

It has been urged that printing is an unhealthy occupation. The mortality known to exist among printers had led people to this conclusion, but when we consider the principal causes producing this result, we find it arises in a great measure from removable evils. For instance, the imperfect ventilation, the impurity of the air being increased by the quantity and bad quality of the gas consumed, and not *least* by the gin, rum, and brandy, so freely imbibed by printers. The chief offices being situated in the most unwholesome localities, are dark and close, and thus become hot beds for the propagation of phthisis.

In the annual reports for the last ten years of the Widows' Metropolitan Typographical Fund, we find the average age of the death of printers was forty-eight years. The number of deaths caused by phthisis and other diseases of that class, among the members in the ten years ending December 31, 1859, was 101 out of a total number of 173, being fifty-eight three-fourths per cent of the whole.

It is too early yet to judge of the effect of this employment upon the health of women, even under careful sanitary arrangements; but I may state that one of my compositors, whom I hesitated to receive on account of the extreme delicacy of her health (inducing a fear of immediate consumption, for which she was receiving medical treatment) has, since she undertook her new occupation become quite strong, and her visits to her doctor have entirely ceased.

The inhalation of dust from the types, which are composed of antimony and lead, is an evil less capable of remedy. The type when heated emits a noxious fume, injurious to respiration, which in course of years occasionally produces a partial palsy of the hands. The sight of the compositor is frequently very much injured, apparently by close application to minute type, but probably, as Mr H. W. Porter remarks in his paper read before the Institute of Actuaries, from the quantity of snuff they take, which cannot fail to be prejudicial. This habit, at all events, is one from which we cannot suppose that the compositors of the Victoria Press will suffer.

It has also been urged that the digestive functions may suffer from the long-continued standing position which the compositor practises at case. This, I believe, nothing but habit has necessitated. Each compositor at the Victoria Press is provided with a high stool, seated on which she can work as quickly as when standing.

There is one branch of printing which, if pursued by the most cultivated class of women, would suffice to give them an independence – namely, reading and correcting for the press. Men who undertake this department earn two guineas a week; classical readers, capable of correcting the dead languages, and those conversant with German and Italian, receive more than this. But before the office of reader can be properly undertaken, a regular apprenticeship to printing must have been worked out; accuracy, quickness of eye, and a thorough knowledge of punctuation and grammar, are not sufficient qualifications for a reader in a printing office; she must have practically learnt the technicalities of the trade. And I would urge a few educated women of a higher class to resolutely enter upon an apprenticeship for this purpose.

But for compositorship it is most desirable that girls should be apprenticed early in life, as they cannot earn enough to support themselves under three or four years, and should, therefore, commence learning the trade while living under their father's roof. Boys are always apprenticed early in life, at the age of fourteen; and if women are to be introduced into the mechanical arts, it must be under the same conditions. I can hardly lay enough stress upon this point; so convinced am I of its truth, that I now receive no new hands over eighteen years of age.

Many applications have been made to me to receive girls from the country; but the want of proper accommodation for lodging them under the necessary influence has hitherto prevented me from accepting them, but I have now formed a plan for this purpose, and when I am assured of six girls from a distance, I shall be able to provide for their being safely lodged and cared for.

In conclusion, I will only attract your attention to the proof of our work; for, while I am unable to produce the numerous circulars, prospectuses, and reports of societies which have been accomplished and sent away during these six months in which we have been at work, I can point to copies of *The English Woman's Journal*, a monthly periodical now printed at the Victoria Press, and also to a volume printed for this Association, both of which can be obtained in the reception room, and which will, I think, be allowed to be sufficient proof of the fact that printing can be successfully undertaken by women.

Women Compositors

(a paper read at the National Association for the Promotion of Social Science, August 1861 and reprinted in *The English Woman's Journal*, September 1861)

After the meeting in Glasgow, last September, a considerable controversy arose respecting the facts contained in my Paper relative to the establishment of the Victoria Press for the employment of women compositors.

It was once again urged that printing by women was an impossibility: that the business requires the application of a mechanical mind, and that the female mind is not mechanical; that it is a fatiguing, unhealthy trade, and that women, being physically weaker than men, would sooner sink under this fatigue and labour; and to these objections an opinion was added, which it is the principal object of this Paper to controvert, namely, that the result of the introduction of women into the printing trade will be the reduction of the present rate of wages.

With reference to the observations respecting the arduous nature of printing, I am quite willing to admit that it is a trade requiring a great deal of physical and mental labour. But with regard to the second objection, I can only say, that either the female mind is mechanical or that printing does not require a mechanical mind – for that women *can* print there is no doubt; and I think every one will accept as a sufficient proof of this the fact that the *Transactions* of this Association at Glasgow is among the volumes printed by the women compositors at the Victoria Press. Let this fact speak for itself, together with another equally important – namely, that the Victoria Press is already self-supporting, which is as much as can generally be said of any business scarcely eighteen months old, and far more than could have been expected of a thoroughly new experiment, conducted by one who had only visited a printing office on two occasions before the opening of the Victoria Press, and who had therefore to buy experience at every step; for although such experience is the most available, it is not the least costly.

The argument that the wages of men will be reduced by the introduction of women into the business was also urged against the introduction of machinery, a far more powerful invader of man's labour than women's hands, but this has fallen before the test of experience. It must be remembered, as is well argued by the author of the 'Industrial and Social Condition of Women', that the dreaded increase of competition is of a kind essentially different from the increase of competition in the labour market arising from ordinary causes – such increase commonly arising from an increased population, either by birth or immigration, or a decrease in the capital available for the labouring population. But in the case we are contemplating this will not occur, since women already form part of the population. Nor will the wages capital be drawn on for the maintenance of a greater number of individuals than it now supports. The real and only consequences will be an increase of the productive power of the country, and a slight re-adjustment of wages; and while heads of families will be relieved of some of the burdens that now press on them so heavily, there is no ground for the fear that the scale of remuneration earned by them will be really injured – the percentage withdrawn will be so small that the loss will be proportionably less than the burden from which they will be relieved, for as the percentage destined for the support of such dependents is necessarily distributed to all men indiscriminately, whether their relations in life require it or not, it is inadequate to meet the real burden borne by such as have these said dependents.

It has been asserted that the 'key note to the employment of women is cheap labour!' – that while the professed cry is to open a new and remunerative field for the employment of women, the real object is to lessen the cost of production.

It is not necessary to give this statement, so far as the printing is concerned, any further denial than that which is found in the fact that the wages paid to the compositors at the Victoria Press are according to the men's recognised scale. The women work together in companies, with 'a clicker' to each companionship, and they write their bills on the same principle and are paid at the same rate as in men's offices.

At present the Victoria Press is labouring under the disadvantage of having no women of the standing of journeymen; the compositors have to serve an apprenticeship of four years, during which they receive apprentices' wages, which, though not large, are still good compared to the wages women receive in most industrial employments. These wages differ according to the amount of work done. When signing the indentures of one of my first apprentices, her father, who is himself a journeyman printer, suggested to me that instead of fixing a weekly salary the apprentices should be paid by the piece, two-thirds of their earnings, according to the Compositors' Scale (English prices), which is indeed higher payment than that of boy apprentices, as they seldom receive two-thirds until the sixth or seventh year of their apprenticeship, whereas it is paid at the Victoria Press after the first six months, during which time no remuneration is given, but a premium of ten pounds required for the instruction received. I think this system more effective than that of an established weekly wage; it is more likely to stimulate exertion, and to make each apprentice feel that she earns more or less according to her attention and industry. It is not correct to suppose that printing simply requires a fair education, sufficient knowledge of manuscript and punctuation, and that all else is simple manipulation.

The difference between a good printer and a bad one is rather in the quality of mind and the care applied to the work than in the knowledge of the work itself. Take the case of two apprentices, employed from the same date, working at the same frame, and with an equally good knowledge of the business; one will earn eighteen shillings a week and the other only ten shillings. The former applies mind to her work, the latter acts as a mere machine, and expends as much time in correcting proofs as the other takes in doing the work well at once. But for every consideration it is necessary that the work should be commenced early; neither man nor woman will make much of an accidental occupation, taken up to fill a few blank years, or resorted to in the full maturity of life, without previous use or training, on the pressure of necessity alone. And those women who become printers, or enter upon any of the mechanical trades, must have the determination to make that sacrifice which alone can ensure the faithful discharge of their work. It is impossible to afford help to those who only consent to maintain themselves when youth is over, and who commence by considering it a matter of injustice and unfair dealing that the work they cannot do is not offered at once to their uninstructed hands. I cannot insist too strongly upon this – every day's experience at the Victoria Press enforces on my mind the absolute necessity of an early training, and habits of precision and punctuality – from the want of it I receive useless applications from the daughters of officers, clergymen, and solicitors, gentlewomen who have been tenderly nurtured in the belief that they will never have any occasion to work for daily bread, but who from the death of their father, or some unforeseen calamity, are plunged into utter destitution, at an age when it is difficult, I had almost said impossible, to acquire new habits of life, and which leaves them no time to learn a business which shall support them. Thus, life's heaviest burdens fall on the weakest shoulders, and, by man's short-sighted and mistaken kindness, bereavements are rendered tenfold more disastrous than they would otherwise have been. The proposal that fathers, who are unable to make some settled provision for their daughters, should train them as they train their sons, to some useful employment, is still received as startling and novel – it runs counter to a thousand prejudices, yet it bears the stamp of sound common sense, and it is at least in accordance with the spirit of Christianity. We have all at some time or other pitied men who, brought up to no business, are suddenly deprived of their fortunes, and obliged to work for their living – we have speculated on the result of their struggles, and if success has followed their efforts, we have pronounced the case exceptional. Is it then a marvel that the general want of training among women meets us as one of the greatest difficulties in each branch of the new employments opening for them? The irreparable mischief caused by it, and the conviction that it is only the exceptional case in either sex which masters the position, determined me on receiving no apprentice to the printing business after eighteen years of age. Boys begin the business very young, and if women are to become compositors it must be under the same conditions.

Still, in spite of all the difficulties we have encountered, I can report a steady and most encouraging progress – the Victoria Press can now execute at least twice the amount of work it was able to accomplish at the time of the Association's last Meeting. We have undertaken a weekly newspaper, the *Friend of the People*, and a quarterly, the *Law Magazine*; we have printed an appeal case for the House of Lords, and have had a considerable amount of Chancery printing, together with sermons and pamphlets from all parts of the kingdom – and I have recently secured the valuable co-operation of a partner in Miss Hays, who has long worked in the movement as one of the Editors of *The English Woman's Journal* and as an active member of the Committee of Management of the Society for Promoting the Employment of Women. We are now engaged in bringing out a volume under Her Majesty's sanction as a specimen of the perfection to which women's printing can be brought. The initial letters are being designed by Miss Crowe, the Secretary to the Society before mentioned, and are being cut by one of the Society's pupils. The volume will be edited by Miss Adelaide Procter, and will be one of considerable literary merit; the leading writers of the day, such as Tennyson, Kingsley, Thackeray, Anthony and Tom Trollope, Mrs Norton, the Author of *Paul Ferrol*, Miss Muloch, Barry Cornwall, Dean Milman, Coventry Patmore, Mrs Gaskell, Miss Jewsbury, Monckton Milnes, Owen Meredith, Gerald Massey, Mrs Grote, and, since my arrival in Dublin, I am grateful to be able to add the name of Lord Carlisle, and many others, have given us original contributions, and with kind and cordial expressions of interest have encouraged us with good wishes for our permanent success in a work the importance of which it is scarcely possible to overestimate.

Isa Craig

(1831–1903)

Isa Craig was the only daughter of a hosier; born in Edinburgh, she was orphaned as a child and brought up by her grandmother. She left school at the age of ten but over the next few years contributed several poems to *The Scotsman*. In 1853, she joined the editorial staff of *The Scotsman* but four years later left in order to take up the position of Assistant Secretary to the National Association for the Promotion of Social Science in London. In 1858 she married her cousin, John Knox, and in the same year became involved with the Langham Place activities. The following year she became a member of the Ladies' Sanitary Association and, shortly afterwards, founded the Telegraph School in order to teach women how to work with the new technology. Isa Craig was also a well-known author; she published several volumes of poetry, including *Poems by Isa* (1856) and *Songs of Consolation* (1874), and a novel, *Esther West* (1870).

Emigration as a Preventive Agency

(a paper read at the National Association for the
Promotion of Social Science, October 1858 and
reprinted in *The English Woman's Journal*,
January 1859)

The existence of this Association and the reception it has met with
is a proof that the men and women of England are fully alive to
the vast national and human interests involved in their present
social condition. That condition is not a gloomy one, but hopeful
in the extreme. It is no healthy activity which can only be roused
in some terrible emergency. But our law reformers are not passing
their resolutions in terror of the scaffold, our sanitarians are not
working under the scourge of a pestilence, nor our social economists deliberating in dread of a famine; yet wiser laws, better
education, better morals, sounder health, and a safer social
standing, are this day sought by the voice of the nation for all its
members. Though crime is decreasing, as a glance at our criminal
statistics will shew, the friends of the reformatory movement and
their exertions are on the increase; and if the country will steadily
give to prevention what it saves on punishment, the interest of the
investment will soon double the capital.

Emigration is one of those wider causes which operate in the
prevention of crime, and to draw the attention of the section to it
as such, may lead, considering the place in which we meet, to a
discussion elucidating the best means for applying it as a preventive
agency. It is only necessary for this purpose to indicate various
points of the question.

The condition of the working classes has the greatest influence
on the production of crime. A man or woman unable to read or
write may be neither a burdensome nor a dangerous member of
society, but a man or woman in want of daily bread and unable
to procure it, must be one or the other, and is in danger of
becoming both. Thus crime is plentiful when employment is
scarce. Labour is the great agent employed in the reformation of

criminals, and a criminal, so far as human judgment goes and so far as human means are concerned, may be held to be reformed who cheerfully submits to continuous toil. So also is labour the great preventive; a principle which has been thoroughly recognised in the economy of our industrial schools. There has unhappily grown up among us a population born in and reared to crime, which it is to be feared will find work for more than one generation of reformatory school-masters and prison disciplinarians, but it is on the whole a weak and a physically, as well as morally, diseased population, and is only kept at its strength by reinforcements from the non-criminal class. The grand recruiting agent for this reinforcement is the want of employment. The young workman, generally a mere lad, sent too early to work to retain much benefit from school instruction, is very often thrown out of employment when his apprenticeship expires. He 'tramps', as it is called, in search of work; he comes to some one of our great cities and finds no opening. The few shillings he arrives with are spent. Wandering about the streets weary, dispirited, exhausted from insufficient food, and perhaps unable to procure a lodging for the night, God alone knows how far he is tempted above what he is able to bear. Is not the best preventive against his joining the ranks of crime to be found in the ship ready to carry the workman to where his work awaits him? And though it may not carry him in the destitute condition described, though it may carry away a goodly portion of the strength and enterprise of the country by whom such trials have already been encountered and overcome, every hundred it does carry may relieve a hundred such at home and give them room to grow to the stature of manhood. Drunkenness is a well-known cause of crime, and that disastrous habit is generally acquired by the workman in those frequent unemployed intervals in which he is fain to resort to some stimulant to deaden his anxieties for the present and enliven his prospect for the future. What was the condition of the people of Ireland before the Irish exodus, which it needed famine and pestilence to accomplish? But the judgments of God are ever mingled with mercy, and the people who left those shores in gloom and anguish went forth to find that the earth 'is full of the goodness of the Lord'. The Irish emigration only slackened when the country was relieved, and the condition of its people has continued rapidly and steadily improving. Wages have risen and work is steadier, and as a consequence, crime has decreased. Within the last three years, convictions in Ireland have fallen from seven thousand to four thousand. In England, too, emigration has been at work as extensively as in Ireland, though the stream has poured out more calmly and constantly and not with such a sudden rush, and here, too, convictions have fallen from twenty-three thousand to fourteen thousand. The dire lack of employment, and consequent debasing struggle for the bare necessaries of life, has told frightfully on the social condition of the humbler women of this country. The most terrible phase in the criminality of the country is the number of its female criminals. One-third of the convicts of the kingdom are women, but that is a shallow calculation. Women are more often the accomplices of crime, its aiders and abettors, than its actual perpetrators. Then also they are the victims of crimes, and the seducers to crimes, which do not come within the power of the law, while inflicting the deadliest wounds on society; and over and above their own lives of crime, they become mothers of criminals. It is well known how brief is the unhappy career which our female criminals run. How they are recruited it is not hard to guess, in a country where there are fifty thousand women working for less than sixpence a day, and a hundred thousand for less than a shilling.

An army of ten thousand able-bodied women pass through our workhouses in a single year. Liverpool alone supplies upwards of two thousand. Many of these women are already criminal, while most of them are miserable specimens of humanity. The Emigration Commissioners could not find acceptance for them in our colonies; thus, for want of a better industrial system, a want beginning to be recognised as a necessity in workhouse management, a noble chance was lost, which it is to be hoped will yet be redeemed, of cutting off a fruitful source of crime, and enabling hundreds of women to emigrate without the brand of convicted felon upon them, to destroy their chance and hope of a better life wherever they go. Caroline Chisholm performed a noble reformatory work when she led out hundreds of destitute women, for it is such personal leadership that our destitute class are so much in need of, to prevent their falling into crime. The government emigration has been steadily accomplishing no mean amount of good, in sending out female emigrants of respectable character, and that emigration is now, by means of unceasing efforts at improvement, almost all that could be desired. A matron accompanies each band of single women sent out by the Commission, and it is contemplated to secure the permanent services of such matrons as have proved themselves capable of their arduous task, that a higher class of persons and a growing efficiency may be gradually attained for this important office.

But is there no hope for the convicted felon? Very little indeed with us. The industrious and honest of his own class shrink from contact with him. Few households will receive into their most menial offices a female convict, however well assured of her repentance and desire to commence a life of honest labour. We can hardly utter in sincerity the 'go and sin no more' of our now happily, to some extent, reformatory prisons, when we thrust forth a convict – especially a woman – into the streets, knowing that no door save that of the house of infamy will open to receive her. The 'Prisoners' Aid Society' might, were the means at its disposal, occupy completely this reformatory field. Emigration is one of the means they have employed in disposing of the prisoners, both male and female, whom they have assisted, and with the best results. It is doubtful whether much publicity concerning the working of such a society is to be desired, except so far as is necessary to secure support and give assurance of usefulness; but it is to be hoped that it will be enabled rapidly and widely to extend its operations.

To come now to the children, whose reformation and prevention from crime is by many considered the most hopeful, if not the only hopeful, reformatory effort. The question is arising in its most practical shape, what is to be done with them on leaving our reformatory and industrial schools? There are the children ready to work, but is the work to be had ready and fit for them? Managers and matrons of schools continually say that there is no difficulty in finding situations for their children, but that so soon as they are placed, especially the girls when received as inmates of respectable families, difficulties arise. Sometimes the parents visit by stealth the houses where they live, and entice them to evil, luring them back to their old evil companionships. Their antecedents are well known, one informing of the other, till it is impossible that they can maintain the powerful preventive principle of self-respect – depending, in all but the strongest minds, on the respect of others. In short, they are frequently tempted to their fall. Besides, every reformed child, whose industrial education has been carefully attended to and who obtains a good situation in consequence, takes the place of the child of the poor but honest working man. Emigration here again presents a solution of the question. Hundreds of boys and a few girls have been sent to the colonies from our reformatory and industrial schools. The matron of the Bloomsbury Industrial School has twice proceeded to Canada with a little band of the picked girls of the institution under her care. The result, so far as can be ascertained, has been most satisfactory. In three hours after her arrival she could have disposed of the whole of the girls, but it was not desirable to place them in one town, where they could hold communication with one another and so create some of the evils which had been felt at home;

they were therefore placed widely apart and with people whose characters were of ascertained respectability. She states that she could then have disposed of two hundred as readily as of twenty. Without a matron to take charge of these girls during the journey and to dispose of them judiciously on their arrival, the dangers of emigration, owing to the temptations that would surround them from the moment they were freed from superintendence, would render such a mode of disposal wholly objectionable. On the other hand, sending out a small number of girls under a matron is an expensive process, and as such is not attainable by many institutions. But might not some plan be adopted to meet this difficulty? Might not a depot as it were, call it 'Industrial Home' or some similar name, be formed in this very town of Liverpool, supported by a union of the industrial institutions throughout the country, with a resident and a travelling matron, whither the children who gained the emigration prize for steadiness and proved honesty might be drafted, for the purpose of being forwarded to the colonies? Government aid at this point would be far more desirable than at any other in the progress of industrial schools, and the good character of those sent out, and consequent readiness of colonists to receive them, might at length prevail on government to grant the children of such an institution free passage to all our colonies.

Thus at every point emigration meets us as a preventive agent. To the destitute but still honest workman, to the repentant felon, to the vagrant and criminal child – the sufferer not from its own sins but from the sins of others – it opens a wide door of hope and of escape from crime, while it benefits those who remain behind; relieving the labour market at home, and creating fresh markets abroad, and this latter is not to be overlooked even in a reformatory view of emigration. One mode of elevating the working classes is to prevent the fall of a portion of them into the criminal class, another is to promote reformation by showing the criminal that crime is a losing game, while lastly we benefit the working classes by strengthening their attachment to the country. Though we may advocate emigration we should not like to see the strength, the energy, and enterprise, of the best of our working population forsaking it. The farmer whose lease is about to expire may exhaust his land, but it is to be hoped that the lease of the English people on English soil is not nearly run out, and that while we send many away to a better life in another country we are looking also to the strengthening of those who remain.

Since the above was written, a pretty wide survey of the reformatory movement, its guiding principles, and the ordering of its details, has been offered to the view of the writer, some features of which it may be interesting to notice.

With regard to the principles which lead to the movement, there is now very little difference of opinion. Here and there an opponent still starts up to denounce reformatory prisons and schools as a premium on crime, but he is met with facts which he fails to dispute and arguments which he declines to answer. He says your criminal statistics prove nothing as to the causes of crime: at one time they are made to prove as its chief cause, ignorance; at another, density of population; at another, drunkenness; and at another, poverty and idleness. No doubt a general analysis of the causes of crime is difficult from their complexity of working. For instance, if a population is superlatively ignorant and poor, yet widely scattered, the absence of temptation and opportunity, from the absence of wealth to be preyed upon, removes one element of the calculation. While in a superlatively educated district, where the population is dense (which only takes place where wealth is accumulated), where poverty alternates with fullness, and idleness with exertion, arising from the greater fluctuations in the distribution of employment and wealth among a population maintained at its highest by the attractions of these, the element of ignorance is to a great extent withdrawn, but the other elements preponderate so largely as to turn the scale completely against the former. Yet it is not necessary to prove that ignorance is *a* cause of crime. Let any one study the composition of the population of several districts relatively to their criminality, and they will find, as was admirably brought out at Liverpool, that where the aggregate of ignorance, density of population, poverty, and drunkenness was greatest, there crime was greatest, and it is at the aggregate of causes that the reformatory movement strikes and not at the removal of any one of them. Take the outcast and vagrant child into the Ragged School, feed his already keenly awakened intellectual faculty with lessons of heavenly truth and of worldly wisdom, which it is happily no longer the fashion to despise, and train him to habits of continuous labour; you cannot say 'I know that child will grow up an honest man, while left on the streets he would infallibly have grown up a thief', but you know that you have increased the first chance and diminished the other a hundredfold. So with the entire movement: no-one can say, under a thoroughly carried out reformatory system, that crime will rapidly decrease down to its lowest point, or that it will recede from the reformatory movement and go on increasing in an alarming ratio, but you have increased the first probability and diminished the other in the same degree.

Two solitary but bitter opponents (Mr Elliott of London and Mr Campbell of Liverpool) stood alone at Liverpool in condemning, not any flaws in the working of the system, but the system itself. Mr. Campbell acknowledged a decrease of crime, but maintained that it could be accounted for in various ways, the chief of these being good harvests and extensive emigration. It was too soon, he said, to trace the effects of reformatories. This is true, as it must be of any great experimental work yet in progress, and all social work is experimental more or less, but its principles have been approved and a sample at least offered of its results. Again, he said, the attempt to elevate the lowest strata of society was utterly futile, and most dangerous to the class immediately above it, by holding out an inducement to take the last step and become criminals. He knew he should be in a minority in such an assemblage of sentimental philanthropists, but as a cold-blooded economist he had come to that conclusion. All these systems had a tendency to make people do everything in the mass and nothing by individual exertion, which was most socially injurious.

To come to the more practical question of individual exertion, which is thus said to be hindered by the operations of societies. The want of individual exertion is easy to be seen and much to be lamented, but the question is, would it be increased if the societies were to withdraw their operations? Have not the societies by which the reformatory movement is carried on, sprung from the necessity for some other mode of action than individual, sprung from the want of scope for such action as would meet the case, tied up as the individual is by the thousand restrictions of our modern society? How are those helpless masses to be dealt with who have fallen out of all connection with individual helping power? To give an instance, and one such might be found every day in the year by any one who did not shut their eyes to it. A stranger crossing the Mall in the early dark of a winter evening sees a young woman asleep on one of the benches, 'no one heeding her'. The sleep might have been that of intoxication, at any rate it was death to lie there on the raw December night. It was not, however, intoxication, but exhaustion.

'Do go home,' said the stranger.

'I have no home,' answered the girl.

'Have you no friends in London?'

'Not one.'

'But you must have lived somewhere lately?'

'I have sometimes a bed in a lodging house, sometimes no bed at all, only a bench in the park.'

'But the workhouse at least is open.'

'I was there. St James's casual ward is full, if I went elsewhere it would be the same. Plenty of us must sleep out in such nights as these.'

She answered thus far quite sullenly; an expression of sympathy caused her to shed tears and answer in a different tone. She spoke of her sufferings, cold and hunger among the least of these. The feeling of utter hopelessness and helplessness. The awakenings from broken sleep on the park bench during the cold dark nights. The shiverings and the cramps that seized her, till in the darkness she fancied she had awakened in some place of torment. She told no fine story: 'All my own fault,' she said. She was not uneducated, and her conversation proved as much.

'There are places of refuge.'

'I know there are, but I have none to help me and I am past helping myself.'

Now in such a case as this what can an individual do? Pass by on the other side, saying 'There is no help for it?' Here is a human being sunk to the lips in sin and suffering, unable to extricate herself, haunted by thoughts of self-destruction. Let her alone: cold, hunger, and disease will soon put an end to her sufferings; or in the kindly December darkness, she may drop into the murky Thames. This, perhaps, is the *'cold-blooded economical'* way of disposing of the case, though we venture to say the economist would not care to put his principle to so severe a practical test. But there is nothing very sentimental in the reformatory mode of disposing of it. The 'cold-blooded economical' is rather the more sentimental of the two. This is the reformatory method.

The stranger could do nothing except give the small immediate aid necessary to procure the sufferer a bed in a model lodging-house, and having ascertained that with all the eagerness of life left in her she grasped at the hope of salvation, send her to one of the ten homes established in different parts of London by one Society – that 'for the Rescue of Young Women and Children' – with the addition of a letter to the secretary, though even that is not necessary. Two hundred thus sent by strangers have been admitted during the past year into these homes. None are sent away for whom accommodation can be found. Some are restored to their friends, but the majority are restored to society as hard-working servants, a class from which the majority have fallen – and not such a bad economical product after all.

It may be mentioned here that it is the rule of this society to receive applicants at once and without any formality; and also as a telling fact that its columns of subscriptions contain a list of upwards of sixty 'former inmates' whose contributions vary from one shilling to four pounds ten.

Thus this and kindred societies aid, instead of superseding, individual effort. Without their help the stranger must pass by on the other side, knowing that he or she can give no effectual assistance. By their help he or she is summoned to individual exertion; summoned not only to add an item to the subscription lists, but to aid the effort and to promote general success.

For the class of degraded women emigration does not offer a very fair field. From the same cause which now forces us to keep our convicts at home and reform them if possible before sending them out from among us – namely, that the colonies will not receive them – must this unhappy class be kept among us at least until they have earned a character which may enable them to cover the stains of the past. The Society we have mentioned, as well as the Reformatory and Refuge Union, which has lately employed female missionaries for the reclaiming of the lost of their own sex, have used, but very sparingly, the agency of emigration. As an indication of the feeling which prevails in the colonies and is rapidly extending, and which ought to guide the leaders of the reformatory movement in availing themselves of the outlet of emigration, the following letter relating to the first emigration from the Bloomsbury School may be given. It may be stated that the experiment was repeated this spring, but still on too small a scale to meet the wants and wishes of the colonists.

Sir, A few days since, you were good enough to insert a few lines from me, announcing the expected arrival of ten girls, about fourteen years of age, under the protection of the matron of the Bloomsbury Industrial School, and specially recommended by the good Earl of Shaftesbury to the favourable notice of M. Hawk.

Upwards of sixty applications resulted from the publication of my letter, an evidence, if any were needed, of the want of such a class of domestic servants.

Mrs Edmond having found at Montreal, and elsewhere on the road, suitable opportunities for placing out these children, very judiciously availed herself of them, though much to the disappointment of the applicants here.

These young persons belonged to an Industrial and *not* a Reformatory School – a distinction to be borne in mind.

The early employment and welcome reception of these young persons, and the great 'demand' for them, will assure the noble lord and the benevolent gentlemen associated with him, that another and larger 'consignment' *next spring* will be acceptable; but we must make it a condition that, should Toronto be their destination, we must be assured of their coming here direct.

Every preparation was made for the suitable reception of Mrs Edmond and her little charges. She arrived on Friday with two of the children, who have been placed out at service; and it is due to Mrs Edmond to say that her deportment made a very favourable impression upon all those with whom she was brought into communication.

I have the honour to be,
Yours faithfully,
H. H.

August 10, 1857

Insanity: its Cause and Cure

(reprinted from *The English Woman's Journal*, September 1859)

We are all more or less acquainted with some of the forms of physical disorder. Few among us but have witnessed the attacks and watched the advances of fatal bodily disease, and beheld the awful mystery of dissolution. When the living principle withdraws from its fellowship with the clay, we know that close following corruption will swiftly turn beauty into hideousness, and that the mortal frame which contained the wisest and purest of spirits must submit without respite to the loathsome process. There is only one condition of humanity more awful to contemplate, more terrible to witness, than disease and death, and that condition is the obscuration and extinction of reason, the attack and triumph of insanity. If the malady takes the form of acute mania, eccentricities of manner make their appearance, speech occasionally rambles, and at length the mental disturbance is manifest; the wildest projects are entertained, and endeavours made to carry them out. Opposition provokes passion over which the unhappy being has lost all control and fearful shrieks and acts of violence proclaim the maniac. Or if it takes the opposite form of melancholia, to which women are more liable than men, the patient loses all hope, all cheerfulness, believes herself lost to happiness, to virtue, to God; doomed to self-destruction, and to the torments of hell, and sinks into the darkness of immovable despair. How terrible to see disorganisation and decay taking possession of the faculties of a human soul; its judgment reduced to helplessness, its passions foaming up into objectless wrath or futile sorrow, its tenderness turned into drivelling folly, its secret faults laid bare! Yet this is the portion of a sadly increasing number of our countrymen and countrywomen in these days of ours.

The reports of the Commissioners in Lunacy tell us that the

disease is actually on the increase. When in 1831 Hanwell was built for five hundred patients, it was supposed to be large enough to meet all the wants of the county. But, two years later it was full; after another two years it was reported to contain one hundred patients more than it had been built to accommodate; after another two years it had to be enlarged for three hundred more; and at this time (Colney Hatch having been meanwhile constructed for the reception of one thousand two hundred lunatic paupers belonging to the same county) Hanwell contains upwards of one thousand patients. Colney Hatch was opened in 1851; within a period of less than five years it became necessary to appeal to the rate-payers for further accommodation; and recent returns show that there are more than one thousand pauper lunatics belonging to the county unprovided for in any of its asylums. What has been going on in the metropolitan county has been going on more or less throughout the whole country. Additional accommodation for the insane has been provided, and further accommodation is still required. We must make allowance for two things to be taken into consideration in inferring, from the increased demand for asylums for the insane, an actual increase in the numbers afflicted with the malady: namely, the great improvement that has taken place during the last twenty years in the management of asylums, and the consequently increased desire to place the insane in institutions where every chance of recovery is afforded them; and the accumulation of chronic cases: the proportion of curable cases of insanity being something like one in five. Still, making allowance for these things, a large progressive increase in the number of lunatics is apparent. By a comparison of the returns of pauper lunatics and idiots, made by the Poor Law Board in the years 1852 and 1857 respectively, it is found that the numbers in the former year were twenty-one thousand one hundred and fifty-eight, and in the latter, twenty-seven thousand six hundred and ninety-three, showing an increase of six thousand five hundred and thirty-five in five years. Of that twenty-seven thousand six hundred and ninety-three, fifteen thousand four hundred and fifty-five were women. In 1852 their proportion to the population was as one to eight hundred and forty-seven, in 1857 it was as one to seven hundred and one. Deductions must also be made from this great apparent increase on account of the tendency to the accumulation of chronic cases in asylums, for when Hanwell was extended and Colney Hatch was opened a vast number of old established cases crowded in, to the exclusion of recent and curable cases.

The causes of insanity must be sought for in the social influences of the age, operating both physically and morally; the moral and physical causes acting and re-acting upon each other. In order to comprehend all the causes of insanity we have only to name two influences, the excessive luxury and the excessive poverty which prevail at the two extremes of the social scale. There is one cause to be found in operation at both ends of that scale, making a prey alike of the enervated and sensitive child of luxury, and of the child of poverty, depressed and dulled by over-work and anxiety; that cause is drunkenness, but that, as we think, is rather a symptom of the disorder than in itself the root of the disease.

With regard to drunkenness, Lord Shaftesbury, as one of the Lunacy Commissioners, stated before a select committee of the House of Commons a few months ago, that a large proportion of the cases of lunacy is ascribable to intoxication. He refers to various medical authorities on the point. Dr Corsellis, of the Wakefield Lunatic Asylum, says, 'I am led to believe that intemperance is the exciting cause of insanity in about one-third of the cases of this institution.' The proportion at Glasgow is about 26 per cent, and at Aberdeen 18 per cent. Dr Browne, of the Crichton Asylum, Dumfries, says, 'The applications for the introduction of individuals who have lost their reason from excessive drinking continue to be very numerous.' In Scotland they have establishments simply and solely for persons who have brought on insanity by intemperance. At Montrose, Dr Poole, the head of the asylum, says, '24 per cent of insane cases from intemperance.' At Northampton, the superintendent of the asylum says, 'Amongst the causes of insanity, intemperance predominates.' Dr Pritchard says, 'The medical writers of all countries reckon intemperance among the most influential exciting causes of insanity.' Esquirol, who has been most celebrated on the continent for his researches into the statistics of madness, and who is well known to have extended his inquiries into all countries, was of opinion that this cause gives rise to one half of the *causes* of insanity that occur in Great Britain. It was found in an asylum in Liverpool, to which four hundred and ninety-five patients had been admitted, that not less than two hundred and fifty-seven had become insane through intemperance. It is needless to multiply authorities. The effects of intemperance are no doubt connected with a previous predisposition to insanity, yet the predisposition would not have been developed but for the intemperance. As soon as the means of obtaining drink are taken away, the cure of such cases is rapid, but a recurrence to the habit of drinking produces a recurrence of the disorder, and that recurrence is what the unhappy beings are unable to avoid. There have been instances of one man having been brought back twenty times in a state of mania in consequence of drink, till the constant recurrence of the disorder became settled, and the man became a chronic madman. 'We visit them,' says Lord Shaftesbury, 'and find them in a state of sanity, yet we know from long experience that those persons, be they men or women, upon being discharged, will in the course probably of one hour go to the nearest gin-shop, and drink to excess, and be furiously mad before the end of the day.'

Of all sanitary conditions that of a sane mind is surely the most important. And in what does a perfectly healthy mind consist? In the vigour of the reasoning faculties, in the subordination of the passions and emotions, in the supremacy of the judgment, in the balance of all the powers. And if these things constitute the state of perfect sanity, then there is a good deal of insanity in the world at large not taken cognisance of by Her Majesty's Commissioners in Lunacy. Undoubtedly there is, just as there is a good deal of dyspepsia and other disease which does not disable people from going about their ordinary business, but which is the source of daily suffering to those afflicted with it, and to all with whom they come in contact. And as the presence of general unhealthiness is due to the same several causes as those which result in fatal disease, and often serves to indicate more clearly their nature and process of development, so the prevalence of restlessness, of excitement, of whimsicalness, of ungovernable temper, or of hereditary intemperance, serves to indicate the sources of mental disease. These are the straws which show how the currents are flowing towards the dreaded gulf of insanity, while some special wind of calamity is supposed to have been the messenger of doom to the wretch who is whirled into the abyss.

In old times the mad were believed to be possessed of devils, and long after the belief had perished, the barbarous treatment to which it led, the whips and chains and darkness which were to subdue the fiend, awaited the hapless sufferer.

When the Committee of 1827 was moved for, a frightful state of thing was revealed. 'Bad as was the evidence then given,' says Lord Shaftesbury, 'I do not think that it stated the real condition of things at all equal to what it was in reality, for I am certain that I can state that I saw and heard things far exceeding anything that appears upon the face of any one of the reports. Just take this fact: in one of the large metropolitan houses, nearly two hundred patients were placed every night under mechanical restraint; and I know that as much as three years after the act of 1829 came into operation, when we were doing all we could to remove those abuses, one of the superintendents admitted to the commissioners that between eighty and ninety patients in the house under his care were to be found in chains every morning. I mention these things because they never can be seen now, and I think that those who come after us ought to know what things have existed within the memory of man. At the present time when people go into an asylum, they see every thing cleanly, orderly, decent, and quiet; and a great number of persons in this generation cannot believe that there ever was anything terrible in the management of insanity. When we began our visitations, one of the first rooms that we went into contained nearly one hundred and fifty patients, in every form of madness; a large proportion of them chained to the wall, some melancholy, some furious, but the noise and roaring were such that we positively could not hear each other; every form of disease and every form of madness was there, horrible and miserable. Turning from that room, we went into a court appropriated to the women. In that court there were from fifteen to twenty women, whose sole dress was a piece of red cloth tied round the waist with a rope, they were covered with filth, crawling on their knees. I do not think I ever witnessed brutes in such a condition. It was known to one or two physicians of the Royal College who visited the place once a year; but they said that although they saw these things they could not amend them.' Dr Conolly has said, 'It is astonishing to witness humane English physicians daily contemplating helpless insane patients bound hand and foot, and neck and waist, in illness, in pain, and in the agonies of death, without one single touch of compunction, or the slightest approach to a feeling of acting either cruelly or unwisely: they thought it impossible to manage insane people in any other way.'

The state of things at York Hospital, the first that became the object of inquiry in 1815, was horrible. It was found that there were concealed rooms in the hospital, unknown even to the governors, and that patients slept in these rooms, which were saturated with filth, and totally unfit for the habitation of any human being; thirteen female patients were crowded in a room twelve feet by seven feet ten inches. Of Bethnal Green the report is still more revolting in its details. Several of the pauper women there, were chained to their bedsteads naked, and only covered with a hempen rug (this was in December). In January 1815 the visitors reported that 'The paupers' department, especially that appropriated to women, was unwholesomely crowded, and that some pauper men were chained upon their straw beds, with only a rug to cover them, defenceless against the cold.' In 1816 it was stated in evidence before the Parliamentary Committee that the patients were subjected to brutal cruelties from the attendants; that they suffered very much from cold (one patient having lost her toes from mort-

ification proceeding from cold, and that they were infested with
vermin). In 1827 it was further stated in evidence that wet, dirty
patients were chained to their cribs, and 'confined, without inter-
mission, from Saturday night till Monday morning'. That was the
constant and universal practice; they were chained at four o'clock
on Saturday afternoon, in crowded and ill-ventilated places, and
liberated about nine or ten on Monday, wallowing in filth, to be
rubbed down with a mop dipped in cold water, like so many
animals. Happily, hardly a vestige of this state of things remains:
if not in their right mind, the wretched things are at least clothed
and fed abundantly, besides being cared for and watched over,
employed, instructed, and amused. When any remains of the old
system are brought to light, there is a universal howl of execration
throughout the land, as witness the late disclosures in Scotland.
And only last year the commissioners found in Armagh Asylum,
Ireland, a female patient strapped down in bed, with body straps
of hard leather, three inches wide, and twisted under the body,
with wrist-locks strapped and locked, and with wrists frayed from
want of lining to the straps; the patient, too, was seriously ill.
Another male patient was found strapped down in bed; in addition
he was confined in a strait-waistcoat, with the sleeves knotted
behind him; and as he could only lie on his back, his sufferings
must have been very great; his arms confined with wrist-locks, his
legs with leg-locks, and the strappings so tight that he could neither
turn nor move. On liberating him he was very feeble, unable to
stand, with pulse scarcely perceptible, and feet dark red and cold,
having been under confinement in this way for four days and
nights. In Omagh Asylum, too, they found a bed in use for
refractory patients thus described. 'It is a wooden bed in the sides,
and there is an iron cover which goes over both rails; it is
sufficiently high to allow a patient to turn and twist, but he cannot
get up; the bars are from twelve to fourteen inches above his
head. The wild-beast-cage system, however, remains only in rare
vestiges like this; the general treatment of the insane is now humane
and tender, though not more humane and tender than is necessary
and wise. Every physical agent for the renovation of health is
secured to them by the enlightenment of the age.' 'Great and awful
is their responsibility,' says Dr Forbes Winslow, 'who thoughtlessly weaken the confidence of the public in the efficacy of the
physical curative agents in the treatment of insanity.' 'I was told,'
said a lady, 'that medicine was of no avail in the affections of the
mind. I went to the clergyman for assistance, he could obtain
none. I have struggled for weeks heroically against the disposition
to suicide, with the prayerbook in one hand and the open razor in

the other. Five times have I felt its keen edge at my throat, but a voice within me suddenly commanded me to drop the murderous instrument; and yet at other times the same voice urged me despairingly on to self-destruction. I knew I was ill, seriously ill, bodily ill; yet no-one pointed out to me the right remedy for my horrible impulse, or recommended me to put myself into the hands of the physician.' Such was the state of a patient who voluntarily subjected herself to medical treatment, and was happily restored to health.

Comparing the food supplied in workhouses and asylums, there is evidence in recent reports to show that the asylums are incomparably the best dieted; in the workhouses the ordinary diet table is of course arranged in such a way as to hold out no inducement to a pauper to remain in the workhouse. In the county asylum, there being no motive of that kind, and it being thought necessary for the benefit of the patients to give them a good diet, they have provided substantial, and nutritious food. The same report recommends a variety of dress, at the choice of the patients, especially of the females, and also that a better description of dress should be provided for Sundays to encourage the healthy feeling of self-respect. The consolations of religion too are offered to their minds. In Hanwell there is a little church of communicants. The last report of the Irish Commissioners recommends 'That the appointment of chaplains should be compulsory on the governors of district asylums, and that proper arrangements should be made for the due celebration of religious worship therein. At the same time,' says the report, 'as the ministrations of the chaplain have a necessary connection with mental exertion on the part of the patient, we consider that the duties of that officer will require on his part great judgment and discretion in their discharge; so that while the consolations of religion are fully afforded, the peculiar mental condition of the patients will not be lost sight of, and that he will carefully abstain from anything calculated to disturb the minds of the patients.'

The state of Pauper Lunatics in our Workhouses is still deplorable. On the 1st of July, 1858, they numbered seven thousand six hundred and sixty-six, close upon one thousand more than they numbered only the year before. Most of these unhappy beings are feeble and diseased in body as well as in mind, and, in a supplement to the twelfth report of the Commissioners in Lunacy, the great increase in their numbers is attributed to the neglect of curative means applied in time to prevent chronic insanity taking the place of mere physical and mental deterioration. We cannot do better than give the substance of this valuable report. It states that the proportion borne by the insane, idiotic, and weak-minded, to the other inmates in the workhouse, varies considerably in the different unions throughout England and Wales, and that it is considered by some that the proportion is greater in remote rural districts than in the more populous localities. Again, as respects the nature of the insanity, a marked difference has been observed between rural and city workhouses. In the former, congenital and imbecile cases have been found to prevail; while in the latter, the weak-minded are held to form a smaller portion, and cases of epilepsy and paralysis to be more frequent. Generally the cases met with in workhouses are those of persons suffering under chronic dementia, melancholia, and epilepsy: they comprise many who are idiotic or imbecile, none of them able to take care of their own interests or welfare, or to conduct themselves discreetly, if left without some governing control. Some reduced to poverty by their disease are of superior habits to those of ordinary paupers, and require better accommodation than a workhouse affords. Many are weak in body and require better diet. Many require better nursing, better clothing, and better bedding. Almost all, and particularly those who are excitable, require more healthful exercise, and all more tender care and more vigilant superintendence. In some of the smaller workhouses, situated in the rural districts, a greater degree of comfort and content is observable than in the larger houses which stand in crowded situations and are hemmed in by other buildings. In the former, the arrangements have a more homely and domestic character, and there are more means of occupation, and of free exercise in the open air. But of the metropolitan work-houses, the large proportion are of great size, old, badly constructed, and placed in the midst of dense populations. The weak-minded and insane inmates are generally crowded into rooms of insufficient size, sometimes in an attic or basement, made to serve for day and sleeping accommodation. Of the six hundred and fifty-five workhouses in England and Wales, somewhat more than a tenth are provided with separate lunatic and idiot wards, and these are ill-suited to the purpose, generally gloomy, ill-ventilated, small, and utterly comfortless; in some instances there being no tables, the patients are compelled to take their meals upon their knees. The supervision is altogether defective. In most cases, indeed, a pauper inmate is the person entrusted with the sole charge of the lunatics. These defects carry with them an almost necessary large adherence to mechanical coercion: in itself a sure and certain test of utter neglect, or of inadequate means of treatment. How sad is the condition of the poor creatures, often incapable of giving correct statements or preferring any complaint, however just, or of making any want known. 'Those who suffer most,' says this blue book, 'are often the least complaining. In a very recent case of semi-starvation at the Bath Union, when the frauds and thefts of some of the attendants had, for a considerable time, systematically deprived the patients of a full half of their ordinary allowance of food, the only complaint made was by the wan and wasted looks of the inmates.' The melancholic and taciturn especially, when (as is often the case) their physical condition is enfeebled by long privation, remain quietly suffering until their malady becomes confirmed and incurable. Placed in gloomy and comfortless rooms, deprived of free exercise in the open air, and wanting substantial nutriment sufficient to promote restoration, they pass their lives in a moody, listless, unhealthy, inactive state, fatal to their chance of ultimate recovery. The insane require both warmer clothing and more nourishing food than are supplied in workhouses, not only for promoting the recovery of those who are curable, but also for checking the tendency to waste and deterioration of the body which frequently attends the disorder in its chronic form. 'Hence it is,' says the report, 'that when the necessity has presented itself, which unhappily of late has very frequently occurred from the overcrowded state of the public asylums, to remove chronic cases of insanity from the latter in order to make room for cases more recent and curable, the immediate change in diet to which patients so removed have been subjected, has proved to be the chief cause of the marked deterioration in their condition which has been found to occur. This deterioration is not confined to bodily health alone; but patients who whilst in the asylum were quite tractable and harmless, have soon become irritable and violent. Restraint and solitary confinement is also extensively practised in workhouses for want of sufficient superintendence. Especial injury and injustice is done to patients recently afflicted. The want of early and proper treatment mainly tends to fill our county asylums with hopeless chronic cases.'

How great is the debt which humanity owes to those who have vindicated, and are still vindicating, the character of the divine Author of our being, and the majesty and universality of those laws by which he governs his moral offspring: to those who have taught, and are still teaching us, that the scourge of pestilence is no outpouring of vindictive wrath, but the product of our own folly in the breaking of some beneficent law of our being, to which the attaching penalty is appointed to bring us to obedience. This great truth has now been recognised in the treatment of mental disease; it is recognised that the individual, or others for him, must have broken one or more of the laws of life, and a return to a simple and entire obedience to these constitutes the remedy to be applied. In the words of Dr Conolly of Hanwell –

'In every well regulated asylum the whole system is strictly hygienic, in the largest sense of the term; comprehending an attention to all that can directly or indirectly promote the health of the body and the mind. The patients enjoy perfect liberty of their limbs. Chains and all mechanical instruments of coercion are unknown; buildings for the reception of many hundreds of insane patients being opened for their reception without one instrument of restraint being provided. Fresh air, clean clothing adapted to the season, good food liberally supplied, comfortable beds, warmth, ventilation, scrupulous cleanliness throughout the house, varied occupations and amusements, social entertainments, religious services judiciously and regularly performed, and spiritual consolation timely and prudently imparted, are now the things which characterise asylums for the insane. The poorest lunatic is introduced to comforts unknown to him before, and which diffuse calming influences over his whole frame of body and soul.' And under these calming influences many recover their reason, from whence it is easy to see that had those calming influences been earlier applied they would never have lost it, which brings us to the grand doctrine of preventability, that great gospel of the grace of God which is being preached among us. True there *is* incurable insanity, but you have only to search back to the cause of that to find it preventable too.

Undoubtedly, extreme poverty is the most fertile source of mental as it is of bodily disease. Its physical and moral influences tend to impair at once the mental and bodily powers. The immense number of pauper lunatics, and the great proportion of incurables among them, establish the fact. We do not mean hard labour and humble fare when we speak of extreme poverty, but of overwork, of insufficient food, and the other bad sanitary conditions which are forced upon a numerous class of the population, especially, though by no means only, in our large towns. 'Want of food,' said Lord Shaftesbury, before the Parliamentary Committee, last March, 'has a very sad and serious effect upon the nervous system, and I have known some instances in which it has superinduced madness. I remember some instances in that most oppressed class, the needle-women and slop-women. I have seen two or three cases in which they have been brought into the house in a state of decided insanity, but in a very short time these poor creatures have been set right, by no other remedy than beef and porter. I have no doubt want of food has a most depressing influence on the nervous system.' The children born of parents under these conditions are, to begin with, weaker as regards physical energy, and they are generally, as a consequence, more excitable. Those who have had to do with criminal or pauper children drawn from this class testify to their frightful excitability. The girls are especially wild in this respect, and the young women of the same class are the terror of workhouse authorities, and some have been sent to gaol for violent conduct, who might with more propriety have been sent to a lunatic asylum. Then the calming influence of the judgment has little opportunity for development; they are hurried with what stock of energy they possess at the earliest possible period into the vortex of toil. That natural moral instinct, which so often supplies the place of judgment, and which often also forms the safeguard of mind and body, and preserves the sanity of both among the sorely tried, is weakened in the case of those whose fall we are tracing, by the repeated triumph of temptation too strong for their powers of resistance, and with-draws its tranquillising and eminently sanitary power. As they grow up to manhood and womanhood, the terrible pressure of anxiety for the supply of the necessities of the body, or the excite-ments of immorality, or trials of temper arising from the irritability of inadequate strength, or the unnatural depression resulting from the same cause, complicated with the physical infirmities which appear alternately as cause and effect, terminate in intemperance which leads to madness, if not directly in madness itself. The children of such parents are the incurables among our pauper lunatics. Look too at the children of our union schools, at the weak and low type of physical and mental conformation which prevails among them. Look at the fact that they are generally unable to rise ubove the condition of pauperism, that they are in reality a race of paupers, that their children are born in workhouses, and that in workhouses they will die, ending life as they began it, their feeble bodies nourished with workhouse gruel, their poor souls solaced with workhouse grumbling. Thank Heaven the necessity for raising the minds and bodies of human creatures out of this slough of despond is beginning to find recognition also, even on the principles of social economy, 'the besetting basenesses of human nature', as they have been called, and sometimes seem, when basely used. It is beginning to be seen that we must give our paupers a good lift over the road to better conditions, if we would not have them come back upon our hands; that we must pay up the interest, at least, of our social sin, if we would not increase the principal of our social burdens. So we are really doing something to restore our paupers to a sanitary condition of body and mind, to enable them to do what sane men and women are able to do, take care of themselves. Bodily disease is readily enough traced to bad sanitary conditions in these days, and it is not difficult to trace mental disorder, and even incapacity, to the same source, while much physical disease can readily be referred to unsanitary mental conditions.

We come now to another class of causes, namely, those engendered by the excessive luxury of the age. Springing directly from this is one very fertile source of mental disease, over-work of the brain. Again to quote Lord Shaftesbury on this point, he says, 'I cannot but hazard the opinion, that if there is not an actual increase of insanity, there is developed a very considerable tendency towards it, and I think it arises from the excitable state of society. It is impossible not to see the effect that is produced by the immense speculation that takes place among all the various small trading classes, and people keeping costermongers shops, and every one who has five pounds that he can invest. All these people are carrying it on to a very great extent, and the number of disappointments, the great ruin that has come upon so many families and individuals, and the horrible distress to which they have been subjected, have had a very considerable effect upon their minds; events succeed each other with great rapidity, society is thus in a state of perpetual agitation. It does not signify whether it is political life or literary life, everyone must see that life is now infinitely more active and stirring than it used to be. The very power of locomotion keeps persons in a state of great nervous excitement, and it is worthy of attention to what an extent this prevails. I have ascertained that many persons, who have been in the habit of travelling by rail, have been obliged to give it up, in consequence of its effect upon the nervous system. I was speaking to one of our commissioners the other day, who had just come off a journey, and he said that his whole nerves were in a state of simmer, and he was not able, without some period of rest, to enter upon business. I think that all these things indicate a very strong tendency to nervous excitement, and in what it may issue I do not know; but I am quite sure, in regard to persons in that class of life entering into trade, and living in, and constantly under the influence of this stir and agitation, that their nervous systems are in a much more irritable state than they were twenty years ago.'

The history of hundreds in our asylums is told in a few sentences such as these. He was in business, seemingly successful, had a fine house and an expensive family, and was accustomed to every luxury; he speculated, failed, and went mad. Ah! If that family had not been so expensive, had been accustomed to labour instead of to luxury, as the true state of their affairs required, the reckless speculation would never have been entered upon, and the husband and father might have been a prosperous man instead of a lunatic and a pauper. Such cases are so numerous as to influence largely the returns of the commissioners, who attribute to it the great increase in the number of pauper lunatics, as compared with those in private asylums, who are generally self-supporting.

While an over-worked brain, the excitement of speculation, and the pressure of business, accounts immediately for mental disease among men of the middle and higher ranks, the lives of the women are given up to an aimlessness equally perilous. To go to the root of the matter, the nurture and education of most women are as enervating as possible. Their physical development is uncared for, if not positively retarded. A species of hot-house culture is forced upon the mind; a certain circle of accomplishments must be mastered, whether a girl has taste for them or no. If she shows little natural aptitude for any particular study, and much natural disinclination to pursue it, so much the worse for her, the drill is increased, the deficiency of nature must be supplied by art. With little or no ear for music, and a consequent hearty hatred or loathing for the preliminary labour by which its practice must be acquired, she must sit with aching back and vacant brain drumming for hours over the piano, in a way sufficient to drive to distraction all within reach of the discord, and which gives her unfortunate musical governess a succession of sick headaches, while powers of observation which would have been, to their owner at least, a source of infinite pleasure, are lying uncultivated, and defraud a judgment wanting only exercise to reach a healthy development. Still more urgent the case may be; even that of an ill-constituted mind calling for the utmost care in the training of the moral powers, and the culture of the qualities of thought in order to preserve its doubtful balance. Yet the same curriculum of accomplishments is deemed necessary for all, and that curriculum is such a crowded one that sense and morals are very often left to take care of themselves. At the same time emulation is encouraged and a system of stimulation applied which has the most painful effect on excitable temperaments, and such a temperament the girl's whole training tends to induce. Having gone through this course of treatment, the young lady comes out perhaps with a more delicate bloom and a more lady-like air than if she had been allowed for the last few years a freer use of her limbs and a more solid diet for her mind. Having come out, her life is passed between two extremes, the extreme of excitement in the season devoted to society, the extreme of aimlessness in the season of seclusion. It must be borne in mind that this is not meant to be a description of the average ladies of England. It is faithful to the class it portrays, faithful to a system which is too generally pursued, but there are thousands of mothers of our middle and higher ranks who give their girls the most careful and judicious training; thousands more who mingle with the system we have described just enough of the leaven of common sense and religion to neutralise its worst effects; and thousands more who have got the length of seeing its evils, without exactly seeing their way out of them. There are enough of the latter, and of the still unreserved upholders of the present system, to call for and justify an earnest appeal in behalf of a better system of female education. What wonder if the course of training and the mode of life we reprobate should sow and cherish the seeds of insanity. Over-excitement and aimlessness are two of the most unsanitary conditions to which the human mind can be subjected, and it is easy to trace to them restlessness, melancholy, and tendency to the painful class of hysterical affections; then comes the overthrow of some cherished hope, the disappointment of some overpowering affection, and the final plunge into the abyss of madness.

Disappointed affection is set down as the immediate cause of a large proportion of the female cases in our lunatic asylums. Of course we have not a word to say against the due development of the affections; we would not have them weakened, we would only have the judgment and the will strengthened, which need not be done at their expense, but ought to contribute to their power and elevation. But if perfect sanity consists in the right balance of all the powers, in the sway of the reason, and in the control of the passions and emotions, then it cannot consist with affections which escape the guidance of reason, with emotions which refuse to be under the control of their possessor, and may at any time throw the whole mental structure into ruin. An undue place is given to the affectional nature of women. They are taught from their infancy that affection is their most lovely and lovable quality. And so it is, but only in conjunction with other and higher qualities. In natures of no great depth of any kind, the result of the stimulants applied is a mannerism of affection fatal to all truth of character, while in natures really affectionate it develops the feelings into morbid power. And what in reality is the worth of that affection which has no discrimination, no foundation in justice and truth, which lavishes equal fondness on a favourite lap-dog and the dearest of friends, which will as readily lend itself to cherish the most selfish propensities of an ignoble nature, as to satisfy the heart of the noblest and worthiest?

Now we begin, we suppose, to show the cloven foot, to make

a demand for strong-minded women. Yes, we own it, while repudiating much that this most abused term has been made to include. Strength is not coarseness; on the contrary, it is nature's foundation for ease and symmetry and grace: and without that foundation, the beautiful superstructure is short-lived and insecure. This is true equally of the graces of person and of mind, as all who have come closely in contact with what are considered the amiable weaknesses will be ready enough to confess. That a woman's strength of judgment and strength of moral purpose should equal the strength of her affections, ought surely to be the guiding maxim upon which her training should proceed, even if the harmony and beauty of her nature were the only things to be considered, and it is only when this perfect balance is approximated to, that we approximate to the perfect woman, high-minded and sincere, and at the same time tender and graceful.

It is the work of the ladies of England to inaugurate an age of such strong-mindedness by using their influence to have the young of their own sex and rank brought under a more strengthening system of education. To discourage mere showy accomplishments, not by cramming with Greek and Latin instead of with music and Italian, but by setting the exercise of the reasoning powers above the exercise of the fingers or even the memory, and by earnestly cultivating the sense of responsibility, and social as well as individual duty. That they have social duties is beginning to be felt uneasily by thousands of the women of England who never entertained the idea before, and taking up the duty that lies nearest them, of preparing others for their share in the world's work, they may assume the ennobling responsibility of endeavouring to rescue their poorer sisters from the pressure of those evils, which, among many other deplorable results, inflict in so many cases the doom of insanity.

Maria Susan Rye

(1829–1903)

The daughter of a solicitor and the eldest of nine children, Maria Rye was born in London and educated at home. Like so many other reformers of her class and generation, it was her involvement with charity work which brought her into contact with feminist causes. She became the Secretary to the Committee to promote the Married Women's Property Bill and a member of the Society for Promoting the Employment of Women. In addition to starting the law copying office in 1859, she helped Emily Faithfull to found the Victoria Press and, with Isa Craig, established the Telegraph School. From 1861, she spent most of her time organising the Female Middle Class Emigration Society and made frequent trips to Australia and Canada to supervise the welfare of the women passengers. Horrified by the conditions on board, the high mortality and subsequent number of orphaned children, she turned her attention to the problem of destitute children. In 1867 she visited a children's home in New York and on her return to England, the following year, she founded a home for pauper children in London. Her efforts were rewarded in 1891 when the Church of England Waifs and Strays Society was founded; henceforth this venture became her main occupation. Always a controversial figure who was reputed to be stubbornly independent and rather fierce, Maria Rye spent the last eight years of her life retired in Hemel Hempstead with her sister.

The Rise and Progress of Telegraphs

(reprinted from *The English Woman's Journal*, November 1859)

The word 'Telegraph' (derived from two Greek words, *Tele* and *Grapho*, i.e., I write afar off) is the name given to any mechanical contrivance for the rapid communication of intelligence by signals.

But although the art of conveying intelligence by signs was practised in the earliest ages, being known even to the rudest savages, and although its importance is not only obvious but continually felt wherever a government is established, it has been allowed to remain in its original state of imperfection down to almost the present day.

Telegraphic communication in an extended sense may be considered to embrace every means of conveying intelligence by gestures and visible signs: such as lanterns, hoisting of flags, beacon fires on the tops of distant hills, carrier pigeons, drums, speaking trumpets (all used by barbarous nations); and more recently, since the invention of gunpowder, by cannons, sky-rockets, and blue lights.

The troops and marines which landed on the coast of America during the war, when scouring the woods in detached parties, were regulated by the notes of the bugle, which were so clearly understood that no false movements were ever made. The immense number of barges and boats which crowd the Imperial Canal of China are directed in their various routes, both by night and day, by the sound of the gong. The Indians of America convey intelligence from hill to hill by throwing out their arms with or without staves in them; and even the Hottentots, the poor degraded Bosjesmans, communicate with each other by arranging fires on the sides of the hills in certain positions.

The use of beacon-fires as a means of giving speedy warning of the approach of an enemy is very ancient, being alluded to by the Prophet Jeremiah, who wrote six centuries before the Christian era, and counselled the Benjamites 'to set up a sign of fire in Bethhaccerem' as evil appeared out of the north, and great destruction.

Beacon-fires were, for many years, a very favourite method of communication in our own country, and in an Act of the Scottish Parliament, 1455, there are directions that one bale or faggot 'shall be warning of the approach of the English in any manner; two bales that they are *coming indeed*; and four bales blazing beside each other, that the enemy are in great force'.

Sir Walter Scott refers to this practice in his *Lay of the Last Minstrel*; and Macaulay, too, in his glorious fragment of *The Armada*, tells us how –

Broader still became the blaze, and louder still the din,
As fast from every village round the horse came spurring
    in.
And eastward straight from wild Blackheath the warlike
    errand went,
And roused in many an ancient hall the gallant squires of
    Kent.
Southward from Surrey's pleasant hills flew those bright
    couriers forth:
High on bleak Hampstead's swarthy moor they started for
    the North.
And on and on without a pause, untired they bounded still;
All night from tower to tower they sprang, they sprang
    from hill to hill,
Till the proud peak unfurled the flag o'er Darwin's rocky
    dales;
Till like volcanoes flared to heaven the stony hills of Wales;
Till twelve fair counties saw the blaze on Malvern's lonely
    height;
Till streamed in crimson on the wind the Wrekin's crest of
    light;
Till broad and fierce the star came forth on Ely's stately
    fane,
And tower and hamlet rose in arms o'er all the boundless
    plain;
Till Belvoir's lordly terraces the sign to Lincoln sent,
And Lincoln sped the message on o'er the wide vale of
    Trent;
Till Skiddaw saw the fire that burned on Gaunt's embattled
    pile,

And the red glare of Skiddaw roused the burghers of
  Carlisle.

That some attempt was made by the ancients to improve upon
such signals is evident from the tenth book of Polybius, who
speaks of two methods of communicating intelligence, one of
which was adopted many centuries afterwards by Bishop Wilkins,
who describes the plan according to the British alphabet in his
curious work entitled *Mercury, or the Secret and Swift Messenger.* In
addition to these alphabetic systems, which depended merely upon
the number or alternate display and concealment of lights, Bishop
Wilkins describes one which rested upon the relative position of
two lights attached to two long poles, and which, he says, 'for its
quickness and speed is much to be preferred before any of the
rest'.

Although the Marquis of Worcester, in his *Century of Inventions,*
1663, tells us 'How at a window, as far as the eye can discover
black and white, a man may hold discourse with his correspondent
without noise made or notice taken,' yet the earliest well-defined
plan of telegraphic communication appears to have been invented
by Dr Hook, whose genius as a mechanical inventor has perhaps
never been surpassed.

This ingenious man delivered, on the 21st of May, 1684, a
discourse to the Royal Society, showing how to communicate
one's mind at distances of thirty, forty, a hundred, or a hundred
and twenty miles, in as short a time *almost* as a man can write
what he would have sent. The learned doctor, however, took to
his aid the then recently invented telescope (or, as Bishop Wilkins
calls it, 'Galileus, his perspective'). This subject appears to have
occupied Dr Hook's attention for some time, and the recent siege
of Vienna by the Turks evidently revived the matter in his mind.
About sixteen or twenty years after Hook's paper, M. Amontous,
of the Royal Academy of Paris, brought forward a very similar
plan in France, which was worked after the following manner.
People were placed in several stations at a certain distance from
one another, and, by the help of a telescope, a man in one station
was enabled to see a signal made in the next before him; he was
then required immediately to make the same signal, so that it
might be seen by persons in the station after him. The signals used
were either large letters of the alphabet, or figures of various shapes
to represent them: the latter being the more valuable, as by a
change of key, the nature of the communication might be kept a
secret from those actually employed in making the signals.
Amontous tried this method in a small tract of land before several

persons of the highest rank at the Court of France. But though Hook's invention and Amontous's modification were published all over Europe, and the former as early as 1684, yet they were not practically applied to any useful purpose until the time of the French revolution.

The telegraph then brought into use, in either 1793 or 1794, was the invention of M. Chappé, and though in general principles it was very similar to the machine invented by Hook, yet in detail it was greatly superior. His first station was on the roof of the Palace of the Louvre; and M. Chappé, having received from the 'Committee of Public Welfare' a message to be forwarded to Lisle, where the French army was then stationed, gave a known signal to Mont Martre, which was the second station, to prepare. At each station there was a watch tower, where telescopes were fixed, and the person on watch gave the signal of preparation. This was repeated all along the line, which brought each person in a state of readiness to receive the intelligence. The master at Mont Martre then received letter by letter the sentence from the Louvre, which he repeated with his own machine, and this was again repeated from the next height with as much rapidity as was possible under the circumstances, until the message finally arrived at Lisle just two minutes after leaving Paris. The upright post which was erected on the Louvre had at the top two transverse arms, movable in all directions by a single piece of mechanism. M. Chappé invented a number of positions for these arms, which stood as signs for the letters of the alphabet, and even these were reduced as much as possible; moreover, as the signs were arbitrary they could be changed every week, so that the sign of B for one day might be the signal for M the next – all that was necessary being that the persons at the extremities should know the key. Two working models of this instrument were executed at Frankfort and sent by Mr W. Playfair to the Duke of York, and hence the plan and alphabet of the instrument came to England.

Like all inventors, M. Chappé met with great opposition and discouragement: the people were averse to the use of telegraphs at all. His first instrument and station were destroyed by the populace, his second shared the same fate, it was burnt to the ground, and M. Chappé himself narrowly escaped with his life, for the populace threatened to burn him along with his telegraphs. Subsequently, as we have already shown, the subject was taken up by the French government, and his telegraph afterwards extensively used on the continent.

This description of telegraph, which was called the *aerial*, was first established in England in 1795, a line of stations being formed from the Admiralty to the sea-coast, and information was by this means conveyed from London to Dover in seven minutes. The expense of maintaining and working the line from London to Portsmouth was three thousand three hundred pounds per annum. We believe the last used in this country was that from Liverpool to Holyhead, which was at work as late as 1852, at a cost of fifteen hundred pounds a year.

Up to this period, however, as Mr Vallance observes, tele-graphic communication had only been a means of intercourse that was serviceable during those portions of the twenty-four hours when the greater light, that ruler of the day, was visible, and when clear weather admitted uninterrupted vision for a distance of ten miles. It had, indeed, been proposed to remedy this disadvantage by nocturnal telescopes, for the lamps of which gas seemed so admirably adapted: but this would do nothing towards lessening the interruption that wet and foggy weather occasions; so the proposed change was not considered worth the great expense which must have been incurred to effect the alteration. Mr Vallance next thought that an incompressible liquid confined in a pipe might be caused to move through the whole length of the tube, by operating on it at either end, and that, too, whether the pipe was one or a hundred miles long. Bossuet had proved the possibility of this for a distance of three miles half a century before. Each end of the pipe was connected to an apparatus which would cause any movement of the water inside to act upon and move a hand. Air confined in small pipes has also been tried, but both systems are attended with many serious disadvantages.

In July, 1747, Dr Watson, Bishop of Landaff, together with several electricians, ascertained the passage of electricity through water by sending shocks across the Thames, which experiment they subsequently repeated on a still larger scale through the New River at Newington; and in the August of the same year they transmitted shocks through two miles of wire and two miles of earth at Shooter's Hill. The passage of electricity through water excited great interest, and these experiments were repeated by Franklin, in 1748, across the Schuylkill at Philadelphia, and in 1749 by De Luc, across the Lake of Geneva.

Although electricity is now the agent used in common for all telegraphic operations, its mode of application has been as manifold as the number of labourers in this most interesting combination of science and art. The electrical plans used for communicating information may be included in the three following divisions: first, that in which simple frictional electricity was alone used; next, the galvanic, where voltaic electricity was employed; and lastly, the electro-magnetic, which combines the agencies of electricity and magnetism. The first method was used from 1747 to 1800; the second from 1800 to 1825; and the third from 1825 to the present time.

The discovery of frictional electricity is of very ancient date. Thales, who lived about six hundred years before the Christian era, is reported to have discovered the power developed in amber by friction; by which it is enabled to attract pieces of straw and other light substances. Theophrastus (B.C. 321) and Pliny (A.D. 70) also refer to this fact; but it does not appear that any of the ancients reasoned upon these observed effects, they simply observed and recorded them as facts, and this knowledge was quietly kept till the commencement of the sixteenth century, when Dr Gilbert instituted a series of experiments upon the subject. He found that this marvellous property possessed by amber was not confined to that substance alone, but belonged to several other bodies: such, for instance, as the diamond, glass, sulphur, sealing wax, resin, etc.

In 1617, a curious book, entitled *Prolusious*, etc., written by a Roman Jesuit named Strada, proves that there was a vague idea floating about concerning a magical magnetic telegraph. In this book there is a fabled contrivance of two magnetic needles, attached to dials bearing a circle of letters, and which possessed the property of always indicating the same letters, so that when one needle was made to point to any particular letter, the other needle, however distant at the time, placed itself so as to point to the same letter. A detailed account of this curious idea will be found in the *Spectator*, No. 241, and in the *Guardian*, No. 119.

Aided by the discoveries and experiments of Sir Isaac Newton, Hawkesbee, M. du Fay, the Abbé Nollet, Dr Watson, Kleist and Muschenbroeck at Leyden and others, electricity made slow but sure progress; but the first real attempt which seems to have been made to render electricity available *for the transmission of signals*, is described by Moigno in his *Traité de Telegraphie Electrique*. It is that of Le Sarge, a scientific Frenchman, who in 1744 established an electric telegraph at Geneva, composed of twenty-four metallic wires, separated from each other, and immersed in non-conducting matter.

In the first volume of Arthur Young's *Travel in France during the Year* 1757 there is the following description of one of the earliest electric telegraphs. 'Mr Lomond,' he says, 'has made a remarkable discovery in electricity: you write two or three words upon paper, he takes them with him into a chamber, and turns a machine in a cylinder case, on the top of which is an electrometer, having a pretty little ball of the pith of a quill, suspended by a silk thread; a brass wire connects it to a similar cylinder and electrometer in a distant apartment; and his wife, on observing the movements of the corresponding ball, writes the words which it indicates. From this it appears that he has made an alphabet of movements, and as the length of the brass wire made no difference, you could correspond at a great distance, as for example, with a besieged city, or *for purposes of more importance.*'

The *Madrid Gazette* of 1796 states that the Prince de la Paix, having heard that M. D. F. Salva had read to the Academy of Sciences a memoir upon the application of electricity to telegraphing, and that he had presented that body with an instrument of his own invention, expressed a wish to examine it, and being delighted with the facility and promptness with which it worked, presented it before the king and court, operating upon it himself: Salva was eventually invited to and entertained at the Court of Madrid. According to Humboldt, a telegraph of this description was established in 1798 from Madrid to Aranjuez, a distance of twenty-six miles. Other writers, on the contrary, say that it was M. Betancourt established this line; but, be this as it may, it is quite certain that in 1787 frictional electricity was used for the purpose of telegraphic communication between these two places.

The next electric telegraph in order of date is that of Mr Francis Ronalds, who in 1816 constructed one by which he was enabled to send signals with considerable rapidity through a distance of eight miles of insulated wire.

In 1823, Mr Ronalds wrote to the Lords of the Admiralty, requesting an inspection of his electric telegraph, strongly recommending its adoption for government purposes; but, alas! the experiments of the philosopher were offered all in vain to that highly respectable body of intelligent men, and with its usual procrastination and supineness the English government could not be induced even to *try* an electric telegraph. 'Lord Melville was obliging enough,' says Mr Ronalds, 'in reply to my application to him, to request Mr Hay to *see me on the subject of my discovery*; but before the nature of it had been known, except to the late Lord Henniker, Dr Rees, Mr Brande, and a few friends, I received an intimation from Mr Brande, to the effect *'that telegraphs of any kind were then wholly unnecessary, and that no other than the one then in use would be adopted.'* I felt very little disappointment,' he continues, 'and not a shadow of resentment on the occasion, because everyone knows that telegraphs have long been great bores at the Admiralty. Should they *again* become *necessary*, however, perhaps electricity and electricians may be indulged by his lordship and Mr Barrow with an opportunity of *proving* what they are capable of in that way.' In 1827, Harrison Grey Dyer, an American, constructed a telegraph at the race-course on Long Island, and supported his wires by glass insulators fixed on trees or poles. From that period to 1837, we have no less than eleven different telegraphs, and in 1837 six different arrangements of this instrument, exclusive of the one patented by Messrs Cooke and Wheatstone in the June of the same year. The deflective telegraph was introduced into Russia in 1822 by Schilling; at Gottingen by Gauss and Weber, in 1830; and into Munich in 1837 by Steenhul. In 1844 the registering telegraph of Professor Morse, employing the electro-magnet, was introduced between Baltimore and Washington. In America as far back as 1852 there were no less than fifteen thousand miles of wire erected and in constant use in that country, at which time we were using the old aerial telegraph on one line at least, viz., between Liverpool and Holyhead!

The first electric telegraph worked in England was on wires laid down between the Euston Square and Camden Town stations: and late in the evening of the 25th of July, 1837, in a dingy little room near the booking office at Euston Square, by the light of a flaring dip candle which simply made the darkness visible, sat Professor Wheatstone with a beating pulse and a heart full of hope. In an equally small room at the Camden Town station, where the wires terminated, sat the co-patentee, Mr Cooke, together with Mr now Sir Charles Fox and Mr Stephenson.

These gentlemen listened with intense anxiety to the first word spelt by that trembling tongue of steel which will only cease to discourse with the extinction of man himself. Mr Cooke in his turn touched the keys, and returned the answer. 'Never did I feel such a tumultuous sensation before,' said Professor Wheatstone, 'as when all alone in the still room I heard the needles click; and as I spelt the words I felt all the magnitude of the invention, now proved to be practical beyond cavil or dispute.' The telegraph thenceforward, so far as its mechanism was concerned, went on without a check; and the modifications of this instrument, which is still in use, have only been made for the purpose of rendering it more economical in its construction and working: two wires at present being employed, and in some cases only one.

After the successful working of the mile and a quarter line, the directors of the London and Birmingham Railway proposed to lay it down to the latter town, if the Birmingham and Liverpool directors would continue it on their line; but they objected, and the telegraph received notice to quit the ground it already occupied. Of course its sudden disappearance would have branded it as a failure in most men's minds, and in all probability the telegraph would have been put back many years had not Mr Brunel, to his honour, determined to adopt it on the Great Western. It was accordingly carried at first as far as West Drayton, i.e. thirteen miles: and afterwards to Slough, a distance of eighteen miles. The wires were not at this early date suspended upon posts, but insulated and encased in an iron tube which was placed beneath the ground.

The telegraph hitherto had been strictly confined to railway business, and in furtherance of this object, Brunel proposed to continue it to Bristol as soon as the line was opened. Here again the folly and blindness of railway proprietors threw obstacles in the way, which, however, led to an unlooked-for application of its powers to public purposes; for it is well to bear in mind that in England telegraphs are of two descriptions, viz., the commercial and the railway. The latter are used for the purpose of sending communications relative to railway matters, while the commercial are employed for the transmission of public or private messages at fixed rates or charges. They are mostly built near the railways, and in some cases a railway company will construct a line and give the use of it to a telegraph company, and as an equivalent the latter lends its aid to expedite their business. But sometimes the telegraph is laid down at the expense of the telegraph company, and that too at an expenditure which is only another instance of that economy, well understood in England, which knows how to make sacrifices bordering almost on prodigality in order to reap afterwards with usury the fruits of its advances.

At a general meeting of the proprietors of the Great Western Railway, in Bristol, a Mr Hayward of Manchester got up and denounced the invention as 'a new-fangled scheme', and managed to pass a resolution repudiating the agreement entered into with the patentees. Thus, within a few years, we find the telegraph rejected by two of the most powerful railway companies, the persons who above all others ought to have welcomed it with acclamation.

To keep the wires on the ground Mr Cooke proposed to maintain it at his own expense, and was permitted by the directors to do so, on condition of sending their railway signals free of charge, and of extending the line to Slough. In return he was allowed to transmit the messages of the public; and here commences the first popular use of the telegraph in England or in any other country. By the end of the year 1845 lines, exceeding five hundred miles in extent, were in operation in England, working Messrs Wheatstone and Cooke's patents, and in the following year the powerful Elec-

tric and International Telegraph Company sprang into existence.
'Jammed in between lofty houses at the bottom of a narrow court
in Lothbury, we see before us a stuccoed wall ornamented with
an electric illuminated clock. Who would think that behind this
narrow forehead lay the great brain – if we may so term it – of
the nervous system of Great Britain; or that beneath the narrow
pavement of the alley lies its spinal cord, composed of two hundred
and twenty-four fibres, which transmits intelligence as imperceptibly as the *medulla oblongata* does beneath the skin? Emerging from
this narrow channel the "efferent" wires branch off beneath the
different footpaths, ramify in certain plexuses within the metrop-
olis, and then shoot out along the different lines of railways, until
the shores of the island would seem to interpose a limit to their
further progress. Not so, however, as is well known, for beneath
the seas, beneath the heaving waves, down many a fathom deep
in the still waters, the moving fire takes its darksome way, until
it emerges on some foreign shore, once more to commence afresh
its rapid and useful career over the wide expanse of the Continent.'

The function of this central office is to receive and redistribute
communications. Of the manner in which these ends are
accomplished little or nothing can be gained from a glance round
the instrument rooms. You see no wires coming in, or emerging
from them: you ask for a solution of the mystery, and one of the
clerks leads you to the staircase and opens the door of what looks
like a long wooden shoot placed perpendicularly against the wall.
This is the great spinal cord of the establishment, consisting of a
vast bundle of wires, insulated from each other by gutta percha.
One set of these conveys the gathered up streams of intelligence
from the remote ends of the Continent and the farthest shores of
Britain, conducts them through London by the street lines underneath the thronging footsteps of the multitude, and ascends with
its invisible despatches directly to the different instruments.
Another set is composed of the wires that descend into the battery
chamber. It is barely possible to realise the fact, by merely gazing
upon this brown and dusty bundle of threads, that we are by them
put into communication with no less than four thousand four
hundred and nine miles of telegraph in England alone.

It must be remembered that although we have only spoken of
the Electric and International Telegraph Company, there are
several other companies in the United Kingdom working different
patents: and if it is a source of wonder to our readers that one
company should virtually possess the monopoly of telegraphic
communication in this country, it must not be forgotten that it
was the first to enter the field, that it came forward with a large

capital, speedily secured to itself the different lines of railway, and bought up, one after another, most of the patents that stood any chance of competing with its own.

From December, 1852, to the same month of the following year, no less than three hundred and fifty thousand five hundred messages were forwarded or received by this company, the receipts of which were £84,184 16s. 4d., thus paying the company dividends at the rate of 7 per cent per annum.

The telegraph company between London and Liverpool receives, or did receive a few years ago, a thousand pounds a year for doing the business of this railway company. *The Times* pays the same sum per annum for the transmission of a certain amount of daily news, paying in addition for all extra communications of importance.

The rate at which a commercial message is charged is a penny a mile for the first fifty miles, and a quarter of this charge for any distance under a hundred miles: some lines, the South-Eastern for instance, are even higher than this in their rates of charges.

There are two kinds of telegraph worked by the company, viz. the Needle Telegraph, which is preferable for all ordinary transactions because it transmits its messages with the greatest rapidity, and Morse's Recording Telegraph. The latter instrument strikes the spectator more perhaps than the nimble working needle apparatus, but its action is equally simple, strips of variable length, representing letters, being punched upon a long strip of paper, called the message strip, which is placed between a revolving cylinder and a toothed spring. Such is the celerity with which the notation is transmitted by this method, that in an experiment performed by M. Le Verrier and Dr Lardner before Committees of the Institute and the Legislative Assembly at Paris, despatches were sent one thousand miles at the rate of nearly twenty thousand words an hour. In ordinary practice, however, the speed is limited to the rate at which an expert clerk can punch out the holes, which is not above a hundred a minute. Where the object is to forward long documents, such as a speech, a number of persons can be employed simultaneously in punching different portions of the message, and thus the message strips can be supplied as fast as the machine can work.

The speed with which the attendants upon these instruments read off the signals made by the needles on the needle telegraph is really marvellous: they do not, in some cases, even wait to spell the words letter by letter, but jump at the sentence before it is concluded; and they have learned by practice, as Sir Francis Head says in *Stokers and Pokers*, to recognise immediately who is telegraphing to them, by the peculiar *expression of the needles* – the long drawn wires thus forming a kind of human antennæ by which individual peculiarities of touch are projected to an infinite distance!

We had the pleasure of visiting the Electric and International Telegraph Office the other day, and rejoiced with a great rejoicing at the fact that the whole of the large and important business is carried on by women, with the exception of that part which belongs to the receipt of the messages, and the transmission of the same by the well known intelligent-faced messengers.

The history of the introduction of young women into this office is most instructive and interesting. It appears that about six years ago Mr Ricardo, M.P., the then chairman of the Company, heard of a young girl, the daughter of one of the railway station-masters, who had for three years carried on day by day the whole of the electric telegraph business for her father, and that too with great intelligence and correctness. The idea then suggested itself of training and employing women as clerks for the telegraph company, and on its being proposed to the committee the proposition was warmly advocated by General Wylde, who has proved a most untiring friend to the cause. Opposition was of course naturally enough shown by the clerks of the establishment, but the experiment was permitted to proceed, and Mrs Craig, the present intelligent matron, appointed to instruct in her own room eight pupils on two instruments. At first, the instruments in one room were worked by young men, and the instruments in the other by young women, and it seemed as though the directors were pitting them against each other, establishing a kind of industrial tournament, to see which description of laborer was worthiest. With what tact, perseverance, and success Mrs Craig and her pupils worked may be gathered from the fact that at Founders' Court alone upwards of ninety young women are now in active employment, the whole of the actual working of the instruments having fallen into their hands. The committee are now perfectly satisfied that the girls are not only more teachable, more attentive, and quicker-eyed than the men clerks formerly employed, but have also pronounced them more trustworthy, more easily managed, and, we may add, sooner satisfied with lower wages. So well pleased, indeed, are they with the result of their experiment, that about thirty more women are now employed at the branch offices, viz., eight at Charing Cross, two at Fleet Street, two at Knightsbridge, etc.; and eventually there is no doubt they will fill posts in all the branch offices in England. As you enter the long room where these young girls are working, the continual clicking of the needles immediately strikes the ear; and a little observation teaches us that in one corner London is holding conversation with Liverpool, while in another Manchester is receiving a long message from London; here Temple Bar is discoursing eloquently of deeds and parchment, there Yarmouth is telling about her fish and shipping. Two girls sit at each machine, the one spelling the words as rapidly as letter succeeds letter, and the other writing it down as the word is pronounced. When the whole of the message is received, it is forwarded to another table, where it is entered, an abstract made, and its number registered; it is then passed on to another table, where another girl prices, seals, folds, and directs the paper, which is then delivered into the hands of the messenger and despatched to its ultimate destination.

The instrumental clerks earn from eight to eighteen shillings per week, and the superintending clerks from twenty to thirty shillings. These latter are responsible that no message is unnecessarily delayed, that the papers are properly filled in, and the words correctly spelt. The instrumental clerks are of course by far the more numerous; they are all young, none being received into the establishment after their twenty-third year, but they may enter as young as sixteen: for, quickness of perception and steadiness of vision being the two great requisites for this business, it will be readily understood that this training cannot commence too early in life. Six weeks is considered the average time for learning the fluctuations of the needle, etc., *after which period payment for service commences, nor is any fee required for instruction*; but if, at the end of two months, the pupil cannot conquer the movement of the hands, she is dismissed as incompetent to master the art.

As the office is obliged to be open twelve hours, there are three staffs, or 'relief guards'. The first works from eight to five, the second from nine to six, and the last from eleven to eight o'clock, thus allotting nine hours to each relay; a period which may be termed long, if considered positively, or short, when viewed comparatively with the twelve or fourteen hours of the miserable needlewoman or dressmaker. But though the hours these young women are on duty are long, we must not forget that the machines are not always in motion, and even when working are far from producing fatigue; we noticed many of the girls employing their spare minutes with knitting pins, light needlework, and books. The young girls now working at Lothbury are chiefly the daughters of small tradesmen, but several are the children of government clerks – Somerset House or Treasury-men – while three or four are the daughters of clergymen.

Should the proposed extension of female clerks to the branch offices be carried out, an inestimable boon will be presented to a very large and most deserving class of women, who, if not gifted with the power of imparting knowledge, have, as is too well known, no resource at present but their needle, for obtaining a livelihood. Other companies, the Magnetic and the London District Telegraph Companies for instance (the offices of both which are in Threadneedle Street) are following the steps of the International, and have already engaged a number of hands, who are now being duly instructed for their employment; but the honour and the credit of the movement is due to the Electric and International Company: nor can we close our paper without offering our most grateful thanks to the committee of that company for the liberal manner and practical form in which they have viewed the important question of female labour.

All communications respecting employment may be addressed to Mrs Craig, International Telegraph Company, Founders' Court, E.C.; or she may be seen there any Saturday, from two until four o'clock in the afternoon, by applicants desirous of being received into the establishment.

On Assisted Emigration

(reprinted from *The English Woman's Journal*, June 1860)

That a country peopled to repletion like our own, and pressed by
anxiety for the right maintenance of its population, as we most
undoubtedly are – that any nation possessing such magnificent
colonies as ours should hold such varied views and display such
apathy on the subject of emigration as is shown in England – is
one of those inexplicable mysteries for which no satisfactory
solution can be offered and scarcely a conjecture hazarded. It is in
vain that our opponents point to the stream of emigrants who for
years past have struggled across the Atlantic as a refutation of our
proposition, for the exodus from these shores (and we do not deny
that it has been a great one) has been effected mainly through the
instrumentality of the colonial governments, and is not and never
has been a national movement, springing spontaneously from the
people themselves, nor with one exception has it received that
encouragement and support from the home government which we
think the importance of the subject demands.

It is perhaps ungracious to say one word against the colonies
from whom we derive the largest if not the whole assistance by
means of which emigration is carried on from these shores, but,
while allowing a due share of praise to be awarded for the help
they have given, we cannot shut our eyes to the fact, that great
selfishness, as well as great assistance, has characterised their
proceedings in this matter. Men and women whose attainments in
physical labour, whose strength, virtue, and known powers would
secure them work and situations wherever they might dwell, are
the only candidates eligible for free or assisted passages. The
following extract from the Colonisation Circular, issued by Her
Majesty's Emigration Commissioners, will sufficiently explain all
that we mean. 'The colonies which promote emigration from the

United Kingdom by means of their public funds are New South Wales, Victoria, South Australia, Tasmania, *some* of the provinces of New Zealand, the Cape of Good Hope, and Natal. The system on which assistance is afforded varies in each colony, but in *all*, the persons assisted must belong strictly to the labouring classes.' From which it will be seen how hopelessly every branch of female labour is, with one exception, excluded from seeking a fresh field wherein to exercise its energies and support life. We desire clearly to point out this feature of the case at once, for this paper, falling as it will into the hands of educated women of limited incomes, to many of whom the subject of emigration is often presented as a means by which their prospects may be improved and their position in life established ought to be especially clear on this head, so again we repeat, '*There is no free and no assisted passage offered to any one colony, for any description of women except household servants.*' Now the sooner this fact is recognised and believed, the sooner some other plan will be organised whereby another and equally deserving class of women may receive assistance. Mind we do not say, or think, or hope, that the colonies will do more than they are now doing, perhaps more ought not to be expected from them, and if what they are now doing were only a little broader in its application perhaps more ought not to be required. No! The help will not come from the colonies; but if it were distinctly known that there was no assisted emigration for any but servants, and that there was a body of women ready to emigrate, as willing and as able to work in other spheres of action as their sisters the servants, surely the hand of charity, of sympathy, and of support would not be wanting or denied by English ladies to start, arrange, and uphold so admirable an institution. When it is remembered that, from circumstances, misfortunes, and losses, such women are often more helplessly placed so far as pecuniary matters are concerned than most household servants, what more can be said in support of a movement from which such great and such important results might be expected to arise?

In a letter containing some sound truths on emigration in the May number of this Journal, we are reminded of a fact which it will be well to bear in mind, viz. 'That the demand for female domestics has never ceased, and never will cease until the relative proportion of the sexes among the settlers is even, for every respectable young woman having the opportunity of marriage soon leaves her original engagement.' And why not, forsooth? Does not the presence of the maiden, household maiden though she be, make the hut of the solitary shepherd to blossom like the rose, and the wilderness to become a pleasant place? Who wonders then that the maidens all marry there, and make fresh homes for themselves and others, rather than remain to work for the families of masters ever so kind, and mistresses not always models of consistency?

No! There is no need to wonder at such a fact. If we wonder at all, it must be at this great truth, overlooked by both the colonial and the home government, viz., that scores of small farmers, owners of sheep-runs, nay even proprietors of large properties both in Australia and in New Zealand, are constantly marrying women beneath them in position and education; and this from the simple reason that there are no educated women there from whom to select a wife, for few, very few, of these men can spare time to cross the 'big pond' to fetch such an help-meet as becomes them, their prospects, or their birth. What then would we propose? To ship a cart-load of educated and polished women, of wives in fact, for the gentlemen of Sydney and Victoria? By no means, but we would assist to the colonies, to the same extent that household servants have been assisted, such women as those who have been accustomed to serve in light business, and the few, who form the daily increasing class of ladies who are not ignorant of or ashamed to join in the household management and duties pertaining to large families.

Such women would find ready employment in the several cities and townships of all our colonies. Offers of one hundred pounds a year have to our knowledge been made to very inferior women to serve as shop-women in mantle and bonnet stores in Melbourne and Sydney. Would not such a position be better for any woman, than the dependent, spirit-wearying life so many are forced to lead in England?

Others, and perhaps this might be the more preferable course to pursue, ought to work their way up the bush, indeed we believe there has been a great, a very great, mistake made on this point by nearly all emigrants. Centralisation may be good, we go further, it is necessary, nay indispensable, but excessive centralisation, even on a small scale, produces the very same evils which arise from overcrowding in the largest city in the world; so that in advising emigrants not to crowd the towns but to push on and into the bush, we are but urging them to take the very identical steps they took when they left their native country, viz., to carry their labour to the best and readiest, because the least supplied, market. There in the open country they might remain settling and establishing way-side schools, answering to our much abused but beloved old dame-schools, as useful in their day and generation as any of the Bell and Lancastrian academies of our own; or again, passing from

house to house, they might act as accoucheurs to those who from
distance and circumstances might require doctor and nurse
combined in one person.

Many an English lady has sat by the cottager's wife in her
hour of trouble, and knows right well how to manage in
such cases, and though she might not care, after reverse of circumstances has compelled her to labour for her own bread, to
undertake such an office here, and thereby appear as rival to the
village Gamp, no such feelings of rivalry or opposition or wounded self-respect could enter the head of the matron in the primeval
forests, where assistance would be duly prized and doubly
welcome.

In this country, too, how often are respectable women, skilled
in cutting out and contriving, found dwelling for weeks together
in the houses of our country gentry, and why should not this plan
be pursued there? Why should not a class of women, superior even
to those so occupied in England, work for their living in this way
in the pleasant homesteads of New South Wales and New Zealand?
It would bring them into contact with many kind and true-hearted,
if not polished, people; and surely a life like this, with everything
around fresh, bright, and abundant, with plenty of work in hand,
and the prospect of a good reward for their labour, surely such a
life, destitute though it might be of many of the elegancies and
refinements of civilisation, must be preferable to the lonely careworn life with its incessant toil and inadequate payment in an over
labour-stocked land like this.

Moreover, the gentlemen in our colonies have married their
maids from necessity, not choice (by-the-by better by far that they
should so act than repeat the disgraces of young Melbourne), but
let a choice be once offered to our countrymen and matters will
soon right themselves on this point, or we are greatly mistaken,
to the advantage of the colony and the inexpressible benefit of
thousands of our countrywomen.

If we were asked to which colony such a class of women might
be sent most advantageously, we should most unhesitatingly
answer New Zealand, because it is a class station; there the preponderating proportion of the people is an educated proportion; order,
and an established church, and collegiate schools are there; the
mania for money is not so rampant as in some of the other colonies,
and life and property and person are amply secured by the character
and general bearing of the great body of the settlers. We would
send our emigrants out in small bodies, say six at first, by assisted
passages, on the principle of the Canterbury Emigration Society,
with this difference that, instead of the Canterbury government

giving half the passage money, the new society which we propose should be started and managed by some of our wealthy English ladies, who should advance that money to the intending emigrants. The plan upon which the government of that province acts is this, the average price for steerage passengers (who of course form the body of emigrants) is seventeen pounds, including provisions; when an eligible person presents herself to their London agent, the question is asked, How much can you afford to pay towards your passage? If the answer is five pounds, then the Canterbury agent promises another five pounds, and the emigrant gives an IOU for the remaining seven pounds; so that the colony doubles whatever sum is put down, but then no-one but labouring people are permitted to offer themselves, so that this plan, admirable though it is, only reaches one class of persons. Of course educated women could not go out as steerage passengers, but the principle upon which these steerage passengers are taken out, would surely work as well for another and higher class of emigrants as for them.

The Government Emigration Officers and Offices for promoting the Emigration of the Labouring Classes are as follows:

S. Walcott, Esq., 8, Park Street, Westminster;
Com. Lean, R.N., 70, Lower Thames Street;
Lieut. Prior, R.N., Stanley Buildings, Bath Street, Liverpool.

The Colonial Agents for assisted passages:

William Field, Esq., 3, Bridge Street, Westminster (for Cape of
   Good Hope);
Messrs. Ridgway & Co., 40, Leicester Square (for Auckland);
Messrs. John Gladstone & Co., 3, White Lion Court (for
   Wellington);
E. Fitzgerald, Esq., 32, Charing Cross (for Canterbury).

The usual length of the voyage to the Australian colonies is about three months and a half, and to New Zealand a little longer: and as, at whatever season of the year it may be made, passengers have to encounter very hot and very cold weather, they should be prepared for both.

The following is a list of the principal articles required; but it cannot be too strongly impressed, as a general rule, that the more abundant the stock of clothing each person can afford to take, the better for health and comfort during the passage.

The Cost of Passage by private ships from London and Liverpool to different Colonies is as follows (from Official Reports)

FROM	TO	CABIN Cost including Provisions				INTERMEDIATE Cost including Provisions			
		£	s	£	s	£	s	£	s
Liverpool	Quebec	15	15	—	—	5	10	—	—
London	Ditto	12	0	to —	—	8	0	—	—
London	New York	15	0	—	0	—		—	—
Liverpool	Ditto	15	0	to —	—	3	10	to 3	15
London	Cape of Good Hope	35	0	,, 50	0	20	0	—	—
Liverpool	Ditto	30	0	,, 35	0	—		—	—
London	Sydney	35	0	,, 80	0	16	0	to 20	0
Liverpool	Ditto	45	0	,, 55	0	20	0	,, 28	0
London	Victoria	35	0	,, 80	0	16	0	,, 25	0
Liverpool	Ditto	40	0	,, 50	0	16	0	,, 25	0
London	Tasmania	35	0	,, 80	0	16	0	,, 25	0
Belfast	Ditto	45	0	,, 55	0	—		—	—
London	West Australia	35	0	,, 80	0	16	0	to 25	0
Belfast	Ditto	40	0	,, 45	0	—		—	—
London	South Australia	35	0	,, 80	0	16	0	to 25	0
Liverpool	Ditto	35	0	,, 45	0	18	0	,, 23	0
London	New Zealand	42	0	,, 80	0	20	0	,, 30	0
Plymouth	Ditto	40	0	,, 60	0	20	0	,, 25	0
London	California	60	0	,, 80	0	35	0	,, 40	0

A single (working) woman's outfit for Australia

		s.	d.
1 warm cloak, with cape		6	0
2 bonnets	each	3	10
1 small shawl		2	3
1 stuff dress		11	0
2 print do.	each	6	0
6 shifts	,,	1	3
2 flannel petticoats	,,	2	6
1 stuff do.		3	9
2 twill do.	each	2	0
1 pair of stays		2	6
4 pocket-handkerchiefs	each	0	3
2 net do., for neck	,,	0	5
3 caps	,,	0	10
4 night-caps	,,	0	7
4 sleeping jackets	,,	1	4
2 pairs of black worsted hose	,,	0	10
4 cotton do.	,,	0	10
1 pair of boots		5	0
6 towels	each	0	4½

Each person will also require:

1 bowl and can	1 tablespoon
1 knife and fork	1 teaspoon
1 deep tin plate	An assortment of needles and
1 pint tin drinking mug	thread, 1s.
2 lbs of marine soap, at 4d.	3 pairs of sheets
1 comb and hair brush	2 pots of blacking
2 shoe brushes	1 strong chest, with lock
1 pair of blankets	1 linen clothes-bag
1 counterpane	1 mattress and pillow

In all therefore the outfit of a single servant costs about five pounds, fifteen shillings; but then it must be remembered that this is a list of the most absolute necessaries, and of course an outfit for cabin passengers would cost considerably more.

We therefore propose that a separate fund be immediately raised 'for promoting the emigration of educated women'. Such money as may be collected to be placed under the control of the Committee for Promoting the Employment of Women, 19 Langham Place, that it may be used on the principles to which we have already referred; the committee at first only sending out small bodies of women (the number in each group not to exceed six persons), who shall be pioneers, and to a certain extent agents for the society, pledging themselves to protect, advise, and aid, to the extent of their power, any further emigrants hereafter to be sent out.

As we believe authentic information on the subject of emigration is exceedingly valuable, we consider ourselves fortunate in being able to offer to our readers extracts from some interesting letters from a poor (but very superior) woman, who, by the assistance of the Emigration Commissioners and the help of a benevolent gentleman in Kent, left this country for South Australia in 1849. The difficulties as well as the advantages of colonial life are here very fairly advanced, and do equal credit to the heart as well as the head of the writer, and we are quite sure that a perusal of their contents will greatly strengthen our first proposition – How is it that, with such colonies as ours, emigration is not carried on with more spirit and regularity from these shores?

Is it indifference or ignorance, or what is it, that is hindering the out-going of an overflowing nation like ours, which keeps our cities crowded to crushing, and lets the fertile plains and valleys of our colonies, quite as much our own though they are thousands of miles away, remain year after year uninhabited wastes without man or beast; hearts broken here, homes wasted there? Oh, fatal indifference and most disgraceful supineness! Happy will be the man or woman who shall arouse once more the spirit of enterprise among the people, and lead them to the fresh pastures and broad acres of our colonial possessions.

Frances Power Cobbe

(1822–1904)

The daughter of Evangelical Protestants, Frances Power Cobbe was educated at home until she attended a school in Brighton for two years. After her father's death in 1856, she travelled to Italy and Greece and became the Italian correspondent for the *London Daily News*. With an inherited income of £200 a year, she was free not to marry and chose instead to pursue a career as a writer and social reformer. She was involved in several welfare causes, advocating special care for the incurably sick and insane, working with Mary Carpenter in Bristol's 'ragged' schools and leading anti-vivisectionist campaigns. She was particularly concerned to reform workhouses and the condition of working women's lives. She met Barbara Bodichon in the 1850s and joined the campaign to protect married women's property. Always a staunch defender of abused young girls and battered wives, she was one of the early suffrage campaigners. Her publications include *The Theory of Intuitive Morals* (1855), *Broken Lights* (1864), *Studies of Ethical and Social Subjects* (1865), *Dawning Lights* (1868), *The Final Cause of Women* (1869), *Doomed to be Saved* (1874) and *The Scientific Spirit of the Age* (1888).

The Preventative Branch of the Bristol Female Mission

(a paper read at the National Association for the Promotion of Social Science, August 1861 and reprinted in *The English Woman's Journal*, November 1861)

I have requested permission to bring before this Association a plan for the protection of young girls of the poorest class, in our great cities. It is not merely as a suggestion more or less plausible that I would urge it on the attention of the members, but as a system of work already tried and proved efficacious on a considerable scale. My respected friend Miss Stephen, of Clifton, devised two years ago the plan which has since been tried at Bristol; and at the present time upwards of *one thousand* young girls have received from it aid and guardianship, which, we cannot doubt, have been the means, humanly speaking, of preserving many and many of them from the peculiar perils of their lot. I hope that the simple statement I shall offer of the nature and success of the scheme may prevail with some benevolent persons, to give it a trial elsewhere. In particular, I would urge that in Dublin, where much effort is making in the way of midnight meetings and refuges, it may also be thought right to endeavour to achieve a still more blessed end and *prevent* the awful woes which such labours can at best but partially *cure*. It was once bitterly remarked to me by a poor governess, 'There is more *bread* in England for one sinner that repenteth, than for ninety-nine innocent women.' I do not believe that this is really the case. I am convinced that if philanthropists saw how they could keep their poor fellow-creatures in the right path, they would gladly double the energies with which they now labour to bring them back when they have gone astray. It can surely only want the knowledge of *a practicable method* of attaining such a purpose which can hinder them from directing their first care to the *prevention* of evil. This method for one class of girls, has, I venture to affirm, been actually found and proved successful to a very considerable extent, therefore (I respectfully submit) it more than *asks*, it *challenges* adoption.

It is an unquestionable result of the experience of philanthropists that a very large proportion of misery and vice in our cities is the result, not of any voluntary and conscious choice of evil in the poor victims, but of conditions of ignorance, distress, and temptation, under which they have almost inevitably succumbed. To relieve young girls from these dangers, to rectify these conditions, is simply, under God, *to save them from falling*. It is not affirmed we can touch all cases where evil is deeper rooted, it is not pretended we can surround young women in our wicked towns with wholly healthful conditions, but, in as far as we can achieve such conditions for the majority, I repeat we are given the power of preserving them from destruction. Let us not faithlessly doubt the trust of this solemn power. An excellent Russian gentleman (son of the late president of the commission for the abolition of serfdom) made to me, a few months ago, this admirable remark, 'I am sometimes overwhelmed by the sight of the miseries caused by overcivilisation in England, and by undercivilisation in Russia; yet must I always believe that God has not so constituted the social condition of His creatures, but that there are laws which, when we have discovered them, and learned to obey them, will remove all this weight of sin and suffering.' This is the true Religious Philosophy of Social Science. There are means of obviating all the misery around us, and God has made it our task to find and use them. We are to drain and ventilate our towns and bring good air, and food, and water, to the lanes and courts, and not sit down and take for granted that cholera and typhus are unavoidable evils which we may *pray* against, but never strive to *hinder*; and *cure* in our hospitals, but never *prevent* in our filthy streets. And in like manner we are bound to purify the moral atmosphere of the poor, to take away the causes of moral disease, and pour in light and mental food, and warmth of kindly sympathies, to the utmost of our power, and not wait till the evil is done, and sin has fastened on its prey, and then begin to bestir ourselves to commit our criminals to reformatories, and our poor fallen women to refuges and penitentiaries. I am speaking for girls especially; let me add one appeal – think what it is to save a woman *at first!* To keep her innocent and good, able in due time to take her happy and honoured place as wife and mother in the great human family!

Among the healthful conditions needful for young girls, the most obvious of all is the protection, and care, and advice of women older than themselves. We all admit this unhesitatingly in the case of girls of the *upper* classes, and surround them perhaps with even unreasonable restrictions in consequence, yet young *ladies* have no such perils to encounter in any case as their humbler sisters. None dare to address them as (I grieve to say it) half the men in our country think they have a right to address a poor girl in her working clothes performing her duties. They are guarded by an ignorance cruelly stripped in very childhood from the others. They have no hard, hungry, toilsome life, no harsh, unfeeling mistress, from whom to escape. Here lies the point of the evil. An immense majority of the girls of the labouring class find their living as domestic servants in small and poor houses; and of all these thousands, and hundreds of thousands, of girls, a vast proportion have no adequate guardianship beyond their mistresses for the time being – their parents being dead or absent, unwilling or unable to attend to them. Again, among these mistresses so many fail in their duty, in one way or other, that the helpless young servant is worse than unprotected. I am not speaking 'without book', but as the result of the investigations of trust-worthy agents and 'missing links'. Mistresses of the humbler class are, of course, as varied in character, for good and evil, as other human beings, but the possession of such irresponsible power as they exercise over their poor drudges is too often a temptation to great and grievous wrong. Some are unkind, harsh, and cruel; some are drunken or ill-conducted; some (careful enough for their own children) send out their servants at all hours, on errands of all sorts – perhaps to the public-house for drink; some starve or overwork the girl; some withhold all her hard-earned wages on pretence of breakages, or of gifts of their own worn-out clothes; some dismiss her at a day's or hour's notice, and (as I have myself known it) actually at night, without a home to go to, or a shilling of money! It will be said, 'Why does not the girl seek for justice?' But the idea of applying at a police-office is the last these poor children would ever entertain, and their mistresses are but too well aware of the fact. It is not wonderful that girls in such circum-stances fall under the temptations which every walk in the streets places in their way – it would be wonderful were they *not* to do so.

To meet these evils was the problem to be solved. In January, 1859, an intelligent woman was installed as agent for a small free Registration Office. Girls from twelve to eighteen, in need of places, soon applied, and also employers needing servants. The agent examined each case, and recommended the girl as the truth might warrant. Such as could not go to service for want of clothes were assisted from a store of good plain ones in the office. When the girl went to her place the agent visited her at intervals, ascertained that all her circumstances were physically and morally healthful, and collected such share of her little earnings as the girl desired to invest in the savings' bank of the institution, which repays fourteenpence on every shilling. When the girl needed to leave her service another was sought for, and she was carefully guarded in safe lodgings, if any interval took place. It may perhaps be imagined that the mistresses would be impatient of such control as this, and decline to take girls from the office. But, on the contrary, it is found that only *bad* employers shrink from the legitimate supervision. All *good* ones rejoice in the added moral influence brought to bear on the conduct of their servants (who, of course, are always admonished in case of fault by the agent) and on the respectable appearance the clothes allowed them enable them to make. The proof that such is the case is this, that the institution grew in a few months with marvellous rapidity. A good house was engaged for a new registration office, agents were multiplied as needed, and girls and employers continued to flock more and more, so that at the proper hour a small crowd was always waiting for the attention of the excellent old lady who from the first presided over the registration. Much of the success of the undertaking must, indeed, be attributed to this good woman's untiring spirit and energy, and the sagacity with which she conducts all her business. Her address is Mrs Bartholomew, 3, Park Row, Bristol; and if any lady should visit that city, and desire to acquaint herself with the working of this institution, she cannot do better than call on her.

At the end of the first year nearly six hundred girls had been guarded and helped by the registration office, and then another want became manifest. Many of the children were utterly ignorant of all domestic duties. In most poor families the eldest daughter is made a sort of drudge and sacrifice to the various little *Molochs*, as Dickens calls her baby brothers and sisters. She is kept away from school to help her mother, and she grows up to sixteen, perhaps, when the other children cease to require her assistance, without knowing how to use a needle, or read or write. For these and many other neglected and ignorant girls it was obviously needed to open a servant's training school. To send them to service in their state of stupid ignorance was only to insure their speedy dismissal. A Home was accordingly opened at some distance from the Registration office. Here as many poor girls as desired it attended day classes for sewing, reading, etc. A certain number from these classes were in succession admitted to the privilege of boarding in the house and learning laundry-work and cookery.

From this Home they could be recommended to the better class of situations.

Still, there was another want. Among the girls who applied for help were many who, it became manifest, would never be suitable for service. Dismissed from place after place for faults of temper or the like, it became impossible honestly to recommend them to any new applicants. What could be done with them? There exists three miles from Bristol a large cotton factory, managed by very good people, and where the general morals of the 'hands' is unusually high. A Factory Home was evidently the proper resource. A small respectable house with a little garden was hired, a kindly matron installed, and the girls gradually established under her charge. After a few weeks, when they have learned their business, their earnings are sufficient to cover the expense of their board, etc.

Such is the whole scheme of the Preventive Branch of the Bristol Female Mission. It was, as I said, devised by Miss Stephen, of Clifton, and carried out by her labours, assisted by other ladies belonging to the Female Mission. The whole expenses (defrayed, of course, by private subscriptions) amount to £500. This includes Registration Office and Agent, Visiting Agents, Training School and Factory Home. As the number of girls assisted exceeds 1,000, we have here an average of less than ten shillings a head for affording them a guardianship which we may safely trust has been the means of preserving *numbers* of them from a fate which the costliest penitentiaries can do little to remedy.

Surely these simple details are enough to excite some desire to imitate in other cities a work so singularly successful in the first trial given to it! There is one class of girls for whom above all others I would plead, and for whom much good may be achieved without any outlay of money, only by the devotion of the leisure time of any lady who would give them guardianship similar to that of Miss Stephen's agents. I speak of the girls who are sent out to service from the Workhouse. I shall not attempt to discuss here the subject of workhouse education; let it suffice to observe that under the best auspices the education of *girls* in large masses, without individual love and care, has never yet been other than a grievous failure. It is all in vain to teach reading and writing, and to gabble formularies of theology, while every element is absent through which woman's nature can develop healthfully and beautifully.

It will not answer to treat a human being as one of a herd of cattle, however carefully fed and housed and driven from yard to yard. With all reverence let us say it, God Himself does not treat us so, but with *individual* care and love; and out of our belief in this *personal* love springs all that is deepest in religion. In like manner, it is the parent's love for the child as an *individual* by which the germs of affection in her nature are kindled, and through such human love she learns to conceive the existence of the love of God. But the poor workhouse girl is the child of an institution, not of a mother of flesh and blood. She is nobody's 'Mary' or 'Kate', to be individually thought of – only one of a dreary flock driven about at certain hours from dormitory to schoolroom and from schoolroom to workhouse yard. The poor child grows up into womanhood, perhaps, without one gleam of affection, and with all her nature crushed down and carelessly trampled on. She has had no domestic duties, no care of a little brother or an old grandparent, to soften her; no freedom of any kind to form her moral nature. Even her hideous dress and her cropped hair are not her own! Yet she is expected to go out inspired with respect for the property of her employer, able to check her childish covetous-ness of the unknown luxury of varied food, and clever enough to *guess* at a moment how to light a fire, and cook a dinner, and dress a baby, and clean a house, for the first time in her life. What marvel is it, these hapless creatures constantly disgust their employers by their ignorance, thievishness, and folly, and fall, poor friendless children! under the temptations which the first errands in our wicked streets will have sufficed to set before them! I will not pretend to speak concerning the Irish poor-house girls, of whose condition such contradictory evidence has lately been given before the Parliamentary Committee; but I can affirm one thing on my own experience of England, and that is this – that one of the largest channels through which young lives are drained down into the Dead Sea which lies beneath all our vaunted civilisation is the Workhouse!

Such a plan, then, as that of Miss Stephen is doubly and trebly needful for these girls, if for none others. With regard to *them*, however, it is possible to effect much of the same benefit by any lady who will devote some of her hours to the work, without any outlay of money for agents or registration office. It has also been tried in Bristol and with entire success. The lady desiring to work the plan should obtain the addresses of girls (from the master of the workhouse or otherwise) immediately on their being sent to service. She should then call on each mistress, express her interest in her little servant, and request permission for her to attend a Sunday afternoon class for workhouse girls. The mistresses are always found to take such visits in good part when they are made with proper courtesy, and are led by them to greater consideration for their servants. The worst of them can no longer treat the poor child as a mere friendless workhouse drudge. She is found to be a human being for whose interests one of higher rank than herself is watchful. Usually the mistresses have been willing to avail themselves of the Sunday school, which, of course, is an excellent 'basis of operations' for all sorts of good, religious and secular, for these poor girls. The main object is effected either way – the children learn to feel affection and reliance on a friend whose influence is wholly directed to keeping them in the path of duty, and whose hand they know will be stretched to help them in case of the dangers of destitution.

I have seldom seen so pretty a sight as that of the Sunday class of workhouse girls, held in a certain dear old house, under the shadow of a cathedral tower; and I cannot but think that anyone who had witnessed it would be tempted to undertake a similar task. The girls came in by twos and threes into the little study, with salutations to their kind teachers, almost uncouth in their warmth; then turned to greet their companions, the only friends they possessed in the wide world. Very plain were the poor children – stunted figures, and faces, in many instances, fearfully scarred by disease. Yet this Sunday parade was not wholly unsuccessful, for the young faces were as bright as cleanliness and pleasure could make them; and the clothes given them by the lady teachers were put on to fullest credit. Business began by grand lodgments of pence – and even, in some marvellous instances, of sixpences – in the savings' bank. Then came changing of books from the little library, with many warm encomiums on the latest perusal, 'Oh, *such* a nice story, ma'am!' Next came a display of copy-books, in which such girls as had had leisure had written either a copy or a recollection of the previous lesson. Afterwards there were repetitions of hymns or texts learnt by heart at pleasure during the week; and then a little reading of the Bible, and some wise kind words from the young teacher. And then there was the great pleasure! The girls chose their own hymns and sung them softly and sweetly enough – the rich tones of the ladies blending with their voices in something better to one's heart than only musical harmony. It was, I say, a pretty sight. England has many like it every Sabbath-day, but none, I think, can well be more touching than that of these poor little workhouse girls – so friendless all their lives before – gathered at last into that little fold of kindness and gentleness at the Deanery in Bristol.

What Shall We Do With Our Old Maids?

(reprinted from *Frazer's Magazine*, November 1862)

In the Convocation of Canterbury for this year of 1862, the readers of such journals as report in full the sayings and doings of that not very interesting assembly were surprised to find the subject of Protestant Sisterhoods, or Deaconesses, discussed with an unanimity of feeling almost unique in the annals of ecclesiastic parliaments. High Churchman and Low, Broad Churchman and Hard, all seemed agreed that there was good work for women to do, and which women *were* doing all over England; and that it was extremely desirable that all these lady guerillas of philanthropy should be enrolled in the regular disciplined army of the Church, together with as many new recruits as might be enlisted. To use a more appropriate simile, Mother Church expressed herself satisfied at her daughters 'coming out', but considered that her chaperonage was decidedly necessary to their decorum.

Again at the Social Science Congress of this summer, in London, the Employment of women, the Emigration of women, the Education of women, and all the other rights and wrongs of women, were urged, if not with an unanimity equal to that of their reverend predecessors, yet with, at the very least, equal animation. It is quite evident that the subject is not to be allowed to go to sleep, and we may as well face it valiantly, and endeavour to see light through its complications, rather than attempt to lecture the female sex generally on the merits of a 'golden silence', and the propriety of adorning themselves with that decoration (doubtless modestly declined, as too precious for their own use, by masculine reviewers), 'the ornament of a meek and quiet spirit'. In a former article ('Celibacy *v.* Marriage' – *Fraser's Magazine* for April, 1862) we treated the subject in part. We now propose to pursue it further, and investigate in particular the new phases which it has lately assumed.

The questions involved may be stated very simply.

It appears that there is a natural excess of 4 or 5 per cent of females over the males in our population. This, then, might be assumed to be the limits within which female celibacy was normal and inevitable.

There is, however, an actual ratio of 30 per cent of women now in England who never marry, leaving one-fourth of both sexes in a state of celibacy. This proportion further appears to be constantly on the increase. It is obvious enough that these facts call for a revision of many of our social arrangements. The old assumption that marriage was the sole destiny of woman, and that it was the business of her husband to afford her support, is brought up short by the statement that one woman in four is certain not to marry, and that three millions of women earn their own living at this moment in England. We may view the case two ways: either

First, we must frankly accept this new state of things, and educate women and modify trade in accordance therewith, so as to make the condition of celibacy as little injurious as possible; or

Second, we must set ourselves vigorously to stop the current which is leading men and women away from the natural order of Providence. We must do nothing whatever to render celibacy easy or attractive; and we must make the utmost efforts to promote marriage by emigration of women to the colonies, and all other means in our power.

The second of these views we shall in the first place consider. It may be found to colour the ideas of a vast number of writers, and to influence essentially the decisions made on many points – as the admission of women to university degrees, to the medical profession, and generally to free competition in employment. Lately it has met a powerful and not unkindly exposition in an article in a contemporary quarterly, entitled, 'Why are Women Redundant?' Therein it is plainly set forth that all efforts to make celibacy easy for women are labours in a wrong direction, and are to be likened to the noxious exertions of quacks to mitigate the symptoms of disease, and allow the patient to persist in his evil courses. The root of the malady should be struck at, and marriage, the only true vocation for women, promoted at any cost, even by the most enormous schemes for the deportation of 440,000 females. Thus alone (and by the enforcing of a stricter morality on men) should the evil be touched. As to making the labours of single women remunerative, and their lives free and happy, all such mistaken philanthropy will but tend to place them in a position more and more false and unnatural. Marriage will then become to them a matter of 'cold philosophic choice', and accordingly may be expected to be more and more frequently declined.

There is a great deal in this view of the case which, on the first blush, approves itself to our minds, and we have not been surprised to find the article in question quoted as of the soundest common-sense. All, save ascetics and visionaries, must admit that, for the mass of mankind, marriage is the right condition, the happiest, and the most conducive to virtue. This position fairly and fully conceded, it *might* appear that the whole of the consequences deduced followed of necessity, and that the direct promotion of marriage and discountenancing of celibacy was all we had to do in the matter.

A little deeper reflection, however, discloses a very important point which has been dropped out of the argument. Marriage is, indeed, the happiest and best condition for mankind. But does anyone think that all marriages are so? When we make the assertion that marriage is good and virtuous, do we mean a marriage of interest, a marriage for wealth, for position, for rank, for support? Surely nothing of the kind. Such marriages as these are the sources of misery and sin, not of happiness and virtue, nay, their moral character, to be fitly designated, would require stronger words than we care to use. There is only one kind of marriage which makes good the assertion that it is the right and happy condition for mankind, and that is a marriage founded on free choice, esteem, and affection – in one word, on love. If, then, we seek to promote the happiness and virtue of the community, our efforts must be directed to encouraging *only* marriages which are of the sort to produce them – namely, marriages founded on love. All marriages founded on interest, on the desire for position, support, or the like, we must discourage to the utmost of our power, as the sources of nothing but wretchedness. Where, now, have we reached? Is it not to the conclusion that to make it a woman's *interest* to marry, to force her, by barring out every means of self-support and all fairly remunerative labour, to look to marriage as her sole chance of competency, is precisely to drive her into one of those sinful and unhappy marriages? It is quite clear we can never drive her into *love*. That is a sentiment which poverty, friendlessness, and helplessness can by no means call out. Nor, on the contrary, can competence and freedom in any way check it. It will arise under its natural conditions, if we will but leave the matter alone. A *loving* marriage can never become a matter of 'cold philosophic choice'. And if *not* a loving one, then, for Heaven's sake, let us give no motive for choice at all.

Let the employments of women be raised and multiplied as much as possible, let their labour be as fairly remunerated, let their education be pushed as high, let their whole position be made as healthy and happy as possible, and there will come out once more, here as in every other department of life, the triumph of the Divine laws of our nature. Loving marriages are (we cannot doubt) what God has designed, not marriages of interest. When we have made it *less* women's interest to marry, we shall indeed have less and fewer interested marriages, with all their train of miseries and evils. But we shall also have more *loving* ones, more marriages founded on free choice and free affection. Thus we arrive at the conclusion that for the very end of promoting marriage – that is, such marriage as it is alone desirable to promote – we should pursue a precisely opposite course to that suggested by the Reviewer or his party. Instead of leaving single women as helpless as possible, and their labour as ill-rewarded – instead of dinning into their ears from childhood that marriage is their one vocation and concern in life, and securing afterwards if they miss it that they shall find no other vocation or concern; instead of all this, we shall act exactly on the reverse principle. We shall make single life so free and happy that they shall have not one temptation to change it save the only temptation which *ought* to determine them – namely, love. Instead of making marriage a case of 'Hobson's choice' for a woman, we shall endeavour to give her such independence of all interested considerations that she may make it a choice, not indeed 'cold and philosophic,' but warm from the heart, and guided by heart and conscience only.

And again, in another way, the same principle holds good, and marriage will be found to be best promoted by aiding and not by thwarting the efforts of single women to improve their condition. It is a topic on which we cannot speak much, but thus far may suffice. The reviewer alludes with painful truth to a class of the community whose lot is far more grievous than either celibacy or marriage. Justly he traces the unwillingness of hundreds of men to marry to the existence of these unhappy women in their present condition. He would remedy the evil by preaching marriage to such men. But does not all the world know that thousands of these poor souls, of all degrees, would never have fallen into their miserable vocation had any *other* course been open to them, and they had been enabled to acquire a competence by honest labour? Let such honest courses be opened to them, and then we shall see, as in America, the recruiting of that wretched army becoming less and less possible every year in the country. The self-supporting, and therefore self-respecting woman may indeed becomes a wife, and a good and happy one, but she will no longer afford any man a reason for declining to marry.

It is curious to note that while, on the one hand, we are urged to make marriage the sole vocation of women, we are simultaneously met on the other by the outpourings of ridicule and contempt on all who for themselves, or even for their children, seek ever so indirectly to attain this vocation. Only last year all England was entertained by jests concerning 'Belgravian mothers'; and the wiles and devices of widows and damsels afford an unending topic of satire and amusement in private and public. Now we ask, in all seriousness, Wherefore all this ridicule and contempt? *If* marriage be indeed the one object of a woman's life – *if* to give her any other pursuit or interest be only to divert her from that one object and 'palliate the symptoms while fostering a great social disease' – then, we repeat, *why* despise these matchmaking mothers? Are they to do nothing to help their daughters to their only true vocation, which, if they should miss, their lives *ought* to be failures, poverty-stricken and miserable? Nay; but if things be so, the most open, unblushing marketing of their daughters is the *duty* of parents, and the father or mother who leaves the matter to chance is flagrantly neglectful. Truly it is a paradox passing all limits of reason, that society should enforce marriage on woman as her only honourable life, and at the same time should stigmatise as dishonourable the efforts of her parents to settle her in marriage.

The spontaneous sentiment of mankind has hit a deeper truth than the theories of economists. It *is* in the nature of things disgraceful and abominable that marriage should be made the aim of a woman's life. It can only become what it is meant to be, the completion and crown of the life of either man or woman, when it has arisen from sentiments which can never be bespoken for the convenient fulfilment of any vocation whatsoever.

But it is urged, and not unreasonably – If it be admitted on all hands that marriage is the best condition, and that only one-fourth of the female sex do not marry, how can we expect provision to be made for this contingency of one chance in four by a girl's parents and by herself in going through an education (perhaps costly and laborious) for a trade or profession which there are three chances in four she will not long continue to exercise?

It must be admitted, here is the great knot and difficulty of the higher branches of woman's employment. It does require farseeing care on the part of the parent, perseverance and resolution of no mean order on that of the daughter, to go through in youth the training which will fit her to earn her livelihood hereafter in any of the more elevated occupations. Nay, it demands that she devote to such training the precise years of life wherein the chances of marriage are commonly offered, and the difficulties of pursuing a steady course are very much enhanced by temptations of all kinds. If she wait till the years when such chances fail, and take up a pursuit at thirty merely as a *pis aller*, she must inevitably remain for ever behindhand and in an inferior position.

The trial is undoubtedly considerable, but there are symptoms that both young women and their parents will not be always unwilling to meet it, and to invest both time and money in lines of education, which *may* indeed prove superfluous, but which likewise may afford the mainstay of a life which, without them, would be helpless, aimless, and miserable. The magnitude of the risk ought surely to weigh somewhat in the balance. At the lowest point of view, a woman is no worse off if she marry eventually, for having first gone through an education for some good pursuit; while if she remain single, she is wretchedly off for not having had such education. But this is in fact only a half view of the case. As we have insisted before, it is only on the standing-ground of a happy and independent celibacy that a woman can really make a free choice in marriage. To secure this standing-ground, a pursuit is more needful than a pecuniary competence, for a life without aim or object is one which, more than all others, goads a woman into accepting any chance of a change. Mariana (we are privately convinced) would have eloped out of the Moated Grange not only with that particular 'he' who never came, but with any other suitor who might have presented himself. Only a woman who has something else than making love to do and to think of will love really and deeply. It is in *real lives* – lives devoted to actual service of father or mother, or to work of some kind for God or man – that alone spring up *real feelings*. Lives of idleness and pleasure have no depth to nourish such plants.

Again, we are very far indeed from maintaining that *during* marriage it is at all to be desired that a woman should struggle to keep up whatever pursuit she had adopted beforehand. In nine cases out of ten this will drop naturally to the ground, especially when she has children. The great and paramount duties of a mother and wife once adopted, every other interest sinks, by the beneficent laws of our nature, into a subordinate place in normally constituted minds, and the effort to perpetuate them is as false as it is usually fruitless. Where necessity and poverty compel mothers in the lower ranks to go out to work, we all know too well the evils which ensue. And in the higher classes doubtless the holding tenaciously by any pursuit interfering with home duties must produce such

Mrs Jellabys as we sometimes hear of. It is not only leisure which is in question. There appear to be some occult laws in woman's nature providing against such mistakes by rendering it impossible to pursue the higher branches of art or literature or any work tasking mental exertion, while home and motherly cares have their claims. We have heard of a great artist saying that she is always obliged to leave her children for a few weeks before she can throw herself again into the artist-feeling of her youth, and we believe her experience is corroborated on all hands. No great books have been written or works achieved by women while their children were around them in infancy. No woman can lead the two lives at the same time.

But it is often strangely forgotten that there are such things as widows, left such in the prime of life, and quite as much needing occupation as if they had remained single. Thus, then, another chance must fairly be added to our one in four that a woman may need such a pursuit as we have supposed. She may never marry, or having married she may be left a childless widow, or a widow whose few children occupy but a portion of her time. Suppose, for instance, she has been a physician. How often would the possibility of returning to her early profession be an invaluable resource after her husband's death! The greatest female mathematician living, was saved from despairing sorrow in widowhood, by throwing herself afresh into the studies of her youth.

It may be a pleasantly romantic idea to some minds, that of woman growing up solely with the hope of becoming some man's devoted wife, marrying the first that offers, and when he dies, becoming a sort of moral Suttee whose heart is supposed to be henceforth dead and in ashes. But it is quite clear that Providence can never have designed any such order of things. All the infinite tenderness and devotion He has placed in women's hearts, though meant to make marriage blessed and happy, and diffusing as from a hearth of warm affections, kindness and love on all around, is yet meant to be subordinated to the great purposes of the existence of all rational souls – the approximation to God through virtue. With reverence be it spoken, God is the only true centre of life for us all, not any creature he has made. 'To live unto God' is the law for man and woman alike. Whoever strives to do this will neither spend youth in longing for happiness which may be withheld, nor age in despair for that which may be withdrawn.

To resume. It appears that from every point of view in which we regard the subject, it is desirable that women should have other aims, pursuits, and interests in life beside matrimony, and that by possessing them they are guaranteed against being driven into unloving marriages, and rendered more fitted for loving ones; while their single life, whether in maidenhood or widowhood, is made useful and happy.

Before closing this part of the subject, we cannot but add a few words to express our amused surprise at the way in which the writers on this subject constantly concern themselves with the question of *female* celibacy, deplore it, abuse it, propose amazing remedies for it, but take little or no notice of the 25 per cent old bachelors (or thereabouts) who needs must exist to match the 20 per cent old maids. *Their* moral condition seems to excite no alarm, their lonely old age no foreboding compassion, their action on the community no reprobation. Nobody scolds them very seriously, unless some stray Belgravian grandmother. All the alarm, compassion, reprobation, and scoldings are reserved for the poor old maids. But of the two, which of the parties is the chief delinquent? The *Zend Avesta*, as translated by Anquetil du Perron, contains somewhere this awful denunciation: 'That damsel who having reached the age of eighteen, shall refuse to marry, must remain in hell till the Resurrection!' A severe penalty, doubtless, for the crime, and wonderful to meet in the mild creed of Zoroaster, where no greater punishment is allotted to any offence whatsoever. Were these Guebre young ladies so terribly cruel, and *mazdiesnans* (true believers) so desperately enamoured? Are we to imagine the obdurate damsels despatching whole dozens of despairing gentlemen in conical caps to join the society in the shades below –

> Hapless youths who died for love,
> Wandering in a myrtle grove!

It takes a vivid stretch of imagination in England, in the nineteenth century, to picture anything of the kind. Whatever other offences our young ladies may be guilty of, or other weaknesses our young gentlemen, obduracy on the one hand, and dying for love on the other, are rarities, at all events. Yet one would suppose that Zoroaster was needed over here, to judge of the manner in which old maids are lectured on their very improper position. 'The Repression of Crime', as the benevolent Recorder of Birmingham would phrase it, seems on the point of being exercised against them, since it has been found out that their offence is on the increase, like poaching in country districts and landlord shooting in Ireland. The mildest punishment we are told, is to be transportation, to which half a million have just been condemned, and for the terror of future evil-doers, it is decreed that no single woman's work ought to be fairly remunerated, nor her position allowed to be entirely respectable, lest she exercise 'a cold philosophic choice' about matrimony. No false charity to criminals! Transportation or starvation to all old maids!

Poor old maids! Will not the Reformatory, Union, or some other friends of the criminal, take their case in hand? They are too old for Miss Carpenter. Could not Sir Walter Crofton's Intermediate System be of some use? There is reason to hope that many of them would be willing to adopt a more honest way of life were the chance offered them.

If the reader should have gone with us thus far, we shall be able better to follow the subject from a point of view which shall in fact unite the two leading ideas of which we made mention at starting. We shall, with the *first*, seek earnestly how the condition of single women may be most effectually improved; and with the *second*, we shall admit the promotion of marriage (*provided it be disinterested and loving*) to be the best end at which such improvements will tend.

In one point there is a practical unanimity between the schemes of the two parties, and this we should desire to notice before proceeding to consider the ways in which the condition of single women may be improved as such. This scheme is that of emigration for women to the colonies. Here we have multitudes of women offered in the first place remunerative employment beyond anything they could obtain at home; and further, the facilitation of marriage effected for large numbers, to the great benefit of both men and women. What there might appear in the plan contradictory to the principles we have laid down above, is only apparent, and not real. The woman who arrives in a colony where her labour, of head or hands, can command an ample maintenance, stands in the precise condition we have desired to make marriage – a matter of free choice. She has left 'Hobson's choice' behind her with the poverty of England, and has come out to find competence and freedom, and if she choose (but *only* if she choose), marriage also.

It is needless to say that this scheme has our entire sympathy and good wishes, though we do not expect to live to see the time when our reviewer's plan will be fulfilled by the deportation of women at the rate of thirty or forty thousand a year.[1]

An important point, however, must not be overlooked. However far the emigration of women of the working classes may be carried, that of educated women must at all times remain very limited, inasmuch as the demand for them in the colonies is comparatively trifling. Now, it is of educated women that the great body of 'old maids' consists; in the lower orders celibacy is rare. Thus, it should be borne in mind that emigration schemes do not essentially bear on the main point, 'How shall we improve the condition of the 30 per cent of single women in England?' The reviewer to whom we have so often alluded does indeed dispose of the matter by observing that the transportation he fondly hopes to see effected, of 440,000 women to the colonies, will at least *relieve the market* for those who remain. We cannot but fear, however, that the governesses and other ladies so accommodated will not much profit by the large selection thus afforded them among the blacksmiths and ploughmen, deprived of their proper companions. At the least we shall have a quarter of a million of old maids *in esse* and *in posse* left on hands. What can we do for them?

For convenience we may divide them into two classes. One of them, without capital or high cultivation, needs employment suitable to a woman's powers, and yet affording better remuneration than woman's work has hitherto usually received. Here we find the efforts of Miss Faithfull, Miss Crowe, Miss Rye, and the other ladies in combination with the society founded by Miss Parkes, labouring to procure such employment for them by the Victoria Printing Press, the Law Copying Office, and other plans in action or contemplated for watchmaking, hair-dressing, and the like. We may look on this class as in good hands; and as the emigration of women will actually touch it and carry away numbers of its members, we may hope that its destinies are likely henceforth to improve.

The other and higher class is that of which we desire more particularly to speak, namely, of ladies either possessed of sufficient pecuniary means to support themselves comfortably, or else of such gifts and cultivation as shall command a competence. The help these women need is not of a pecuniary nature, but a large portion of them require aid, and the removal of existing restrictions, to afford them the full exercise of their natural powers, and make their lives as useful and happy as Providence has intended. Of *all* the position is at the present moment of transition worthy of some attention, and suggestive of some curious speculations regarding the future of women. Channing remarks that when the negro races become thoroughly Christianised we shall see a development of the religion never known before. At least equally justly may we predict that when woman's gifts are at last expanded in an atmosphere of freedom and happiness, we shall find graces and powers revealed to us of which we yet have little dreamed. To the consideration, then, of the condition and prospects of women of the upper classes who remain unmarried, we shall devote the following pages.

All the pursuits of mankind, beside mere money-getting, may be fitly classed in three great orders. They are in one way or another the pursuit of the True, the Beautiful, or the Good. In a general way we may say that science, literature, and philosophy are devoted to Truth; art in all its branches (including poetic literature) to the Beautiful; and politics and philanthropy to the Good. Within certain limits, each of these lines of action are open to women; and it is in the aspect they bear as regards women's work that we are now to regard them. But before analysing them further, I would fain be allowed to make one remark which is far too often forgotten. Each of these pursuits is equally noble in itself; it is our fitness for one or the other, not its intrinsic sanctity or value, which ought to determine our choice; and we are all astray in our judgments if we come to the examination of them with prejudices for or against one or the other. In these days, when 'the icy chains of custom and of prejudice' are somewhat loosened, and men and women go forth more freely than ever of old to choose and make their lives, there is too often this false measurement of our brother's choice. Each of us asks his friend in effect, if not in words – 'Why not follow my calling rather than your own? Why not use such a gift? Why not adopt such a task?' The answer to these questions must not be made with the senseless pedantry of the assumption, that because to *us* art or literature, or philanthropy or politics, is the true vocation, therefore for all men and women it is the noblest; and that God meant Mozart to be a statesman, and Howard a sculptor, and Kant a teacher in a ragged school. The true, the beautiful, and the good are all revelations of the Infinite One, and therefore all holy. It is enough for a man if it be given him in his lifetime to pursue any one of them to profit – to carry a single step further the torch of humanity along either of the three roads, every one of which leads up to God. The philosopher, who studies and teaches us the laws of mind or matter – the artist, who beholds with illumined eyes the beauty of the world, and creates it afresh in poetry or painting – the statesman or philanthropist, who labours to make Right victorious, and to advance the virtue and happiness of mankind – all these in their several ways are God's seers, God's prophets, as much the one as the other. We could afford to lose none of them, to undervalue none of them. The philosopher is not to be honoured only for the goodness or the beauty of the *truth* he has revealed. All truth is good and beautiful, but it is to be prized because it is *truth*, and not merely for its goodness or beauty. The artist is not to be honoured only for the truth or the goodness of the *beautiful* he has revealed. The beautiful is necessarily good and true, but it is to be loved because it is *beautiful*, and not merely for its truth or goodness. Like the old Athanasian symbol, we may say, 'The Truth is divine, the Beautiful is divine, and the Good is divine. And yet they are not three divine things, but three revelations of the One Divine Lord.' If men would but feel this each in his own pursuit, and in judging of the pursuits of others, how holy and noble would all faithful work become! We are haunted yet with the Romish thought that a life of asceticism, of preaching, of prayer, of charity, is altogether on a different plane of being from a life devoted to other tasks. But it is not so. From *every* field of honest human toil there rises a ladder up into heaven. Was Kepler further from God than any Howard or Xavier when, after discovering the law of the planetary distances, he bowed his head and exclaimed in rapture, 'O God, I think Thy thoughts after Thee!' Was Milton less divine than any St Theresa locked in her stony cell, when his mighty genius had soared 'upon the seraph wings of ecstasy' over the whole beautiful creation, and he poured out at last his triumphant Psalm –

These are Thy glorious works, Parent of Good –
Almighty!

Of these three great modes of Divine manifestation, it would appear, however, that, though equal in sanctity and dignity, the pursuit of the True and of the Beautiful were designed for comparately few among mankind. Few possess the pure abstract love of Truth in such fervour as to fit them to become the martyrs of science or the prophets of philosophy. Few also are those who are endowed with that supreme sense of the Beautiful, and power to reproduce it in form, colour, or sound, which constitute the gifts of the artist. Especially does this hold good with women. While few of them do not feel their hearts warmed with the love of goodness, and the desire to relieve the sufferings of their fellows, a mere fraction, in comparison, interest themselves to any extent in the pursuit of the abstract truths of philosophy or science, or possess any powers to reproduce the Beautiful in Art, even when they have a perception of its presence in nature. We may discuss briefly, then, here the prospects of the employment of women in the departments of Truth and Beauty, and in a future paper consider more at length the new aspect of their philanthropic labours and endeavours to do Good.

Till of very late years it was, we think, perfectly justifiable to doubt the possibility of women possessing any creative artistic power. Receptive faculties they have always had, ready and vivid perception of the beautiful in both nature and art, delicate discrimination and refined taste, nay, the power (especially in music and the drama) of reproducing what the genius of man had created. But to originate any work of even second-rate merit was what no woman had done. Sappho was a mere name, and between her and even such a feeble poetess as Mrs Hemans, there was hardly another to fill up the gap of the whole cycle of history. No woman has written the epics, nor the dramas, nay, nor even the national songs of her country, if we may not except Miriam's and Deborah's chants of victory. In music, nothing. In architecture, nothing. In sculpture, nothing. In painting, an Elisabetta Sirani, a Rosalba, an Angelica Kauffman – hardly exceptions enough to prove the rule. Such works as women did accomplish were all stamped with the same impress of feebleness and prettiness. As Mrs Hemans and Joanna Baillie and Mrs Tighe wrote poetry, so Angelica Kauffman painted pictures, and other ladies composed washy music and Minerva-press romances. If Tennyson had spoken of woman's *Art*, instead of woman's passions, he would have been as right for the one as he was wrong as regards the other. It *was*

> As moonlight is to sunlight
> And as water is to wine.

To coin an epithet from a good type of the school – it was all 'Angelical', no flesh and blood at all, but super-refined sentiments and super-elongated limbs.

But there seem symptoms extant that this state of things is to undergo a change, and the works of women become remarkable for other qualities beside softness and weakness. It may be a mere chance conjunction, but it is at least remarkable, that the same age has given us in the three greatest departments of art – poetry, painting, and sculpture – women who, whatever be their faults or merits, are pre-eminently distinguished for one quality above all others – namely, strength. *Aurora Leigh* is perhaps the least 'Angelical' poem in the language, and bears the relation to *Psyche* that a chiselled steel corslet does to a silk boddice with lace trimmings. The very hardness of its rhythm, its sturdy wrestlings and grapplings, one after another, with all the sternest problems of our social life – its forked-lightning revelations of character – and finally, the storm of glorified passion with which it closes in darkness (like nothing else we ever read since the mountain-tempest scene in *Childe Harold*) – all this takes us miles away from the received notion of a woman's poetry.

And for painting, let us look at Rosa Bonheur's canvas. Those droves of wild Highland black cattle, those teams of tramping Norman horses – do they belong to the same school of female art as all the washed-out saints, and pensive ladies, and graceful bouquets of Mesdemoiselles and Signorine Rosee, and Rosalba, and Panzacchi, and Grebber, and Mérian, and Kauffman? We seem to have passed a frontier, and entered a new realm wherein Rosa Bonheurs are to be found.

Then for Sculpture. Will woman's genius ever triumph here? We confess we look to this point as to the touchstone of the whole question. Sculpture is in many respects at once the noblest art and the one which tasks highest both creative power and scientific skill. A really good and great statue is an achievement to which there must contribute more elements of power and patience than in almost any other human work, and it is, when perfected, one of the most sublime. We know generally very little of this matter in England. We possess pictures by the great masters sufficient in number and excellence to afford a fair conception (though of course an incomplete one) of the powers of painting. But notwithstanding the antique treasures in the Elgin and Arundel Collections, and a few fine modern statues to be found in private houses in this country, it is, I believe, to every one a revelation of a new agency in art when he first visits Italy and beholds the 'Laocöon', the 'Apollo', the 'Niobe', and the 'Psyche' of Praxiteles. Hitherto sculpture has appeared to be merely the production of beautiful forms, more or less true to nature. Now it is perceived to be genius breathing through form, the loftiest thoughts of human souls. 'Apollo Belvedere' is not the mere figure of a perfect man in graceful attitude, as we thought it from casts and copies in England. It is Power itself, deified and made real before our eyes. The 'Laocöon' is not the hapless high-priest writhing in the coil of the serpent. It is the impersonation of the will of a giant man, a Prometheus struggling with indomitable courage against the resistless Fate in whose grasp meaner mortals are crushed helplessly. The 'Niobe' is not merely a woman of noblest mould inspired by maternal anguish. She is glorified MOTHERHOOD, on whose great bosom we could rest, and round whose neck we could throw our arms. And the 'Psyche' in the Museo Borbonico? – is this a poor fragment of a form, once perhaps graceful and fair, but now a mere ruin? No! It is the last gleam of the unknown glory of ancient art, the one work of human hands which we forget to admire because we learn to love it – the revelation to each of us of our innermost ideal of friend or wife, the sweetest, purest of our dreams made real before our eyes.

Not untruly has sculpture been named the *Ars Divinior*. A deep and strange analogy exists between it and the highest we know of the Supreme Artist's works. Out of the clay, cold and formless, the sculptor slowly, patiently, with infinite care and love, moulds an image of beauty. Long the stubborn clay seems to resist his will, and to remain without grace or proportion, but at last the image begins, faintly and in a far-off way, to reflect that prototype which is in the sculptor's mind. The limbs grow into shape, and stand firmly balanced, the countenance becomes living and radiant. And last of all, the character of true sculpture appears; there is calm and peace over it all, and an infinite divine repose, even when the life within seems higher and fuller than that of mortality. The moulding is done, the statue is perfected.

But even then, when it should seem that the sculptor's great work is achieved, and that his image should be preserved and cherished evermore, what does he in truth do with his clay? Return hither, oh traveller, in a few short days, and the image of clay is gone, its place knows it no more. It has returned to the earth whence it was taken, thrown by, perchance for ever, or else kneaded afresh in some new form of life. Did he make it, then, but for destruction, and mould it so carefully but to crush it out at last in dust? Look around with illumined eyes! In the great studio of the universe the Divine image is still to be found, not now moulded in clay and ready to perish, dull of hue and dead in lustre, but sculptured in eternal marble, white, and pure, and radiant; meet to stand for ever in the palaces on high.

Sculpture is the noblest of the arts; nay, it is above all others in this very thing which has been pointed at as its bane and limitation. Its aim must ever be the expression of calmness and repose. No vehement wildness of the painter's dream, no storm of the musician's harmony, no ecstasy of the poet's passion; but the stillness and the peace of which earth knows so little. To bring our souls into sympathy with a great work of sculpturesque repose, is to bring them into the serener fields of the upper air, where the storms approach not, nor any clouds ascend. We do not naturally in the earlier moral life feel in union with things calm and still like these. The struggle in our own breasts, the lordly will wrestling with the lower powers for mastery, leaves us rather able to sympathise with all nature's warfare of wind and wave, all human death-battles, than with the repose in which the saint's soul rests, loving the cloudless sky and waveless sea, and the smile of a sleeping child nestled in the long sweet grass of summer. To reach that rest of the whole nature, which is at the same time absolute repose and absolute action of every power and every faculty in perfect balance, is the 'Beulah land',

Where blessed saints dwell ever in the light
Of God's dear love, and earth is heaven below.
For never doubt nor sin may cloud their sight,
And the great PEACE OF GOD calms every human woe.

The art which is the idealising, the perpetuation of repose is, then, the divinest art – the art to be practised only by great souls – great races of men. Egyptians and Greeks were races of sculptors; Hindoos and Mexicans stone cutters of goblins. We repeat that the sharpest test to which the question of woman's genius can be put is this one of sculpture. If she succeed here, if a school of real sculpturesses ever arise, then we think that in effect the problem is solved. The greater includes the less. They may still fall below male composers in music, though we have seen some (inedited) music of wonderful power from a female hand. They may produce no great drama – perhaps no great historical picture. Yet if really good statues come from their studios, statues showing at once power of conception and science of execution, then we say, women can be artists. It is no longer a question whether the creative faculty be granted to them.

Now, we venture to believe that there are distinct tokens that this solution is really to be given to the problem. For long centuries women never seem to have attempted sculpture at all; perhaps because it was then customary for the artist to perform much of the mechanical labour of the marble-cutter himself; perhaps because women could rarely command either the large outlay or the anatomical instructions. But in our time things are changed. The Princesse Marie d'Orleans, in her well-known Joan of Arc, accomplished a really noble work of sculpture. Others have followed and are following in her path, but most marked of all by power and skill comes Harriet Hosmer, whose Zenobia (now standing in the International Exhibition, in the same temple with Gibson's Venus) is a definite proof that a woman can make a statue of the very highest order. Whether we consider the noble conception of this majestic figure, or the science displayed in every part of it, from the perfect *pose* and accurate anatomy, to the admirable truth and finish of the drapery, we are equally satisfied. Here is what we wanted. A woman – aye, a woman with all the charms of youthful womanhood – can be a sculptor, and a great one.

Now we have arrived at a conclusion worthy of some little attention. Women a few years ago could only show a few weak and washy female poets and painters, and no sculptors at all. They can now boast of such true and powerful artists in these lines as

Mrs Browning, Rosa Bonheur, and Harriet Hosmer. What account can we give of the rise of such a new constellation? We confess ourselves unable to offer any solution, save that proposed by a gifted lady to whom we propounded our query. Female artists hitherto always started on a wrong track; being persuaded beforehand that they ought only to compose sweet verses and soft pictures, they set themselves to make them accordingly, and left us Mrs Hemans' Works and Angelica's paintings. *Now*, women who possess any real genius, apply it to the creation of what they (and not society for them) really admire. A woman naturally admires power, force, grandeur. It is these qualities, then, which we shall see more and more appearing as the spontaneous genius of woman asserts itself.

We know not how this may be. It is at all events a curious speculation. One remark we must make before leaving this subject. This new element of *strength* in female art seems to impress spectators very differently. It cannot be concealed that while all true artists recognise it with delight, there is no inconsiderable number of men to whom it is obviously distasteful, and who turn away more or less decidedly in feeling from the display of this or any other power in women, exercised never so inoffensively. There is a feeling (tacit or expressed) 'Yes, it is very clever, but somehow it is not quite feminine.' Now we do not wish to use sarcastic words about sentiments of this kind, or demonstrate all their unworthiness and ungenerousness. We would rather make an appeal to a better judgment, and entreat for a resolute stop to expressions ever so remotely founded on them. The origin of them all has perhaps been the old error that clipping and fettering every faculty of body and mind was the sole method of making a woman – that as the Chinese make a lady's foot, so we should make a lady's mind; and that, in a word, the old alehouse sign was not so far wrong in depicting 'The Good Woman' as a woman without any head whatsoever. Earnestly would we enforce the opposite doctrine, that as God means a woman to *be* a woman and not a man, every faculty he has given her is a woman's faculty, and the more each of them can be drawn out, trained, and perfected, the more *womanly* she will become. She will be a larger, richer, nobler woman for art, for learning, for every grace and gift she can acquire. It must indeed be a mean and miserable man who would prefer that a woman's nature should be pinched, and starved, and dwarfed to keep on his level, rather than be nurtured and trained to its loftiest capacity, to meet worthily his highest also.

That we quit the subject of woman's pursuit of the Beautiful, rejoicing in the new promise of its success, and wishing all prosperity to the efforts to afford female students of art that sound and solid training, the lack of which has been their greatest stumbling-block hitherto. The School of Art and Design in London is a good augury with its eight hundred and sixty-three lady pupils!

But for woman's devotion to the True in physics and meta-physics, woman's science and woman's learning, what shall we venture to say? The fact must be frankly admitted – women have even more rarely the powers and tastes needful to carry them in this direction than in that of art. The love of abstract truth as a real passion is probably antithetic in some measure to that vivid interest in persons which belongs to the warm sympathies and strong affections of women. Their quickness of perception mili-tates against the slow toil of science, and their vividness of intuitive faith renders them often impatient of the discussions of philosophy. Many women love truth warmly enough, and for religious truth female martyrs have never been wanting since the mother of the Maccabees. But few women complete their love of truth by such hatred of error as shall urge them to the exertion of laboriously establishing and defining the limits of the truths they possess. These natural causes again have been reinforced by endless artificial hindrances. The want of schools and colleges, the absence of such rewards as encourage (though they cannot inspire) the pursuit of of knowledge, popular and domestic prejudices rendering study disfavoured, difficult access to books or leisure from household duties, the fluctuating health fostered by the unwholesome habits of women; and last, the idleness and distractions of those very years of youth in which education can rise above the puerile instruction of a girl's school-room.

Far be it from us to wish to force all women into courses of severe study – to put (as has been well said of late) Arabian horses to the plough, and educate directly against the grain; only we desire that much, that those women who do possess the noble love of knowledge and are willing to undergo the drudgery of its acquirement, should have every aid supplied and every stumbling block removed from their paths. The improvements which in our time are making in these directions may be briefly stated. First, popular prejudice against well-educated women is dying away. It is found they do *not* 'neglect infants for quadratic equations', nor perform in any way less conscientiously the various duties of life after reading Plato or even Kant. Second, the opening of ladies' colleges, such as Bedford-square and Harley-street, where really sound and solid instruction is given by first-rate teachers at a cost not equal to half that of the shallow and superficial boarding-school of twenty years ago. Third, women have benefited even more than men by the general progress of the times, the facilitation of travelling (formerly impossible to them without protection), the opening of good lending-libraries, cheap books and postage. The dead sea of ennui in which so many of them lived is now rippled by a hundred currents from all quarters of heaven, and we may trust that the pettiness of gossip which has been the standing reproach of the sex will disappear with the narrowness of life which supplied no wholesomer food for conversation or thought. To cramp every faculty and cut off all large interests, and then complain that a human being so treated is narrow-minded and scandal-loving, is precisely an injustice parallel to that of some Southern Americans whom we have heard detail those vices of the negroes *which slavery had produced*, as the reason why they were justified in keeping so degraded a race in such a condition. It would be indeed a miracle often if a woman manufactured on some not unpopular principles were anything else than a very poor and pitiful piece of mechanism. The further improvements which may be sought in these directions are of various kinds. The standard of ordinary female education cannot perhaps be elevated above that of the ladies' colleges already mentioned, but *this* standard will become not (as now) the high-water mark for a few, but the common tide-line for all women of the middle and higher classes supposed to be fairly educated. Above this high standard, again, facilities and encouragements may be given to women of exceptionally studious tastes to rise to the levels of any instruction attainable. One important way in which this last end may be reached – namely, the admission of women to the examinations and honours of the London University – has been lately much debated. The arguments which have determined its temporary rejection by the senate of the University (a rejection, however, only decided by the casting vote of the chairman), seem to have been all of the character discussed a few pages ago – the supposed necessity of keeping women to their sole vocation of wives and mothers, and so on. The benefits which would accrue from the measure were urged by the present writer before the Social Science Congress,[2] and were briefly these – that women need as much or more than men a stimulus to carry their education to a high pitch of perfection and accuracy; that this stimulus has always been supplied to men by university examinations and rewards of honour; that it ought to be offered to women, as likely to produce on them the same desirable results; lastly, that the University of London requiring no collegiate residence, and having its examinations conducted in special apartments perfectly unobjectionable for women's use, it constitutes the one university in the kingdom which ought to admit women to its examinations.

Intimately connected with this matter is that of opening to women the medical profession, for which university degrees would be the first steps. The subject has been well worn of late; yet we must needs make a few remarks concerning it, and notably to put a question or two to objectors. Beloved reader (male or female, as the chance may be), did it ever happen to you to live in a household of half a dozen persons in which some woman was *not* the self-constituted family physician, to whom all the other members of the party applied for advice in ninety-nine cases out of a hundred? A cold, a cough, a rheumatism, a sprain, a cut, a burn, bile, indigestion, headaches and heartaches, are they not all submitted to her counsel, and the remedies she prescribes for them devoutly taken? Usually it is the grandmother or the housekeeper of the family who is consulted; but whichever it may chance to be, mistress or servant, it is always a *woman*. Who ever dreamed of asking his grandfather or his uncle, his butler or footman, 'what he should do for this bad cold', or to 'be so kind as to tie up this cut finger'? We can hardly imagine the astonishment of 'Jeames' at such a request; but any woman abovestairs or below would take it as perfectly natural. Doctoring is one of the 'rights of women', which albeit theoretically denied is practically conceded so univer-sally that it is probable that all the M.D.s in England, with the apothecaries to boot, do not order more drugs than are yearly 'exhibited' by their unlicensed female domestic rivals. It is not a question whether such a state of things be desirable; it exists, and no legislation can alter it. The two differences between the authorised doctors and unauthorised doctoresses are simply these – that the first are paid and the second unpaid for their services, and the first have *some* scientific knowledge and the second none at all. It behoves us a little to consider these two distinctions. First, if patients choose to go for advice to women, and women inspire them with sufficient confidence to be consulted, it is a piece of interference quite anomalous in our day to prevent such services being rewarded, or in other words, to prevent the woman from qualifying herself legally to accept such reward. A woman may or may not be a desirable doctor, just as a dissenter may or may not be a desirable teacher; but unless we are to go back to paternal governments, we must permit patients and congregations to be the judges of what suits them best, and not any medical or ecclesiastical corporation. It is not that *women* are called on to show cause why they should be permitted to enter the medical profession and obtain remuneration for their services, but the *doctors*, who are bound to show cause why they should exclude them and deprive them of the remuneration which there are abundance of patients ready to bestow. This is the side of the rights of the doctor. But are we not still more concerned with the second point of difference, which involves the safety of the patient? As we have said, men and women *will* go continually to women for medical advice in all those thousand contingencies and minor maladies out of which three-fourths of the mortal diseases of humanity arise. There is no use scolding, and saying they *ought* to go to the apothecary or the M.D. People will *not* do so, least of all will delicate women do so when it is possible to avoid it. The only question is, whether the advice which in any case they will get from a woman will be good advice or bad advice – advice founded on some scientific knowledge, or advice derived from the wildest empiricism and crassest ignorance.

We have sometimes lamented that we have lacked the precaution of making memoranda of the wonderful remedies which have become known to us in the course of time, as applied by that class of domestic doctoresses of which we have spoken. They would have afforded a valuable storehouse of arguments to prove that, if 'the little knowledge' of medicine (which we are told is all women could hope to acquire in a college) is 'a dangerous thing', the utter absence of all knowledge whatever which they at present display, is a hundred times more perilous still. Well can we recall, for instance, in the home of our childhood, a certain admirable old cook who was the oracle in medical matters of the whole establishment. Notwithstanding the constant visits of an excellent physician, it was to her opinion that recourse was had on all emergencies; and the results may be imagined when it is avowed that in her genius the culinary and therapeutic arts were so assimilated, that she invariably *cooked* her patients as well as their dinners. On one occasion a groom having received an immense laceration and excoriation of the leg, was treated by having the wound *rubbed with salt, and held before a hot fire!*

At the opposite end of the social scale we can remember a lady of high degree and true Lady Bountiful disposition pressing on us, in succession, the merits of Morison's pills, hydropathy, and brandy and salt; 'and if none of them cure your attack, there is St John Long's remedy, which is *quite* infallible'. It would not be easy to calculate how often such practitioners might incur the same chance as a grandmother of our own, who, asking an Irish labourer his name, received the *foudroyante* reply – 'Ah! and don't you know me, my lady? And didn't your ladyship give the dose to my wife, and she died the next day? – *long life to your ladyship!*'

All this folly and quackery – nay, the use of quack medicines altogether – would be vastly diminished, if not stopped, by the training of a certain number of women as regular physicians, and the instruction derived through them of females generally, in the rudiments of physiology and sanitary science. It is vain to calculate whether individual lady physicians would be as successful as the ordinary average of male doctors. To argue about an untried capacity, *a priori*, seems absurd; and such experience as America has afforded us appears wholly favourable. But the point is, not whether women will make as good doctors as men, but how the whole female sex may be better taught in a matter of vital importance, not only to themselves, but to men whose health is modified through life by their mother's treatment in infancy. As the diffusion of physiological knowledge among women *generally* must unquestionably come from the instruction of a few women *specially* educated, the exclusion of females from courses of medical study assumes the shape of a decree that the sex on whom the health of the community peculiarly depends, shall for ever remain in ignorance of the laws by which that health is to be maintained.

With the highest possible education for women in ladies' colleges, with University examinations and the medical profession opened to them, we have little doubt that a new life would enter into many, and the pursuit of knowledge become a real vocation, where it has been hitherto hardly more than an amusement. Many a field of learning will yield unexpected flowers to a woman's fresh research, and many a path of science grow firm and clear before the feet which will follow in the steps of Mrs Somerville. Already women have made for themselves a place, and a large one, in the literature of our time; and when their general instruction becomes deeper and higher, their works must become more and more valuable. Whether doctoresses are to be permitted or not, may be a question; but authoresses are already a guild, which, instead of opposition, has met kindliest welcome. It is now a real profession to women as to men, to be writers. Let any one read the list of books in a modern library, and judge how large a share of them were written by women. Mrs Jameson, Mrs Stowe, Miss Brontë, George Eliot, Mrs Gaskell, Susan and Katherine Winkworth, Miss Martineau, Miss Bremer, George Sand, Mrs Browning, Miss Procter, Miss Austen, Miss Strickland, Miss Pardoe, Miss Mulock, Mrs Grey, Mrs Gore, Mrs Trollope, Miss Jewsbury, Mrs Speir, Mrs Gatty, Miss Blagden, Lady Georgiana Fullarton, Miss Marsh, and a dozen others. There is little need to talk of literature as a field for woman's future work. She is ploughing it in all directions already. The one thing is to do it thoroughly, and let the plough go deep enough, with good thorough drainage to begin upon. Writing books ought never to be thought of slightly. In one sense, it is morally a serious thing, a power of addressing many persons at once with somewhat more weight than in common speech. We cannot without offence misuse such a power, and adorn vice, or sneer at virtue, or libel human nature as all low, and base, and selfish. We cannot without offence neglect to *use* such a power for a good end; and if to give pleasure be the object of our book, make it at least to the reader an ennobling and refining pleasure. A book ought always to be *the high water-mark* of its author – his best thoughts, his clearest faith, his loftiest aspiration. No need to taunt him, and say he is not equal to his book. His book ought not to be merely the average of his daily ebb and flow, but his flood-line – his spring-tide, jetsam of shells and corallines, and all 'the treasures of the deep'.

And again, writing is an Art, and as an art it should be seriously pursued. The true artist spirit which grudges no amount of preparatory study, no labour of final completion – this belongs as much to the pen as to the pencil or the chisel. It is precisely this spirit which women have too often lacked, fondly imagining their quickness would do duty for patience, and their tact cover the defect of study. If their work is (as we hope and believe) to be a real contribution to the happiness and welfare of mankind hereafter, the first lesson to be learned is this – conscientious preparatory study, conscientious veracity of expression, conscientious labour after perfection of every kind, clearness of thought, and symmetry of form. The time will come, we doubt not, when all this will be better understood. Writing a novel or a book of travels will not be supposed to come to a lady by nature, any more than teaching children to a reduced gentlewoman. Each art needs its special study and careful cultivation; and the woman who means to pursue aright either literature or science, will consider it her business to prepare herself for so doing, *at least* as much as if she purposed to dance on the stage or make bonnets in a milliner's shop.

Then, we believe we shall find women able to carry forward the common progress of the human race along the path of the True, as well as of the Beautiful and the Good; nay, to give us those views of truth which are naturally the property of woman. For be it remembered, as in optics we need two eyes to see the roundness and fulness of objects, so in philosophy we need to behold every great truth from two stand-points; and it is scarcely a fanciful analogy to say, that these stand-points are provided for us by the different faculties and sentiments of men's and women's natures. In every question of philosophy there enters the intuitive and the experimental, the arguments *a priori* and *a posteriori*. In every question of morals there is the side of justice and the side of love. In every question of religion there is the idea of God as the Father of the world – the careful Creator, yet severe and awful Judge; and there is the idea of God as the Mother, whose tender mercies are over us all, who is grieved by our sins as our mothers were grieved by them, and in whose infinite heart is our only refuge. At the highest point all these views unite. Absolute Philosophy is both intuitive and experimental; absolute Morality is both justice and love; absolute Religion is the worship (at once full of awe and love) of the 'Parent of Good, Almighty', who is both parents in One. But to reach these completed views we need each side by turns to be presented to us; and this can hardly be better effected than by the alternate action of men's and women's minds on each other.

NOTES

1 We rejoice to hear that Miss Maria S. Rye, who has already done so much for this cause, is on the point of sailing to Otago with one hundred female emigrants, to superintend personally the arrangements for their welfare. This is doing woman's work in working style truly.
2 *Female Education, and how it would be affected by University Education.* A Paper read before the Social Science Congress.

Criminals, Idiots, Women and Minors. Is the Classification Sound?

A Discussion of the Laws concerning the Property of Married Women

(reprinted from *Frazer's Magazine*, December 1868)

There was an allegory rather popular about thirty years ago, whose manifest purpose was to impress on the juvenile mind that tendency which Mr Matthew Arnold has ingeniously designated 'Hebraism'. The hero of the tale descends upon earth from some distant planet, and is conducted by a mundane cicerone through one of our great cities, where he beholds the docks and arsenals, the streets and marts, the galleries of art, and the palaces of royalty. The visitor admires everything till he happens to pass a graveyard. 'What is that gloomy spot?' he asks of his companion.

'It is a cemetery,' replies the guide.

'A – what did you say?' inquires the son of the star.

'A graveyard; a place of public interment; where we bury our dead,' reiterates the cicerone.

The visitor, pale with awe and terror, learns at last that there is in this world such a thing as *Death*, and (as he is forbidden to return to his own planet) he resolves to dedicate every moment left to him to prepare for that fearful event and all that may follow it.

Had that visitor heard for the first time upon his arrival on earth of another incident of human existence – namely, *Marriage*, it may be surmised that his astonishment and awe would also have been considerable. To his eager inquiry whether men and women earnestly strove to prepare themselves for so momentous an occurrence, he would have received the puzzling reply that women frequently devoted themselves with perfectly Hebraistic singleness of aim to that special purpose; but that men, on the contrary, very rarely included any preparation for the married state among the items of their widest Hellenistic culture. But this anomaly would be trifling compared to others which would be revealed to him.

378

'Ah,' we can hear him say to his guide, as they pass into a village church, 'What a pretty sight is this! What is happening to that sweet young woman in white, who is giving her hand to the good-looking fellow beside her; all the company decked in holiday attire, and the joy-bells shaking the old tower overhead? She is receiving some great honour, is she not? The Prize of Virtue, perhaps?'

'Oh, yes,' would reply the friend; 'an honour certainly. She is being Married.' After a little further explanation, the visitor would pursue his inquiry:

'Of course, having entered this honourable state of matrimony, she has some privileges above the women who are not chosen by anybody? I notice her husband has just said, "With all my worldly goods I thee endow." Does that mean that she will henceforth have the control of his money altogether, or only that he takes her into partnership?'

'*Pas précisément*, my dear sir. By our law it is *her* goods and earnings, present and future, which belong to him from this moment.'

'You don't say so? But then, of course, his goods are hers also?'

'Oh dear, no! not at all. He is only bound to find her food; and, truth to tell, not very strictly or efficaciously bound to do that.'

'How! Do I understand you? Is it possible that here in the most solemn religious act, which I perceive your prayer book calls "The Solemnization of Holy Matrimony", every husband makes a generous promise, which promise is not only a mockery, but the actual reverse and parody of the real state of the case: the man who promises giving nothing, and the woman who is silent giving all?'

'Well, yes; I suppose that is something like it, as to the letter of the law. But then, of course, practically . . .'

'Practically, I suppose few men can really be so unmanly and selfish as the law warrants them in being. Yet, some, I fear, may avail themselves of such authority. May I ask another question? As you subject women who enter the marriage state to such very severe penalties as this, what worse have you in store for women who lead a dissolute life, to the moral injury of the community?'

'Oh, the law takes nothing from them. Whatever they earn or inherit is their own. They are able, also, to sue the fathers of their children for their maintenance, which a wife, of course, is not allowed to do on behalf of *her* little ones, because she and her husband are one in the eye of the law.'

'One question still further – your criminals? Do they always forfeit their entire property on conviction?'

'Only for the most heinous crimes; felony and murder, for example.'

379

'Pardon me; I must seem to you so stupid! Why is the property of the woman who commits Murder, and the property of the woman who commits Matrimony, dealt with alike by your law?'

Leaving our little allegory, and in sober seriousness, we must all admit that the just and expedient treatment of women by men is one of the most obscure problems, alike of equity and of policy. Nor of women only, but of all classes and races of human beings whose condition is temporarily or permanently one of comparative weakness and dependence. In past ages, the case was simple enough. No question of right or duty disturbed the conscience of Oriental or Spartan, of Roman or Norman in dealing with his wife, his helot, his slave, or his serf. '*Le droit du plus fort*' was unassailed in theory and undisturbed in practice. But we, in our day, are perplexed and well nigh overwhelmed with the difficulties presented to us. What ought the Americans to do with their negroes? What ought we to do with our Hindoos? What ought all civilised people to do with their women? It seems very easy to go on driving down the 'high *a priori*' road of equal rights for all human beings, but, as it is quite clear that children and idiots cannot be entrusted with full civil and political rights, the question always resolves itself into the further one; where shall we draw the line? When has a human being fairly passed out of the stage of pupilage, and attained his majority?

At the head of this paper I have placed the four categories under which persons are now excluded from many civil, and all political rights in England. They were complacently quoted last year by *The Times* as every way fit and proper exceptions; but yet it has appeared to not a few, that the place assigned to Women amongst them is hardly any longer suitable. To a woman herself who is aware that she has never committed a crime; who fondly believes that she is not an idiot; and who is alas! only too sure she is no longer a minor – there naturally appears some incongruity in placing her, for such important purposes, in an association wherein otherwise she would scarcely be likely to find herself. But the question for men to answer is: Ought Englishwomen of full age, in the present state of affairs, to be considered as having legally attained majority? or ought they permanently to be dealt with, for all civil and political purposes, as minors? This, we venture to think, is the real point at issue between the friends and opponents of 'women's rights', and it would save, perhaps, not a little angry feeling and aimless discussion, were we to keep it well in view, and not allow ourselves to be drawn off into collateral debates about equality and abstract rights. Let us admit (if it be desired) that the pupilage in which women have been hitherto kept has been often inevitable, and sometimes salutary. The question is, should it be prolonged indefinitely?

In the present paper we shall attempt to consider the most striking instance wherein the existing principle presses upon women, and where its injustice appears most distinctly – namely, in the regulation of the Property of Married Women under the Common Law. We shall endeavour to do this with all possible fairness and equanimity. The acrimony which too often creeps into arguments on this subject is every way needless and mischievous. Of course it is not pleasant to women to be told they are 'physically, morally, and intellectually inferior' to their companions. Nevertheless, they are foolish to be angry with the man who in plain words says straightforwardly that, in his opinion, such is the case. After all, he pays them a better compliment than the fop who professes to adore them as so many wingless angels, and privately values them as so many dolls. In any case all such discussion is beside our present aim. We shall endeavour, in these pages, neither to talk with one party, as if all instinct and feeling were the creatures of law, and could be altered by 'An Act to Revise the Constitution of Human Nature'; nor with another, as if the particular sentiment of our age and country about 'Woman's Sphere' were the only possible standard of legislation for all time. If, as Pope said, 'the world were inhabited by men, women, and Herveys', we should endeavour to write like a Hervey, to do justice to both the other parties!

Mr G. Shaw Lefevre last summer carried through two readings in Parliament, and obtained a favourable report upon, 'A Bill to Amend the Law with respect to the Property of Married Women.'[1] Let us briefly state what is the existing law which it is proposed to amend; what may be urged in its behalf; and what may be said against it.

By the Common Law of England a married woman has no legal existence, so far as property is concerned, independently of her husband. The husband and wife are assumed to be one person, and that person is the husband. The wife can make no contract, and can neither sue nor be sued. Whatever she possess of personal property at the time of her marriage, or whatever she may afterwards earn or inherit, belongs to her husband, without control on her part. If she possess real estate, so long as her husband lives he receives and spends the income derived from it; being only forbidden to sell it without her consent. From none of her property is he bound to reserve anything, or make any provision for her maintenance or that of her children. This is the law for all, but practically it affects only two classes of women, viz., those who marry hurriedly or without proper advisers, and those whose property at the time of marriage is too small to permit of the expense of a settlement; in other words, the whole middle and lower ranks of women, and a certain portion of the upper ranks. Women of the richer class, with proper advisers, never come under the provisions of the common law, being carefully protected therefrom by an intricate system elaborated for the purpose by the courts of Equity, to which the victims of the Common Law have for years applied for redress. That system always involves considerable legal expenses, and an arrangement with trustees which is often extremely inconvenient and injurious to the interests of the married couple; nevertheless it is understood to be so great a boon that none who can afford to avail themselves of it, fail to do so.

What, then, is the principle on which the Common Law mulcts the poorer class of women of their property and earnings, and entails on the rich, if they wish to evade it, the costs and embarrassment of a marriage settlement? There is, of course, a principle in it, and one capable of clear statement. There are grounds for the law; first of Justice, then of Expediency, lastly (and as we believe) most influential of all, of Sentiment. Let us briefly describe them as best we can.

First, the grounds of Justice.

Man is the natural breadwinner. Woman lives by the bread which man has earned. Ergo, it is fit and right that the man who wins should have absolute disposal, not only of his winnings, but of every other small morsel or fraction of earnings or property she may possess. It is a fair return to him for his labour in the joint interest of both. He supports her, pays any debts she has incurred before or after marriage, and provides for the children which are hers as well as his. For all this, it is but just he should receive whatever she has to give. The woman's case is that of a pauper who enters a workhouse. The ratepayers are bound to support him; but if he have any savings they must be given up to the board. He cannot both claim support and keep independent property.

Then for Expediency. 'How can two walk together except they be agreed?' says the Bible. 'How can they walk together except one of them have it all his own way?' says the voice of rough and ready John Bull. Somebody must rule in a household, or everything will go to rack and ruin; and disputes will be endless. If somebody is to rule it can only be the husband, who is wiser, stronger, knows more of the world, and in any case has not the slightest intention of yielding his natural predominance. But to give a man such rule he must be allowed to keep the purse. Nothing but the power of the purse – in default of the stick – can permanently and thoroughly secure authority. Besides, for the good of the whole family, for the children and the wife herself, it is far more expedient that all the resources of the family should be directed by a single hand, and that hand the one that can best transact business of all kinds. Equally then, as a matter of Justice to the husband, and of Expediency for the interests of the family at large, the law of England has decreed, as aforesaid, that all a woman's present and prospective property becomes on marriage the property of her husband.

But where women are concerned, English law ceases to be a dry system, regardful only of abstract justice and policy. Themis, when she presides at the domestic hearth, doffs her wig, and allows herself to be swayed by poetical, not to say romantic, considerations. We are rarely allowed, in debate, to examine accurately the theory of conjugal justice. We are called upon rather to contemplate the beautiful ideal of absolute union of heart, life, and purse which the law has provided for, and which alone it deigns to recognise. If it so happen that happy married couples do not want the law to provide for them, and that the troubles of unhappy ones are greatly aggravated by the law *not* providing for them, we are told that it is an inconvenience to be regretted, but that it is counterbalanced by the great public benefit of the existing system. That the legislative judgment of England should hold up before the world a perfect picture of what it understands that married life *ought* to be, is affirmed to be of much more consequence than that it should try to mend cases which must be bad at the best.

Now, let us admit heartily that there is much sense in these arguments of justice and expediency, and much beauty in this ideal of absolute union of interests. In what may fairly be taken as typical marriages, where the man labours all day in the field or the office, and the woman provides for the household at home, the woman *has* no earnings independently of her husband, and what she has earned or inherited before marriage is employed for some purpose common to the family. There is no injustice here. When we remember the thousands of husbands and fathers who thus labour all their lives long for their wives and children – so commonly that it is only the exceptional selfishness we notice, never the rule of manly unselfishness – it may appear the plainest justice that he on whom all depends (the 'houseband', as our ancestors well called him) should have all the power as well as the toil. True that men have other motives for work beside the love of their families; they have interest in their pursuits, ambition, and pride. Many a bachelor, with none to come after him to inherit his store, labours as sedulously to increase it as the most devoted of parents. But with how many hundreds and thousands is it otherwise! How many men long and pine to cast down the spade or the pen, to leave the bleak field for the fireside, the gloomy shop or office for the streets and the hills; and *could* do so in a moment and live in comfort with a quarter of their present toil, were it not for the thought of the wife who is sitting at home rocking the cradle, or the young daughters who are asking for all the luxuries and flipperies of fashion! We have heard a boy remark that when he grew up he would never marry, because he noticed that when men married their wives enjoyed everything, and they had only to work harder than before. There was a good deal of truth in the remark; as doubtless the *Saturday Review* would readily corroborate. In the large sense and the common run of life, men are wonderfully unselfish towards women; and the general feeling of society has actually constituted it a rule that they should be expected to be so. Is it not, then, plainly just that he who plants the vineyards should eat – or at least have the distribution – of *all* the fruit thereof?

Then, again, for Expediency. How ignorant are most women in money concerns! How little they understand the commonest transactions, and how liable they are to be cheated, when they flatter themselves they do understand them! In the lower classes, as a general rule, women are more stupid than men; the feminine brain, such as it is, less well bearing rough usage, and the education of girls being inferior to that of boys. For the benefit of both husband, wife, and children, is it not every way expedient to make the wiser of the two keep the common purse?

Lastly, for the Sentimental view. How painful is the notion of a wife holding back her money from him who is every day toiling for her support! How fair is the ideal picture of absolute concession on her part of all she possesses of this world's dross to the man to whom she gives her heart and life! How magnificent in its unreserve is Portia's endowment of Bassanio, as quoted by Mr Lefevre:

> Myself and what is mine, to you and yours
> Is now converted. But now I was the lord
> Of this fair mansion, master of my servants,
> Queen o'er myself; and even now, but now,
> This house, these servants, and this same myself
> Are yours, my lord!

And in the humbler ranks, how sweet is the corresponding idyllic picture! The young man and maiden, after years of affection, and careful laying by of provision for the event, take each other at last, to be henceforth no more twain, but one flesh. Both have saved a little money, but it all now belongs to the husband alone. He lays it out in the purchase of the cottage where they are henceforth to dwell. Day by day he goes forth to his labour, and weekly he brings home his earnings, and places them in his wife's lap, bidding her spend them as she knows best for the supply of their homely board, their clothing which her deft fingers will make and many a time repair; and at last for their common treasures, the little children who gather around them. Thus they grow old in unbroken peace and love, the man's will having never once been disputed, the wife yielding alike from choice and from necessity to his superior sense and his legal authority.

Surely this ideal of life, for which the Common Law of England has done its utmost to provide, is well worth pondering upon before we attempt to meddle with any of its safeguards? Who will suggest anything better in its room?

Alas! There are other scenes besides idylls of domestic peace and obedience promoted by the law we are considering. We must look on the dark side as well as on the bright, before we determine that its preponderating influence is beneficial. But of these we shall speak hereafter. Before doing so we must traverse once more, and a little more carefully, the ground we have gone over. Is the Justice, is the Expediency, is the Sentiment of the Common Law all that appears at first sight?

What, in the first place, of the Justice of giving all a woman's property to her husband? The argument is, that the wife gets an ample *quid pro quo*. *Does* she get it under the existing law? That is the simple question.

In the first place, many husbands are unable, from fault or from misfortunes, to maintain their wives. Of this the law takes no note, proceeding on reasoning which may be reduced to the syllogism:

A man who supports his wife ought to have all her property;
MOST *men support their wives;*
Therefore, ALL *men ought to have all the property of their wives.*

Let us suppose the managers of a public institution to engage with a contractor, to pay him £1,000 on the nail for the supply of the institution with provisions for a year. At the end of a month the contractor has spent the £1,000 on his own devices and is bankrupt. The institution starves accordingly. What, in such case, do we think of the managers who gave the £1,000 without security for the fulfilment of the contract, and what do we think of the contractor? But are not hundreds of husbands in the position of the contractor, yet rather pitied than blamed by public opinion? And is not the law in such cases precisely in the position of the reckless managers? When all that a woman possesses in the present and future is handed over unreservedly by the law to her husband, is there the smallest attempt at obtaining security that he on his part *can* fulfil that obligation which is always paraded as the equivalent; namely, the obligation to support her for the rest of her life? Nay, he is not so much as asked to promise he will reserve any portion of her money for such purpose, or reminded of his supposed obligation. If he spend £10,000 of her fortune in a week in paying his own debts, and incapacitate himself for ever from supporting her and her children, the law has not one word to say against him.

But waiving the point of the *inability* of many husbands to fulfil their side of the understood engagement, one thing, at all events, it must behove the law to do. Having enforced her part on the woman, it is bound to enforce his part on the man, *to the utmost of his ability*. The legal act by which a man puts his hand in his wife's pocket, or draws her money out of the savings' bank, is perfectly clear, easy, inexpensive. The corresponding process by which the wife can obtain food and clothing from her husband when he neglects to provide it, what may it be? Where is it described? How is it rendered safe and easy to every poor woman who may chance to need its protection? When we are assured that men are always so careful of the interests of the women for whom they legislate, that it is quite needless for women to seek political freedom to protect themselves, we might be inclined to take it for granted that here, if anywhere, here where the very life and subsistence of women are concerned, the legislation of their good friends and protectors in their behalf would have been as stringent and as clear as words could make it. We should expect to find the very easiest and simplest mode of redress laid open to every hapless creature thus reduced to want by him to whom the law itself has given all she has ever earned or inherited. Nay, seeing the hesitation wherewith any wife would prosecute the husband with whom she still tries to live, and the exceeding cowardice and baseness of the act of maltreating so helpless a dependant, it might not have been too much had the law exercised as much severity in such a case as if the offender had voluntarily starved his ass or his sheep, and the Society for the Prevention of Cruelty to Animals were his prosecutors.

But this is the imaginary, what is the actual fact? Simply that the woman's remedy for her husband's neglect to provide her with food, has been practically found almost unattainable. The law which has robbed her so straightforwardly has somehow forgotten to secure for her the supposed compensation. Since 1857, if the husband altogether forsake his home for years together, the wife may obtain from the magistrate a Protection Order, and prevent him from seizing her property. But, if he come back just often enough to keep within the technical period fixed as desertion, and take from her everything she may have earned, or which charitable people may have given her, then there is absolutely no resource for her at all. The guardians of her union, if she ask to be admitted into the workhouse, may, if they please, receive her, and prosecute her husband, at the petty sessions, for putting the parish to the expense of supporting his wife. But the guardians are not obliged to admit her, and the trouble and cost of prosecution is an argument which frequently weighs with them against doing so. Then, as if to add insult to injury, when the poor wretch, driven from the shelter of the workhouse, and perhaps on the point of bearing a child to the man who is starving her, goes to the magistrate to implore protection, what answer does she receive? She is told that he cannot hear her complaint; that she cannot sue her husband, as he and she are one in the eye of the law.[2]

Again, the common law fails to secure justice to the wife, not only during her husband's life, but after his death. The following story was published many years ago in the *Westminster Review*, as having then recently occurred. We cannot vouch otherwise for its veracity, and must quote from memory, but, if it be only taken as a hypothetical case, what a lesson does it convey! A gentleman, of landed estate, in the north of England, became involved in debt, and finally ruined, and reduced to actual want. His wife, a lady of ability and spirit, finding him incapable of any effort for their joint support, opened a little shop for millinery in the county town. Her old friends gave her their custom, and her taste and industry made it a thriving business. For many years she maintained her husband and herself, till at last having realised a small competency, and grown old and feeble, she sold her shop, and retired to spend, as she hoped, in peace with her husband, the remaining years of her life. After a short time, however, the husband died, duly nursed and tended to the last by his wife. When he was dead he was found to have left a will, by which he bequeathed every shilling of his wife's earnings to a mistress he had secretly maintained. Either the wife had originally married without a settlement, or her settlements had not contemplated so singular a fact as her earning a fortune. The husband's will, therefore, was perfectly valid, *and was executed.*

So much for the Justice of the Common Law. What now shall we say to its Expediency? The matter seems to lie thus. Men are usually more wise in worldly matters than women; more generally able and intelligent, and their wives habitually look up to them with even exaggerated confidence and admiration. Such being the case, it would naturally happen, were there no law in the case, that the husband should manage all the larger business of the family. The law, then, *when the husband is really wise and good* is a dead letter. But for the opposite cases, exceptions though they be, yet alas! too numerous, where the husband is a fool, a gambler, a drunkard, and where the wife is sensible, frugal, devoted to the interests of the children – is it indeed Expedient that the whole and sole power should be lodged in the husband's hands; the power not only over all they already have in common, but the power over all the wife can ever earn in future? Such a law must paralyse the energy of any woman less than a heroine of maternal love. How many poor wives has it driven to despair, as one time after another they have been legally robbed of their hard won earnings, who can calculate? One such hapless one, we are told, when her lawful tyrant came home as usual, drunk with the spoils of her starving children, took up some wretched relic of their ruined household and smote him to death. She was a murderess. In former times she would have been burnt alive for 'petty treason' for killing her lord and master. But what was the law which gave to that reckless savage a power the same as that of a slave-holder of the South over his slave? Another case, still more recent, will be in the memory of many of our readers. Susanna Palmer was indicted on the 14th of January, 1869, at the Central Criminal Court, for wounding her husband in a struggle, in which it appeared he had, while drunk, endeavoured to wrench a table knife from her hand at supper. The evidence, which has since been carefully sifted and amply corroborated, showed Susanna Palmer to be a most industrious and sober woman. For twelve years since her marriage with James Palmer she has managed to support herself and her four children, having received from him during that period the sum of *five shillings* for the purpose. He has been four or five times in gaol for beating her, knocking out her teeth, and nearly killing her boy. Each time he returned from prison only more brutal and rapacious, and seized whatever money or furniture she had managed to obtain, breaking up her home over and over again. She applied to the magistrates at Clerkenwell for a Protection Order, to enable her to retain her earnings, but was refused it as her husband had not 'deserted' her; and, of course, had not the slightest intention of doing so. The law, as it at present exists, has absolutely no help to offer, and the charitable persons who desired to aid her have been compelled to place their contributions in the hands of the Ordinary of Newgate, in trust for her benefit. (See *The Times*, January 15th and 16th, 1869.) Such cases, we believe, might be multiplied by scores; but it is rare that the woman's sobriety and industry do not break down under such trials, and the whole family go to ruin together.

It is continually repeated *in this connection only* that laws cannot take note of exceptional cases; they must be laid down to suit the majority, and the minority must do as best they can. But is there any other department of public justice in which the same principle is applied? What else is law *for*, but to be 'a terror to evil doers'? – always, as we trust, in a minority in the community. The greater number of people are honest, and neither steal their neighbour's goods nor break into their houses. Yet the law takes pretty sharp account of thieves and burglars.

Setting up an ideal of perfect marriage union sounds very well. But what would it be to set up an ideal, say, between rich and poor, and to assume that what ought to be their relation in a Christian country actually is so? A new Poor Law based on the hypothesis that the Sermon on the Mount forms the rule of English life, to which the exceptions are too trifling to be regarded, would be at all events a novelty in legislation. Or rather, would it not correspond in spirit with the law we have been considering? The poor woman whose husband has robbed her earnings, who leaves her and her children to starve, and then goes unpunished because the law can only recognise the relation of husband and wife as it ought to be – and he and she are one before the law – such a woman's case would resemble closely enough that of a pauper who should be told that the law can only recognise the relation of rich and poor as it ought to be; and that, as everyone who has two coats must be assumed to give to him who has none, and from him that would borrow nobody can be supposed to turn away, the striking of a Poor's Rate in a Christian land must be wholly superfluous.

It is one of the numerous anomalies connected with women's affairs, that, when they are under debate, the same argument which would be held to determine other questions in one way is felt to settle theirs in another. If, for instance, it be proved of any other class of the community, that it is peculiarly liable to be injured, imposed on, and tyrannised over (e.g. the children who work in factories), it is considered to follow as a matter of course, that the law must step in for its protection. But it is the alleged helplessness of married women which, it is said, makes it indispensable to give all the support of the law, *not* to them, but to the stronger persons with whom they are unequally yoked. 'Woman is physically, mentally, and morally inferior to man.' Therefore it follows – what? – that the law should give to her bodily weakness, her intellectual dullness, her tottering morality, all the support and protection which it is possible to interpose between so poor a creature and the strong being always standing over her? By no means. Quite the contrary, of course. The husband being already physically, mentally, and morally his wife's superior must in justice receive from the law additional strength by being constituted absolute master of her property. Do we not seem to hear one of the intelligent keepers in the Zoological Gardens explaining to a party of visitors: 'This, ladies and gentlemen, is an inoffensive bird, the *Mulier Anglicana*. The beak is feeble, and the claws unsuited for grubbing. It seems to be only intelligent in building its nest, and taking care of its young, to whom it is peculiarly devoted, as well as to its mate. Otherwise it is a very simple sort of bird, picking up any crumbs which are thrown to it, and never touching carrion like the vulture, or intoxicating fluids like the maccaw. Therefore, you see, ladies and gentlemen, as it is so helpless, we put that strong chain round its leg, and fasten it to its nest, and make the bars of its cage exceptionally strong. As to its rudimentary wings we always break them early, for greater security; though I have heard Professor Huxley say that he is convinced it could never fly far with them, under any circumstances.'

But the great and overwhelming argument against the Expediency of the common law in this matter is the simple fact that no parent or guardian possessed of means sufficient to evade it by a marriage settlement ever dreams of permitting his daughter or ward to undergo its (alleged) beneficial action. The parent who neglected to demand such a settlement from a man before he gave him his daughter would be thought to have failed in the performance of one of his most obvious and imperative duties. Even the law itself in its highest form in the realm (that of the Court of Chancery) always requires settlements for its wards. How then can it be argued that the same rule is generally considered Expedient, yet invariably evaded by all who are able to evade it?

Again. There is the test of experience. Are married couples with settlements obviously less harmonious, are they less united in affection, are their children less well brought up than those who undergo the action of the law? When a woman has money of her own, so settled that she really has it for her separate use, do we find her always opposing her husband, and do her children seem to suffer from parental dissensions? Nay, let us go to the countries where no common law like ours exists at all, or where it has been repealed. In Russia marriage makes no difference in a woman's possession of property, to which also are attached the same political and municipal rights as belong to male proprietors. All that we know of Russian households is their peculiar harmony and mutual good feeling. And in the State of New York, where the Common Law was repealed in 1860, in Vermont, where it was changed in 1847, in Pennsylvania, where it was changed in 1848, and in Massachusetts, where it was changed in 1855, the report of the action of the new law, whereby the woman holds her own property and earnings, is entirely satisfactory. The following are some of the testimonies to the fact, collected by the Parliamentary Committee:

Mr Washbourne, formerly Governor of Massachusetts, and now Professor of Law at Harvard University, and who allows that he viewed the change with apprehension that it would cause angry and unkind feelings in families, and open the door for fraud, now admits that he is so far convinced to the contrary, that he would not be one to restore the common law if he could. Any attempt to go back to it would meet with little favour at this day. The oral evidence we have received from members of the Vermont and Massachusetts bars, from Mr Cyrus Field, of New York, and from the Hon. J. Rose, Finance Minister of Canada, is to the same effect. They state that the change has given entire satisfaction; that it has not caused dissension in families . . . that the benefit has chiefly accrued to women of small means. Mr Wells, Judge of the Supreme Court of Massachusetts, says: "That for which the law seems to me most commendable is the power which it gives to women of the poorer classes to control the fruits of their own labour. Many women of that class are left to struggle against the hardships of life, sometimes with a family of children, abandoned by their husbands, or, still worse, with a drunken, thriftless, idle vagabond of a man, claiming all the rights of a husband, and fulfilling none of the duties of the relation. When such men could take the hard earnings of their wives from service in the mills, and waste it upon their indulgences, no woman could have courage to struggle long in such a hopeless effort. In our manufacturing towns there are a great many women thus situated, who are saved from the most hopeless poverty and slavery by this most just provision, which gives them the right to receive and to hold the wages of their own labour. The misfortune has been that the more ignorant and degraded men were, the more rigorously they insisted upon and exercised their marital rights. . . . The law, by this change in the relative rights of husband and wife, has brought to the women of the poorer class a relief which touches the spring of hope and energy." Mr Dudley Field says of it, "Scarcely one of the great reforms which have been effected in this State have given more satisfaction than this." '3

With such examples before us, it truly seems impertinent to talk of Expediency. The only persons for whom the existing law is expedient are fortune-hunters, who, if they can befool young women of property so far as to induce them to elope, are enabled thereby to grasp all their inheritance. Were there no such law as the cession of the wife's property on marriage, there would be considerably fewer of those disgusting and miserable alliances where the man marries solely to become possessed of his wife's money.

But, as we have said already, there is an argument which has more force in determining legislation about marriage than either considerations of Justice or of Expediency. It is the Sentiment entertained by the majority of men on the subject; the ideal they have formed of wedlock, the poetical vision in their minds of a wife's true relation to her husband. Legislators talk in Parliament with a certain conviction that the principles of fairness and policy are the only ones to be referred to *there*. But whenever the subject is freely discussed, in private or in a newspaper, there is sure to burst out sooner or later the real feeling. Nothing can be more amusing than to watch such spontaneous outbreaks of the natural man in the dignified columns of *The Times*, or the hard-hitting periods of a well-known writer in the *Pall Mall Gazette*. Let us try to fathom this sentiment, for till we understand it we are but fighting our battles in the dark. Is it not this: that a woman's whole life and being, her soul, body, time, property, thought, and care, ought to be given to her husband; that nothing short of such absorption in him and his interests makes her a true wife; and that when she is thus absorbed even a very mediocre character and inferior intellect can make a man happy in a sense no splendour of endowments can otherwise do? Truly I believe this is the feeling at the bottom of nearly all men's hearts, and of the hearts of thousands of women also. There is no use urging that it is a gigantic piece of egotism in a man to desire such a marriage. Perhaps it is natural for him to do so, and perhaps it is natural for a great number of women to give just such absorbed adoring affection. Perhaps it is a tribute to the infinite nature of all love that for those who know each other best, as a wife knows her husband, there is no limit to human affection. At all events it seems a fact that the typical man (if we may call him so) desires such love, and the typical woman is ready to give it to him. He is impatient at the notion of a marriage in which this conception of absolute absorption of his wife's interests in his own shall not be fulfilled; and, so far as legislation can create such an ideal, he is resolved that it shall do so.

So far all is plain, but the question is this: Supposing such marriages to be the most desirable, do men set the right way about securing them, by making such laws as the Common Law of England? Is perfect love to be called out by perfect dependence? Does an empty purse necessarily imply a full heart? Is a generous-natured woman likely to be won, and not rather to be alienated and galled, by being made to feel she has no choice but submission? Surely there is great fallacy in this direction. The idea which we are all agreed ought to be realised in marriage is that of the highest possible Union. But what *is* that most perfect union? Have we not taken it in a most gross commercial sense, as if even here we were a nation of shopkeepers? Let us go into this matter a little carefully. It is rather instructive.

Husband and wife, in the eye of the poet, the divine, and, shall we say, the Judge of the Divorce Court? are 'not twain, but one flesh'. I know not whether Mr Darwin will sanction that theory concerning the Origin of Species, which tells us that

> Man came from nothing, and by the same plan
> Woman was made from the rib of a man;

or whether Dr Carpenter and Professor Huxley have verified the anatomical doctrine held by our nurses, that in consequence of Adam's sacrifice of his rib, men have ever since had one rib fewer than women. Still, however learned physiologists may decide this obscure problem, we shall all agree that it is a noble oriental metaphor to describe a wife's relation to her husband as 'bone of his bone, and flesh of his flesh'. But the union of two human beings may, as preachers say, be considered three ways. Firstly, there is the sort of union between any friends who are greatly attached to one another; a union oftenest seen, perhaps, between two sisters, who each have full liberty to come and go, and dispose of their separate resources, but who yet manage commonly to live in harmony and affection, and not unfrequently to bring up a whole batch of little nephews and nieces in their common abode. Two such we know, who for many years have kept the same account at their banker's, and say that they find only one serious objection to the plan – they can never make each other a present! Secondly, there is the union of the celebrated Siamese twins, who are tied together – not by Mother Church but by Mother

Nature – so effectually that Sir William Fergusson and Sir William
Wilde are equally powerless to release them. Each of them has,
however, the satisfaction of dragging about his brother as much
as he is dragged himself; and if either have a pocket, the other
must needs have every facility of access thereto.

Lastly, for the most absolute type of union of all, we must seek
an example in the Tarantula spider. As most persons are aware,
when one of these delightful creatures is placed under a glass with
a companion of his own species, a little smaller than himself, he
forthwith gobbles him up, making him thus, in a very literal
manner, 'bone of his bone' (supposing tarantulas to have any
bones) 'and flesh of his flesh'. The operation being completed, the
victorious spider visibly acquires double bulk, and thenceforth may
be understood to 'represent the family' in the most perfect manner
conceivable.

Now, of these three types of union, it is singular that the only
one which seems to have approved itself, in a pecuniary point of
view, to the legislative wisdom of England should be that of the
Tarantula. Unless a man be allowed to eat up the whole of a
woman's fortune, there is apparently no union possible between
their interests. Partnerships, limited liabilities, and all other devices
for amalgamation of property are here considered inadmissible.
The way in which brothers and sisters settle their affairs when they
reside under the same roof, would never suffice, it seems, to keep
things straight between those who hold a yet more tender and
trustful relationship.

Englishmen have, perhaps beyond all men, generous hearts and
chivalrous natures. They delight in such glorious lines as that of
their own poet:

> Yet were life a charnel, where
> Hope lay coffined with Despair;
> Yet were Truth a sacred lie,
> Love were lust – if Liberty
> Lent not life its soul of light,
> Hope its iris of delight,
> Truth its prophet's robe to wear,
> Love its power to give and bear.[4]

Is it possible that one of them, whose eye kindles over such
words, seriously believes that his own mother, sister, daughter, is
made of such different clay from himself, as that for *her*, abject
dependence is calculated to create and foster love, while for *him* it
would be gall and wormwood, turning his affection into bitterness
and revolt?

Truly I am persuaded it is not *thanks* to the Common Law, but in *spite* thereof, that there are so many united and happy homes in England.

To sum up our argument. The existing Common Law is not *just*, because it neither can secure nor actually even attempts to secure for the woman the equivalent support for whose sake she is forced to relinquish her property.

It is not *expedient*, because while in happy marriages it is superfluous and useless, in unhappy ones it becomes highly injurious; often causing the final ruin of a family, which the mother (if upheld by law) might have supported single-handed. It is also shown not to be really considered expedient by the conduct of the entire upper class of the country, and even of the legislature itself, in the system of the Court of Chancery. Where no-one who can afford to evade the law fails to evade it, the pretence that it is believed to be generally expedient is absurd. Further, the classes which actually evade it, and the countries where it is non-existing, show in no degree less connubial harmony than those wherein it is enforced.

Lastly, it does not tend to fulfil, but to counteract, the *sentiment* regarding the marriage union, to which it aims to add the pressure of force. Real unanimity is not produced between two parties by forbidding one of them to have any voice at all. The hard mechanical contrivance of the law for making husband and wife of one heart and mind is calculated to produce a precisely opposite result.

The proposal, then, to abolish this law seems to have in its favour Justice, Expediency, and even the Sentiment which has hitherto blindly supported the law. As the Parliamentary Committee report, they are strongly of opinion 'that the Common Law of this country, which gives the wife's property to her husband, should be repealed, and that the wife should have control over her property and earnings; and that her disability to contract and sue and be sued in respect of them should be removed'.

That certain difficulties must arise in carrying out so extensive a change is obvious, yet they are probably less than might be supposed; and a brief trial of the working of a new law would enable the legislature to find out the weak point (if any) of their present Bill. As the committee remark: 'Questions of importance arise in settling details of such a matter. Whether, for instance, the poor law liability of the father for the maintenance of the children should be extended to the mother; whether the change should be confined to future marriages only, or should be applied to existing marriages where other property is acquired' etc.

One thing, however, was unanimously agreed upon, and it is an important point in question:

It does not appear to be necessary to make any alteration in the liability of a husband to maintain his wife in consequence of such a change in the law with regard to the property of married women. A married woman, living apart from her husband, can only bind him for what is necessary, and the possession of property of her own, *pro tanto*, negatives the authority arising from necessity. A married woman, living with her husband, has an authority which, in spite of some fluctuations and uncertainty of judicial decisions, seems to be regulated by the general principle of the law of agency. Agency is a mixed question of law and fact, and the courts will give due weight to such a fact as the possession of property by a married woman, without any express statutable direction.'[5]

That such a change could not entail injurious consequences is guaranteed by two facts: First, there follow no injurious consequences to the richer classes in England, by whom the law is practically set aside; second, there have followed no injurious results, but very beneficial ones, to the lower classes in the American States, by whom the law has been repealed. We have already cited the testimony of the distinguished American lawyers, Mr Dudley Field, Judge Welles, Governor Washbourne, and others, to this point.

Justice, Expediency, a truly guided Sentiment, and such experience as is yet attainable – all these, then, point unanimously to the repeal of the existing Common Law, as it touches the property of married women.

But leaving this special, though typical, case of the Property of Married Women, may we not for a moment try to answer, if it be but vaguely, the larger question in which it is involved: What ought to be the general tone of legislation, the general line of policy pursued in these days by English men towards English women? It is clear enough that we have come to one of those stages in human history which, like a youth's attainment of majority, makes some change in the arrangements of past time desirable, if not imperative. There is no use reverting, on the one side with pertinacious dogmatism, and on the other with scorn and indignation, to old Eastern, or Classic, or Feudal relations between men and women. Anyone who has lived in southern and eastern lands can perfectly understand, from the nature of the women of those passionate races, how such states of things arose at first, and have been maintained ever since without blame or cruelty. In Feudal times, also, the blended chivalry and tyranny of men towards women was rather to be admired, for the chivalry then condemned for a tyranny which probably fell more lightly on women than on any inferior class of men in the social scale. But all these things are changed for us. Our Teuton race, from the days of Tacitus, has borne women whose moral nature has been in more than equipoise with their passions; and who have both deserved and obtained a freedom and a respect unknown to their sisters of the South. As the ages of force and violence have passed away, and as more and more room has been left for the growth of gentler powers, women (especially in England) have gradually and slowly risen to a higher place. It is indeed quite possible still to point out thousands who are unfit for any important exercise of freedom, who are mere dolls, or something worse. Half the discussions which go on about women would be stopped at the outset, if the speakers could settle *what* women they are going to talk of; the women of strong characters, or the women who have as little character as their own looking-glasses. One woman lives for affection, for duty, for elevated and refined pleas-ures of taste and intellect; not incapable of devoted love, yet not living with love alone in her thoughts; pleased to adorn her person, yet not dreaming and chattering of dress from morning till night. Another woman lives for admiration and passion, for low pleasures of vanity and sense; having for her sole ambition to befool the men who surround her, and for her sole serious employment to deck herself for their gaze. To one the society of men and women is equally interesting, provided each be equally intelligent. To the other, the presence of a man, be he almost an indiot, is so exciting and delightful that every woman in company is forgotten, and the most ludicrous changes of tastes and opinions are effected at a moment's notice, to fall in with his pleasure, as if they were the furniture of a lodging-house, to be moved to suit a new lodger. As George Sand says: if the minds of such women have received any impression over night, it is carefully smoothed down next morning, like a gravel walk, *avec le rateau*, to be quite ready to receive a fresh impression from the next visitor.

Such are the differences, the contrasts rather, between two orders of women; and it is not unnatural that when 'women's rights' are under discussion and one interlocutor is thinking of one sort of woman, and the other of the other, they should not readily agree to what is either just or expedient to be done for them. It seems equally out of question to withhold the franchise from Florence Nightingale when she asks for it,[6] or to grant it to the 'Girl of the Period'. Unfortunately, as strong minded women are apt to associate only with the strong of her own sex, and as men are apt to be a good deal more familiarised with the man-adoring type of women than with them, it is common when they argue for each to go on contradicting the other without the slightest hope of coming to an understanding.

But it must be granted, we think, that the numbers of those of whom Pope could affirm that

> Most women have no characters at all,

has a tendency to diminish year by year; and the numbers of the women with characters to increase. How much faster the alteration will go on under improved education, if such splendid schemes as that of Miss Davies' and Madame Bodichon's College can be carried out, is hard to judge. Already the classification of which we have already spoken, with the 'idiots' and the 'minors', seems hardly such as the scientific intellect would be satisfied with in other departments of zoology. Shall we say it resembles the botanical scheme of the governess who informed her pupils that 'plants are divided into Monandria, Bulbous Roots, and Weeds'?

We wish that we could persuade men more often to try and realise for themselves what is actually the life of a woman. Not as an appeal for compassion. It is very much to be questioned whether the warm affections and simple hearts of the better sort of women do not make life sweeter to them than to most men. 'Happiness,' says Paley, 'is to be found no less with the purring cat than with the playful kitten.' Enjoyment is a hardy little plant which grows at all altitudes above the level of actual starvation. There are glories of the nursery and ambitions of the kitchen which fill human hearts no less than the contests of the senate and the triumphs of the battle field. To the majority of men the life of a woman with its narrow household cares, its small social emulations, and its slightly flavoured pleasures, seems dull and insipid to the verge of disgust. Very few would hesitate to repeat the thanksgiving of the Rabbins for 'being born of the human race, and not a brute; a Jew, not a Gentile; a man, and not a woman'. Yet happiness is quite sufficiently elastic to shrink into the narrow circle of domestic life even while it is capable of stretching itself to the wide bounds of imperial power. Maria Theresa, and Catherine the Great might have made themselves content, the one perhaps as the mistress of a well frequented inn, or the other as an actress at a provincial theatre. Women who are not utterly ground down by the sordid cares of poverty, are quite as cheerful and a good deal more resigned to the decrees of Providence than their lords. It is, therefore, with a pity not dashed with compassion, but partaking of the tenderness wherewith we watch a child pleased with its doll and its baby-house, that men usually regard the lives of those dearest to them in the world. Were they ever to ask themselves how such an existence would suit *them*, they might perhaps be startled at the reflections which would suggest themselves. Any way I believe they would thenceforth carefully endeavour that none of the little patrimony of women's pleasures should be retrenched, none of the bounds of their interests and duties made narrower than nature herself has drawn them by the laws of their physical constitutions and their domestic affections.

Last summer *The Times* remarked that 'when working men desired to have votes *they* threw down the park palings, but that women have not shown their wish for the same privilege by any such proceedings'. Were we not on that same enchanted ground whereon all arguments are turned topsy turvy, we should have supposed that the mob who attacked the police and spoiled the public park, and the women who stopped at home and signed Mr Mill's petition, had respectively shown the one their *un*fitness, the other their fitness for the franchise of a law-respecting nation. But, in truth, women very rarely throw down *any* palings, either material or only imaginary; and they generally hurt themselves cruelly when they do so. Not for that reason ought men to refuse to them whatever rights may seem for them fairly established. Among these I trust, in the present paper, I have placed that of Married Women to the use of their own earnings and inheritances.

In conclusion, I would make one remark on the general question. Much time and more temper have been lost in debating the sterile problem of the 'equality' of men and women, without either party seeming to perceive that the solution either way has no bearing on the practical matters at issue; since civil rights have never yet been reserved for 'physical, moral, and intellectual' equals. Even for political rights, among all the arguments eagerly cited last year against extending the franchise, no-one thought it worth while to urge that the class proposed to be admitted to them was, or was not, physically, intellectually, or morally inferior to the classes which already possessed it. As for civil rights – the right to hold property, to make contracts, to sue and be sued – no class, however humble, stupid, and even vicious, has ever been denied them since serfdom and slavery came to an end. If men choose to say that women are their inferiors in *everything*, they are free and welcome then to say so. Women may think that they are the equivalents, if not the equals of men; that beauty is as great a physical advantage as the strength which man shares with the ox; that nimble wits and quick intuitions are on the whole as brilliant, though not as solid intellectual endowments as the strong understanding and creative imaginations of men; and finally, that for morality,[7] that aged man is happy whose conscience as he leaves the world is as void of grave offence as that of the majority of aged women. But whatever a woman may think on these subjects, she has no need to argue, much less to grow shrill and angry about it. 'Granted,' she answers to all rebuffs; 'let me be physically, intellectually, and morally your inferior. So long as you allow I possess moral responsibility and sufficient intelligence to know right from wrong (a point I conclude you will concede, else why hang me for murder?) I am quite content. It is *only* as a moral and intelligent being I claim my civil rights. Can you deny them to me on that ground?'

NOTES

1 Since Mr Lefevre's accession to office, the care of the Bill has been undertaken by Mr Russell Gurney.
2 A horrible instance in point occurred near Gainsborough, in Lincolnshire. The evidence given on the inquest was published in the *Lincolnshire Chronicle*, July 5, 1863.

The parish surgeon wrote thus to the clergyman of the parish, who was also a magistrate:

Dear Sir – I have today seen Mrs Seymour. I found her in a wretchedly weak state. She is nursing a baby, which office she is not able to perform effectually from her exhausted condition. Her husband, she says, does not allow her the necessaries of life, which he, in his position, could find if he liked. Without some means be taken to provide her with good diet, etc. or to make her husband do so, she must die of starvation at no very distant period. If you could, in your official capacity, help the poor creature, you would confer a great blessing on the poor woman, and oblige yours faithfully,

J. C. Smallman

The clergyman found, however, that he had no power as a magistrate to take cognisance of the case, unless the guardians would give the wife relief, and prosecute the husband; and this they declined to do. In vain did the poor half-starved wretch appear before them, and pray to be admitted into the workhouse. She was refused admission on the ground that her husband earned good wages; and so she went home, and, after lingering a while, probably fed now and then by her neighbours, she died. The husband escaped without any punishment whatever. The jury who tried him [*men*, of course!] gave him the benefit of a doubt as to the cause of his wife's death, and acquitted him.

3 *Special Report of Parliamentary Committee on Married Women's Property Bill.* It is satisfactory to know that separate property and the right of contract, has been accorded to married women by the new law of India, compiled by some of the ablest lawyers in this country: Lord Romilly, Sir W. Erle, Mr Justice Willes, Sir Edward Ryan, and Mr Lowe.

4 Shelley's *Hellas*.

5 *Special Report from the Select Committee on Married Women's Property Bill*, p. vii.

6 As she has done, along with such women as Mrs Somerville, Harriet Martineau, and Anna Swanwick, etc.

7 It must be confessed that, to a woman, the claim of superior *morality* for men sounds supremely absurd. Look at the three most hateful forms of vice – cruelty, drunkenness, unchastity – are they most common in women or in men? Watch for the first, the devil-vice of cruelty, among children. See how the little girl tends her birds and animals, and, as Chaucer describes her, 'all conscience and tender heart', 'greting' when anyone strikes her dog. See how her brother (brought up just as tenderly) begins in the nursery to pull flies to pieces, to worry the cat, then to terrify the sheep, to lay traps in the snow for sparrows. Observe how it is always his *mother's* soft words, his sister's tears, which win him at last, and make of him that really tender-hearted being, a perfect English gentleman. It is never his schoolfellows who correct him, rarely his master. Watch the class below. Is it the poor wild street girls who persecute and stone to death the hapless lost dogs of London? Read the reports of the Society for the Prevention of Cruelty to Animals, and observe whether it be men or women who are commonly prosecuted for torturing domestic creatures. Would any *woman's* devotion to science (does the reader think) lead her to practise vivisection? Nay, but it is hard for a man to tell the misery and disgust, rising almost to revolt against the order of the world, which fills many a woman's heart when she sees daily around her the instances of man's wanton and savage cruelty to the harmless creatures for whom she can only plead and pleads usually in vain. As I have been actually writing these pages, some dozen young men, of the labouring class, have passed under my window, pursuing, with volleys of heavy stones, a hapless little canary, which had escaped out of its cage, and, in its feeble flight, was striving to find shelter among the trees below. Is it needful to say there was no woman among the gang, and that the appeal of other women beside myself to give up their cruel chase, was unheeded? '*It ought to be killed*!' shouted one young ruffian in reply. A canary worthy of death! I sit down to pursue the theme of woman's moral inferiority. But where was I? Did I hear anybody say that women were more cruel than men? – or, perhaps, that cruelty is not the very crown of – shall we call it, Moral Superiority?

Emily Davies
(1830–1921)

Sarah Emily Davies, as she was christened, was the daughter of Mary Hopkinson and the Reverend John Davies. After a strict Evangelical upbringing and little formal education, she realised the disadvantages of her sex when her elder brother went on to pursue a distinguished career in Cambridge. When she was twenty-four, she met Elizabeth Garrett, who would become a close and supportive friend in future campaigns, and, shortly afterwards, Barbara Bodichon and Bessie Rayner Parkes. But it was not until her father died in 1861 that Emily Davies was able to move to London, become involved with the Langham Place Group and support Elizabeth Garrett's attempt to gain a medical qualification. Emily Davies considered embarking on a medical career herself but, having decided that her sketchy education and the needs of her widowed mother would impede her progress, she directed her energies towards campaigning for women's higher education. When her attempt to induce London University to admit women students failed, she turned her attention to Oxford and Cambridge. In 1864, she successfully campaigned for girls to be included in the Schools' Enquiry Commission and, two years later, published *The Higher Education of Women*. A member of the Kensington Society, she clashed with Helen Taylor over the issue of suffrage (Emily Davies thought that it would be prudent to ask for the vote for unmarried women only whilst Helen Taylor believed that women should be enfranchised on the same terms as men) and concentrated instead on her plan to establish a women's college. In 1866, she set up a fund-raising committee; her efforts were rewarded initially with the college at Hitchin in 1869 and, finally, when Girton College was founded in 1873. Having dropped out of any involvement in the suffrage campaign lest it harm the progress of women's higher education, Emily Davies felt that she could lend her support once Girton had been secured: in 1879 she gave her name to a list of eminent women approving of suffrage; ten years later she became a member of the general committee of the London National Society for Women's Suffrage; in 1891 she joined the Executive Committee and became an active suffrage campaigner; and, in 1919 she was one of the few early suffrage workers still alive to record her vote.

Female Physicians

(reprinted from *The English Woman's Journal*, May 1862)

Ladies,

The elaborate and apparently well-considered observations of 'A Physician of Twenty-one Years' Standing', in *The English Woman's Journal* of last month, call for some notice on the part of those who believe the Medical Profession to be a sphere of usefulness especially suited to women.

Your correspondent, after expressing his general sympathy with the efforts made for the 'expansion of woman's responsibilities and work', proceeds to remark, that 'we shall fail in our attempts if they are not consonant with those laws of our physical and moral nature which are the necessary basis upon which alone any ethical or political structure can be raised, that shall not prove the mere "baseless fabric of a vision".' Is it not the question in dispute whether there is anything in the practice of medicine by women which must necessarily contravene these laws?

'A Physician' asks us to consider the question under two aspects, corresponding to two main elements which determine the choice of a young man in selecting a profession: his own aptitude, and the sphere into which his profession may throw him.

First, as to aptitude, by which I conceive is meant a general liking for some particular pursuit, combined with a certain amount of ability. I scarcely suppose that the most vehement objectors to female physicians would argue that, as a class, women have less taste for medicine than men. An ignorant love of doctoring is one of the recognised weaknesses of women. Their intellectual and physical incapacity requires to be proved by 'something more stringent than the dogmatic opinion of any writer'. Whether the mental powers of women are on the whole equal to those of men is a wide and difficult question, on which it is needless to enter, inasmuch as we claim only the right to exercise such powers as we possess, be they great or small. 'A Physician' speaks of the previous training medical students have received as boys, as if it were impossible that girls should receive the same. But is not some training of this sort just what women want? On this point, I may be allowed to quote from a well-known author:

'Women's education must be made such as to ensure some accuracy and reasoning. This may be done with any subject of education, and is done with men, whatever they learn, because they are expected to produce and use their acquirements. But the greatest object of intellectual education, the improvement of the mental powers, is as needful for one sex as the other, and requires the same means in both sexes. The same accuracy, attention, logic, and method, that are attempted in the education of men, should be aimed at in that of women.'

And again:

'It is a narrow view of things to suppose that a just cultivation of women's mental powers will take them out of their sphere – it will only enlarge that sphere. The most cultivated women perform their common duties best. They see more in those duties. They can do more. Lady Jane Grey would, I dare say, have bound up a wound or managed a household with any unlearned woman of her day. Queen Elizabeth did manage a kingdom; and we find no pedantry in her way of doing it.'

That lady students, entering upon the course without preliminary training, do so at an immense disadvantage, we are quite ready to admit. It is perhaps the strongest point in our case, as regards mere power, both physical and intellectual, that women have been able to do so much while debarred from the advantages of early education open to most men.

'Supposing the difficulties of the student's life surpassed, you then come to the troubles and difficulties of incipient practice.' And here the physical weakness of women is the argument. That, as a whole, men are stronger than women, no-one denies; but does that justify us in assuming that every individual man is stronger than any individual woman? We learn from 'A Physician' what our own observation confirms, that many members of the medical profession are feeble in constitution and scarcely fit for the struggle of life; but we do not therefore condemn them to complete inaction, nor do we propose any regulation for limiting the profession to men of herculean frames. On the other hand, we learn from our own observation, though not from your correspondent, that in various parts of the country women of the lower classes go through an amount of labour under which a gentleman would probably break down. I have myself been told by an eyewitness that in Staffordshire, women are doing, 'not men's work, but horses work'; and it is an unquestionable fact that in manufactories where women and girls are employed, the low, rough, exhausting work is given over to them, while the higher branches, in which some intelligence is required, are reserved for men. The same may be said of brick-making and other laborious outdoor work. Let it not be supposed that we look with satisfaction upon this over-tasking of the physical strength of women. On the contrary, we believe that by opening out occupations in which intelligence goes for something, these poor degraded women may gradually be drawn up from a condition in which common morality is almost an impossibility; and so, while delivering the upper classes from the curse of idleness, we may at the same time effectually help those least able to help themselves. But we do think that while women are showing themselves to be capable of such an amount of physical exertion, the comparatively far easier career of a physician should not be closed to us on the ground of physical weakness. It is remarked, that 'unless she can cope with men in all the various branches of medical inquiry and practice, she will, in the race of life, necessarily go to the wall; and the struggle, which will be unavoidable, must be to the stronger'. Be it so. Women are so much in the habit of going to the wall that the position will not alarm them by its novelty, and their fate will only be the same as that of all members of the profession who are not able to cope on equal terms with their superior brethren.

As we look round upon medical men, we cannot help observing many physicians and surgeons who do not appear to be superior in ability to average women; and as for many years only women somewhat above the average in mental and physical strength will dare to think of entering the profession, perhaps they would *not* always go to the wall. At any rate, their position could scarcely be worse than that of governesses. A practice of four or five hundred a year is not thought much of among physicians; but ladies, who can seldom, even by hard work during their best years, earn more than, say, £200 a year, will not despise the crumbs which fall from the rich man's table.

'A Physician' proceeds to inquire, 'Is there a proper field for the employment and support of female physicians?' We unhesitatingly reply that all the diseases to which women and children are liable would naturally come within the province of the female physician, and surely that is a domain wide enough, without encroaching upon the sphere of men. But your correspondent is confident that ladies would not consult female doctors. On this point my experience is widely different from his. I can well believe that ladies, being suddenly questioned, would reply at once that they would not have confidence in a woman. Hastily assuming that the female physician would be either a shallow, superficially taught lady, or a sort of superior nurse, they naturally feel that they would prefer the services of an able and experienced man. But ladies who have had time to think are almost unanimous in declaring that if they could secure the attendance of equally well-educated women (and this can be certified by a degree), they would give them the preference. I speak not from hearing, but from actual personal knowledge, when I say that this feeling is much stronger among refined women of the poorer classes, who are more at the mercy of young men and the inferior order of practitioners. The feeling is strongest of all among young girls. I believe that to many of them the sympathy and tenderness of a woman would be absolutely more curative than the possibly superior skill of a man – of which, indeed, they often refuse to avail themselves.

Finally, your correspondent inquires from whence you would draw your supply of females who are to study medicine and become physicians? To which I reply, from whence do we draw our supply of governesses? Of them there appears to be an abundant, nay an excessive, supply. A female medical student need not 'devote herself heart and soul to celibacy'. She might indeed exercise a more independent choice, because she would not be driven into marriage by the mere longing for some satisfying occupation; but if suitable marriage came in her way, her profession need be no hindrance. To have passed a few years in patient study and earnest work would, surely, be an admirable preparation for married life; and she would be better off than other women in having a profession to fall back upon in case of widowhood or other misfortune. This question of marriage, in fact, amounts to this – Are all women to be shut out from any and every method of earning money by honest and intelligent work lest they should grow too independent of their natural supporters, or are they to be encouraged and urged to use their gifts as those who must give account? It is beginning to be believed that women have certain gifts of hand, and that it is not unfeminine to use them. Let us hope that in a generation or two it will also be admitted that they have heads, and that this being so, it is their bounden duty 'sincerely to give a true account of their gift of reason, to the benefit and use of men'. How they may best labour to this end can surely be satisfactorily proved only by experience. There may be much confident assertion on both sides, but till the experiment has been fairly tried, we have no right to decide positively that women can or cannot go through the medical course uninjured; that they will or will not find patients. And if ladies show some reluctance in coming forward as students, let us not hastily draw unfavourable conclusions. We are reminded by your correspondent that the training must commence in early life; and it would be folly to expect that girls of sixteen will eagerly press for admission into a profession, 'into which', as they are told by 'A Physician of Twenty-one Years' Standing', 'they are to be forced against the dictates of Nature and all the usages and requirements of society'. They may indeed suspect that their interest and delight in medical study and in doctoring (not merely nursing) is in itself a 'dictate of Nature', and that 'the usages of society' are in this case, as they have sometimes been before, unreasonable and wrong. But modest, well-brought up girls are slow (can we wish them to be less so?) to act upon their own convictions against the authority of their more experienced friends, and for them to enter upon such a struggle unaided would be clearly impossible. On the other hand, women whose convictions have grown with their growth, and who have arrived at an age at which they are at liberty to judge for themselves find it too late to enter upon the medical course. The spring and energy which might have been turned to account for the service of God and man has been exhausted, frittered away in desultory, unsatisfying effort, if it has not found an outlet for itself in actual mischief.

Your correspondent candidly admits, that 'You know, and the readers of this Journal know, the female heart better than he can.' It is indeed so. Men, the most liberal and the most generous, do not know, and never will know, what women are suffering, who, to the eye of the world, are 'very happy'. Young ladies are not all so thoughtless as they seem. The injunction to 'make themselves happy' in luxurious idleness is as much a mockery to them as to Rasselas and Neyakah in the Happy Valley. To such happiness, unblessed of God and unhallowed of men, may they never learn to reconcile themselves.

I am, etc.
'A. C. R.'
Emily Davies

Medicine as a Profession for Women

(a paper read at the Social Science Congress, June 1862)

In speaking of Medicine as a profession for women, it is not my intention to enter upon the general question of the employment of women. I may be allowed, however, in passing, to protest against a notion which seems to have taken possession of many minds, that those who are endeavouring to extend the range of women's labour are desirous of adding to the severity of their toil. Women already work hard, and it ought scarcely to be said that we wish to increase the aggregate amount of their labour. What we are striving for is rather a re-adjustment of the burden, a somewhat different apportionment of mental and physical labour as relatively distributed between men and women. We desire to see such a condition of society as is described by Coleridge, who, in picturing an imagined golden age, speaks of it as a time 'when labour was a sweet name for the activity of sane minds in healthful bodies'. It is not too much to say that the great mass of women are much less healthy, both in mind and body, than they might be if they had a fair chance of physical and mental development. Many ladies are sickly and hysterical, not, strictly speaking, from want of work, but from the want of some steady occupation, sufficiently interesting and important to take them out of themselves. The very poor, on the other hand, are worn down by an amount and a kind of physical toil, for which their frames were never intended, their minds being utterly uncultivated, while their earnings are so small that it is impossible for them to maintain themselves in decency and comfort.[1] Of neither of these classes can it be fairly said that they are in that state of life into which it has pleased God to call them. Some other agency must be at work, some disturbing cause, hindering them from filling their appropriate position. It is to help them to find their place, and to occupy it when found, that our efforts are directed.

If it be true, as the most experienced persons tell us, that what women want in the way of employment is something which gives room for the exercise of their mental activities, without excessive physical toil, we are led to inquire in what professions and occupations these conditions can be obtained. For ladies, it is also requisite that the occupation should not involve the forfeiture of social position. A parent may reasonably say, 'I feel that my daughter would be better and happier with some definite work, but what can I bring her up to?' The practice of Medicine among women and children, as being to all appearance essentially a woman's work, naturally occurs first, and we have now to consider whether it fulfils the before-mentioned conditions. As to the first – no-one doubts that the study and practice of Medicine afford ample scope for the use of the mental powers. Some persons have indeed expressed a fear that, the minds of women being naturally inferior, the strain on their faculties would be too great. There seems little reason, however, to apprehend danger on this score, as a little observation proves that the most highly cultivated women, whose mental energies are at least as much in use as those of average doctors, are not less healthy-minded than others, but rather the reverse. With regard to bodily exertion, there is no doubt that a physician in full practice goes through a very considerable amount of work. But, after all, walking, and riding, and driving about, are among the recognised means of gaining health, and even the night work, of which some share falls to the lot of all doctors, is perhaps not much more trying to the constitution than the night work habitually performed by ladies of all ages, in heated rooms, and under other unfavourable circumstances. It should be understood throughout that in making these comparisons, I speak of the general run of doctors all over the country, not of a few picked men at the head of their profession, on whose energies the demand must be extraordinarily great, and with whom it would not be necessary for ladies to compete.

The last-named condition, that the profession should not involve the sacrifice of social position, is the one which marks out Medicine as eminently suitable for women of the middle class. We are constantly told that women are made to be nurses, and that a better class of nurses is urgently required. But it seems to be forgotten that though a few philanthropic ladies may undertake nursing in hospitals or among the poor, as a work of charity, without loss of social rank, the business of hired nurse cannot be looked upon as a profession for a lady. The salary of a hospital nurse is less than the wages of a butler or a groom; and even supposing that superior women would command higher remuneration, the position of a nurse is in every way too nearly allied to that of an upper servant to be in the least appropriate for the daughters and sisters of the mercantile and professional classes.

Apart from the foregoing considerations, which apply chiefly to the want of some outlet for the mental energies of women, there is another aspect of the question which ought not to be overlooked. I refer to the want of women in the medical profession. The existence of this want is not generally admitted by medical men, but I submit that they are not likely to be the best judges. It is an unquestionable fact – and here I speak, not from hearsay or conjecture, but from personal knowledge obtained by extended inquiry – that women of all ranks do earnestly desire the attendance of physicians of their own sex. The want is most strongly felt by those who cannot command the services of the higher class of medical men. It is equally unquestionable, and here again I speak from authority, that women wish to enter the profession. Is not the mere existence of these two corresponding facts a sufficient reason for giving leave to try the experiment? If we fail, we fail; and having fairly tried, we shall be content to abide by the result. That an innovation *is* an innovation is not a sufficient ground for opposing it. The opponents of a change are bound to give reasons for their resistance. In the case under consideration, I am ready to admit that they have done so freely. Some of the objections seem indeed to cancel each other. For instance, one asks, 'Where are your lady students to come from?' while another complains, 'What is to become of the men, if women crowd into this already overstocked profession?' At one time, women are ordered to keep their place, while at another they are assured that their place is at the bedside of the sick. Those who are most anxious to see women waiting upon male patients as nurses consider it an outrage upon propriety that they should attend their own sex as physicians.

There are, however, more serious difficulties than these thoughtless cavils. It cannot be denied that there are grave objections to the study of Medicine by male and female students in mixed schools, and although a few exceptional women might be willing, for the sake of others, to go through the medical course, even under existing arrangements, it is evident that for female students generally, some modification of these arrangements would be necessary. Such a modification might easily be effected, if the demand for it were clearly made out. Separate classes might be formed for lady students, in connection with the existing schools. There would be no difficulty in obtaining the services of eminent medical men as teachers. Some of those who most strongly object to the admission of ladies into the schools for men have expressed their willingness to give separate instruction. The examinations must, of course, be the same for both sexes, as a security that the standard of proficiency should not be lowered for women, but to that there can be no objection. The difficulties of the case arise, neither from a want of aptitude on the part of women, to whom the practice of Medicine seems to come more naturally than to men, nor from the opposition of the medical authorities, many of whom have shown marked liberality and freedom from prejudice. The real obstacles are the unwillingness of young women to incur the reproach of singularity and self-sufficiency, and the less excusable unwillingness of their parents and friends to aid them in overcoming difficulties which they cannot conquer alone. The medical course ought to be begun early in life, and young women cannot be expected to force themselves into a profession against the wishes of those to whom they have learnt to look up for advice and guidance. At the same time, it should be remembered that no class are more sensitively alive to the influence of public opinion than the parents of daughters. Many people who would be favourable to women-physicians, in the abstract, would shrink from giving the least encouragement to their own daughters to take a single step out of the beaten path. And it is here that we can all do something. We can at least refrain from joining in the thoughtless cry of horror and astonishment at the idea of women-physicians. Ladies may help much by simply making known in the proper quarters their wish for the medical attendance of women. By so doing they would encourage ladies to offer themselves as students, and would afford to them a moral support which they much need. We cannot, indeed, save them from the prominence which must be the lot of the pioneers in any movement – a prominence which has little attraction for those thoughtful women, who, feeling the responsibilities of life more strongly than others, are more earnest in desiring to take their modest share in the work of the world. A certain amount of notoriety is unavoidable, but it rests with the public to decide whether it shall be an unmerited stigma or an honourable distinction.

NOTE

1 Those who have come into immediate contact, as I have, with the female workers in glass-houses, paper-mills, brick-yards, etc., will confess that this is no exaggerated statement.

The Influence of University Degrees on the Education of Women

(reprinted from *The Victoria Magazine*, June 1863)

In considering the education of women in connection with recent proposals for its improvement by means of examinations for University Degrees, it may be well to inquire at the outset, what *is* a Degree? In what does its value consist?

A University degree is neither more nor less than a certificate. At Oxford and Cambridge it certifies that the graduate has lived during a certain number of terms in a college or hall, has been devoting his time chiefly to study, and has passed divers examinations which were meant to test his ability and knowledge. The degrees of the University of London also certified in the beginning that graduates in Arts and Laws had been students during two years, at one or other of the affiliated institutions, which were to the University of London what the colleges are to the Universities of Oxford and Cambridge. Few will deny the advantages of residence for two or three years in a college; and it may be easily seen how such residence, and the intercourse between students which it implies, may be made very greatly to lessen the dangers and disadvantages from which mere examination, taken alone, can scarcely be wholly free. It is possible that a young man, preparing at home for his degree, may be sufficiently crammed to pass, and may even find his name somewhere in the list of honours; and yet mistake knowledge for wisdom, and a retentive memory for genius. But in a college, such a man would be pretty sure to find his true level. He would find among his companions some who, with far less than his own powers of memory or application, would still unquestionably be his superiors. He would be made to feel quite easily, and almost without knowing how useful a lesson he was learning, that processes are almost as valuable as results; that what a man is, is of far more importance than what at any given time he can do; and that there are a thousand excellences that can find no room for display in any University examination whatever. Moreover, residence for two or three years in a college implies comparatively easy circumstances, and ought, therefore, to imply all that society expects from gentlemen; and though many of the colleges connected with the University of London required no extravagant expenditure, and were, perhaps, not half so costly as those of Oxford and Cambridge, yet the term of residence was generally longer, being in many of them as long as five years.

The University of London, however, was intended to promote the education, not only of gentlemen, and of persons who could afford to live for several years at a college, but of all classes of Her Majesty's subjects, without any distinction whatever; and accordingly in the new Charter it was provided that persons not educated in any of the institutions connected with the University should be admitted as candidates for matriculation, and degrees, 'other than degrees in medicine or surgery, on such conditions as the Chancellor, Vice-Chancellor, and Fellows by regulations in that behalf should from time to time determine; such regulations being subject to the provisos and restrictions contained in the Charter'. This change was regarded with considerable disfavour by many of those who had graduated under the old regulations, and who imagined that the value of their degrees would be reduced when similar degrees were conferred upon those who had never been to a college at all. It is obvious however, that the colleges must look for their prosperity to their own intrinsic worth; and that the University should confer degrees upon all those who could pass the examination prescribed, wherever they might have been educated, was clearly in harmony with the original intention of the University. The want of college training, and especially of the indirect advantage of association with men whose favourite studies lie in different directions, and who possess very different kinds of ability, was partly counteracted by the wide range of subjects in which candidates for degrees were required to pass. Nor has the change as yet done much more than recognise a right which it would have been invidious to withhold. Scarcely any of those who have taken honours during the last few years, have come to their examinations from 'private study', and sixteen out of the twenty who have taken the degree of Bachelor of Science are from the colleges connected with the University. But after all, if a man can read Livy or Thucydides, Plato's *Republic*, or Aristotle's *Ethics*, it really matters little how he obtained his knowledge of Greek and Latin; and if it be expedient to found a University at all, and if degrees are of any use, then the man who can prove that he possesses the requisite knowledge has a fair claim to have that fact certified.

But if the want of money, and, what amounts to very much the same thing, the want of leisure are to be no impediment to the recognition of a man's real worth and attainments, so far as examination can test them, why should any impediments whatever be allowed to remain? Why especially should difference of sex be an impediment?

The question was raised so early as 1856, in which year a lady applied for admission to the examinations of the University of London. The advice of counsel was taken, and an opinion was given that such admission could not legally be granted. No further steps were taken until April, 1862, when another lady preferred a request to be admitted as a candidate at the next Matriculation Examination. On that occasion a resolution was passed: 'That the Senate, as at present advised, sees no reason to doubt the validity of the opinion given by Mr Tomlinson, July 9th, 1856, as to the admissibility of females to the Examinations of the University.' The matter was not allowed to rest here. On April 30th the following memorial was laid before the Senate.

Gentlemen – An application having been made by my daughter for admission to the Examinations of your University, and refused on legal grounds, we beg respectfully to request that the question may receive further consideration.

It appears to us very desirable to raise the standard of female education, and that this object can in no way be more effectually furthered than by affording to women an opportunity of testing their attainments in the more solid branches of learning. It is usually admitted that examinations are almost essential as a touchstone of successful study, and as a stimulus to continuous effort. Such a touchstone, and such a stimulus, are even more necessary to women than to men; and though we should be most unwilling to obtain these advantages by the sacrifice of others still more precious, we are of opinion that in the University of London our object might be obtained without any contingent risk. Many of the candidates for degrees would probably be furnished by the existing Ladies' Colleges, and as the University requires no residence, and the examinations involve nothing which could in the slightest degree infringe upon feminine reserve, we believe that by acceding to our wishes you would be conferring an unmixed benefit.

We are informed that a new Charter of the University is about to be submitted to Parliament. We beg therefore to suggest that the technical legal objection, which appears to be the only obstacle to the admission of women, may be removed by the insertion of a clause expressly providing for the extension to women of the privileges of the University. I beg to enclose a list of ladies and gentlemen who have given their sanction to the proposal.

I have the honour to be, Gentlemen,
Your obedient Servant,
NEWSON GARRETT

On May 7th a resolution was moved by the Vice-Chancellor, Mr Grote, and seconded by the Right Hon. R. Lowe, M.P., to the effect, 'That the Senate will endeavour, as far as their powers reach, to obtain a modification of the Charter, rendering female students admissible to the Degrees and Honours of the University of London, on the same conditions of examination as male students, but not rendering them admissible to become Members of Convocation.' After an earnest and protracted discussion, the Senate divided. The numbers being equal, ten on each side, the motion was negatived by the casting vote of the Chancellor. The following reply to the Memorial was addressed to Mr Garrett.

'Sir – I am directed to inform you that, after a full consideration of your Memorial, the Senate have come to the conclusion that it is not expedient to propose any alteration in the Charter, with a view of obtaining power to admit females to the Examinations of the University.

I think it well to add that this decision has not been the result of any indisposition to give encouragement to the higher education of the female sex – a very general concurrence having been expressed in the desire stated in your Memorial, that an opportunity should be afforded to women of testing their attainments in the more solid branches of learning; but it has been based on the conviction entertained by the majority of the Senate, that it is not desirable that the constitution of this University should be modified for the sake of affording such opportunity.

I remain, Sir,
Your obedient Servant,
W. B. CARPENTER

The matter has since been brought forward in the Convocation of the University. On the 26th March a Resolution was passed by the Annual Committee, and afterwards embodied in the Report to Convocation, to the following effect: 'That this Committee, recognising the desirableness of elevating the standard of female education, recommend Convocation to represent to the Senate the propriety of considering whether it might not forward the objects of the University, as declared in the Charter, to make provision for the examination and certification of women.' After a lengthened discussion the resolution was negatived by a considerable majority.

The question having thus been fairly raised – a definite application having been made – it clearly becomes the duty of those who decline to accede to a request which appears so reasonable, to show cause for their refusal. The *onus probandi* undoubtedly rests with the opponents of the measure. And it must be confessed that they have not been backward in accepting the challenge, whatever may be thought of the quality of the arguments brought forward. They resolve themselves, for the most part, into an 'instinct', a prejudice, or an unproved assertion that women ought not to pursue the same studies as men; and that they would become exceedingly unwomanly if they did. A woman so educated would, we are assured, make a very poor wife or mother. Much learning would make her mad, and would wholly unfit her for those quiet domestic offices for which Providence intended her. She would lose the gentleness, the grace, and the sweet vivacity which are now her chief adornment, and would become cold, calculating, masculine, fast, strongminded, and in a word, generally unpleasing. That the evils described under these somewhat vague terms are very real, and do actually exist at this moment, cannot be denied by any one who is at all conversant with English society. That any scheme of education which might tend to foster them ought to be energetically resisted, will scarcely be disputed by any – least of all by the advocates of extended mental culture for women.

It may be well to examine first that theory of the difference between manhood and womanhood which underlies most of the objections commonly brought against the thorough culture of women; and which, if it were true, would render all further argument superfluous. The differences between a man and a woman are either essential or conventional, or both. In any case it is difficult to understand how they affect the right of a woman to pass an examination and to take a degree. The differences themselves are often exaggerated, both by women and by men. So far as they are manifested by any external acts, they are almost entirely conventional; and of those which are essential, and which belong to the inmost being of woman or man, it seems difficult to understand how any information can be obtained, or comparison instituted. For how can things be compared which *ex-hypothesi* are wholly unlike? How can we possibly know or learn that to which there is nothing analogous in ourselves? We understand the nature of animals because, and in so far as, we are animals ourselves. To the same extent possibly a dog might understand a man; but no ingenuity could ever impart to an animal the knowledge of the human spirit, with all its endless resources, its freedom, its aspirations, its power to 'look before and after'. Nothing could make a brute religious, or explain to a brute what religion is; and, on the other side, are we not taught that we can know God only so far as we are partakers of the Divine nature; only because God created man in His own image? If there be then in woman a mystic something to which nothing in a man corresponds; if woman has what man wants, or wants what man has; if this difference be natural, essential, and therefore forever unalterable, it simply marks out a region of utter unlikeness which is protected by that unlikeness from intrusion or visitation. Perhaps then we may leave altogether out of the question those mystic differences which can give no clear proof of their own existence, which have no faculty of speech, no means of expressing what they are.

But at any rate, there are differences, we are told, which can manifest themselves. The strength of the woman, we are told, is in the heart; the strength of the man, in the head. The woman can suffer patiently; the man can act bravely. The woman has a loving care for the individual; the man an unimpassioned reverence for the general and universal. These, and such as these, are represented as the outward tokens of essential differences, which cannot be mistaken, and ought never, in any system of education or work of life, to be overlooked.

If these are natural differences, it is idle to ask whether we should praise or blame them, for the nature of a thing has no moral qualities whatever. A tiger may be dangerous, but is certainly not cruel; a fox may be cunning, but cannot be dishonest; and if dogs delight to bark and bite, because God hath made them so, who shall find fault with them? But natural differences should certainly guide our systems of education; and if it is really in the nature of a woman to have very much feeling and very little sense, were it not a kind of fighting against Providence to attempt to rescue her from this very dangerous form of insanity? Yet, surely, it may be affirmed with the utmost confidence, that a woman's affections ought to be as well regulated as a man's; that she should know how to give as well as to receive, and be prompt to act as well as patient to suffer. She should not sacrifice the many for the one, nor the long endless future for the passing moment. And do we really wish to people the world with male creatures devoid of all gentleness and affection, losing sight of the individual in the mass, irritable and impatient under the irremediable discomforts and reverses of life? Does religion include no tender affections for the man, no intellectual strength for the woman? And do we not read that God created man in His own image, in the image of God created He him, male and female created He them? Should not a man's thoughts of God be a woman's thoughts also? And why should that compassion of the Almighty, which is spoken of in Scripture as womanly, be strange to the heart of man? A woman surely ought to have a sense of the law of justice, and a man, of the law of love. Moreover, a genius for detail is quite worthless if the parts are not fittingly arranged and subordinated to the whole.

In truth, it is exactly in this subordinating of the whole to its parts that even the charity and affection of women has often done great mischief; and is capable of doing any amount of mischief, if it were not restrained by that power of generalisation and order which now women sometimes find in men, and ought to find in themselves. A beggar dying in the streets of starvation should be relieved by anybody who is able to relieve him; his individual life is not to be sacrificed for any theory or system, however comprehensive. If it is a man who sees him perishing with want he would be bound, and we may fairly hope he would be willing, to save him. On the other hand, the majority of street-beggars are impostors, and certainly ought not to be relieved. To relieve them is a direct encouragement of idleness and vice. Even the little children, who will certainly be cruelly flogged unless they take home a fair amount of money after a day's suffering and shame, would never be employed in so shameful a business as begging if ill-regulated kindness had not made it profitable. Individually they may be as greatly in need of assistance as any sufferers whatever; the reasons why they are not to receive alms are reasons derived from the careful combination and comparison of very many facts of very different kinds. Is it really thought desirable, then, that women should be ignorant of those facts, and the general rules deduced from them? Is the wisdom of the male sex to be forever fighting against the tender-heartedness of the female sex? And is the thought of man to form wise and useful rules of conduct, only that the impulsiveness of woman may break them? But why do women look to the individual rather than to the many, and deal with separate examples rather than with general rules? It is surely not necessary to look for any recondite and essential ground of this difference if we can find one obvious and conventional, which will account equally well for the phenomenon. Women, in fact, have never been instructed in general principles. A man talks to a man about the statistics of poverty or crime; they carefully consider together what are the causes which, in the majority of cases, have produced either of these gigantic evils; causes, such as ignorance, drunkenness and the like. They do their best, therefore, not to collect money to give away in alms to any beggar who may ask their assistance, but they establish a school, provide places of refreshment and amusement, orderly and well-conducted, and where, by satisfying natural desires, the temptation to unnatural excesses may be reduced to a minimum. They take care, or at least they know that they *ought* to take care, that the relief of poverty shall be of a kind to remove as far as possible the causes of poverty, and every new experiment they make for the relief of misery and the prevention of crime, widens their theories and improves their rules of practice. But it has not been the habit of men to talk with women, and act with them, after this manner. Without a word of instruction about the reasons for what they are about to do, they are asked to visit some poor man's cottage, and administer what relief they may think necessary; or to visit some school or work-house, or to collect money, or to make clothes, like Dorcas. It is surely not very surprising that women confine themselves to that sort of work which alone has been entrusted to them from generation to generation. It is not wonderful that they do that sort of work well, nor does it require any mystic difference between the sexes to account for the fact that they do not know what, through hundreds of generations, they have neither been required nor encouraged to learn.

We are told, however, that the course of study required for obtaining a degree in the University of London is altogether unfit for women. 'Do the advocates of the Burlington House degrees know,' asks a writer on female education, 'what is actually required by the London University for ordinary graduates? Why, the candidate is required to pass in nearly the whole range of pure arithmetical science – in geometry, plane and solid; in simple and quadratic equations; in the elements of plane trigonometry; in elementary Latin; in the history of Rome to the death of Augustus; in English composition, and English history to the end of the seventeenth century; in either French or German; in statics and dynamics treated with elementary mathematics; in an experimental knowledge of physics and optics, and a general conception of plane astronomy; in animal physiology; in elementary Greek, and Greek history up to the death of Alexander; and in the elements of logic and moral philosophy. Does anyone in his (or her) senses suppose that the understanding of average young ladies would be the better for passing this examination well, or for trying to pass it anyhow, as the proper aim of their education? We might get one or two clever women, several Miss Cornelia Blimbers, and many Miss Tootses – if we may suggest an intellectual sister to Mr Toots – out of such a system, but certainly not an improved standard for ordinary women. I believe that we should have half the young women in the country in brain fever or a lunatic asylum, if they were to make up their minds to try for it.'

It is perhaps equally probable that we should have half the young *men* in the country in brain fever or a lunatic asylum, if they were to make up *their* minds to try for it. Graduates are a very small minority of the men of England, and yet their education has determined the education of the great majority who are not graduates. It is by no means obvious that it would do women any harm to know enough for the B.A. (London) pass-examination. They are already expected to learn not much less at Queen's College, in Harley Street; and a degree would be to women, in their present stage of cultivation, what honours are to men.

Women are expected to learn *something* of arithmetical science, and who shall say at what point they are to stop? Why should simple equations brighten their intellects, and quadratic equations drive them into a lunatic asylum? Why should they be the better for the three books of Euclid, which they are required to master at Queen's College, and 'stupefied' by conic sections or trigonometry? Why should Latin give them a deeper insight into the philosophy of language, and introduce them to a literature and history which may raise them above the narrowness or the extravagance of their own age, and the language of the New Testament be forbidden, as too exhausting a labour, a toil fruitful only of imbecility or death? Is it really necessary that women should be shut out from the knowledge of the physical sciences? Would a knowledge of physiology make them worse mothers, and an acquaintance with the chemistry of food less fit to superintend the processes of cooking? It is not asked, be it remembered, that one single woman should be compelled to take a degree, or held disgraced for being without one; but simply that she may try if she chooses, and that if she chooses and succeeds, then she shall receive that certificate of her strength and culture which will be fairly her due.

But the value of degrees in female education would be far greater indirectly than directly; they would raise the standard of excellence by a sure process, even though it might be slow, of every school and every teacher in the kingdom. A very small proportion of girls would attempt to take them; fewer still would succeed; fewer still would take honours. But every schoolgirl in the land would very soon become aware of the fact that women might hope and strive for a thorough culture which has never yet been generally offered to them. The Arts regulations of the University of London would guide the studies of women as gently and effectually as they now guide the studies of boys and men. A very simple example of this may be given. There is an increasing neglect of the Greek and Latin Classics in ordinary education. The reason why these languages are still taught in the majority of middle-class schools is neither more nor less than this: that some knowledge of them is required for the B.A. degree, and even for matriculation in the University of London. That which in the case of boys seems drawing near to death, is, in the case of girls, just beginning to live; and the classic languages in girls' schools and colleges have to force their way to general acceptance through many difficulties and prejudices. The same influence which arrests the decay in one case would favour the growth in the other case. Whether the reasons for the study of the classical languages be understood or not, reasons of the utmost cogency do actually exist. They have been considered and reconsidered over and over again, and in all variety of circumstances, by those who are best qualified to judge; and they still retain their place of highest honour and prime necessity in thorough human culture. The study of them justifies itself in every case where they are really studied, and not simply acquired as accomplishments. It would be a very great advantage, and especially in a country so devoted to commerce as our own, that they should be studied, even though very few might perceive the reasons why. That they were necessary for a certificate of merit, or for a University degree, would be a satisfactory answer for teachers to give to that large class of parents who really know nothing about genuine education, but who feel that they must obtain for their children what other children have, and a reputation for knowledge at any rate, if not knowledge itself.

In the foregoing observations it is not intended to assert that the curriculum of the London University is absolutely the best that could possibly be devised for women. There are differences of opinion as to whether it is absolutely the best that could be devised for men. But, in the meantime, here it is, ready made to our hands. Men accept it, admitting it to be imperfect, as the best at present attainable. Women are desirous of sharing its advantages and disadvantages. They need, even more than men, 'an encouragement for pursuing a regular and liberal course of education' *after* the period at which their school education ceases. To found a separate University for them would be a work of enormous difficulty and expense, and one which the existence of the University of London renders unnecessary. If indeed there were no University having the power to examine and confer degrees without collegiate residence, a new institution would undoubtedly be required. As it happens, however, that quite irrespective of the claims of women, the constitution of the University of London has already been so modified as exactly to meet their requirements, the suggestion to found a new University may be regarded as simply a device for getting rid of the question.

Those who entertain the fear that an enlarged course of study would, by overworking the female brain, eventually produce widespread idiocy, should remember that mental disease is produced by want of occupation as well as by an excess of it. It has been stated to us by a physician at the head of a large lunatic asylum near London, having under his charge a considerable number of female patients of the middle class, that the majority of these cases were the result of mental idleness. It is a well-known fact that in those most melancholy diseases known by the names of hysteria, and nervous affections, under which so large a proportion of women in the well-to-do classes are, more or less, sufferers, the first remedy almost invariably prescribed is interesting occupation, change of scene, anything, in fact, that may divert the mind from the dull monotony of a vacant life.

The strongest arguments which can be used in favour of offering some stimulus to the higher intellectual culture of women are in fact those which have been thoughtlessly advanced on the other side. Amazons have never been persons of high intellectual attainments, nor have the most learned women shown any tendency to rush into Bloomerism and other ugly eccentricities. It is true, indeed, and a fact of the utmost significance, that women with great natural force of character do, when denied a healthy outlet for their energy, often indulge in unhealthy extravagances, simply because it is a necessity of their nature to be active in some way or other. But the fast women and the masculine women are not those who sit down to their books and devote themselves to an orderly course of study. It may be asserted with still greater emphasis that the hard and cold women are precisely those whom a consciousness of their unimportance to the world in general has made callous to everything but their own petty, personal interests, and in whom the sense of duty and responsibility, or, in other

425

words, the conscience, has been deadened and seared by fashionable frivolity.

Great stress has been laid on the alleged fact that women do not themselves want University examinations and degrees. It is always difficult to ascertain the 'sense' of women on any given subject. Many shrink from even affixing their names to a memorial, and there is no other recognised method by which they can, in any corporate manner, express their opinions. There can be no doubt that among the more thoughtful, there are many who are eager to obtain for younger women educational aids of which they cannot themselves enjoy the benefit. The cordial support given to this proposal by Mrs Somerville, Mrs Grote, Mrs Gaskell, Mrs Mary Howitt, etc., and by a large proportion of the ladies concerned in the management of Queen's College and Bedford College, sufficiently attest the fact.

It is probably equally true that there are many others who are not very anxious for any alteration in existing systems of education. This ought not to be surprising to a reflecting mind. It is perfectly natural that people who do not know by experience the value of learning, and who are pretty well satisfied with themselves as they are, should not care much about securing to others advantages which they are incapable of appreciating. The tendency, almost the professed object, of their education has been to make them unreasonable. It would be strange indeed, if on this one subject they should be able to reason and judge. *Their* indifference is much less astonishing than that of men, who willingly forego for their daughters opportunities of intellectual advancement which they well know how to appreciate, and which they consider of the highest importance for their sons.

There is one part of this subject which is of special practical importance, and also of peculiar difficulty: the right of women to take degrees in Medicine. This, it should be remembered, is wholly distinct from the general question which it has been the object of this paper to discuss. The course of study and of practice necessary for the M.B. or M.D. degree, is by no means a necessary part of that human culture which every man and every woman should be encouraged and urged to seek. But the right to practise as a physician would be valuable as opening the way for useful and remunerative employment to those ladies who do not wish to be governesses, or to engage in ordinary trade; and as affording to all women the alternative of being attended by physicians of their own sex. It cannot be denied that a large number of women find very great satisfaction in some kind or other of doctoring, and do actually practise it, whether they know anything about it or not; yet this is so grave a matter that it has been thought necessary, quite recently, to bring the practice of medicine more completely under legal control. The want of skill or care may so easily and quickly produce fatal mischief, and even murder itself may be so easily hidden under the disguise of the unskilfulness of a physician that it has been thought necessary to require the surest guarantees of competency from all those to whose professional attention the health and lives of their patients are so often entrusted. Here, however, as in Arts, what has been asked on the part of women is not a lower standard of medical skill, not easier examinations, but that they should be allowed, in medical schools of their own, to acquire such knowledge as would enable them to pass the examinations and acquire the skill which are now thought necessary and sufficient in the case of men.

The holding of degrees by women is not without precedent. In the Italian Universities, and in that of Göttingen, women have held high positions. Towards the end of the last century a female physician graduated at Montpelier. In 1861, the degree of *Bachelier ès-Lettres* was conferred on Mlle Daubié by the Academy of Lyons, and within the last few months another French lady, Mlle Chenu, passed her examination for the degree of *Bachelier ès-Sciences* at the University of the Sorbonne. It appears not unreasonable to hope that before many years have elapsed, Englishwomen will be placed in a not less favourable position than their continental neighbours, and that whatever advantages may belong to University examinations and degrees will be thrown freely open to them.

On Secondary Instruction, as Relating to Girls

(a paper read at the National Association for the Promotion of Social Science, 1864)

In the great controversy which, having been begun by the debates on the Report of the Public Schools' Commission, is now extending itself over almost the whole department of secondary instruction, there is an omission which seems to call for remark. Throughout the discussion, voluminous as it has been, the question has hitherto been treated exclusively in reference to boys, it having been tacitly assumed that male education only is a matter of concern to the general community. This feature is the more remarkable, inasmuch as it is peculiar to the present agitation. In the effort made some years ago for the improvement of primary education, ignorant boys and ignorant girls were recognised as having similar needs and similar claims. National and British Schools for girls are inspected, mistresses are trained, female pupil-teachers are apprenticed and, speaking generally, the education of the daughters of the labouring classes is as carefully watched over as that of their sons. Why is the case altered when we advance a few steps higher in the social scale? With regard to the public schools, the reason is obvious enough. As there are no Etons for girls in existence, they could not be made the subject of investigation. Probably the sisters of public school boys are, for the most part, taught by governesses at home. Their education is therefore clearly beyond the scope of a commission of inquiry, and though it does not follow that it is a matter in which the nation has no interest, it is natural enough that it should not appear in the discussion called forth by the Commissioners' Report. But this consideration does not apply to the daughters of the middle class, and it is difficult to understand why their early training should be regarded as a matter of less importance than that of their brothers. That it is so regarded appears to be implied by the almost total silence of the thinkers and writers to whom the nation looks for guidance. It is needless to bring proofs of what no-one will deny. It is a simple fact that in the mass of speeches, articles, reviews, pamphlets and volumes which have lately been before the public on the subject of secondary instruction for boys, there is scarcely so much as a passing allusion to that of girls. This side of the question has been, by general consent, completely ignored.

There is no reason for attributing this silence to ungenerous motives. It no doubt arises in a great degree from a sort of inadvertence. Public writers are occupied with the busy world around them, in which men only are to be seen, and it is perhaps not much to be wondered at, if they think only of training the boys, who are hereafter to do the more conspicuous part of the world's work. Some, and those the men most worth listening to, are unwilling to speak of what they imperfectly know, and it is difficult for them to know much about girls or women. When they speak of boys, they have at any rate their own experience to go upon, and it is not unnatural that they should by preference confine themselves to that side of the subject of which they have personal cognisance. Others are no doubt insensibly influenced by the view of education which regards it merely as a means of making a living. It has been remarked that 'a great part of the confusion in which the question of education is involved, arises from the division of public feeling as to the value of knowledge'. There are many persons who value it only as a weapon to be used in the struggle for material existence, and as women are, theoretically, never required to fight, it may seem superfluous to supply them with arms.

Women, on their part, are largely responsible for the general carelessness. It could scarcely be expected that they should very keenly appreciate advantages of which they have had no experience, and they are generally ready enough to profess themselves perfectly satisfied with things as they are, and to echo doubts as to whether 'so much education is necessary for girls'. Some, who are conscious of their own deficiencies, are afraid that the manifestation of a desire to help others may be mistaken for an assumption of great enlightenment in themselves. Others, who by unusual energy and perseverance have succeeded in gaining knowledge and the power that it brings with it, are, by their very superiority, cut off from the multitude. They look down from their heights, with little sympathy, on the mass of women tamely giving way before difficulties which they have known how to overcome. Others again shrink from prominence in any cause whatever; their dread of publicity is so overpowering that they would rather see a whole generation drowning before their eyes in ignorance and sloth than run the slightest risk of being spoken of as having taken part in the rescue. I should be sorry to speak of this reserve with anything like disrespect; I believe it is seldom absent from the finest natures. But I submit that it is one of the duties imposed upon the women of this generation to speak out, careless of the cost, on those questions of which they can most fitly judge. Silence and inaction are not justified by any of the reasons here suggested; for whatever may be the causes – or the excuses – the result is the same. The impression is conveyed to the public mind that the education of girls is an affair of very little consequence – that it is, in fact, one of the things which may safely and properly be left to take care of themselves. It is no wonder that so agreeable an untruth should meet with ready acceptance.

In venturing to raise a protest against both the doctrine itself and the policy which it involves, I do not propose to enter upon an inquiry into the condition of girls' schools, and the systems of teaching pursued. It is one of the results of the prevailing indifference, that nobody knows enough of the interior of girls' schools to speak with authority about them. The data for forming a general conclusion are not within the reach of any individual. But there is a method by which we may test the quality of the schools – we can look at the quality of the thing produced. Anybody, or at least any woman, may know what girls are after leaving school, and we may fairly judge of the process by its results, making allowance, of course, for extenuating circumstances in the shape of vitiating home influences.[1]

I ask then, what are girls worth when their education is finished? What are they good for? Are they in vigorous health of mind and body? What is there that they care about? How are their lives filled up? What have they to talk about? What do they read? I am speaking, let it be remembered, not of children, but of grown-up women. Does anybody care for their opinions on any but the most trivial matters? Have they a thought beyond the circle of petty cares?

To all these questions favourable answers might be returned as regards many exceptional women. But if we look at the great mass, we shall find much to be ashamed of. On all sides there is evidence that, as regards intelligence and good sense, English women of the middle class are held in small esteem. 'A woman's reason' means, in popular phrase, no reason at all. A man who lets it be known that he consults his wife endangers his own reputation for sense. A habit of exaggeration, closely verging upon untruthfulness, is a recognised feminine characteristic. Newspaper writers, expressing the prevailing sentiment, assume towards women an indulgent air which is far from flattering, giving them credit for plenty of good intentions, but very little capacity, and the tone in which many ladies speak of the capabilities of women is still more depreciatory than that adopted by men. No doubt this is partly exaggerated and unjust. All *classes*, as such, are now and then maligned, and so long as women are unfortunately regarded as a class, they will come in for their share of ridicule. But without taking the current raillery too much *au sérieux*, it will be admitted that the popular estimate of a woman's mental worth is somewhat low.

This condition of mental weakness might not be looked upon as so very grave a misfortune, if it was made up for by bodily strength. We are learning more and more the importance of physical health to the life of a nation, and a training which should produce a thoroughly sound physique, even at the expense of feebleness of mind, would have much to recommend it. But women are not healthy. It is a rare thing to meet with a lady, of any age, who does not suffer from headaches, languor, hysteria, or some ailment showing a want of stamina. Shut out, in towns especially, from wholesome sources of excitement, they either resort to such as are unwholesome, or else fall into indolent habits, losing strength from want of exercise, and constantly requiring change of air and scene, as a substitute for the healthy stimulus of regular exertion. Dullness is not healthy, and the lives of ladies are, it must be confessed, exceedingly dull. Men recall pictures of homely households in earlier times, and imagine that such things are, or might be, going on still. They forget the prosaic fact that the continually increasing use of all sort of machinery for the supply of household wants has completely altered the aspect of our domestic interiors. The rounded life of our grandmothers, full of interest and variety and usefulness, is a thing of the past. Some of us may look back upon it with regret, but it can never be recalled. How can women, living in towns where they can buy almost every article in domestic use cheaper than they could make it, unless they reckon their time and eyesight as worth nothing at all, work with spirit at tasks which are obviously futile? It is not in human nature. It is not in women's nature even, mysteriously inconsequent as that nature is believed to be. I may seem to be wandering from the point, but it will be seen, I hope, that if the old avocations, involving abundant exercise of all the faculties, are being taken away, it becomes necessary to supply their place by new interests and occupations. A hundred years ago, women might know little of history and geography, and nothing at all of any language but their own – they might be careless of what was going on in the outer world – ignorant of science and of art – but their minds were not therefore necessarily inactive. Circumstances provided a discipline which is now wholly wanting, and which needs to be supplied by wider and deeper cultivation. I dwell upon this point because I am sure that busy people, and especially busy men, have a very faint and feeble conception of what dullness is. They overtax their own brains, and by way of compensation they have invented the doctrine of vicarious rest, according to which men are justified in wearing themselves out so long as women can be kept in a state of wholesome rust. We hear a great deal of the disastrous effects which would follow if women were to abandon the habits of elegant leisure by which the balance is supposed to be redressed. The *otium* SINE *dignitate* of drawing-rooms presents itself to men's minds in enviable contrast with the bustle and turmoil of an active career. They 'hearken what the inner spirit sings, There is no joy but calm.' And they think dullness is calm. If they had ever tried what it is to be a young lady, they would know better.

The system tells in different ways, according to the individual character. Some girls fret and pine under it; others, satisfying their souls with husks, are content to idle about from morning till night, acquiring, as has been already said, indolent and desultory habits, hard to break through when in later life the demand for steady methodical exertion comes upon them. Some take to works of charity, doing some harm, and no doubt also some good. Their usefulness is at any rate seriously lessened by the want of the cultivated judgment to guide and control benevolent impulse. Some, I gladly admit, lead noble lives, filling their leisure with worthy pursuits, and in spite of difficulties, tracing out for themselves a useful and happy career.

It may seem to be entering upon somewhat low ground to speak of women's talk, but it may not be out of place, seeing that, as things are, it forms a chief part of their business. And what do ladies talk about at morning calls and evening parties? Children, servants, dress, and summer tours – all very good subjects in themselves, but so treated, partly through sheer ignorance, that as the conversation advances, tedium grows, till at last all signs of intelligence disappear, and the weary countenances too faithfully reveal the vacancy within. Of literature, women of the middle class know next to nothing. I am not speaking of religious literature, which is extensively read by some women, and to which they owe much. I speak of general literature, and of ordinary women, whose reading is for the most part confined to novels, and of novels not the best. The catalogue of a bookseller's circulating library, in which second-rate fiction largely preponderates, is a fair criterion of the range and the taste of middle-class lady readers. Newspapers are scarcely supposed to be read by women at all. When *The Times* is offered to a lady, the sheet containing the advertisements, and the births, deaths, and marriages, is considerately selected.

This almost complete mental blankness being the ordinary condition of women, it is not to be wondered at that their opinions, when they happen to have any, are not much respected. In those cases, indeed, where natural sagacity is a sufficient guide, women often form just conclusions, but manifestly, wherever a knowledge of facts is required, they are almost sure to be at fault. And very few questions of any importance can be decided without such knowledge. Of what is going on in the world women know little and care less. When political or social questions are forced upon their notice, they commonly judge them from some purely personal point of view. Right and wrong are elements which scarcely enter into the calculation.

In taking this melancholy view of the middle-class female mind, I am aware that I lay myself open to the attacks of two classes of objectors. By one class the picture will be condemned as a caricature; by the other it will be accepted as faithful, but it will be maintained that the defects pointed out are traceable, not to want of education, but to the natural inferiority of the female intellect. To the first I can only reply that I speak from personal knowledge, supported by the experience of other observers, and that, for all that has been said, I could, if space permitted, adduce abundant evidence. The second objection is not easy to meet, in the paucity of material for proof on either side. I believe I may say, however, on behalf of the advocates of female education, that any objector is welcome to assert anything he likes about the inferiority of the female intellect, if only he does not rate it so low as to be incapable of improvement by cultivation. We are not encumbered by theories about equality or inequality of mental power in the sexes. All we claim is that the intelligence of women, be it great or small, shall have full and free development. And we claim it not specially in the interest of women, but as essential to the growth of the human race. This is not the place to discuss whether women have, or ought to have, any other than merely domestic relations. I take the commonly received theory that except as wives, mothers, daughters or sisters, women have no *raison d'être* at all; and on this neutral ground I urge the impolicy of neglecting female education. For now, more than ever before, the mutual influence of the sexes makes it impossible to serve one without the other. Of this fact, often enough asserted in theory though little regarded in practice, the revelations of the Royal Commission have furnished a new and striking demonstration. In one of the recent debates, it was pointed out by Mr Gladstone that the idleness and ignorance of public school boys are largely attributable to the overindulgent atmosphere of the homes in which they are brought up, and the Commissioners' Report contains repeated testimonies to the same effect. Mr Matthew Arnold says of our highest class that its culture has declined. Young men at the universities exhibit 'a slackness', 'a sleep of the mind', which he traces to 'a torpor of intellectual life, a dearth of ideas, an indifference to fine culture or disbelief in its necessity, spreading through the bulk of our highest class and influencing its rising generations. . . . Never,' he says, 'in all its history, has our whole highest class shown such zeal for enjoying life, for amusing itself.' Is this surprising? Is it not precisely what might have been expected in a society which, for at least one generation, has been content to bring up its girls to be mere elegant triflers? Is it not true that to amuse themselves and other people is the great object in life of women of the non-working classes, and is it possible that their sedulous devotion to this one object can fail to react upon the men with whom they associate? Who gives the tone to the lax and luxurious homes of the wealthy? Who teaches the boys that hard work is foolish self-torture, that an easy life is more to be desired than the fine gold of intellectual attainment? Not their fathers, for though they too may be led away by the prevailing passion for play, they have had a nobler ideal set before them. What is the ideal presented to a young girl? Is it anything higher than to be amiable, inoffensive, always ready to give pleasure and to be pleased? Could anything be more stupefying than such a conception of the purposes of existence? And is it likely that, constituted as society now is, young men will escape the snare which has been spread for their sisters?

In a lower social grade, the temptations assume a more sordid character. We get the trifling without the elegance. Mr Arnold has told us in the most eloquent and convincing language, what the middle class wants. Its virtues and its defects, what it has and what it needs, have been held up to view, and those whose knowledge of that great class is most intimate will most promptly recognise the admirable faithfulness of the portrait. We are told that it is 'traversed by a strong intellectual ferment' – that it has 'real mental ardour, real curiosity'. Whether it will attain to 'a high commanding pitch of culture and intelligence', depends on 'the sensibility which it has for perfection, on its power to transform itself'. And 'in its public action this class has hitherto shown only the power and disposition to affirm itself, not at all the power and disposition to transform itself. Here again, we are reaping what our fathers have sown. A young man of the middle class, who enters upon life with generous instincts and aspirations after perfection, is apt gradually to lose them. He becomes day by day less public-spirited, more engrossed by selfish aims. The more home-loving he is, the more likely is this to be the case. In his best moments, where is he to look for sympathy? His highest thoughts and feelings cannot be shared by those nearest and dearest to him. Any expression of them is likely to be met by a blank, uncomprehending stare. If there is any question of a small sacrifice to be made for the good of his town or parish, he is advised against it. That his first duty is to think of his children, or, in other words, always to make the aggrandisement of his own family his primary consideration, is a maxim about which his wife feels not the slightest doubt, and which she never fails to impress upon him. In the home circle, the conversation is inevitably restricted to petty subjects. The master of the house may discourse upon politics, or literature, or any other topic that may interest him, but there can be no intelligent response, no interchange of thought, no pleasant discussion of things worth talking about. He may lay down the law on matters of which he knows nothing whatever, betraying the grossest ignorance of elementary facts, in full confidence that his conclusions, whether true or false, will be accepted with equal indifference. He will learn unconsciously, but very surely, that the great thing for him to do is to stick to his business, think of nothing else, talk of nothing else, aspire after nothing else. Making money and getting on in the world by means of it are things that his wife and his mother and his daughters can understand and care for. They know all about the advantages of having a carriage and servants, and 'a position', and plenty of money to do what they like with. If he wants to please them, the way is plain. It may not be the way he would have chosen. He may have had unselfish impulses, some 'aptitude for ideas', some longings after a nobler career. But a fire which for fuel is perpetually fed with cold water, soon dies out. The man who was teachable, impressible, growing, hardens into the mere man of business, worldly-minded, narrow-hearted, self-satisfied. I do not mean this statement to be taken in a universal sense. Of course it is sometimes the other way. The wife is cultivated and aspiring, and the husband drags her down. But I believe I have given a tolerably accurate account of the tendencies in the great mass of English homes of the middle class.

Why should this unsatisfactory state of things be allowed to continue? Why should not our English homes be animated by a spirit of truth and of sacrifice – pervaded by an atmosphere of light and warmth in which all high thoughts and generous impulses should live and grow, all mean and selfish ends be, by common consent, disowned and utterly renounced? Why might not the family circle be a place where 'example teacheth, company comforteth, emulation quickeneth' – our daily domestic intercourse like iron sharpening iron, mutually kindling, and stimulating to noble thoughts and deeds? What a change would then come over the whole aspect of our national life! What problems would be solved, what terrible enigmas disappear! How little need should we then have of philanthropic schemes for elevating the poor! How naturally would they share in all social reforms, how inevitably would they be refined and civilised by the insensible influence – the best of all influences – of the employing class, whose ideas, unconsciously communicated to their subordinates, gradually leaven all the classes below them. Masters and mistresses reveal in their everyday life in what their ideal of blessedness consists, and that ideal becomes, with some modifications, that of the humbler homes of working men and women. I say with modifications, because working men are through their mutual association subject to counteracting influences, and it is chiefly in so far as that of wives and mothers prevails over others scarcely less strong, that the ideas of the employing class penetrate and govern. That through this medium they do act, inconspicuously but most powerfully, on the labouring class, will probably be admitted. It cannot, I am afraid, with truth be denied, that the principle, 'Every man for himself' – or, to say the least, every family and order for itself – of which mistresses complain so loudly when it is adopted by servants, but upon which they too commonly rule their own households, is by their example extended into circles far beyond the range of their direct and conscious influence. The want of hearty sympathy, not only between the classes which are divided by broad and easily recognised distinctions, but between those which are separated by lines so shadowy that, looked at from above or below, they are scarcely discernible – is one of the most serious impediments to social progress, and it is one which a better and more widely diffused culture might do much to remove. Not, indeed, that the education of youth, even taking the word in its deepest sense, is to be regarded as the only, or even the chief, agency for the improvement of society; but it happens to be the point towards which attention is at this moment directed. We are taught to expect great things from a reform in secondary instruction, and this being so, it is surely reasonable to ask that such reforms as may be possible shall be on the widest basis, not omitting any really important section of society.

It will be understood, I hope, that those who make this appeal on behalf of girls are not proposing the introduction or the enforcement of any particular scheme of instruction. It may be that the curriculum most commonly pursued, or at least professed, is as good as any that is likely to be devised, and that we only want better methods and more encouragement. On questions of detail we are not in the least inclined to dogmatise. It would be rash indeed to fix upon any particular course of instruction as absolutely the best for girls, while as to that of boys, on which so much more thought has been bestowed, we are still in a state of confusion and bewilderment. There seems to be as yet no body of opinion formed out of the floating mass, unanimous enough to be authoritative and competent to pronounce upon what branches of study are in themselves most worthy, what are most useful as educational instruments, what proportion of time should be allotted to each, and the many other complicated questions which must be answered before a perfect scheme of education can be produced. When that happy discovery shall at last have been made, it will probably be found also that the same course is, in the main, the best for both boys and girls, the object being substantially the same, that of awakening and strengthening and adorning the human spirit. That this great work should at least be well begun during the period allotted to secondary instruction is especially necessary in the case of women, because with the first stage their education ends. I do not mean, of course, that a girl necessarily lays aside all study on leaving school, any more than a man does on taking his degree, but that the end of the school course is the same kind of educational terminus to a woman that graduation is to a man. When a girl leaves school, her strictly professional studies assume a greater prominence. In using the word professional, I do not refer to any trade or business, but to the profession which absorbs the great majority of women, that of marriage. For this calling, some technical preparation is required. The amount cannot be great, as under existing social arrangements, a thorough acquaintance with needle-work and cookery – the very easiest of arts – includes I believe all the special knowledge required by the mistress of a household. But setting aside the question whether it is desirable that the merely professional training should begin so early – 'the second and finishing stage of a liberal education' being altogether omitted – it seems obvious enough, that if regular, methodical instruction is to cease at the age of eighteen, it is the more imperative that the culture, up to that period, should be wide and deep and humane in the highest possible degree. A man has some chance of making up at the university the deficiencies of his school training; or if he passes direct from school to business there is a possibility that he may find in his daily work something of the mental and moral discipline that he needs. But a girl who leaves school unawakened, is not likely to be roused from her lethargy by anything in her home life. The dissipation to which, in the absence of any spur to wholesome activity, so many girls give themselves up, completes the deadening process begun at school.

I have endeavoured to set forth, very imperfectly, but at least without exaggeration, some of the reasons for devoting to this subject more attention than has hitherto been bestowed upon it. Once again I would venture to urge, with the utmost insistance, that it is not a 'woman's question'. Let me entreat thinking men to dismiss from their minds the belief, that this is a thing with which they have no concern. They cannot help exerting a most serious influence upon it. Silence sometimes teaches more eloquently than words, and while they refrain from giving encouragement, their apparent indifference damps and chills. The matter is in their hands, whether they choose it or not. So long as they thrust it aside, it will not come before the mind of the nation as worthy of serious thought. The Scriptural maxim, 'That the soul be without knowledge is not good' will still be interpreted as applying to the souls of men only. We want to have the question settled. If the proposition, often enough vaguely affirmed, that the true greatness of a nation depends as much on its women as on its men, be anything more than a rhetorical flourish, let it be acted upon. Let it be accepted as a fact, if it be a fact, and if not, let it be contradicted and disproved, that in so far as education is worth anything at all, it is just as desirable for girls as it is for boys. We have little fear but that when once the question gets its fair share of consideration, something, and probably the right thing, will be done. Some efforts have indeed already been made, and so far as they have gone the results have been encouraging. In London, the ladies' colleges, in which men of the highest ability take part, have done much, not only within their own walls but by their influence over other teachers, to raise the standard and improve the tone of education generally. In the country, we have the school at Chantry, near Frome, founded in 1857 by Mr Allen and Mr Fussell – the training-school for governesses at Bolham, in Devonshire, where 'teaching to teach' is made a prominent study – Miss Clough's school at Ambleside – and others of greater or less importance, all steps in the right direction. But these isolated attempts require to be followed up. The provision of secondary instruction for girls is impeded by the usual hindrance, the want of funds. It is found very difficult to supply really good teaching on such terms as middle-class parents are able and willing to pay, and there is scarcely any assistance forthcoming in the shape of old endowments. The 547 ancient grammar schools scattered throughout England are, as is well known, almost entirely filled by boys. The other endowed schools, of which there are about 2,000, take in a much larger proportion of girls, but they are of the poorer class. The endowed schools which are attended by pupils of the upper and middle classes do not include girls. It may be a question for consideration whether some of these endowments might not, without much divergence from the intentions of the original donors, be used for the foundation of a few first-rate girls' schools, or in some other way be made available for the advancement of female education. At any rate, wherever a new institution, such for instance as the Albert Memorial School, in Suffolk, is being founded, it would seem reasonable to make a fair division of the funds, of course taking into consideration any special local circumstances. Again, where we have a St Nicolas' College, or a first-rate proprietary school, for boys, let there be some corresponding foundation for girls. Let schemes of examination and inspection designed to raise the character of boys' schools be extended to girls also. In a word, let female education be encouraged – let it be understood that the public really cares whether the work is done well or ill – and the minor practical questions will ere long find for themselves a satisfactory solution.

NOTE

1 In fairness to the schools it ought perhaps to be remarked that they are moulded by public opinion. Many school-mistresses supply what society demands, very much against their own judgment and inclination.

Elizabeth Garrett
(1836–1917)

One of twelve children, Elizabeth Garrett was born in London and educated at home. Her mother, Louise Dunnell, was a deeply religious woman who opposed her struggle for medical training; her father, Newson Garrett, ran a pawnbroker's shop in London but later bought a corn and coal warehouse in Aldeburgh, Suffolk and became quite wealthy. When she was eighteen, Elizabeth Garrett met Emily Davies who, in turn, introduced her to Barbara Bodichon. She trained as a nurse at the Middlesex Hospital, London, but in 1860 was refused admission to medical schools. She continued to study, dissecting cadavers in her bedroom when she was denied access to dissecting rooms. Eventually she was allowed to take the Apothecaries' Examination and, a year after she qualified, in 1866, she opened St Mary's Dispensary for Women (later to become the New Hospital for Women and Children). She actively supported the admission of women to the University of Edinburgh while she obtained her own full professional qualification from the University of Paris. A member of the Kensington Society, she joined the committee to collect signatures for the suffrage campaign and, in 1866, she and Emily Davies delivered the petition to Westminster for John Stuart Mill to present to Parliament. She became a lecturer and later the Dean and President of the London School of Medicine for Women. She was the first and only woman member of the British Medical Association from 1873 to 1892. When she was elected Mayor of Aldeburgh in 1908, she was the first woman mayor in England. When her husband, James Skelton Anderson, died in 1907, she joined the militant branch of the suffragette movement and, the following year, at the age of seventy-two, she was involved in a raid on Parliament.

Hospital Nursing

(a paper read at the National Association for the
Promotion of Social Science, 1866)

The question of hospital nursing is one which has received, during
the last ten years, considerable attention, and which excites interest
among people not immediately connected with hospital administration. It may be noticed, in the first place, that in the discussion
of the question, no doubt has been raised as to the value of good
nursing. Thanks to Miss Nightingale, most people have some
notion of what nursing should be – everyone wishes it to be good,
and everyone agrees that, to be so, it should be in the hands of
trustworthy and intelligent women. Unanimity even goes a step
beyond this; for those who are in a position to decide upon the
merits of our present system agree in saying that it wants reform.
The point of divergence is reached when we ask for a plan upon
which the reform shall be based. Hospital nursing, like most other
employments, may be undertaken in either of two ways – that is,
in what may be briefly described as the commercial way, where
the work is chosen primarily for the sake of the income to be
gained by doing it, or in the philanthropic or religious way, where
the work is done gratuitously. The words 'commercial' and
'religious' must be understood as referring only to the motive for
the choice of an employment, not necessarily to the spirit in which
it is done. Commercial work may be done religiously, or religious
work commercially.

The commercial method is that which has, till quite recently,
prevailed in all our hospitals. The main point at issue between
those who discuss the question of hospital reform is, whether it
shall be continued or whether it shall give place to the religious or
volunteer method. It will clear the ground for the consideration of
this question to state briefly the distinctive features of the present
system and its rival.

In the majority of English civil hospitals, the nursing department is under the control of the matron. Choosing the nurses and over-looking them form two of her most important duties. The nursing staff consists of two classes – the head nurses and the under nurses. The former are in some hospitals called sisters, to distinguish them from the under nurses. These are again divided into night and day nurses. The head nurses are responsible for from thirty to fifty patients; they give medicines, attend to the surgical dressings, receive the medical directions for each patient, keep order in the wards, serve out the dinners, and see that the actual attendance upon the patients is given by the under nurses. As a rule, they are skilful, experienced, and kindly people, very well suited to their work. They usually belong to the lower section of the middle class, are the widows of small tradesmen or clerks, or less frequently they have been confidential domestic servants. Their salary varies from £20 to £50 a year, with board and residence.

The under nurses wait upon the patients, assist the sister in her duties, and in many cases clean the ward. One nurse is found to be enough for fourteen or fifteen patients, so that every head nurse has two or three under nurses beneath her. The latter are, as a rule, vastly inferior to the head nurses, both in intelligence and character. They are commonly below the class of second or even third-rate domestic servants; if they were not nurses, one would expect them to be maids-of-all-work, scrubs, or charwomen. They receive about £10 or £12 a year, with partial board or board wages.

From them, again, there is an apparent descent to the night nurses. I believe it is apparent only, and that actually they are much on a level, the night nurses seeming worse only because more is required of them, and because they are left for several hours entirely without supervision. When they do not live in the hospital, they eke out their scanty incomes by working the best part of the day, and, consequently, they come to the hospital hoping to be able to sleep the greater part of the night. On the whole, ordinary hospital nursing may be described as a mixture of good, indifferent, and bad – the head nurses being often very good, the under nurse fairly good when under supervision, and bad when left without it.

In contrast to this, the volunteer method puts the nursing department into the hands of ladies who, having elected to do the work, are interested in doing it well. The main difference is, that the control no longer rests with the matron, and that at least the higher part of the nursing is done gratuitously. The head nurses are replaced by ladies, to whom the under nurses are directly responsible. At King's College and University College Hospitals, in London, where this method has been introduced, there is but one opinion as to the immense improvement in the nursing since the change was effected. The *Lancet* has recently given emphatic testimony on the same point. Referring to the volunteer help given during the cholera epidemic, it says: 'The nursing by ladies is the very best nursing that England has yet seen'; and it prophesies that we cannot long refuse to adopt a system 'which embodies intelligence, the keenest sympathy, refinement', and, as it might have added, 'economy'. In fact, the advantages to the patients and to the hospitals are so great and so obvious, that it is astonishing to find anyone blind to them. It is all gain to them to get in the place of paid servants ladies who are willing to do the work for nothing in a peculiarly admirable manner. But admitting the superiority of ladies as nurses, it is still possible to question the wisdom of asking them to take up nursing as a profession. No amount of medical testimony in favour of their fitness for the work is of much avail when we are asking, 'Is the work fit for them?' The *Lancet* says it is, apparently on the ground that the volunteer cholera nurses, in spite of very hard work, continued in excellent health. And, in truth, the 'health and strength' argument, as it may be called, is entirely with those who advocate nursing by volunteers. There is very little room for doubt that most ladies would find the work of hospital nursing positively invigorating. Constant exercise in large and airy wards, employment of the kind which prevents morbid introspection or continuous mental exertion, absence of anxiety, regular and early hours, simple diet, and a life at least much less dull than that of most single women, combine to form a sum of conditions under which the health of most ladies would rapidly improve.

The volunteer nurses in the cholera hospitals were by no means above the average standard of health, and among them there was but one opinion as to the hygienic effect of the work. One lady who had suffered daily from neuralgia for seven years lost it entirely from the day she came to the hospital; several agreed in saying they took more food in a day than they had before taken in a week, and in all there was the unmistakable look of healthy vigour. But the argument drawn from these facts has less weight when we reflect upon the beneficial influence of any regular work done with spirit and interest. It tells strongly in favour of doing something, but it does not decide what it is best to do. The question remains, is it for the advantage of the whole community that hospital nursing should be accepted as an unpaid profession by women of the educated classes? To answer this, it is necessary to consider the subject of unpaid *versus* paid labour somewhat broadly, not merely with reference to the special point at issue. It will probably be conceded that, wherever the circumstances of society and of the individual permit a choice of work, there are two points to be considered – namely, the appropriateness of the individual for any special work, and of that particular work for him. A small amount of thought shows us that these two points require consideration in a kind of inverse proportion. The quality which our American friends have named, 'faculty', fits its possessor to acquire skill in doing almost anything he attempts to do, but the power of doing small things well ought not to be used as a fetter to bind him perpetually to the doing of them. The same is true of women. A lady who, with very little training, does hospital nursing in a first-rate way is, *a priori*, likely to be able to do much more difficult things, and the question is whether it is desirable, for the sake of saving money to the hospital, to limit her permanently to work of so subordinate a character. What we want to know is, if hospital nursing can only be done well by gentlewomen – if the qualities which fit them for many employments pledge them, as it were, to this? For it must be remembered that, in virtue of their position and their advantages, cultivated women are bound to discriminate in the choice of work. As education multiplies power, the moral obligation of making a choice is also increased. If the highest work is to be done at all, those capable of doing it must be content to leave the easier work to others – to recognise that they are bound not to do it, but to leave it undone for the sake of those to whom it is the highest possible. True social economy demands not only that everyone should do something, but that everyone should do his best. The advantage of getting moderately easy work exceptionally well done for nothing is apparent only if those who do it are prevented from doing other equally useful work for which those whom they displace are entirely unfit. It is admitted generally now that, in a well-ordered household, the mistress ought not to do the domestic work herself if she can afford to keep servants, although, in virtue of her superior refinement, she is peculiarly capable of doing it well. For experience has shown that when she gives up her time to petty domestic businesses, the higher duties of her position get neglected, so that as there are appropriate people glad to do her cooking and dusting, as a means of getting their living, her duty is to see that they do them, and to reserve herself for work which they cannot do. I would suggest that what is true of domestic management is true also of hospital nursing. Admirably as ladies can nurse, the actual work of nursing is not much more appropriate to them than that of cooking or dusting in their own houses. It is not true that hospital nursing cannot be well done by women of inferior rank and culture, and therefore it cannot be entirely desirable that those of a higher class should spend their time in doing it.

The difficulties in the way of good hospital nursing would, I believe, be completely removed by the introduction of two reforms into the old commercial system. In the first place, the scale of wages should be uniformly raised to the maximum rate. In the official report on hospitals, made to the Privy Council in 1863 by Dr Bristowe and Mr Holmes, much of the improvement observed in the nursing at St Thomas's Hospital is attributed to the higher salaries given to the nurses since the Nightingale Training Institution was associated with the hospital. The reporters state that while the old rate of wages was, for the head nurses, £40 to £50 a year, without board, and, for the under nurses, 10s. to 13s. a week, without board, the present rate is £50 and £21 respectively, with board, and that this higher scale has been sufficient to gain for the hospital the services of a very superior class of women. Respectable clever women will not take the post of under nurse at the present minimum rate of hospital pay, and of course where the salaries are so low that none but intemperate charwomen will think of taking them, the nursing is as bad as intemperate charwomen can make it. The wages should be sufficient to attract respectable women of the rank of good domestic servants – that is, they should be somewhat above that which the people who are wanted could get in service, as an under nurse's life is necessarily less comfortable than that of most domestic servants.

In the second place, I would suggest that the supervision now confined to the day should be extended to the night. Nursing requires more thought and attention than the routine work of domestic servants, and therefore even fairly good under nurses should have over them one who would give them even more than the supervision which a careful mistress gives to her servants. It is not easy to see why the superior work of supervision should be done by unpaid labourers. It is the kind of work which many women who have to support themselves could do exceedingly well, and the keen demand for remunerated work among women of the educated class makes it desirable to open as many such situations as possible. The amount of employment thus opened would not be great, as probably not more than 200 such situations could be offered to women if all the hospitals in the United Kingdom agreed to use the services of paid lady superintendents. Excluding workhouse infirmaries, there are only about 100 hospitals having more than fifty beds, in England, Scotland, and Ireland. Two or three of these in the rural districts are too small to require more supervision than the matron ought to be able to give, and this is the case also with a few of the special hospitals in London. On the other hand, several of the large metropolitan hospitals could perhaps employ three ladies, so that the rough calculation of two for each hospital containing more than fifty beds will not be far from accurate.

It may be said that the objections here expressed to ladies doing the work of head nurses do not apply to those who, though very much in need of employment, are not likely to do anything higher than nursing. It sounds very plausible to say, 'Here are a number of unemployed women, pining for work, not in need of payment, glad, indeed, to do the work of head nurses for nothing, and not at all likely to enter into any more difficult work. Surely they may offer thus to give their time to the service of the sick poor?'

I admit that to say 'No' sounds somewhat hard, but the hardship is removed by the simple expedient of their taking the salary which should rightly go with the work. It is not fair to the women to whom work is bread that those to whom it is luxury should come into the market and cheapen its price by giving what the others have to sell. The notion that there are crowds of women eager to do hard work for nothing very much increases the difficulty of those who have to live by their work. It would be far better that it should be accepted as a point of honour among women, as it is among professional men, to take without question the salary or fee which belongs to any post or work, even when the recipient is not without some private income.

The difficulty of spending the extra money need never be great or permanent, or the salary could be returned indirectly to the hospital.

But it may farther be asked, why have not ladies the right to give their services when the hospital physicians and surgeons give theirs? The answer to this is that the cases are in no degree parallel. True, the medical staff usually receive no payment for their services, and even where a medical school is connected with the hospital, the fees received by its teachers are too small to be of any moment. But, on the other hand, the immense advantage of hospital practice more than repays anyone enjoying it for the time and labour it costs; the amount expended being, indeed, very much less than it would be in the case of a lady who made the wards her home.

Perhaps the only class of volunteer nurses to whom the objections now raised do not apply are those to whose exertions we owe the recent renewal of the discussion – those, namely, who come forward to give extra help in times of emergency. But there is no reason, because the ordinary staff of nurses are paid, why in times of sudden and unusual difficulty extra volunteer help should not be both offered and accepted. To help heartily for a month or two is very different from taking the routine work as an unpaid profession. In fact, it may fairly be doubted if the whole benefit of the help in the cholera wards would have remained had volunteer nurses been quite *en règle* in the hospitals. Their presence was then all the more valuable, because no one could take it quite as a matter of course. Half the good they did (and it would be difficult to say how much this was) in cheering and encouraging everyone, was due to the fact that neither the patients, the medical officers, nor the regular nurses were accustomed to their presence. The stimulus was felt the more from its being a novelty. Briefly recapitulating, in conconclusion, the opinions now expressed, it is contended –

1. That hospital nursing can be very well done by the women of the lower middle class.

2. That the payment necessary to secure the services of appropriate people need not exceed £50 a year for the head nurses, and £21 a year for the under nurses, with board and residence.

3. That each head nurse thus paid could, if the size and arrangement of the wards permitted it, attend to not less than fifty patients, and every under nurse, in ordinary circumstances, to fourteen or fifteen.

4. That the influence of a lady superintendent over the nurses would be exceedingly good, as combining the principal advantage of the volunteer method with the advantages of the present system.

5. That the office of lady superintendent is one which should be held by a trained and qualified person, and that the salary should be what a lady of the educated class would be glad to take; for instance, not less than £150, with board and rooms.

6. That the employment which a general adoption of this plan would open to educated women is too limited to justify its advocates in thinking of nursing as a profession for ladies, in the sense in which the word 'profession' is commonly used. Two hundred such situations represent the maximum number ever likely to be offered, and the probable number would be very much below this.

Elizabeth Blackwell
(1821–1910)

Elizabeth Blackwell was born in Bristol but emigrated to America with her family at the age of eleven. The daughter of liberal, progressive parents, who supported social reform, women's rights, temperance and the abolition of slavery, Elizabeth became determined to seek a career in medicine. In 1849, she became the first woman to gain a medical degree in the United States. After further study in Paris at La Maternité, where she contracted purulent ophthalmia and lost her sight in one eye, she set up a one-room dispensary in a tenement district of New York where she treated over 200 poor women in the first year. In 1857, after four years of fund-raising, she was able to expand the original dispensary and open the New York Infirmary for Women and Children. Her plan to attach a medical college for women, a nursing school and a Chair of Hygiene to the Hospital was delayed by the Civil War (during which time she and her sister, Emily, were involved in the selection and training of nurses) but it eventually opened in 1868 and functioned for the next thirty years until 1899 when Cornell University's Medical School opened its doors to women. In 1869, Elizabeth Blackwell returned to England and built up a large and successful practice in London. Two years later, she and her supporters founded the National Health Society and helped Sophia Jex-Blake and Elizabeth Garrett to establish the London Medical School for Women where she accepted the Chair of Gynaecology in 1874.

Extracts from the Laws of Life, with special reference to the Physical Education of Girls

(reprinted from *The English Woman's Journal*, May 1858)

Observe how in all ages our ancestors have endeavoured to express their ideals by beautiful forms, through which the spirit might freely shine; they saw more clearly than we do that the condition of our present life is the *union* of body and soul, that we cannot live as disembodied spirits, but must necessarily express ourselves through a material frame – that our aspirations are often limited by the body, and that the condition of our material organisation reacts most powerfully upon the soul. They saw that weakness, ugliness, and disease deaden our power, cripple all our activities, and render our lives discordant – therefore they figured their gods and goddesses and heroes, under forms of surpassing beauty; their bodies were well proportioned, the features regular; every muscle had a living development, every sense a vigorous organ; and all these forms, though perfect, were infinitely varied – the beauty of Juno was not the beauty of Diana – the perfection of Jupiter differed from that of Apollo – but it was not the beauty of material form as an end, that they aimed to reach, but the grand truth that the loftiest qualities of the soul find their highest expression in corresponding beauty of form.

When we read in the chronicles of past ages the many feats recorded of physical power – of a body that knew neither weakness nor fatigue, an iron strength of endurance and action – it seems to us like the echo of a distant age with which we have nothing to do. We cannot realise the strength of the beautiful Cymburga, wife of the stalwart Duke Ernest of Austria, who could crack nuts with her fingers, and drive a nail into a wall with her hand, as far as others with a hammer. When we hear of the lofty Brinhilda, who bound her offending lover with her girdle, and slung him to a beam of the ceiling, we do not recognise that the myth which represents the wild strong life of that distant age has a lesson for us, and we should ponder the question whether in our modern days we have not lost much stout virtue, with the failure of our bodily powers. The breakfast feats of good Queen Bess and her maids, on rounds of beef and mugs of ale, seem incredible in our poor dyspeptic days – what would not our delicate ladies and gentlemen give for that vigorous life, which could spring out of bed at five o'clock, full of energetic activity, digest and enjoy plain substantial fare, and pursue every occupation of the day, with the power of robust health?

And if the tone of the muscles is destroyed, if they are weak, relaxed, unfit for duty – the tone of all the organs will be destroyed in corresponding degree. Thus from the neglect of exercise during youth, we have this formidable result to the body, a weakness of the whole muscular system. Now the time would fail me to trace out all the bodily evils, all the diseases that inevitably spring from this condition of weakness. The crooked spines, with other vices of growth, may be directly traced to it, and its injurious influence on the functions of adult life, I shall soon have occasion to dwell upon.

Let me recapitulate the special evils which will thus arise to the whole material frame when the muscular system is not called into exercise, and developed as its structure and important functions demand. I have called your attention, first to the congestion of the various organs, and consequent impairment of their functions. Second, to the stagnation of the venous circulation, from the absence of muscular stimulus. Third, to the deficiency of heat and electricity, which are produced by muscular contraction. Fourth, to the irritability and undue excitement of the nervous system, which must arise when the motor nerves are not called into action. Fifth, to the loss of tone in the whole body, from the weakness of the muscular system. Now, all these evils, more and more formidable as they will seem, the more you reflect upon them in detail, are still minor evils, because they do not refer to the *great object* of the muscular system, which is to furnish a varied and powerful instrument for the expression of the soul.

We need muscles that are strong and prompt to do our will, that can run and walk in doors and out of doors, and convey us from place to place, as duty or pleasure calls us, not only without fatigue, but with the feeling of cheerful energy; we need strong arms that can cradle a healthy child, and toss it crowing in the air, and backs that will not break under the burden of household cares, a frame that is not exhausted and weakened by the round of daily duties. We want faces that can smile and light up with every noble sentiment, and not be rigidly set to vacancy, or wrinkled by care, faces that will greet the stranger with a welcome that he can feel; that will *show* to the loved ones the rich affections of the heart; that can lighten with indignation, or glow with honest approbation: we need faces that know how to move and express true feelings, instead of remaining like an icy barrier, through which the warm feelings of the heart strive in vain to break. We need developed muscles that shall make the human body really a divine image, a perfect form rendering all dress graceful, and not requiring to be patched and filled up and weighed down with clumsy contrivances for hiding its deformities. Bodies that can move in dignity, in grace, in airy lightness, or conscious strength, bodies erect and firm, energetic and active – bodies that are truly sovereign in their presence, the expressions of a sovereign nature. Such are the bodies that we need, prompt to do and to feel, truly our own. And such nature intends us to have. In order to give us so perfect and beautiful an instrument, the muscular frame was constructed, so rich in every way, so obedient to the mind. Exercise, then, the means by which the muscular system may be developed, assumes its true position, as of primary importance during the period of youth. It is the grand necessity which everything else should aid. We have seen how the organic involuntary life needs our aid but indirectly, but this education of exercise is immediately under our control, and demands imperatively our direction. Let us consider what we have to do in this important matter.

The young infant is almost withdrawn from our control. Nature says to us, 'stand by, and watch my work!' This delicate life will admit of no trifling, no neglect, no experiment; but watch the infant how it kicks, and cries, and works, not arms and legs alone, but every part of its body in pain or pleasure. We sit and smile, or silently weep; but the baby puts every muscle in motion; if it is pained or angry, it will scream with its whole life, and contract every little fibre, and strain and wriggle in infantile rage, to the intense alarm of its mother. We may leave it to nature for exercise; it will be well attended to, and carried through an efficient course, reaching every muscle of the body, that we should find difficult to imitate by art.

Letter to Young Ladies Desirous of Studying Medicine

(reprinted from *The English Woman's Journal*, February 1860)

I am often consulted by young ladies in relation to the way in which a woman may enter the medical profession; I therefore willingly comply with the suggestion of friends, to write down the results of my experience as to the best method of study that can at present be pursued by a woman who desires to become a physician, and the qualifications which the student should possess.

Let me say, however, first of all, that though a woman may now become a legally qualified practitioner of medicine, the task is still a very arduous one, and should not be lightly undertaken. Independently of the difficulties involved in the study itself, there are moral and social difficulties which are far greater. Society has not yet recognised this study as fit woman's work. Gossip and slander may annoy the student, and want of confidence on the part of women, with the absence of social and professional support and sympathy, will inevitably make the entrance of the young physician into medicine a long and difficult struggle. There is a noble and useful life to be gained by the conquest of these difficulties, but they must not be overlooked nor underrated by anyone who desires to become a physician; and they require perseverance, courage, and self-reliance to overcome them.

Should the mind, however, be clearly made up on these points and the resolution formed to pursue the study, I think the following preliminary qualifications necessary. The student should be between the ages of twenty and thirty; the health and constitution should be good, and she should have enjoyed a good education. Not only is a liberal English education a prerequisite, but familiarity with French and Latin, and some knowledge of Greek. The two former languages are indispensable to a student of science, and a certain amount of Greek is equally necessary –

the mastery for instance, of such a book as Anthon's Greek Lessons. When possessed of these qualifications, the student must look forward to four years of special medical study, the last two years of which, under existing circumstances, must be spent abroad.

I suggest the following division of these four years. The first to be spent at home, i.e. wherever the student may happen to be, in medical reading, under the direction of a physician or surgeon. The second to be spent, six months as nurse in a hospital, and six months in a laboratory, and in private classes, if such openings can be found. A year and a half must then be spent in America, to obtain a college education, and medical degree; and the remaining six months should be passed in La Maternité, Paris, where an invaluable acquaintance with midwifery may be obtained. This is a general outline of the four years' study, variations being made according to circumstances: for instance, should no openings for really valuable study occur in the second year, except the period of nursing, it would then be better to go at once to America, and reserve the additional six months for the study of disease in Paris, after the period passed in La Maternité, or it might be that, by that time, some new openings in England might be found. These variations may occur, but the essential points to observe are four years definite medical study: the first passed in patient preparatory study; one portion in a hospital; another period in America; some time in La Maternité; and the rest wherever the best opportunities for medical instruction may be found.

Let me say a few words on each of these periods. The first year's private study is needed, not only for the good of the study, but as a test of the student's own purpose, when being in no way committed to any future plan, she can drop the whole matter if it do not suit her taste, etc. It is an injurious thing to give up anything once resolutely undertaken, and in so serious a matter as this, a year of reflection is absolutely needed. This reading should be directed by a medical practitioner, who should also examine the student on the subjects of study, and give a certificate of the examinations at the end of the year. There would be a great advantage to the student in having such a friend at hand, and I should counsel her strongly to seek for a respectable medical practitioner, who would take an interest in this year of study, and direct it. I will mention here the text books commonly used by students on the various branches of medical study, though other works on the same subject may be used if more convenient. Carpenter's *Physiology*, Wilson's *Anatomy*, Pereira's *Materia Medica*, Watson's *Practice of Medicine*, Druitt's *Surgery*, Churchill's

Midwifery, Churchill's *Diseases of Women*, Alison's *Pathology*, Fownes' *Chemistry*, Bell's *Legal Medicines*. Only a portion of these could be studied during this year, and the selection should be made by advice. Anatomy, physiology, and chemistry might form the commencement, and the subjects for examination. One piece of advice I would give the student: make your study as practical as possible; do not rely on simple reading. If you study anatomy, try and get access to some little museum, see the bones themselves, study the prepared skeleton, look at plaster or papier-maché models, dissect birds, or a cat or dog – a single glance will often be worth more than pages of description. If you study chemistry, try and get admission to an apothecary's, see the substances spoken of, learn the taste, smell, and look of the various articles of the materia medica; if you can handle medicines and put up prescriptions, so much the better. During some period of your study, you must enter and work in a laboratory. If you can see sick people and learn to observe symptoms, feel the pulse, examine the tongue, etc., by all means do so; it will wonderfully assist your memory in reading on the practice of medicine; seek for ways in which you can assist the memory by aid of the senses and judgment.

In relation to the second period of study, six months may be passed with great advantage in a hospital as nurse. No woman can now enter a hospital except in this capacity, but the advantages of seeing practice in a great hospital are so indispensable, that no-one who has the true spirit for this work in her, will hesitate to accept the wearisome details of the nurse's duty, for the sake of the invaluable privilege of studying disease on a large scale. All pride and assumption of superiority must be laid aside; and while diligently performing the distinct duties of the poor you accept, observe, and privately make a record of whatever belongs to your proper medical work. The menial drudgery that formerly was associated with the nurse's work is being laid aside in some of the London hospitals. I have ascertained that a lady can enter in such a capacity as I here recommend, without injury to health, and, with a little womanly tact and real earnestness in the work, this residence may be made a most valuable time of study. I would add that as, later, it will belong to your duty as physician, to superintend nurses and carefully attend to the hygienic and other arrangements of the sick room, it will be an advantage to you to have actually done the work of an intelligent nurse, and familiarised yourself with this important part of the care of the sick. As also the prevention of disease and care of health is half the physician's work, all experience which bears upon these subjects will be of great use.

In respect to residence in the Maternité, which I strongly advise: it had better be deferred to the end of the course, not only on account of the prejudice that exists in relation to an English woman's studying medicine in France, and the advantage of enlarged experience before doing so, but because there are a great many old midwife prejudices and practices clinging to that institution which you can better discriminate and avoid at the end of your education than at the beginning. The great practice of the institution will be invaluable to you, and the vastly increased medical experience which you will possess after a six months' residence there will fully repay you for the immense discomforts of the position. You will see every variety of midwifery practice, perform a large amount yourself, and acquire the skilful touch so necessary in the profession. The price of tuition is very low. A certificate of baptism, good character, and vaccination, with a knowledge of reading and writing, are the only qualifications required. Though the community-life of the institution is trying to English feeling, and the style of living, food, etc., of the plainest description, the arrangements of time and occupation are all made for the benefit of the pupil.

The time spent in America will give not only the drill of college, but the degree of a legal practitioner. There is no school of medicine open to women in Europe, but there are several open in America, and though a foreign degree is not necessarily recognised in England, i.e. though the council which registers properly qualified medical practitioners may or may not accept the degree as evidence of suitable study, still the probabilities are that it would be accepted, if evidence of the whole course of study were furnished, and the application for registration made in the proper way. You can practise in England without this registration. The chief disadvantages of doing so (independently of the loss of the prestige of registration) are the inability to compel the payment of fees, or to take part in established hospitals, neither of which, I think, would much affect you. All physicians holding foreign diplomas labour under the same difficulty. All you can do, however, is to obtain the best diploma accessible to you; and I think that the enlarged experience, as well as real knowledge, to be gained by American study, are well worth the proposed expenditure of time. The best methods of studying in America may be obtained without difficulty when the time comes for carrying out this part of the plan.

It is difficult to make a calculation of the sum of money required for carrying out such a plan of education as is here laid down, as it will vary greatly, according to the expenditures made for private instruction, this instruction being as expensive as it is valuable. But I think I may safely state that £100 per annum will be necessary, exclusive of travelling expenses, clothes, books, and instruments, but inclusive of board, public tuition, and some private instruction. To this I must add that means of support must be possessed to some extent during the first years of practice, for no one should calculate on a rapid success in practice.[1]

NOTE

1 Communications from any young lady seriously desirous of studying the medical profession, may be addressed to Dr E. Blackwell, care of the Editors of *The English Woman's Journal.*

Medicine as a Profession for Women*

(reprinted from *The English Woman's Journal*, May 1860)

In inviting consideration to the subject of medicine as an occupation for women, it is not a simple theory that we wish to present, but the results of practical experience. For fourteen years we have been students of medicine; for eight years we have been engaged in the practice of our profession in New York; and during the last five years have, in addition, been actively occupied in the support of a medical charity. We may therefore venture to speak with some certainty on this subject; and we are supported by the earnest sympathy of large numbers of intelligent women, both in England and America, in presenting this subject for the first time to the public.

The idea of the education of women in medicine is not now an entirely new one; for some years it has been discussed by the public, institutions have been founded professing to accomplish it, and many women are already engaged in some form of medical occupation. Yet the true position of women in medicine, the real need which lies at the bottom of this movement, and the means necessary to secure its practical usefulness and success, are little known. We believe it is now time to bring this subject forward and place it in its true light, as a matter not affecting a few individuals only, but of serious importance to the community at large; and demanding such support as will allow of the establishment of an institution for the thorough education of women in medicine.

When the idea of the practice of medicine by women is

*This lecture was prepared by Drs Elizabeth and Emily Blackwell, as an exposition of the effort now being made in the city of New York to open the profession of medicine to women. It was delivered in Clinton Hall, on the 2nd of December, 1859.

suggested, the grounds on which we usually find sympathy expressed for it are two. The first is that there are certain departments of medicine in which the aid of *women* physicians would be especially valuable to women. The second argument is that women are much in need of a wider field of occupation, and if they could successfully practise any branches of medicine it would be another opening added to the few they already possess. In some shape or other, these two points are almost universally regarded (where the matter has been considered at all) as the great reasons to be urged in its behalf.

Now, we believe that both these reasons are valid, and that experience will fully confirm them; but we believe also that there is a much deeper view of the question than this; and that the thorough education of a class of women in medicine will exert an important influence upon the life and interests of women in general, an influence of a much more extended nature than is expressed in the above views. The question of the real value to the community of what women may do in medicine is an eminently practical matter, for upon it is based the aid which they may ask for its accomplishment; and upon the position of women in medicine depends the kind and extent of education which should be given to fit them for it. A great deal of well-meant effort has been, and is still being, expended upon the institutions which have been established for this purpose. Sometimes we have heard much discouragement expressed at the slight result that has followed from them; while, on the other hand, it is often said, 'After all, it is a matter for women to settle for themselves, if they can be doctors, and want to, they will find the way to do it, there is no need of doing any thing in the matter.' Now, as I have said, we believe it to be by no means a matter concerning only the limited number of women who may be actually engaged in the pursuit itself; and it is also certain that to insure the success of the work it is not enough that women should wish to study, the co-operation and support of public sentiment is needed to enable them to do so. We hope, by showing the value of the work, to prove it to be the interest of the community to carry it out; and we desire to show the means by which this may be done.

Let me then say a few words on the influence which would be exerted on society by the opening of medicine as a profession to women. The interests and occupations of women, as they actually are at present, may be referred to four distinct forms of effort: – Domestic life; the education of youth; social intercourse; and benevolent effort of various kinds. All these avocations, by unanimous consent, are especially under the superintendence of women, and every woman, as she takes her place in society, assumes the responsibility of participation in some of them.

While these pursuits have always formed the central interest of the majority of women, their character, and the requirements which they make for their proper performance, have widened, with the advance of modern society, in a remarkable degree. Social intercourse – a very limited thing in a half civilised country – becomes in our centres of civilisation a great power, establishing customs more binding than laws, imposing habits and stamping opinions, a tribunal from whose judgment there is hardly an appeal. All who are familiar with European life, and the life of our great cities, know what an organised and powerful force it ever tends to become.

In like manner, benevolent efforts have little influence in new countries, but in Europe, especially in England, the extent of such work, and the amount of it which is done by women would be incredible, did we not see here, in our midst, the commencement of a similar state of things.

Domestic life is not less affected by the growth of the age; the position and duties of the mother of a family call for very different qualifications, in the wide and complicated relations of the present, from what was needed a century ago.

Now it is evident that the performance of all these forms of work, extended and organised as they are, is in its practical nature a business requiring distinct knowledge and previous preparation, as much as actual trades and professions. This fact would be more commonly recognised were it not that there is so much moral and spiritual life interwoven into woman's work by the relations upon which it is founded, and out of which it grows, as to make it more difficult to separate this business aspect of her work from her personal life, than is the case with the business life of men; consequently its practical character is too often considered entirely subordinate, or lost sight of. Every woman, however, who brings thought and conscience to the performance of everyday duties, soon realises it in her own experience. The wider the view she takes of life, the higher her ideal of her domestic and social relations, the more keenly she will feel the need of knowledge with regard to this matter of fact basis upon which they rest. The first and most important point in which she will feel the want of this previous training will be in her ignorance of physiological and sanitary science, in their application to practical life; of the laws of health and physical and mental development; of the connection between moral and physical conditions, and the influences which our social and domestic life exert upon us. These and similar questions will meet her at every step, from the commencement of her maternal life, when the care of young children and of her own health bring to her a thousand subjects of perplexity, to the close of her career, when her children, assuming their positions as men and women, look to her as their natural counsellor.

It may be said, at first sight, that in these things it is not so much knowledge as common sense and earnestness that are wanted; that as health is the natural condition, it will be secured by simply using our judgment in not positively disregarding what our natural instincts teach us in regard to our lives. This would be true if civilisation were a simple state directed by instinct; but every advance in social progress removes us more and more from the guidance of instinct, obliging us to depend upon reason for the assurance that our habits are really in accordance with the laws of health, and compelling us to guard against the sacrifice of our physical or moral nature while pursuing the ends of civilisation.

From the fact, then, that our lives must be directed more by reason than instinct, arises at once the necessity for a science of health, and that comprehension of it which will lead to its daily application. Take in illustration the simplest physical need, that which is most completely instinctive in its character – the question of food. Animals make no mistake on this point, being governed infallibly by instinct, but what conflicting theories it has given rise to among men! It is very rare to find among women, the heads of families, any clear idea of what are the requisites for a healthy table; and what is true of this very simple material want is still more so with regard to higher questions of physical law, those more intimately connected with the intellect and affections, and the family and social relations growing out of them. Nothing is more striking in a wide observation of daily life than the utter insufficiency of simple common sense to secure wise action in these matters. Numbers of people, of very good common sense in other things, violate the fundamental laws of health without knowing it; and when they think upon the subject they are just as likely to follow some crude popular theory as to find out the truth.

That progress is needed in sanitary matters is widely admitted; sanitary conventions are held; the medical profession and the press are constantly calling attention to defects of public and private hygiene, pointing out the high rate of mortality amongst children, etc.; but it is far from being as generally recognised how essential to progress it is that women, who have the domestic life of the nation in their hands, should realise their responsibility, and possess the knowledge necessary to meet it.

In education, as in domestic life, the same necessity for hygienic knowledge exists. Statistics show that nine-tenths of our teachers are women, and it is obviously a matter of great importance that they should be familiar with the nature and needs of the great body of youth which is intrusted to their care. It is not possible that our systems of education should be really suited to childhood, training its faculties without cramping or unduly stimulating the nature, unless those by whom this work is done understand the principles of health and growth upon which school training should be based. Our school education ignores, in a thousand ways, the rules of healthy development; and the results, obtained with much labour and expense, are gained very generally at the cost of physical and mental health.

If, then, it be true that health has its science as well as disease; that there are conditions essential for securing it, and that everyday life should be based upon its laws; if, moreover, women, by their social position, are important agents in this practical work, the question naturally arises, how is this knowledge to be widely diffused among them? At present there exists no method of supplying this need. Physiology and all branches of science bearing upon the physical life of man are pursued almost exclusively by physicians, and from these branches of learning they deduce more or less clear ideas with regard to the conditions of health in everyday life. But it is only the most enlightened physicians who do this work for themselves; a very large proportion of the profession, who are well acquainted with the bearing of this learning upon disease, would find it a difficult matter to show its relation to the prevention of disease, and the securing of health, by its application to daily life. If this be the case with regard to physicians, it must evidently be impossible to give to the majority of women the wide scientific training that would enable them from their own knowledge to deduce practical rules of guidance. This must be done by those whose avocations require wide scientific knowledge – by physicians. Yet the medical profession is at present too far removed from the life of women; they regard these subjects from such a different stand-point that they cannot supply the want. The application of scientific knowledge to women's necessities in actual life can only be done by women who possess at once the scientific learning of the physician, and as women a thorough acquaintance with women's requirements – that is, by women physicians.

That this connecting link between the science of the medical profession and the everyday life of women is needed, is proved by the fact that during the years that scientific knowledge has been accumulating in the hands of physicians, while it has revolutionised the science of medicine, it has had so little direct effect upon domestic life. Twenty years ago, as now, their opinion was strongly expressed with regard to the defects in the adaptation of modern life and education to the physical well-being of society, and particularly of its injurious results to women. Yet, as far as these latter are concerned, no change has been effected. In all such points women are far more influenced by the opinions of society at large, and of their elder women friends, than by their physician, and this arises from the fact that physicians are too far removed from women's life; they can criticise but not guide it. On the other hand, it is curious to observe that, as within the last few years the attention of a considerable number of women has been turned to medicine, the first use they have made of it has been to establish a class of lectures on physiology and hygiene for women. They are scattered all over the country; the lectures are generally as crude and unsatisfactory as the medical education out of which they have sprung; but the impulse is worthy of note, as showing the instinctive perception of women, as soon as they acquire even a slight acquaintance with these subjects, how directly they bear upon the interests of women, and the inclination which exists to attempt, at least, to apply them to their needs. As teachers, then, to diffuse among women the physiological and sanitary knowledge which they need, we find the first work for women physicians.

The next point of interest to be noticed is the connection of women with public charities and benevolent institutions.

In all civilised nations women have always taken an active share in these charities; indeed, if we include those employed in the subordinate duties of nurses, matrons, etc., the number of women actually engaged would much outnumber that of men. How large a part of the character of these institutions, and of the influence exerted by them upon society, is dependent upon this great body of women employed in them and connected with them, may readily be imagined. Yet it is certain, and admitted by all who have any acquaintance with the matter, that this influence at present is far from being a good one. It is well known how much the efficiency of women as managers or supporters of public institutions is impaired by the lack of knowledge and practical tact to second their zeal; and business men who have dealings with them in these relations are very apt to regard them as troublesome and uncertain allies, rather than as efficient co-workers. With those employed in the active care of the institutions the case is still worse; the very term hospital nurse conveys the idea of belonging to a degraded class.

How to obviate this great evil has become an important question. In England, where all public institutions, hospitals – civil and military – workhouses, houses for reformation, prisons, penitent-iaries, etc., form a great system, dealing with the poorer classes to an immense extent, and having a social importance too serious to be overlooked, the question has assumed sufficient weight to be discussed earnestly by government and the public at large.

In Catholic countries this is accomplished to a certain extent – that is, so far as the domestic and nursing departments are concerned – by the religious orders, the sisters of charity and others. Everyone who is familiar with such institutions must have been struck by the contrast between the continental and English hospitals, etc., caused by this one thing, by the cheerful and respectable home-like air of well-managed French establishments, as compared with the gloomy, common aspect of even wealthy English or American charities; and must have observed the salutary influence upon patients, students, and all connected with these places, of the presence and constant superintendence of women who, instead of being entirely common and subordinate, are universally regarded with respect and confidence, and by the poorer classes almost with veneration.

It is very common among both Catholics and Protestants to consider these sisterhoods as the result entirely of religious enthusiasm, and to assert that large bodies of women can only be induced to accept these occupations, and carry them out in this efficient manner, from this motive. When efforts have been made in England and Germany to establish anything of the kind among Protestants, it is always to the religious element that the appeal has been made. Many such efforts have been made, with more or less success, in Germany. In England, the results have been very imperfect, and have entirely failed to secure anything approaching in practical efficiency to the Catholic sisterhoods.

Now these failures are very easily comprehended by anyone who has seen much of these sisters in actual work, for such persons will soon perceive that the practical success of these orders does not depend upon religious enthusiasm, but upon an excellent business organisation. Religious feeling there is among them, and it is an important aid in filling their ranks and keeping up their interest; but the real secret of their success is in the excellent opening afforded by them for all classes of women to a useful and respected social life. The inferior sisters are plain, decent women, nothing more, to whom the opportunity of earning a support, the companionship, protection, and interest afforded by being members of a respected order, and the prospect of a certain provision for age, are the more powerful ties to the work, from the fact that they are generally without means, or very near connections, and would find it difficult to obtain a better or so good a living. The superior sisters are usually women of character and education, who, from want of family ties, misfortune, or need of occupation, find themselves lonely or unhappy in ordinary life; and to them the church, with its usual sagacity in availing itself of all talents, opens the attractive prospect of active occupation, personal standing and authority, social respect, and the companionship of intelligent co-workers, both men and women – the feeling of belonging to the world, in fact, instead of a crippled and isolated life. For thought it is common to speak of the sisters as renouncing the world, the fact is, that the members of these sisterhoods have a far more active participation in the interests of life than most of them had before. No-one can fully realise the effect this has upon them, unless they have at once seen them at their work, and are aware how welcome to great numbers of women would be an active, useful life, free from pecuniary cares, offering sympathy and companionship in work and social standing to all its members, with scope for all talents, from the poorest drudge to the intelligent and educated woman – an offer so welcome as to be quite sufficient to overcome the want of attraction in the work itself at first sight.

As we have said, every effort so far to introduce a corresponding class of women into English institutions has proved a failure, for there is no such organisation in external life in Protestant churches as there is in the Catholic; it is contrary to the genius of the nation; and the same results would certainly follow in America.

The only way to meet the difficulty, to give a centre to women who are interested in such efforts, and to connect intelligent women with these institutions, is to introduce women into them as physicians. If all public charities were open to *well* educated women physicians, they would exert upon them the same valuable influence that is secured by the presence and services of the superiors of these orders; they would bring in a more respectable class of nurses and train them, which no men can do; they would supervise the domestic arrangements, and give the higher tone of womanly influence so greatly needed.

They would be at the same time a connecting link between these establishments and women in general life, enlisting their interest and active services in their behalf, far more effectually than could be done by any other means. A real and great want would thus be supplied, and one which no other plan yet proposed has proved at all adequate to meet.

We come now to the position of women in medicine itself. The fact that more than half of ordinary medical practice lies among women and children, would seem to be, at first sight, proof enough that there must be here a great deal that women could do for themselves, and that it is not a natural arrangement that in what so especially concerns themselves they should have recourse entirely to men. Accordingly we find that, from the very earliest ages a large class of women has always existed occupying certain departments of medical practice. Until within half a century, a recognised position was accorded to them, and midwives were as distinct a class as doctors. Even now, in most European countries, there are government schools for their instruction where they are most carefully trained in their own speciality. This training is always given in connection with a hospital, of which the pupils perform the actual practice, and physicians of standing are employed as instructors. In Paris, the great hospital of La Maternité, in which several thousand women are received annually, is entirely given up to them, and Dubois, Professor of Midwifery in the medical school of Paris, is at the head of their teachers. Until within a few years, it was common for eminent French physicians to receive intelligent midwives as their private pupils, and take much pains with their education. They were also admitted to courses of anatomical instruction in the Ecole Pratique, and an immense amount of practice was in the hands of these women. The whole idea of their education, however, planned and moulded entirely by men, was not to enable these women to do all they could in medicine, but to make them a sort of supplement to the profession, taking off a great deal of laborious poor practice, and supplying a certain convenience in some branches where it was advantageous to have the assistance of skilful women's hands. With the advance of medical science, however, and its application to all these departments of medicine, this division of the directing head, and the subordinate hand, became impossible. Physicians dismissed, as far as possible, these half-educated assistants, excluded them from many opportunities of instruction under their authority, and in the government schools, which popular custom still upholds, they have materially curtailed their education. Nor is it possible or desirable to sanction the practice of any such intermediate class. The alternative is unavoidable of banishing women from medicine altogether, or giving them the education and standing of the physician. The broad field of general medical science underlies all specialities, and an acquaintance with it is indispensable for the successful pursuit of every department. If the popular instinct which called women so widely to this sort of work represent a real need, it can only be met now by a class of women whose education shall correspond to the wider requirements of our present medical science.

Moreover, experience very soon shows that it is not these special branches of practice that will chiefly call for the attention of women in medicine. The same reason which especially qualifies women to be the teachers of women, in sanitary and physiological knowledge, viz., that they can better apply it to the needs of women's life, holds good in regard to their action as physicians. So much of medical practice grows out of everyday conditions and interests, that women who are thoroughly conversant with women's lives will, if they have the character and knowledge requisite for the position, be as much better qualified in many cases to counsel women, as men would be in similar circumstances to counsel men. At present, when women need medical aid or advice, they have at once to go out of their own world, as it were; the whole atmosphere of professional life is so entirely foreign to that in which they live that there is a gap between them and the physician whom they consult, which can only be filled up by making the profession no longer an exclusively masculine one. Medicine is so broad a field, so closely interwoven with general interests, dealing as it does with all ages, sexes, and classes, and yet of so personal a character in its individual applications, that it must be regarded as one of those great departments of work in which the co-operation of men and women is needed to fulfil all its requirements. It is not only by what women will do themselves in medicine, but also by the influence which they will exert on the profession, that they will lead it to supply the needs of women as it cannot otherwise.

Our own experience has fully proved to us the correctness of this view. We find the practice, both public and private, which comes naturally to us is by no means confined to any special departments, and where patients have sufficient confidence in us to consult us for one thing, they are very apt to apply in all cases where medical aid is needed. The details of our medical work during the number of years that we have been connected with the profession cannot be given to the public, but they have fully satisfied us that there will be the same variety in the practice of women as exists in that of men; that individual character and qualification will determine the position in practice, rather than pre-conceived ideas with regard to the position; and that there is no department in which women physicians may not render valuable services to women.

It is often objected to this idea of professional and scientific pursuits for women that it is too much out of keeping with their general life, that it would not harmonise with their necessary avocations in domestic and social life; that the advantages to be gained from the services of women physicians would not compensate for the injurious effect it would have upon the women themselves who pursued the profession, or the tendency it might have to induce others to undervalue the importance of duties already belonging to them.

This objection, the prominent one which we usually meet, appears to us based on an entire misapprehension of what is the great want of women at the present day. All who know the world must acknowledge how far the influence of women in the home, and in society, is from what it should be. How often homes, which should be the source of moral and physical health and truth, are centres of selfishness and frivolity! How often we find women, well meaning, of good intelligence and moral power, nevertheless utterly unable to influence their homes aright. The children, after the first few years of life, pass beyond the influence of the mother. The sons have an entire life of which she knows nothing, or she has only uneasy misgivings that they are not growing up with the moral truthfulness that she desires. She has not the width of view – that broad knowledge of life, which would enable her to comprehend the growth and needs of a nature and position so different from hers; and if she retain their personal affection, she cannot acquire that trustful confidence which would enable her to be the guardian friend of their early manhood. Her daughters also lack that guidance which would come from broader views of life, for she cannot give them a higher perception of life than she possesses herself. How is it, also, with the personal and moral goodness attributed to woman, that the tone of social intercourse, in which she takes so active a part, is so low? That, instead, of being a counterpoise to the narrowing or self-seeking spirit of business life, it only adds an element of frivolity and dissipation.

The secret of this falling short of their true position is not a want of good instinct, or desire for what is right and high, but a narrowness of view, which prevents them from seeing the wide bearing of their duties, the extent of their responsibilities, and the want of the practical knowledge which would enable them to carry out a more enlightened conception of them. The more connections that are established between the life of women and the broad interests and active progress of the age, the more fully will they realise this wider view of their work. The profession of medicine which, in its practical details, and in the character of its scientific basis, has such intimate relations with these everyday duties of women, is peculiarly adapted as such a means of connection. For what is done or learned by one class of women becomes, by virtue of their common womanhood, the property of all women. It tells upon their thought and action, and modifies their relations to other spheres of life, in a way that the accomplishment of the same work by men would not do. Those women who pursued this life of scientific study and practical activity, so different from woman's domestic and social life and yet so closely connected with it, could not fail to regard these avocations from a fresh stand-point, and to see in a new light the noble possibilities which the position of woman opens to her; and though they may be few in number, they will be enough to form a new element, another channel by which women in general may draw in and apply to their own needs the active life of the age.

We have now briefly considered the most important grounds on which the opening of the profession of medicine to women is an object of value to society in general, and consequently having a claim upon the public for aid in its accomplishment. Let us now state briefly what are the means needed for this purpose.

The first requirement for a good medical education is, that it be practical, i.e., that the actual care of the sick, and observation by the bedside, should be its foundation. For this reason, it must be given in connection with a hospital. This essential condition is equally required for the more limited training of the nurse, which, though perfectly distinct in character and object from that of the physician, agrees with it in this one point of its practical nature. In Europe, the shortest period of study required for a physician's degree is four years, and at least ten months of each year must be spent in attendance upon the course of instruction. This course comprises not only lectures on the different branches of medicine, but thorough practical study of chemistry, botany, anatomy, etc., in the laboratory, gardens, museums, etc. Attendance on the hospitals is also required, where, for several years, the student is occupied with subordinate medical and surgical duty. This hospital training is the foundation of their education, and the lectures are illustrative of it, not a substitute for it. In England, no medical school can confer a degree that has not attached to it a hospital of as many as one hundred beds. And in many of the best schools as that of St Bartholomew's, of London, the college department will only number forty or fifty students, who perform all the assistants' duty of a hospital of five hundred beds, with an out practice of eighty thousand patients annually. In America, though so extensive and thorough an education is not legally required, yet all students who attain any standing in the profession pass through essentially the same course, because nothing short of it will enable them to meet the responsibilities of practice with success.

The chief difficulty in the way of women students at present is, as it always has been, the impossibility of obtaining practical instruction. There is not in America a single hospital or dispensary to which women can gain admittance, except the limited opportunities that have been obtained in connection with the New York Infirmary. This difficulty met us during our own studies, and we were obliged to spend several years in Europe to obtain the facilities we needed. Even there, no provision is made for the admission of women, but there are so many great hospitals in both London and Paris that only those distinctly connected with medical schools are crowded with students. There are many large institutions attended by distinguished physicians, comparatively little frequented by them, and in these a lady, with good introductions, can, if she will give the time and patience, find good opportunities for study.

This troublesome and expensive method is still the only way in which a woman can obtain anything that deserves to be called a medical education, but it is evidently beyond the means of the majority of women. The instruction that they have hitherto been able to obtain in the few medical schools which have received them has been purely theoretical. It consists simply of courses of lectures, the students being rigorously excluded from the hospitals of the city, which are only open to men. Some three hundred women have attended lectures in these schools, the majority of them being intelligent young women, who would probably have been teachers had they not chosen this profession. They enter the schools with very little knowledge of the amount and kind of preparation necessary, supposing that by spending two or three winters in the prescribed studies they will be qualified to begin practice, and that by gaining experience in practice itself they will gradually work their way to success. It is not until they leave college, and attempt, alone and unaided, the work of practice that they realise how utterly insufficient their education is to enable them to acquire and support the standing of a physician. Most of them, discouraged, having spent all their money, abandon the profession; a few gain a little practical knowledge and struggle into a second-rate position. No judgment can be formed of women as physicians under such circumstances. It would be evidently an injustice to measure their capacity for such occupation by their actual success, when all avenues to the necessary instruction are resolutely closed to them.

Realising the necessity of basing any system of instruction for women on actual practice, we resolved, seven years ago, to lay the foundation of such an institution as was needed. A number of well-known citizens expressed their approval of the undertaking, and kindly consented to act as trustees. We then took out a charter for a practical school of medicine for women. This plan was founded upon those of European hospital schools. It is as follows: To a hospital, of not less than one hundred beds, lectureships are to be attached, for the different branches of medical science, with clinical teachers to give instruction in the wards. The students should be connected with it for four years, and should serve as assistants in the house, and in outdoor practice. Amongst the professorships attached to the hospital should be one of sanitary science, of which the object is to give instruction on the laws of health, and all points of public and private hygiene, so far as science and practical life have taught us with regard to them. This professor should also supervise the sanitary arrangements of the hospital itself, and should be the chief of the system of instruction for nurses. We believe that this professorship would be of real and important value, not only in giving the students a thorough acquaintance with the laws and conditions of health, and fully imbuing them with the idea that it is as much the province of the physician to aid in preventing as in curing disease, but also as affording to teachers and mothers the opportunity of obtaining that sort of knowledge which we have shown they so much need, and yet have no means of acquiring. In this hospital we would also establish a system of instruction for nurses.

This is a slight sketch of the mode in which we wish to carry out the three-fold object of the institution, viz., the education of physicians, the training of nurses, and the diffusion of sanitary knowledge amongst women.

It is evident that to organise such a hospital school would be a costly undertaking. It could not be self-supporting, for students are generally barely able to pay for their own direct instruction; and the hospital foundation, the apparatus for teaching, and the professorships, must be at least in part supported by endowment. It would require, therefore, a very large sum to organise such an institution of the size I have described, and it could not be efficiently carried out on a smaller scale, but could we awaken in the public a conviction of the value of the object, we believe that any amount really needed to accomplish it would be raised.

When we took out our charter we knew that, having few friends to aid in the effort, we must work gradually toward so large an end. We accordingly began the New York Infirmary, as a small dispensary, in a single room, in a poor quarter of the city, open but a few hours during the week, and supported by the contributions of a few friends. Three years ago we had grown sufficiently to take the house now occupied by the institution, No. 64, Bleecker Street, and with the same board of trustees and consulting physicians we organised a small house department. This year the number of patients treated by the infirmary is about three thousand seven hundred. Although the institution is much too small to enable us to organise anything like a complete system of instruction for students or nurses, we have received into the house some of the elder students from the female medical schools, and a few women who have applied for instruction in nursing. We have thus become more familiar with their needs, and better able to shape the institution toward meeting them.

Although we cannot yet realise the ultimate objects toward which we are working, the institution, even of its present size, is of very great value. In the first place, the fact that the entire medical practice of such an institution is performed by women is the best possible proof to the public of the possibility of the practice of women, since, being public in its character, its results are known, as those of private practice cannot be. Secondly, it is already a valuable medical centre for women. The practice of a public institution, however small, establishes connections between those who conduct it and others engaged in various public charities; and from the relations thus formed we have already been able to obtain facilities for students in the city dispensaries, and in private classes, that could not be obtained had we not such a centre to work from. Indeed, so effectual has it proved already in this manner, that were it established on a permanent basis, we could, by its assistance, and our connections with the profession here and in Europe, enable individual students, possessing the requisite means, to obtain a good medical education before the institution itself can offer the complete education which I have described.

It is, moreover, a charity which is of much value to poor women, as being the only one where they can obtain the aid of women physicians. We have only been able to keep a very small number of beds, but they are constantly occupied by a succession of patients, and we could fill a much larger number if we were able to support them. Our dispensary practice is constantly increasing.

We believe, therefore, that, quite independent of the broader work that may be ultimately accomplished, in its present shape as a charity to poor women, as a proof of women's ability to practise medicine, and as a medical centre for women, this institution is well worthy of support.

What we ask from those who are interested in the objects we have stated is to assist in raising a fund for endowment which shall place the institution on a secure foundation. It has hitherto been

475

supported almost exclusively by the subscriptions of a few friends, who pledged themselves for certain sums during three years. It has been a principle of management distinctly laid down, that the infirmary should not go into debt or on credit; that every year's expenses should be collected in advance, and should never be allowed to exceed the sum in the treasury at its commencement. This rule will be steadily adhered to, and no extension of operations undertaken until the funds are actually collected for that purpose. But so long as we are obliged to collect the income by subscription only from year to year we are not able even to lease a house, or make any arrangement for more than one year, but are obliged to devote to the work of its material support the time and attention that should be given towards organising and furthering the objects of the institution. New York is the true centre of medical education. One hundred and fifty thousand patients received free medical aid last year; no other city in the Union compares with this in its need of medical charity. It is here, therefore, that a college hospital for women should be established. We have been urged to commence this work in England, and offers of valuable aid have been made for this purpose. But this medical work has originated here, and we believe that it is better suited to the spirit of this than of any other country. As America, therefore, has taken the initiative in this medical reform, let us do the work well.

I said to English friends before I left them, 'You must send us over students, and we will educate them in America to do the same work in England.' The cordial reply was, 'We will send them over if we cannot prevail upon you to return to us.'

Now, therefore, America must help us to redeem the pledge of education which we have given in her behalf.

Help us to build up a noble institution for women, such an institution as no country has ever yet been blessed with, a national college hospital, in which all parts of the Union shall join. Let it not be a name merely, but a substantial fact, wisely planned and liberally endowed.

Surely this awakening desire of women to do their duty in the world more earnestly, and to overcome, for a great and good end, the immense difficulties which stand in their way, will enlist the sympathy and support of every generous man and woman.

Help us, then, friends! Join the little band of workers that has borne so bravely with us the odium of an unpopular cause. Help us fight this good fight, and achieve the victory, the victory of erecting a noble centre of instruction for women, which shall be not only a glory to the New World, but a blessing to the Old World too!

Index